Alice 19th

volume **6** *Blindness*

Alice 19th
volume 6 Blindness
shôjo edition

STORY & ART BY
Yuu Watase

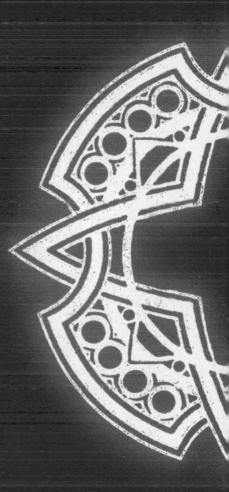

English Adaptation/Lance Caselman
Translation/JN Productions
Touch-Up Art & Lettering/Walden Wong
Cover Design & Layout/Judi Roubideaux
Editor/Frances E. Wall

Editor in Chief, Books/Alvin Lu
Editor in Chief, Magazines/Marc Weidenbaum
VP of Publishing Licensing/Rika Inouye
VP of Sales/Gonzalo Ferreyra
Sr. VP of Marketing/Liza Coppola
Publisher/Hyoe Narita

Printed in Canada

Published by VIZ Media, LLC
P.O. Box 77010 · San Francisco, CA 94107

10 9 8 7 6 5 4
First printing, August 2004
Fourth printing, August 2007

viz media
www.viz.com
store.viz.com

volume **6** *Blindness*

story and art by **Yuu Watase**

Alice 19th™

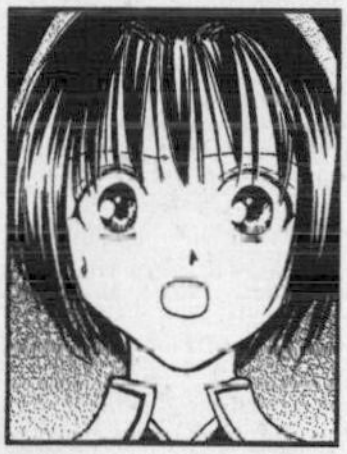
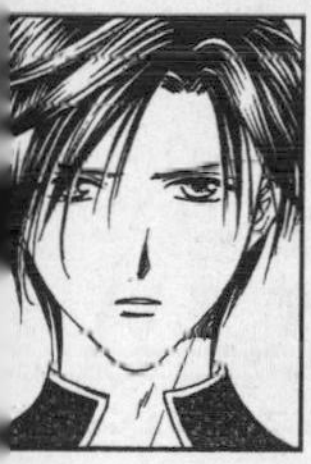
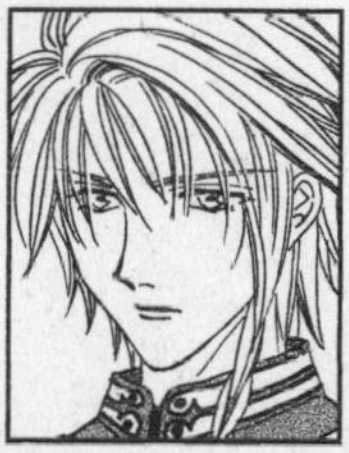
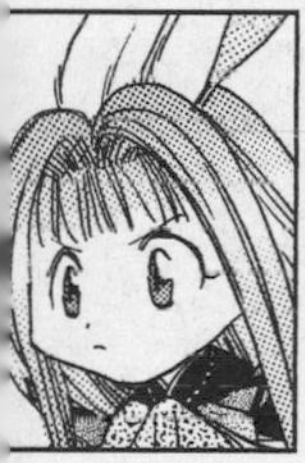
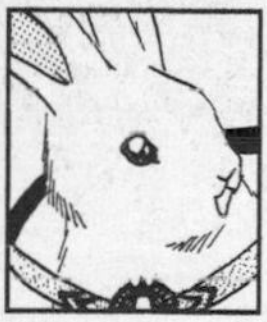

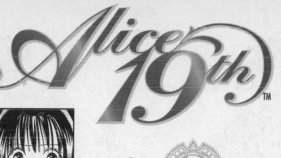

Story thus far

Mayura is still in the Metropolitan Building in Tokyo, where Darva, the embodiment of evil, is slowly consuming her. Darva has unleashed a Barrier of Evil over Tokyo, enabling the Maram Masters to control the city's inhabitants by manipulating the Mara in their hearts. Servants of Mara repeatedly attack the Lotis Masters, but Kyô, Alice, Chris, and Frey have been able to defeat them... so far. It's getting harder to fight off these evil forces, though, and Chris reminds Kyô and Alice that they must study the Lotis words diligently if they expect to have a prayer of conquering Darva and saving Mayura. The Maram Masters keep trying to lure Kyô over to the darkness, and Kyô may have secrets in his past concerning the death of his father...

Young Lotis masters Billy MacDowell, from America, and Pai Mei Lin, from China, arrive in Japan to help fight Darva. Billy talks to Kyô and explains the curse that Mayura placed upon him, which would cause Kyô to die if Alice confessed her love to him. Kyô then understands that Alice loves him, too, but is forbidden from expressing her feelings. Billy and Mei Lin join the other Lotis Masters as they approach the Tokyo Metropolitan Building, ready to confront Darva...

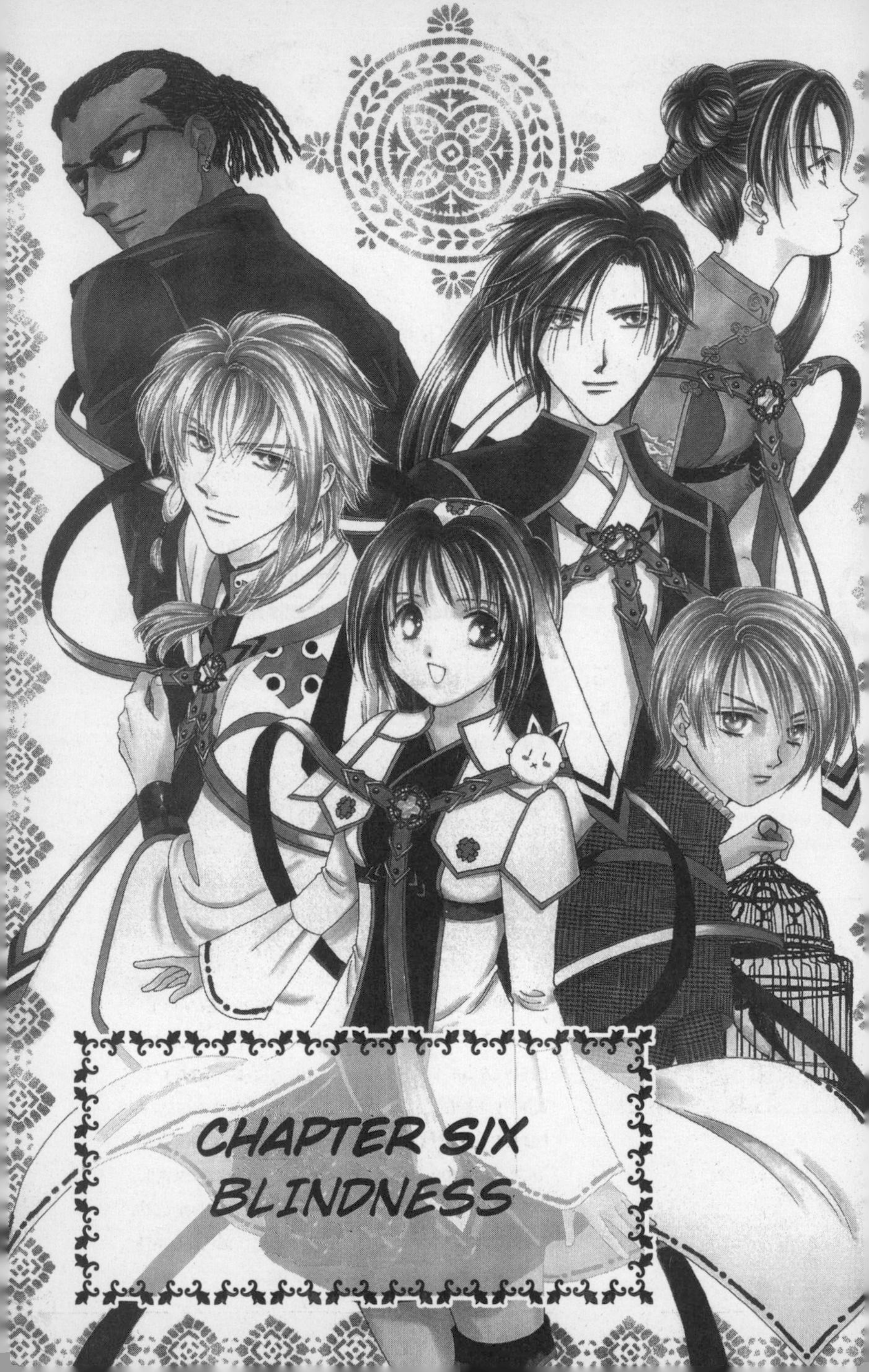
CHAPTER SIX
BLINDNESS

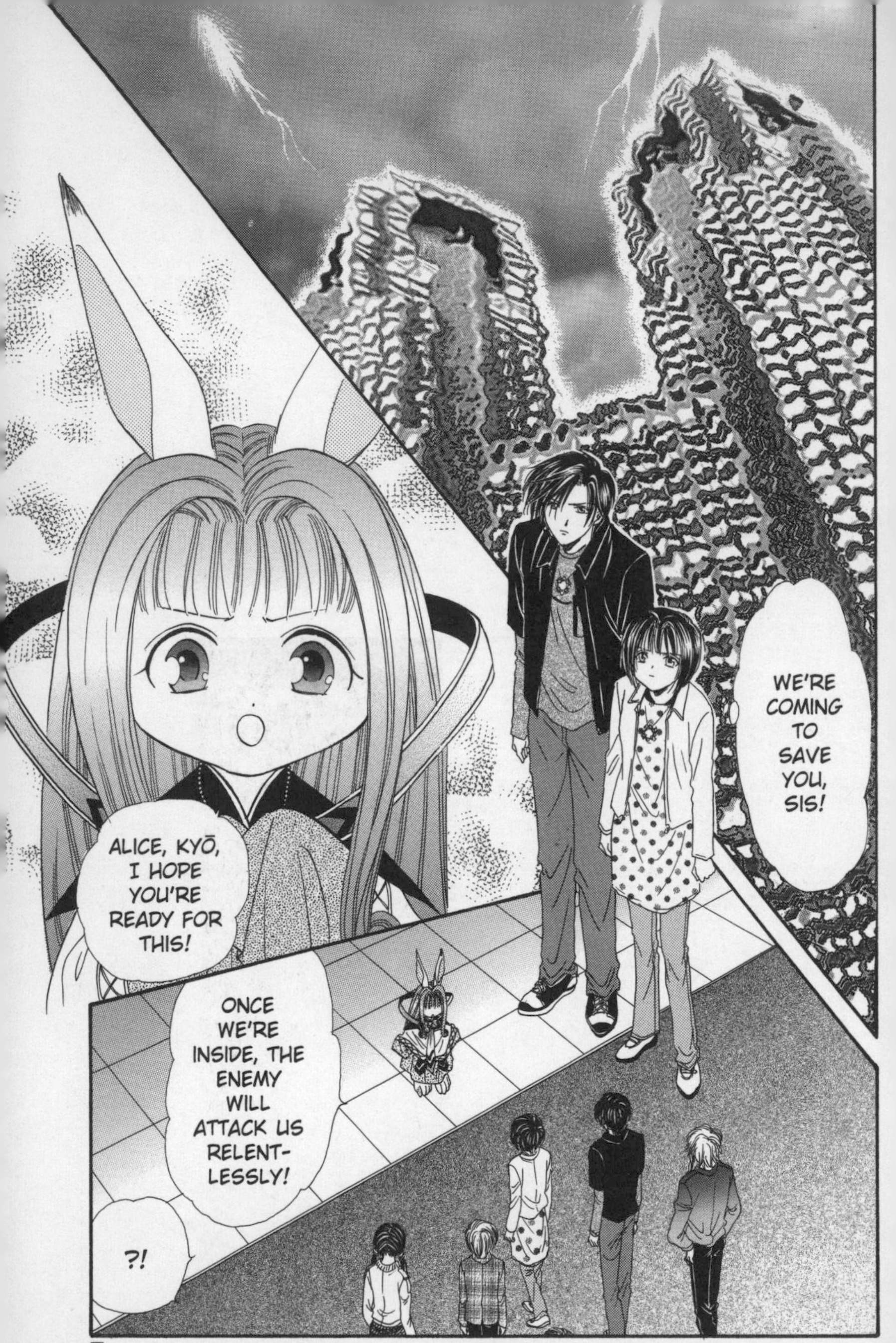
WE'RE COMING TO SAVE YOU, SIS!
ALICE, KYŌ, I HOPE YOU'RE READY FOR THIS!
ONCE WE'RE INSIDE, THE ENEMY WILL ATTACK US RELENT-LESSLY!
?!

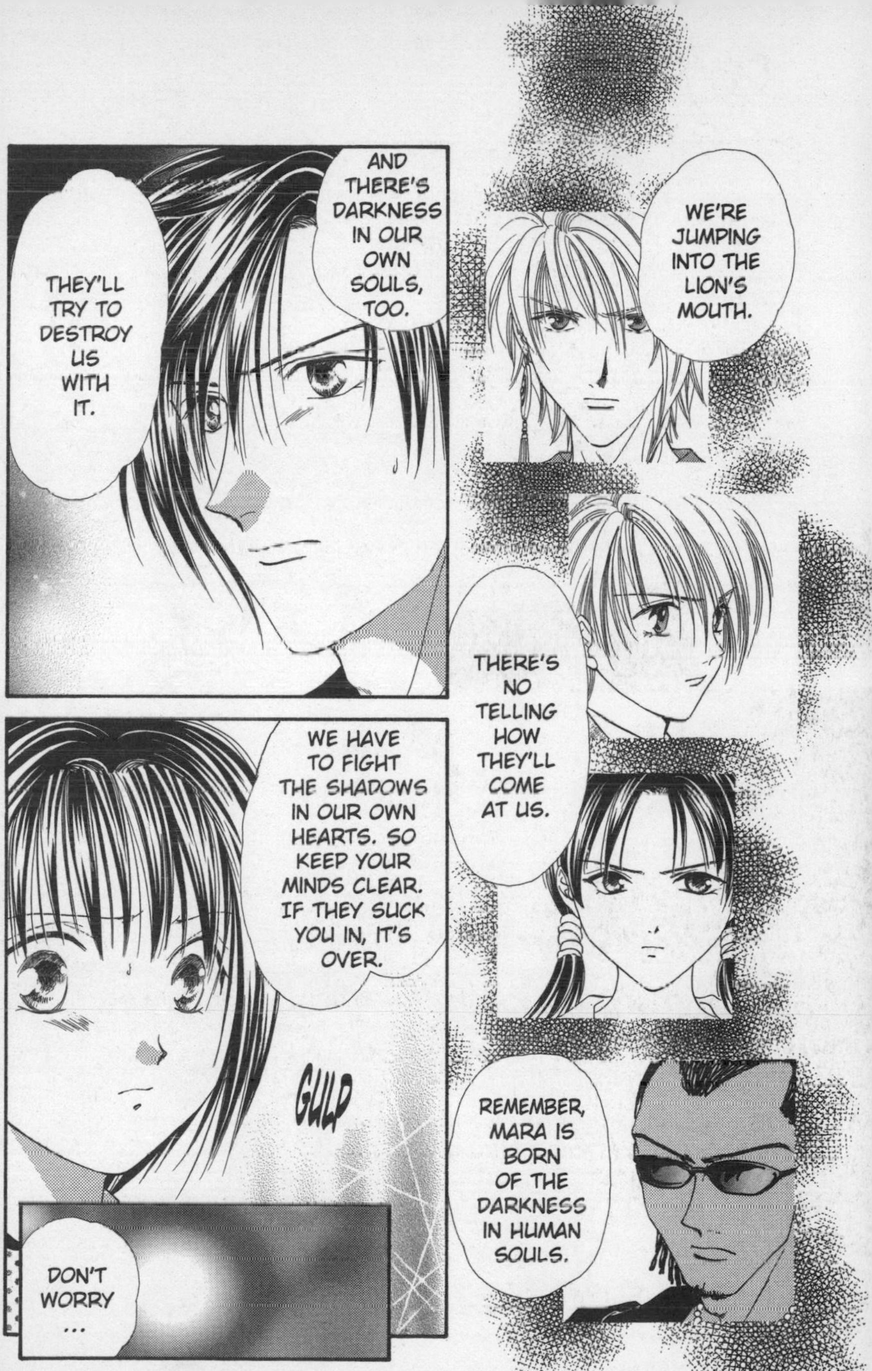
WE'RE JUMPING INTO THE LION'S MOUTH.
THERE'S NO TELLING HOW THEY'LL COME AT US.
REMEMBER, MARA IS BORN OF THE DARKNESS IN HUMAN SOULS.
AND THERE'S DARKNESS IN OUR OWN SOULS, TOO.
THEY'LL TRY TO DESTROY US WITH IT.
WE HAVE TO FIGHT THE SHADOWS IN OUR OWN HEARTS. SO KEEP YOUR MINDS CLEAR. IF THEY SUCK YOU IN, IT'S OVER.
GULP
DON'T WORRY ...

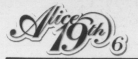

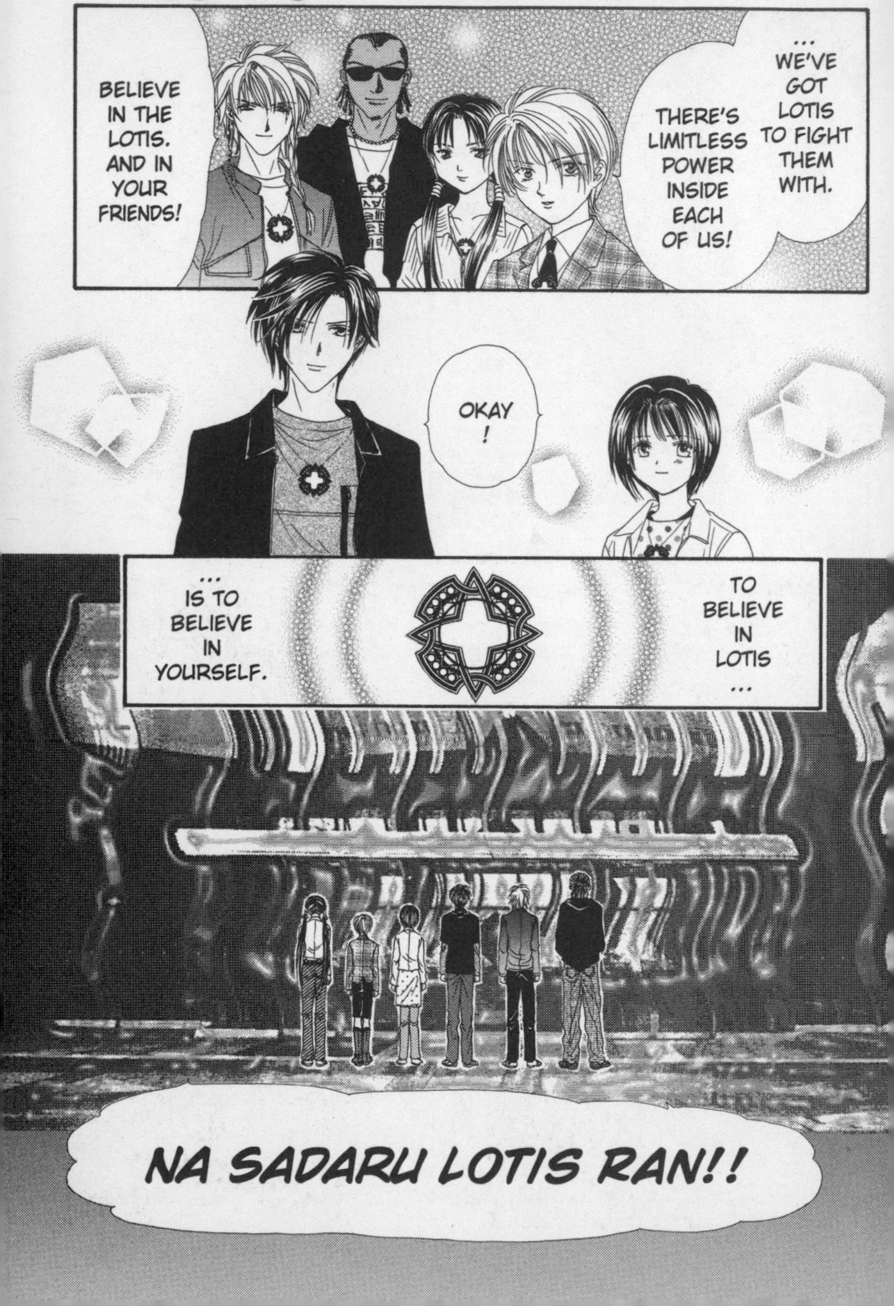
... WE'VE GOT LOTIS TO FIGHT THEM WITH.
THERE'S LIMITLESS POWER INSIDE EACH OF US!
BELIEVE IN THE LOTIS. AND IN YOUR FRIENDS!
OKAY!
TO BELIEVE IN LOTIS ...
... IS TO BELIEVE IN YOURSELF.
NA SADARU LOTIS RAN!!

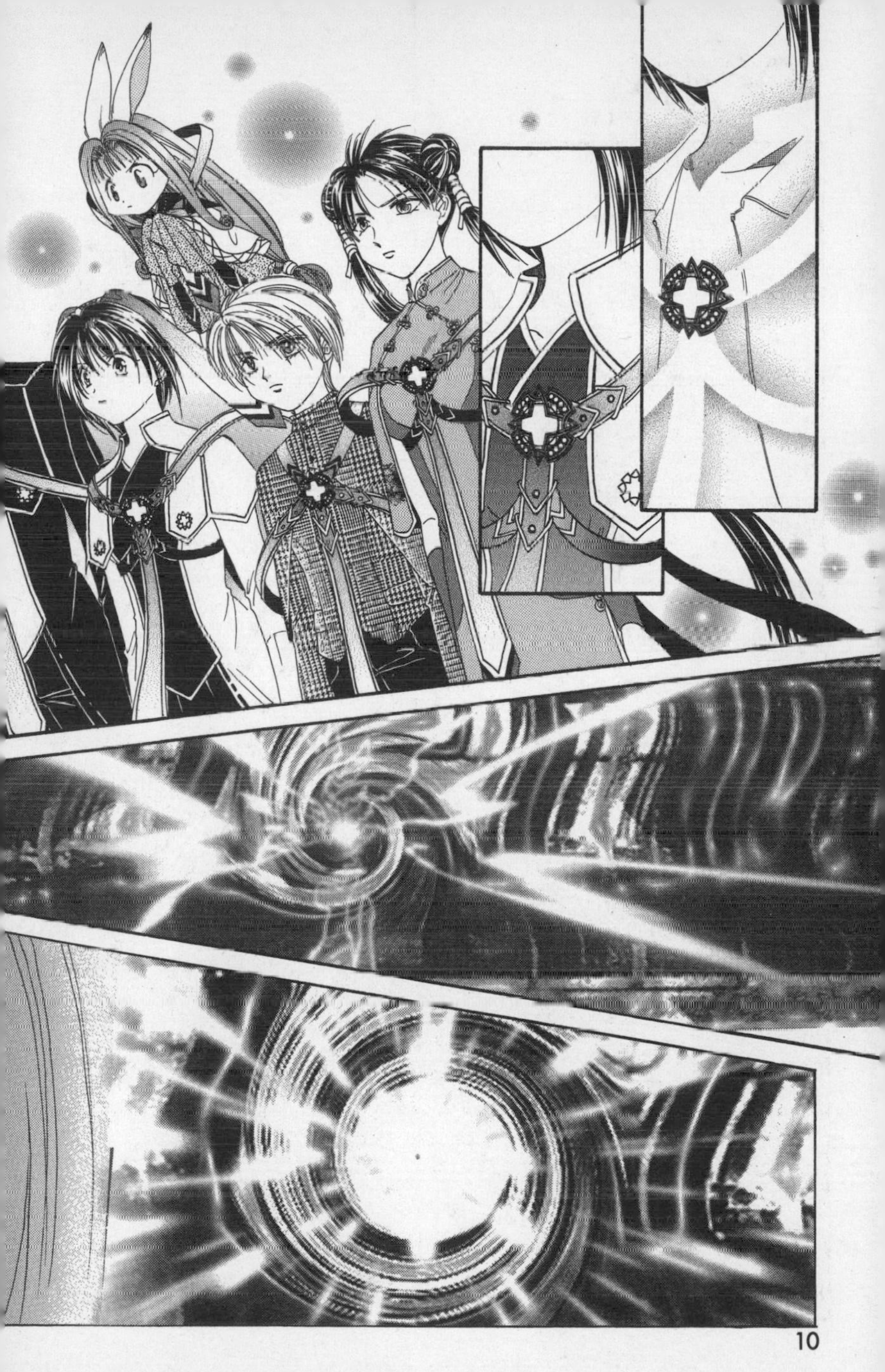

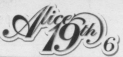

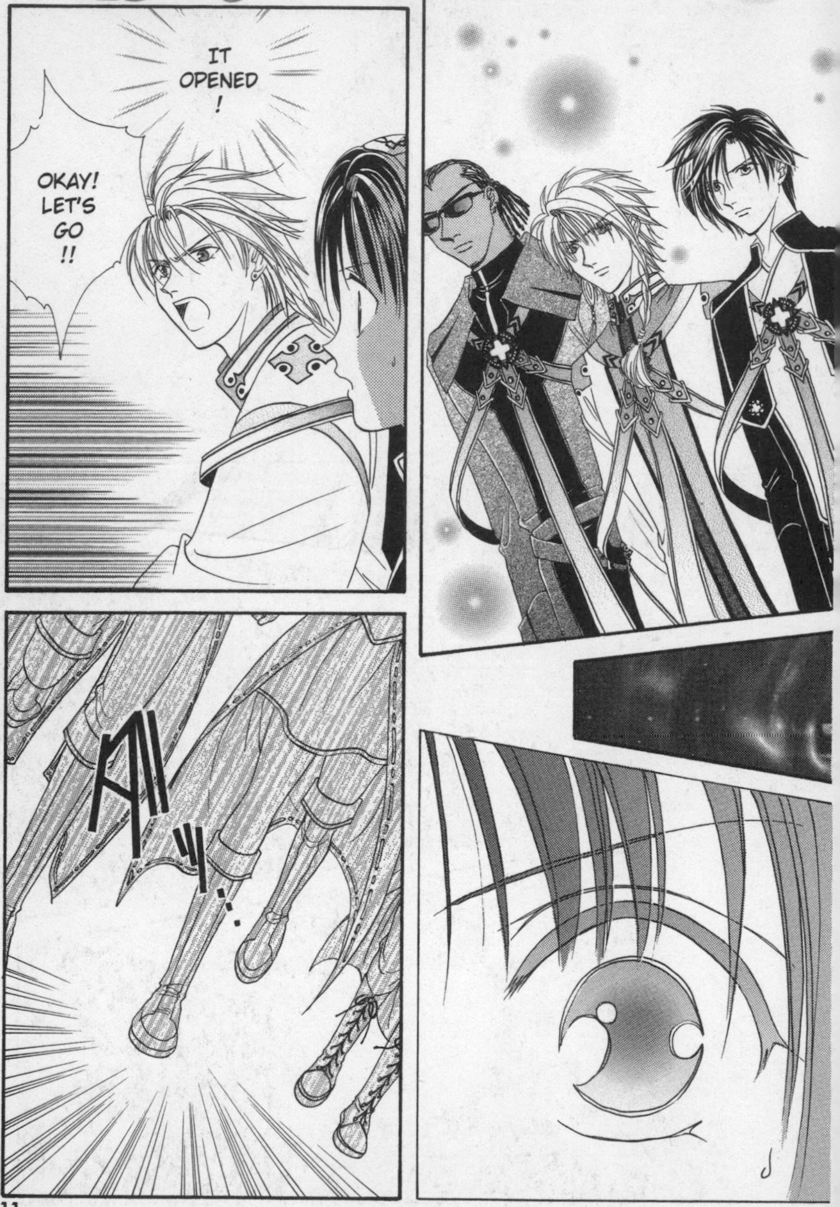
IT OPENED !
OKAY! LET'S GO !!

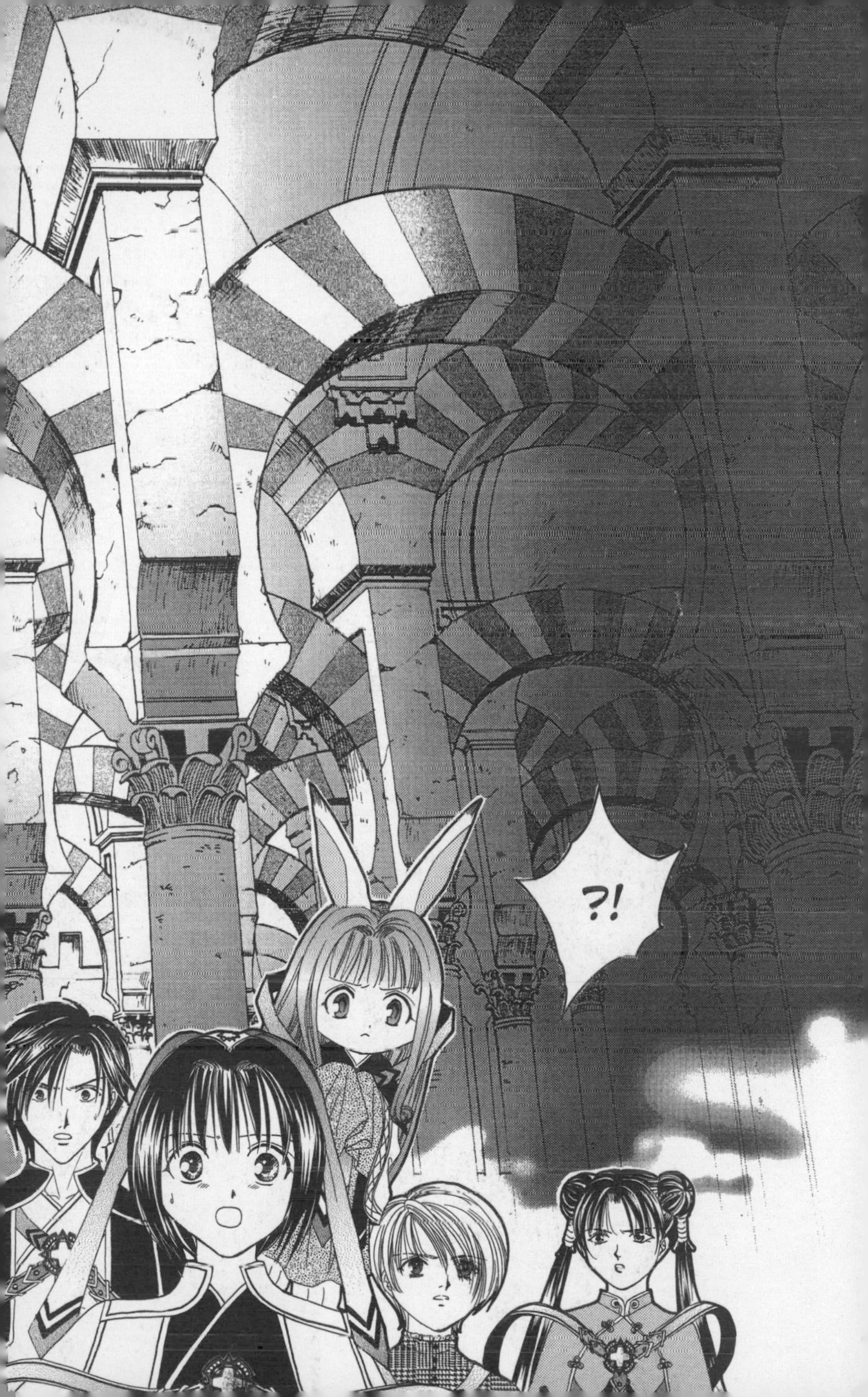
?!

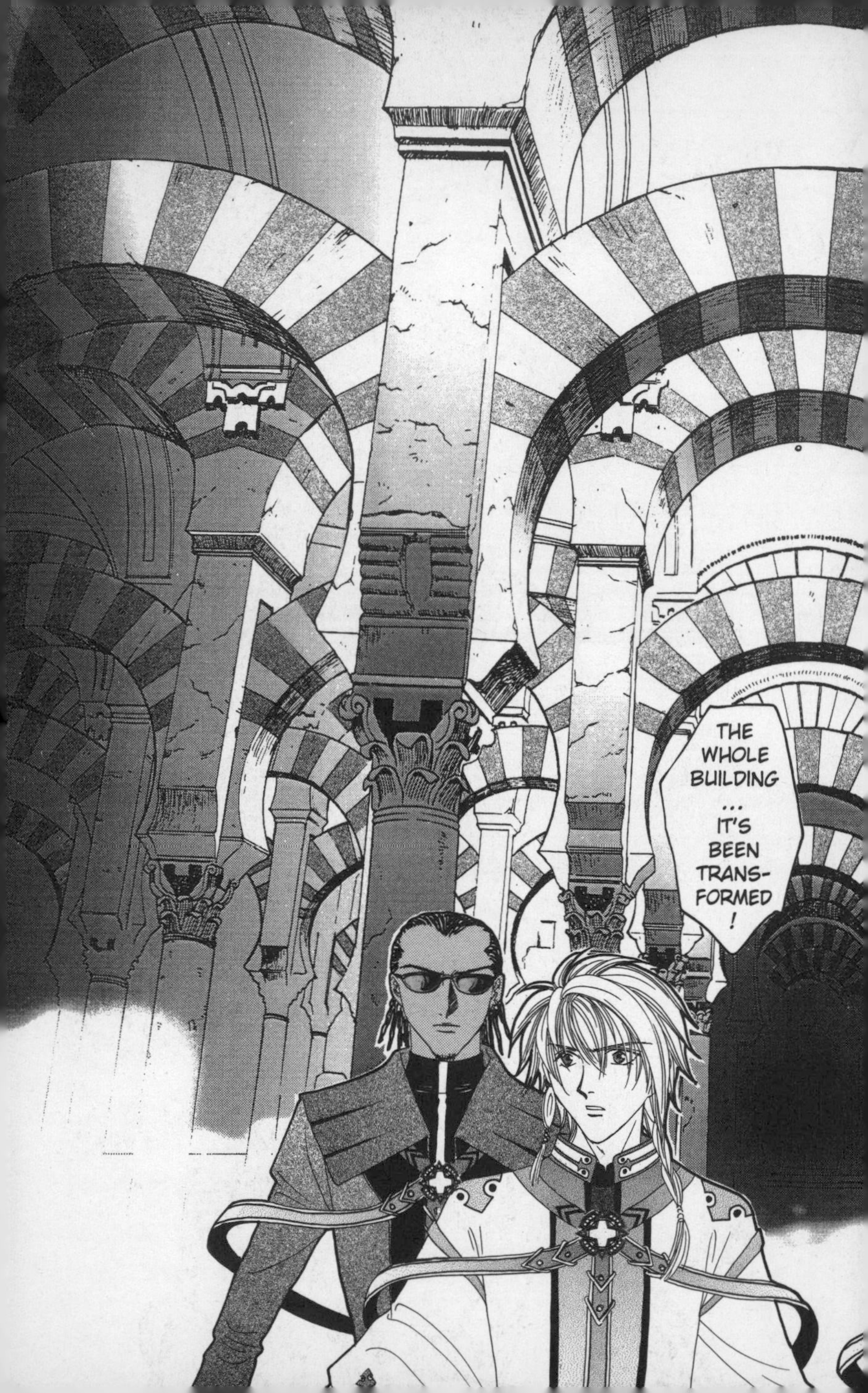
THE WHOLE BUILDING ... IT'S BEEN TRANS-FORMED!

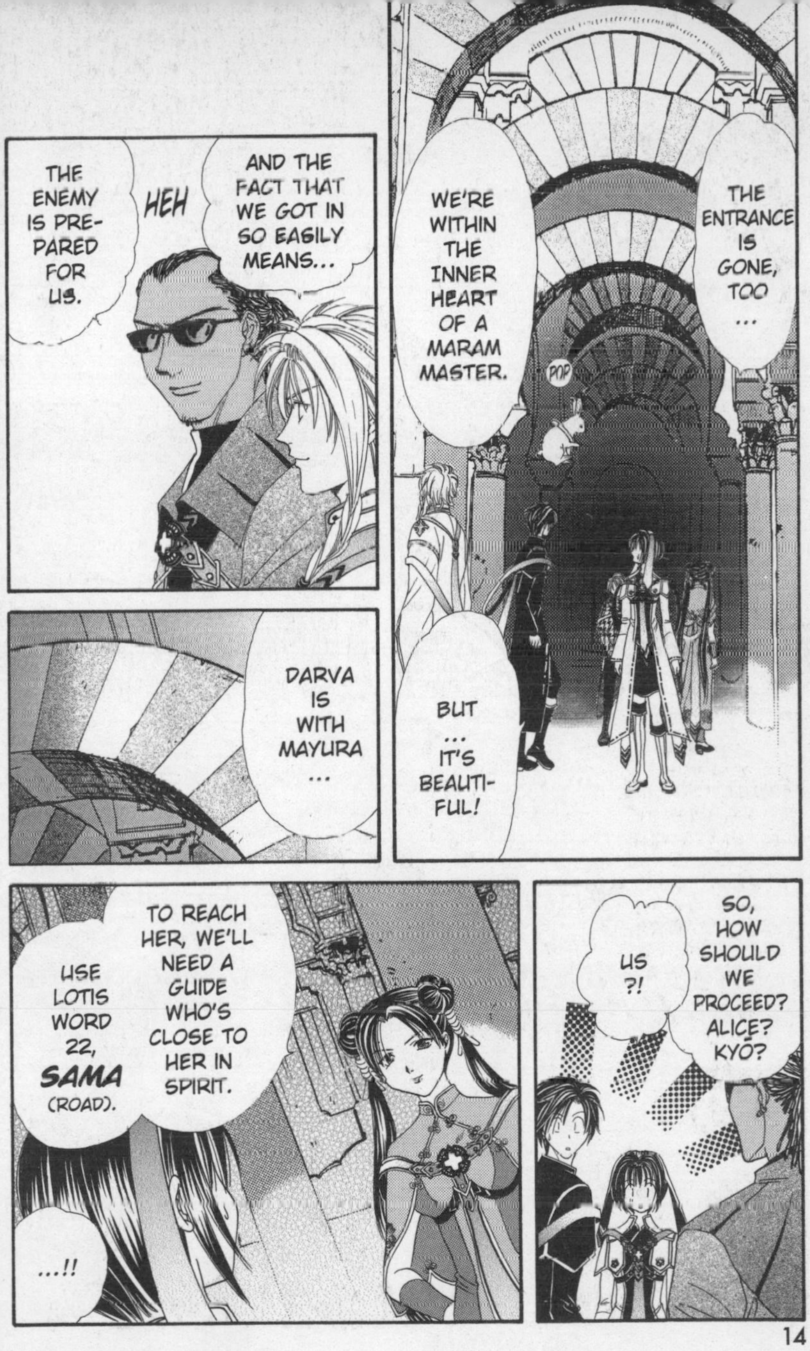
THE ENTRANCE IS GONE, TOO ...
WE'RE WITHIN THE INNER HEART OF A MARAM MASTER.
POP
BUT ... IT'S BEAUTIFUL!
AND THE FACT THAT WE GOT IN SO EASILY MEANS...
HEH
THE ENEMY IS PRE-PARED FOR US.
DARVA IS WITH MAYURA ...
SO, HOW SHOULD WE PROCEED? ALICE? KYO?
US ?!
TO REACH HER, WE'LL NEED A GUIDE WHO'S CLOSE TO HER IN SPIRIT.
USE LOTIS WORD 22, **SAMA** (ROAD).
...!!

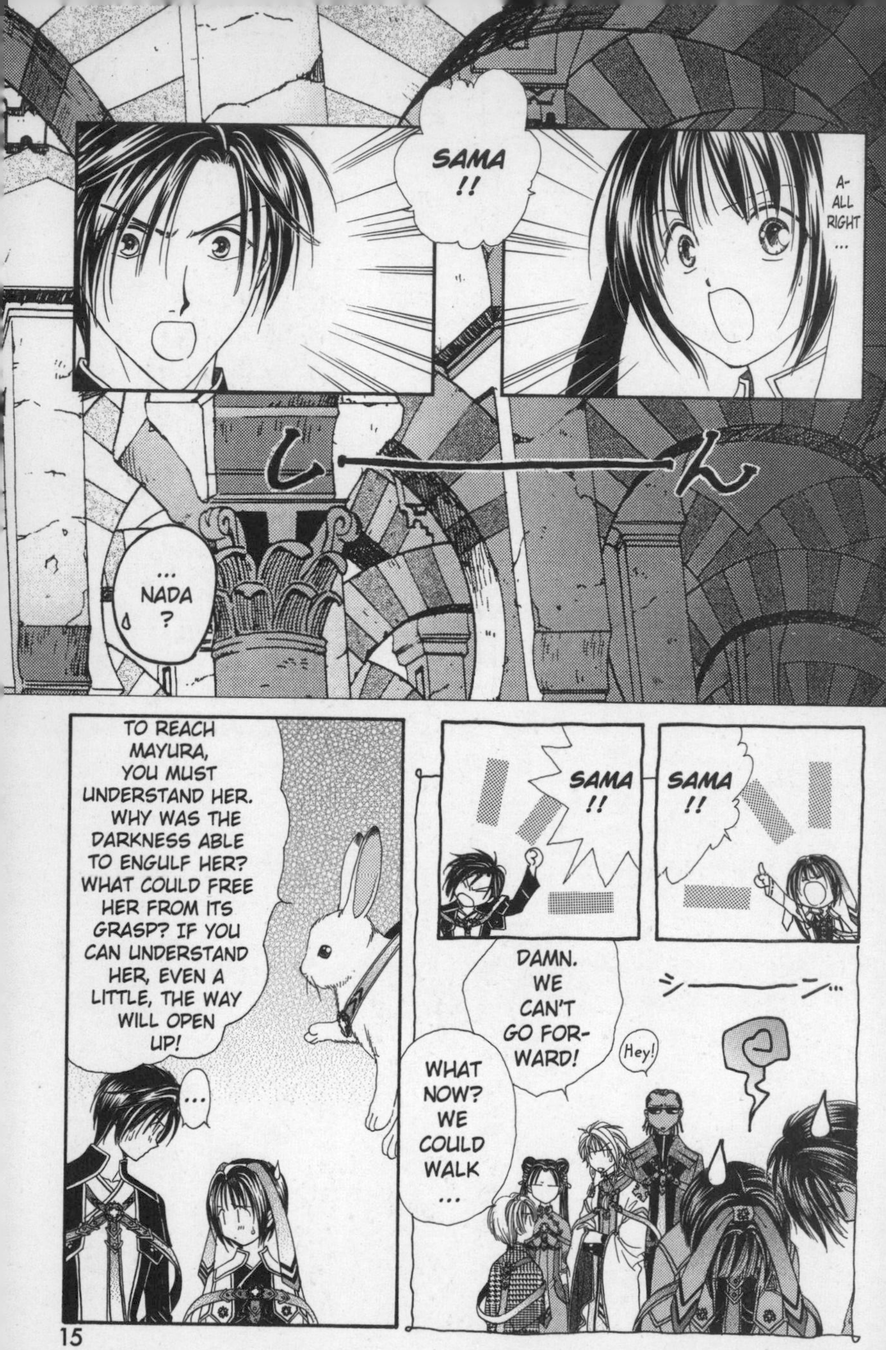
A- ALL RIGHT ...
SAMA !!
し———ん
... NADA ?
SAMA !!
SAMA !!
シ————ン…
Hey!
DAMN. WE CAN'T GO FOR-WARD!
WHAT NOW? WE COULD WALK ...
TO REACH MAYURA, YOU MUST UNDERSTAND HER. WHY WAS THE DARKNESS ABLE TO ENGULF HER? WHAT COULD FREE HER FROM ITS GRASP? IF YOU CAN UNDERSTAND HER, EVEN A LITTLE, THE WAY WILL OPEN UP!
...

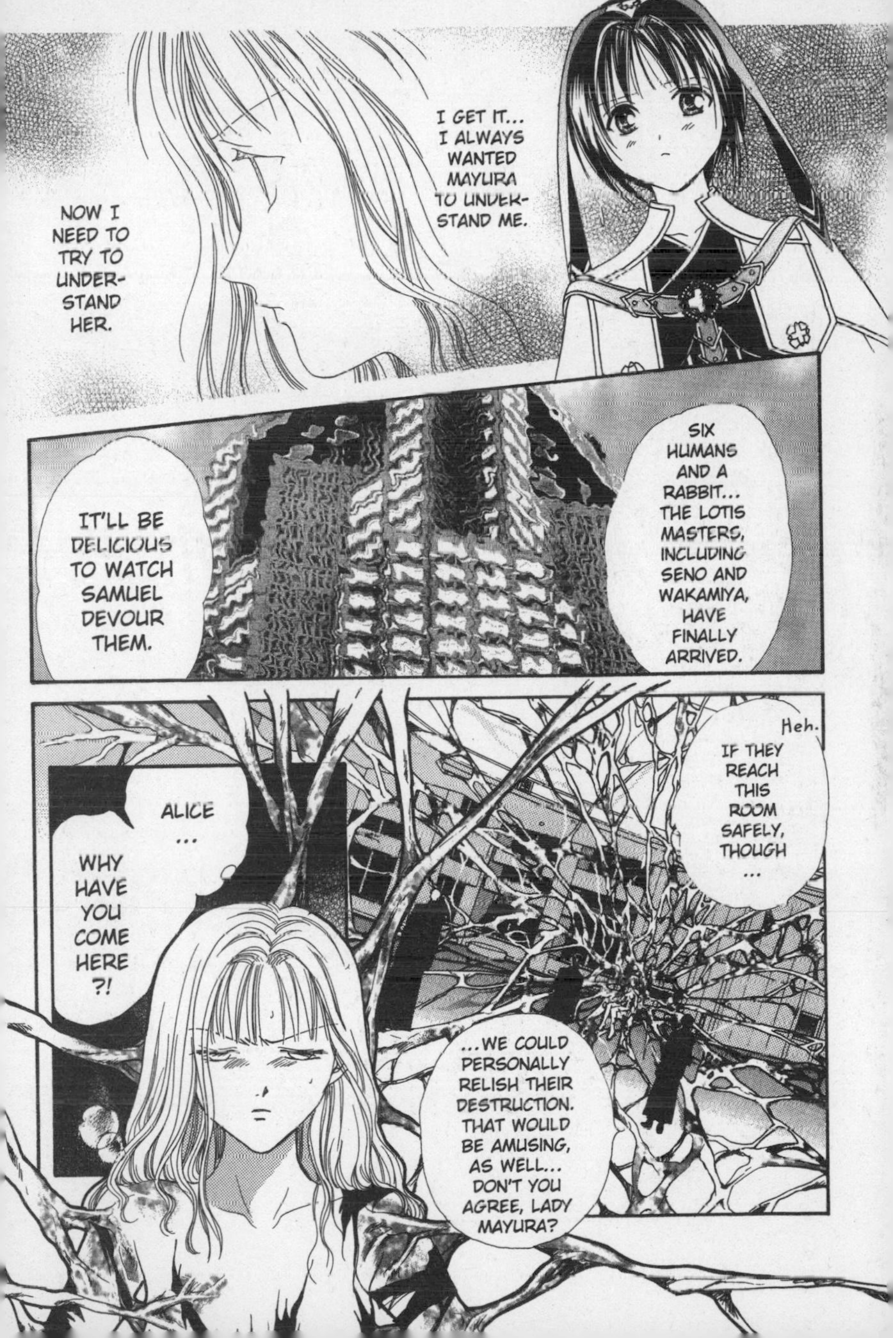
I GET IT... I ALWAYS WANTED MAYURA TO UNDER-STAND ME.
NOW I NEED TO TRY TO UNDER-STAND HER.
SIX HUMANS AND A RABBIT... THE LOTIS MASTERS, INCLUDING SENO AND WAKAMIYA, HAVE FINALLY ARRIVED.
IT'LL BE DELICIOUS TO WATCH SAMUEL DEVOUR THEM.
Heh.
IF THEY REACH THIS ROOM SAFELY, THOUGH...
...WE COULD PERSONALLY RELISH THEIR DESTRUCTION. THAT WOULD BE AMUSING, AS WELL... DON'T YOU AGREE, LADY MAYURA?
ALICE... WHY HAVE YOU COME HERE?!

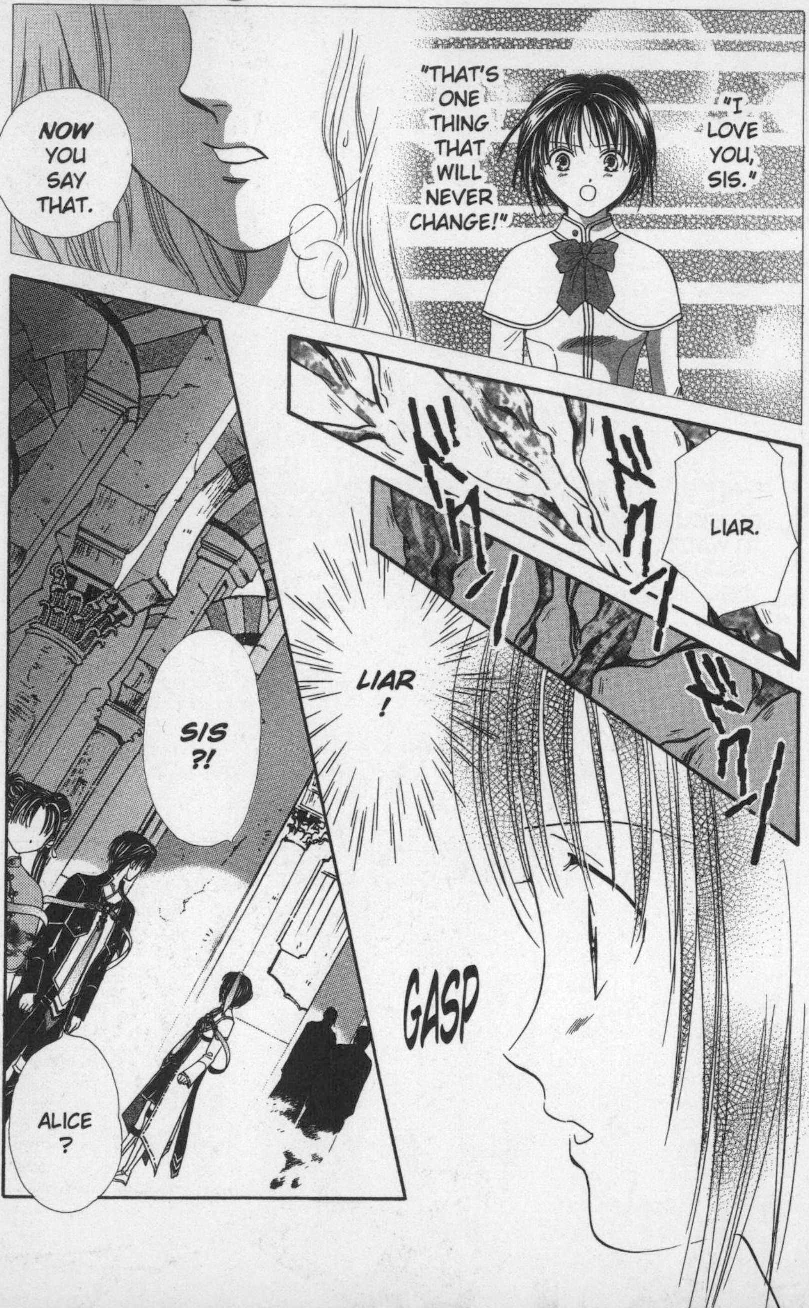
"I LOVE YOU, SIS."
"THAT'S ONE THING THAT WILL NEVER CHANGE!"
NOW YOU SAY THAT.
LIAR.
LIAR!
GASP
SIS?!
ALICE?

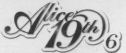

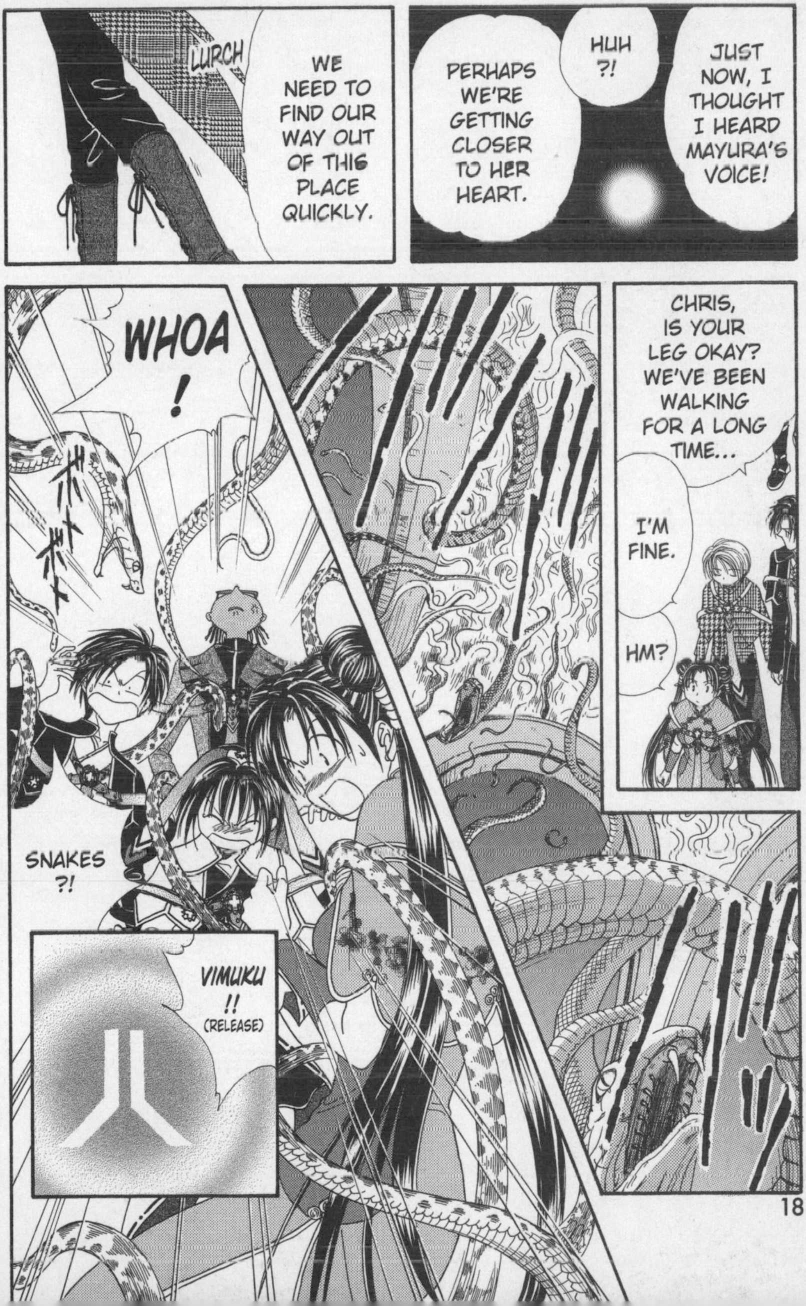

JUST NOW, I THOUGHT I HEARD MAYURA'S VOICE!
HUH ?!
PERHAPS WE'RE GETTING CLOSER TO HER HEART.
WE NEED TO FIND OUR WAY OUT OF THIS PLACE QUICKLY.
LURCH
CHRIS, IS YOUR LEG OKAY? WE'VE BEEN WALKING FOR A LONG TIME...
I'M FINE.
HM?
WHOA !
SNAKES ?!
VIMUKU !!
(RELEASE)

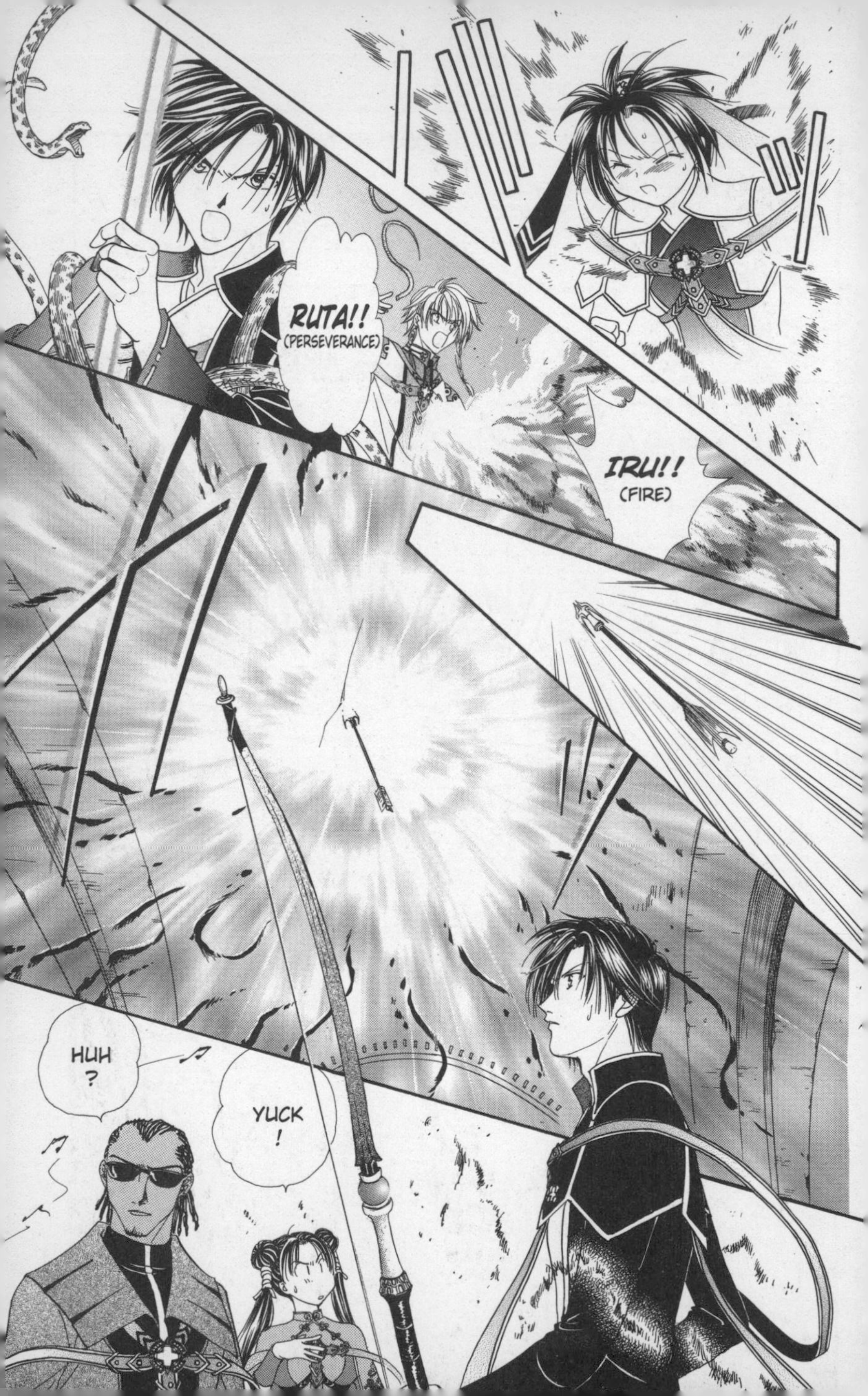
RUTA!!
(PERSEVERANCE)
IRU!!
(FIRE)
HUH
?
YUCK
!

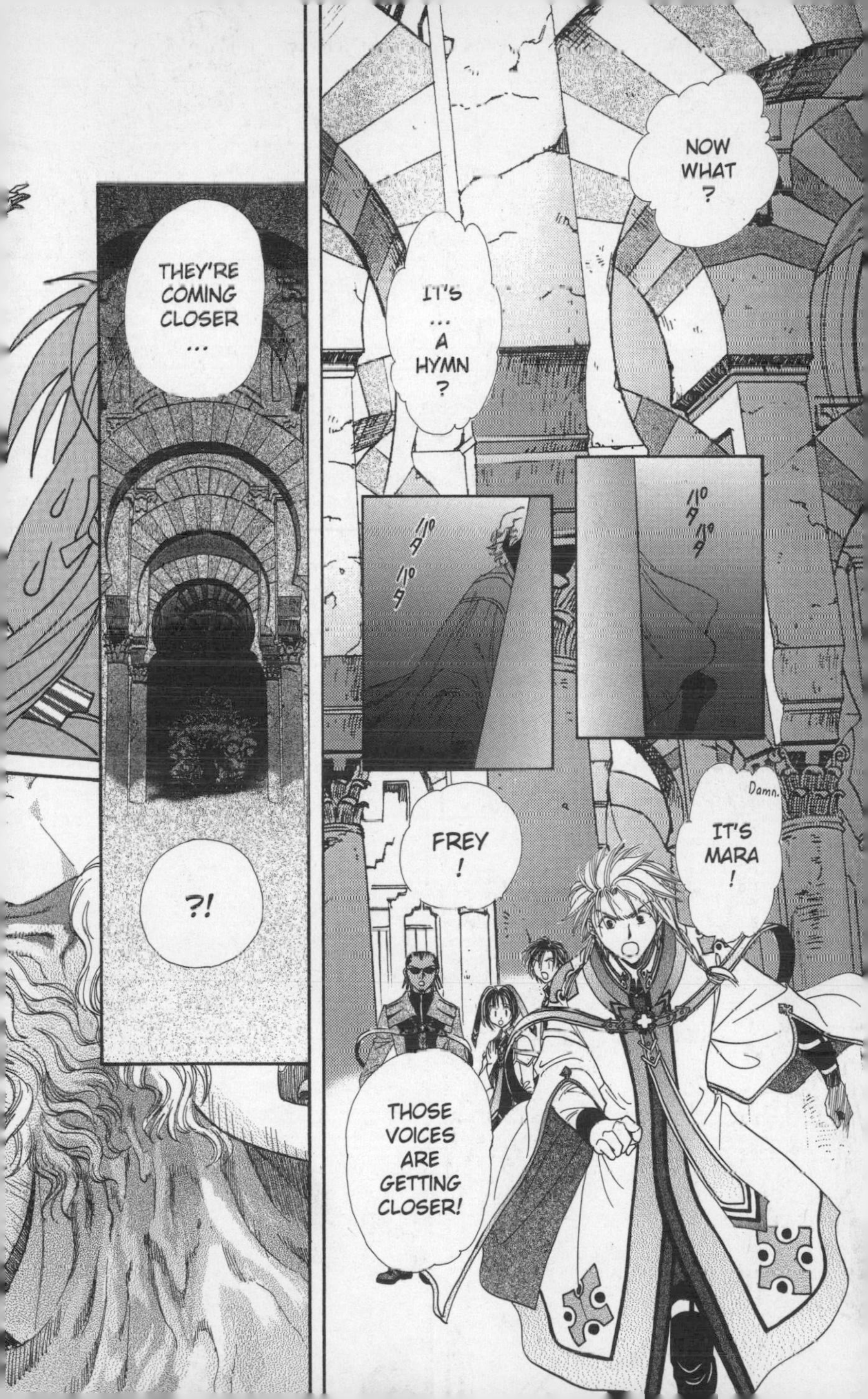
NOW WHAT?
IT'S... A HYMN?
パタパタ
パタパタ
Damn.
IT'S MARA!
FREY!
THOSE VOICES ARE GETTING CLOSER!
THEY'RE COMING CLOSER...
?!

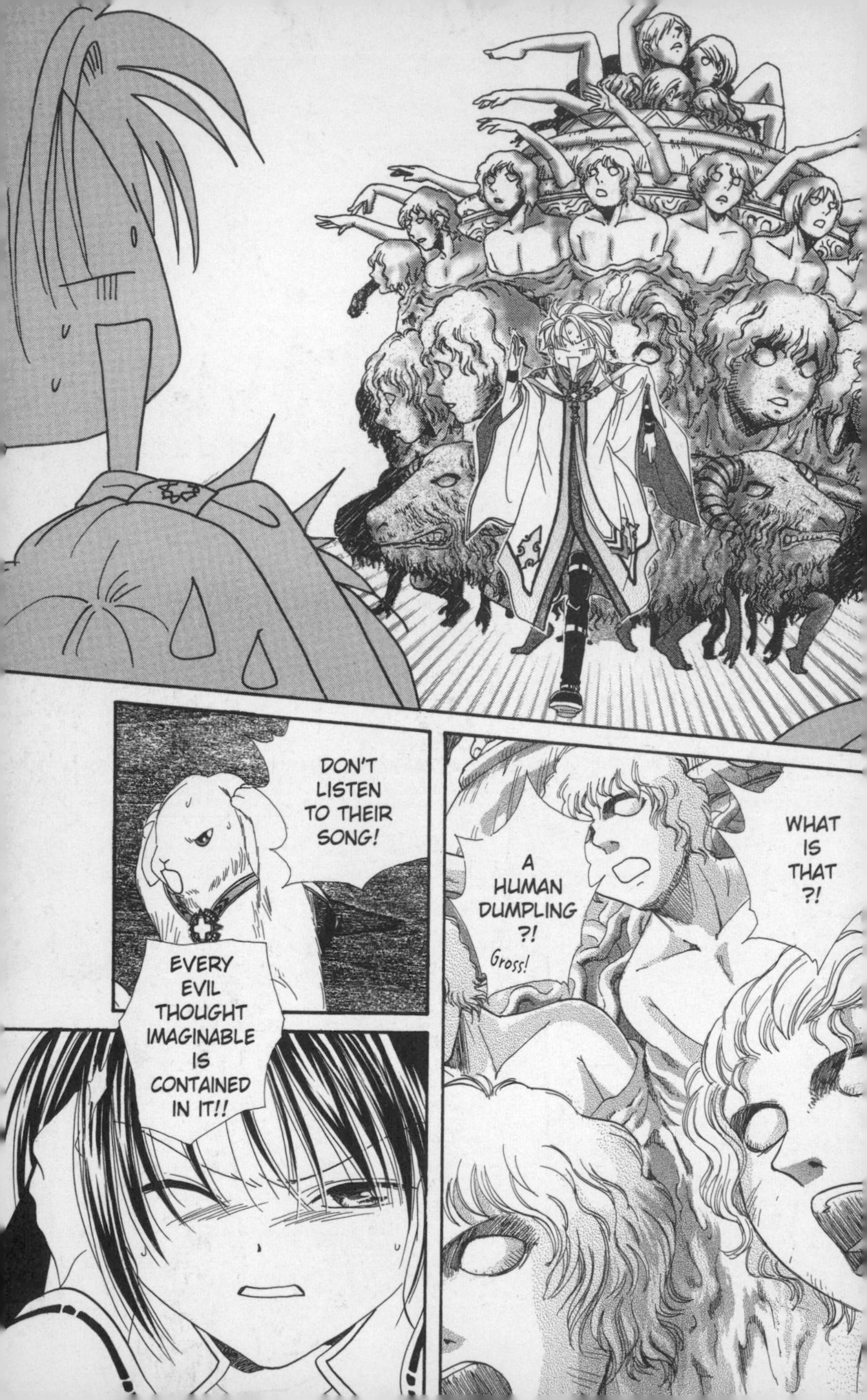
WHAT IS THAT ?!
A HUMAN DUMPLING ?!
Gross!
DON'T LISTEN TO THEIR SONG!
EVERY EVIL THOUGHT IMAGINABLE IS CONTAINED IN IT!!

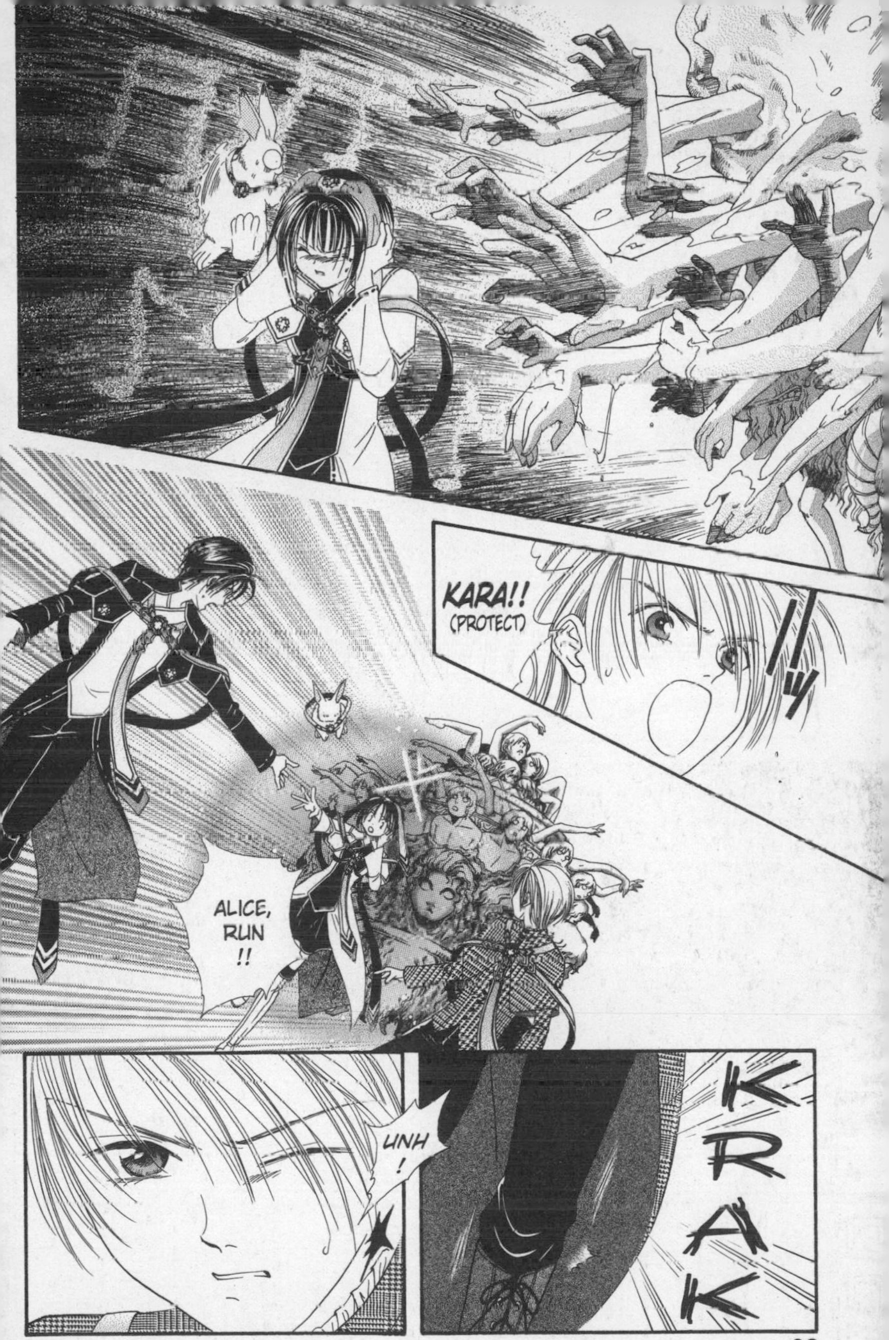
KARA!!
(PROTECT)
ALICE, RUN!!
KRAK
UNH!

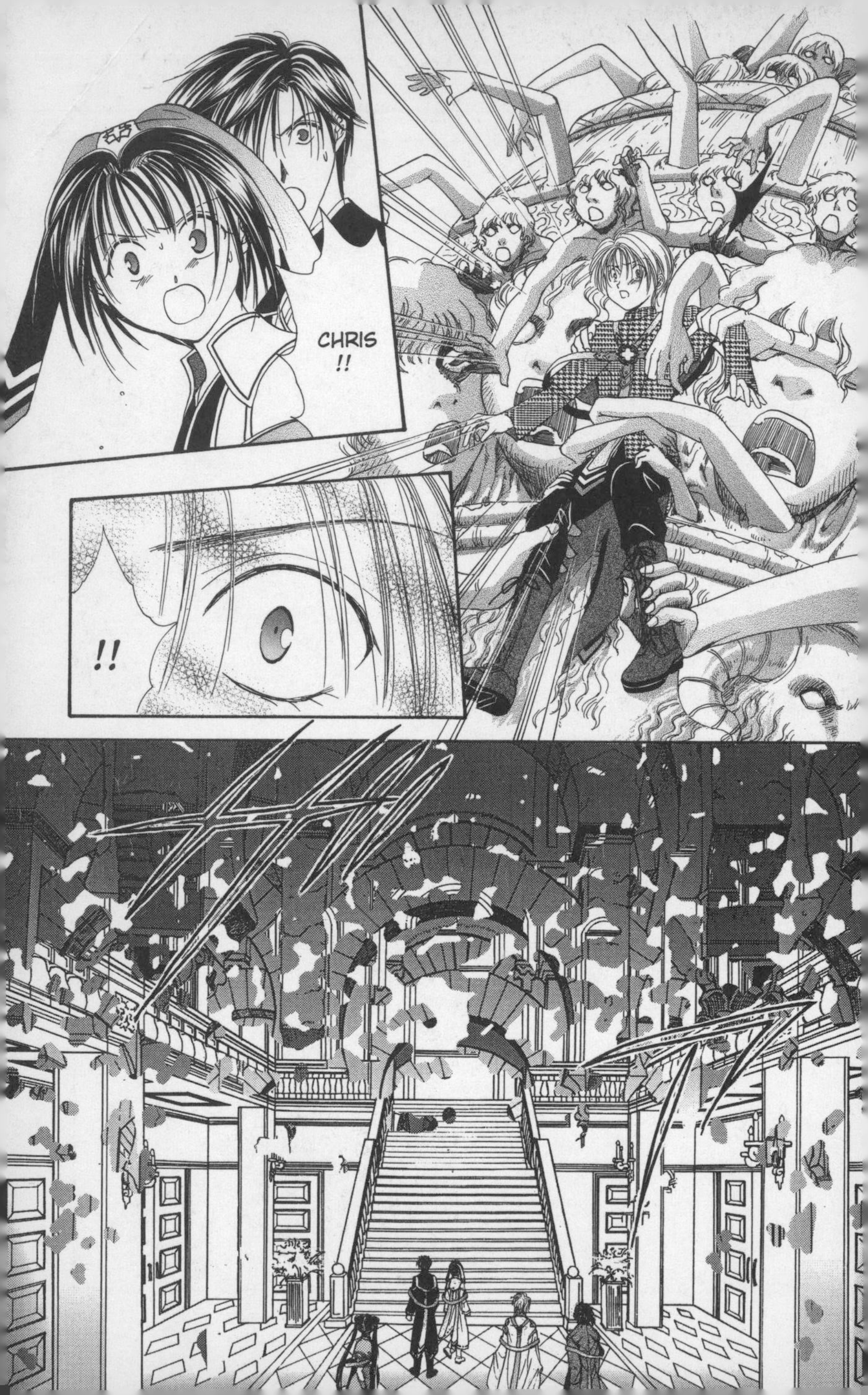
CHRIS !!
!!

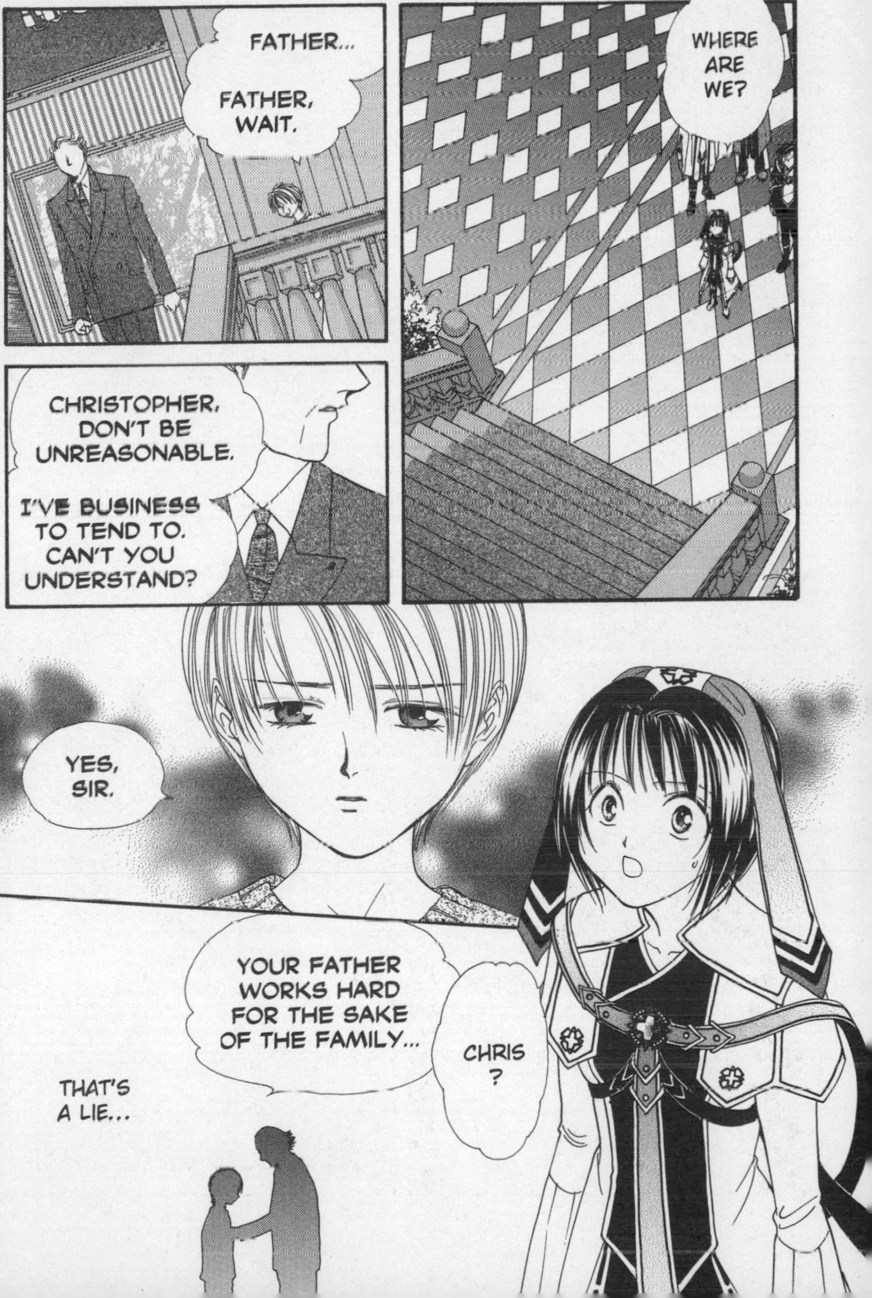
WHERE ARE WE?
FATHER...
FATHER, WAIT.
CHRISTOPHER, DON'T BE UNREASONABLE.
I'VE BUSINESS TO TEND TO. CAN'T YOU UNDERSTAND?
YES, SIR.
CHRIS ?
YOUR FATHER WORKS HARD FOR THE SAKE OF THE FAMILY...
THAT'S A LIE...

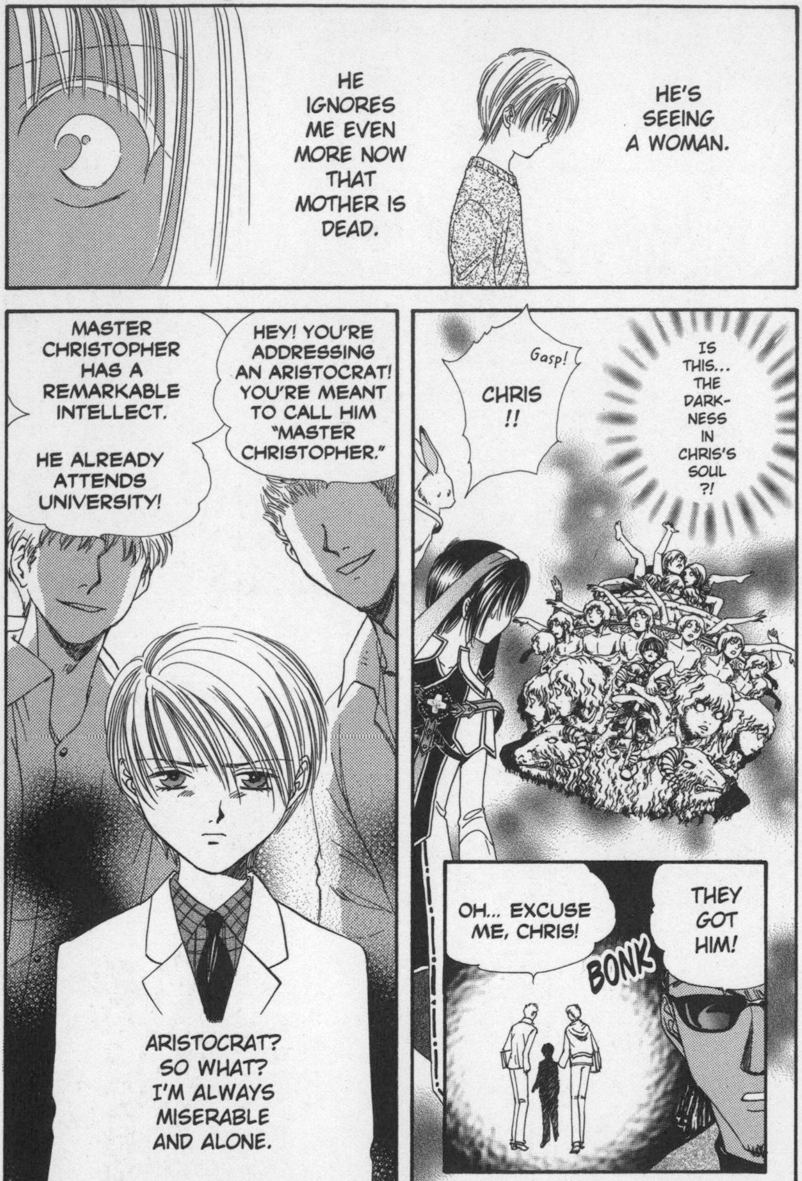
HE'S SEEING A WOMAN.
HE IGNORES ME EVEN MORE NOW THAT MOTHER IS DEAD.
IS THIS... THE DARKNESS IN CHRIS'S SOUL ?!
Gasp!
CHRIS !!
THEY GOT HIM!
BONK
OH... EXCUSE ME, CHRIS!
HEY! YOU'RE ADDRESSING AN ARISTOCRAT! YOU'RE MEANT TO CALL HIM "MASTER CHRISTOPHER."
MASTER CHRISTOPHER HAS A REMARKABLE INTELLECT.
HE ALREADY ATTENDS UNIVERSITY!
ARISTOCRAT? SO WHAT? I'M ALWAYS MISERABLE AND ALONE.

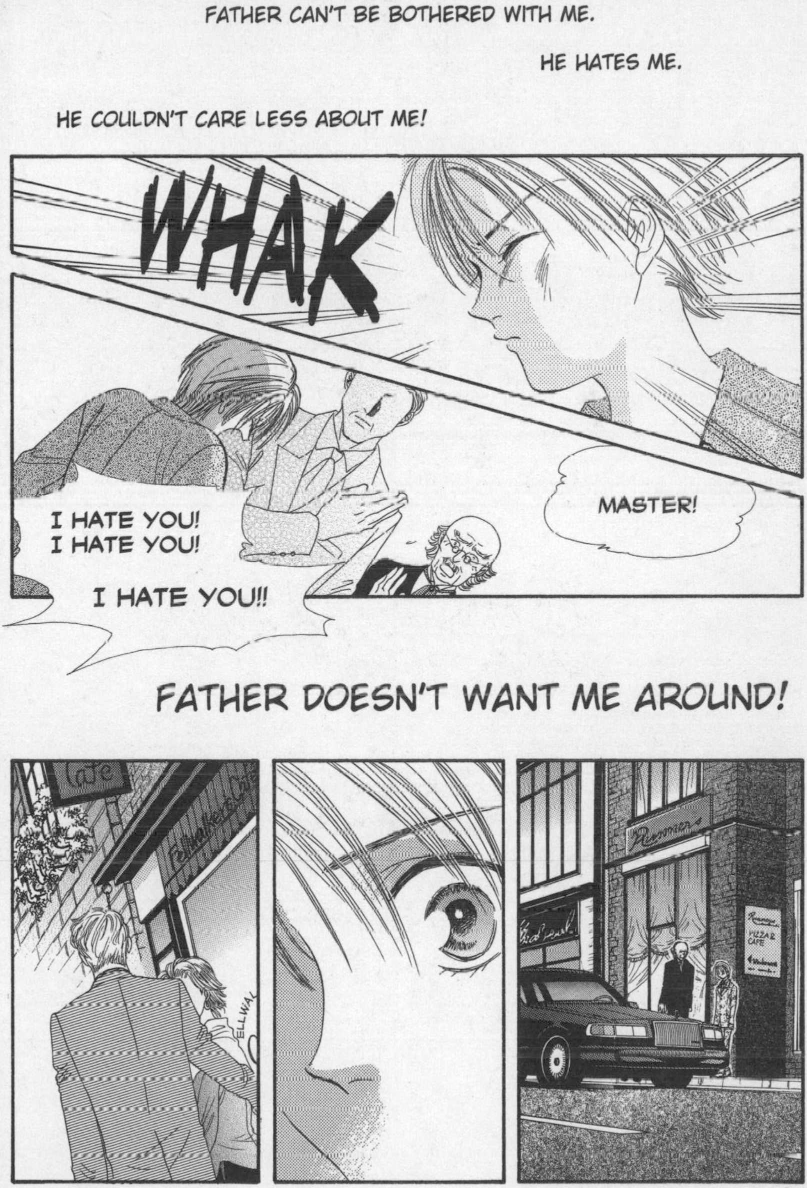
FATHER CAN'T BE BOTHERED WITH ME.
HE HATES ME.
HE COULDN'T CARE LESS ABOUT ME!
WHAK
MASTER!
I HATE YOU! I HATE YOU!
I HATE YOU!!
FATHER DOESN'T WANT ME AROUND!
PIZZA & CAFE
ELLWAL

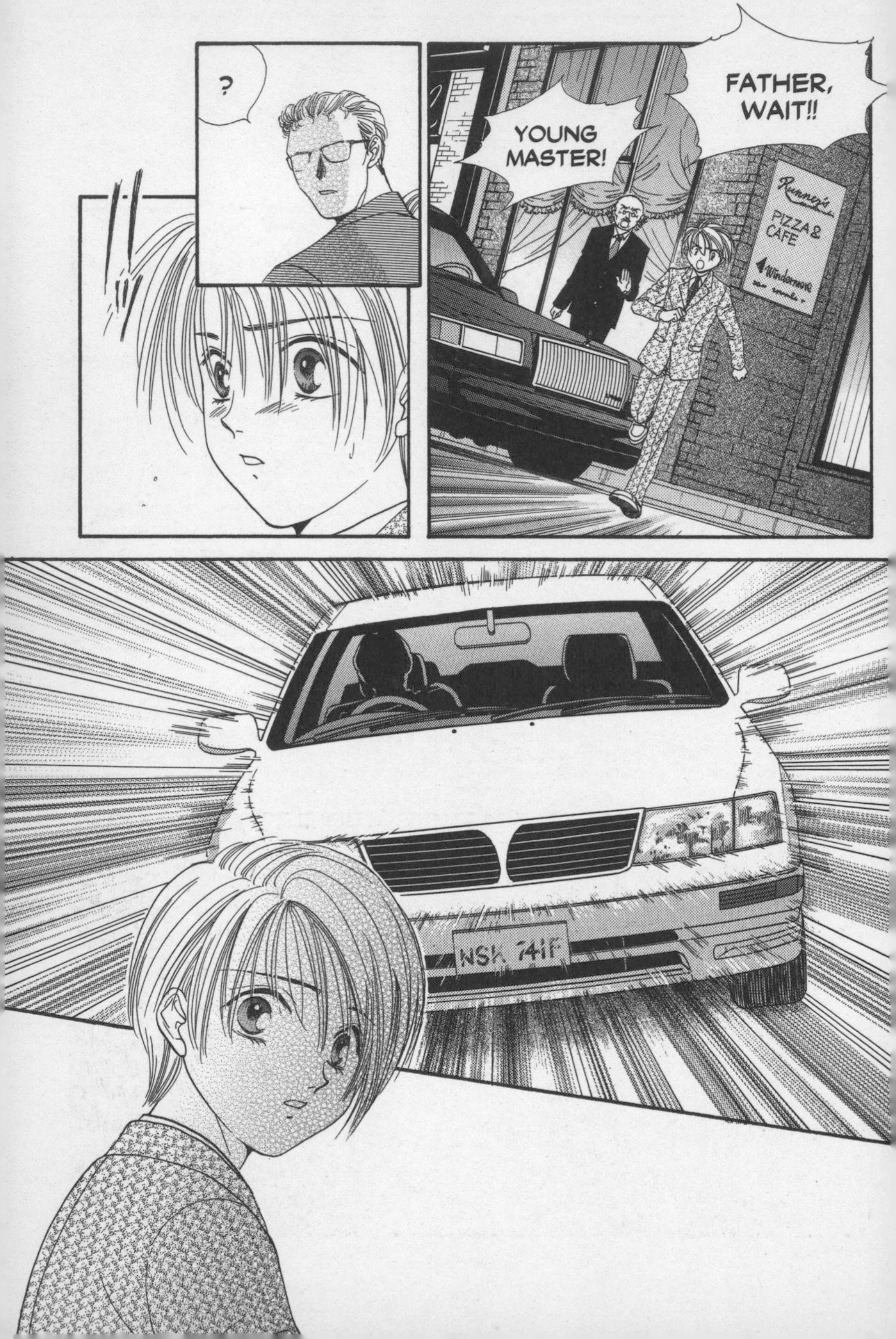
FATHER, WAIT!!
YOUNG MASTER!
PIZZA & CAFE
?

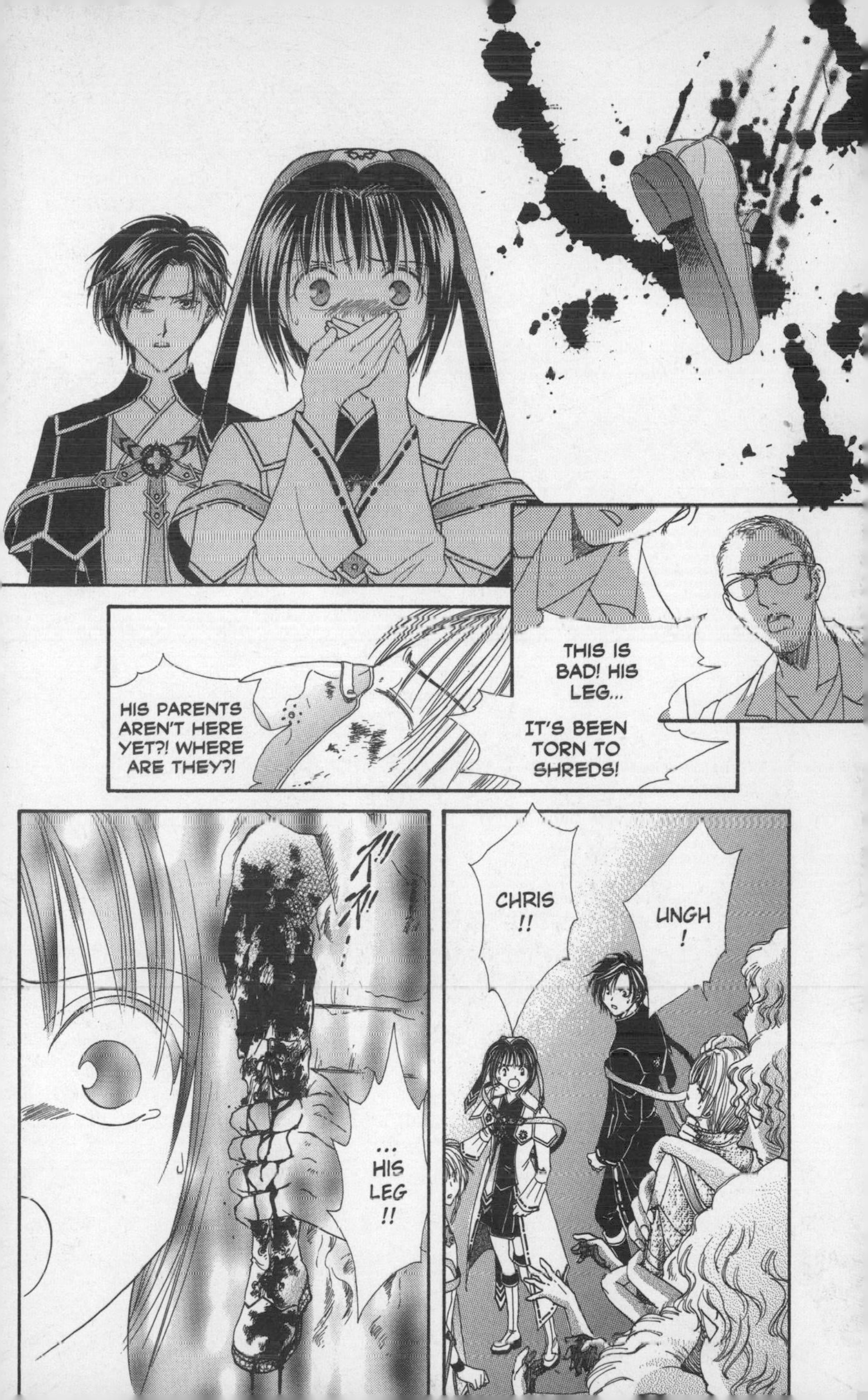
THIS IS BAD! HIS LEG...
IT'S BEEN TORN TO SHREDS!
HIS PARENTS AREN'T HERE YET?! WHERE ARE THEY?!
UNGH!
CHRIS!!
...HIS LEG!!

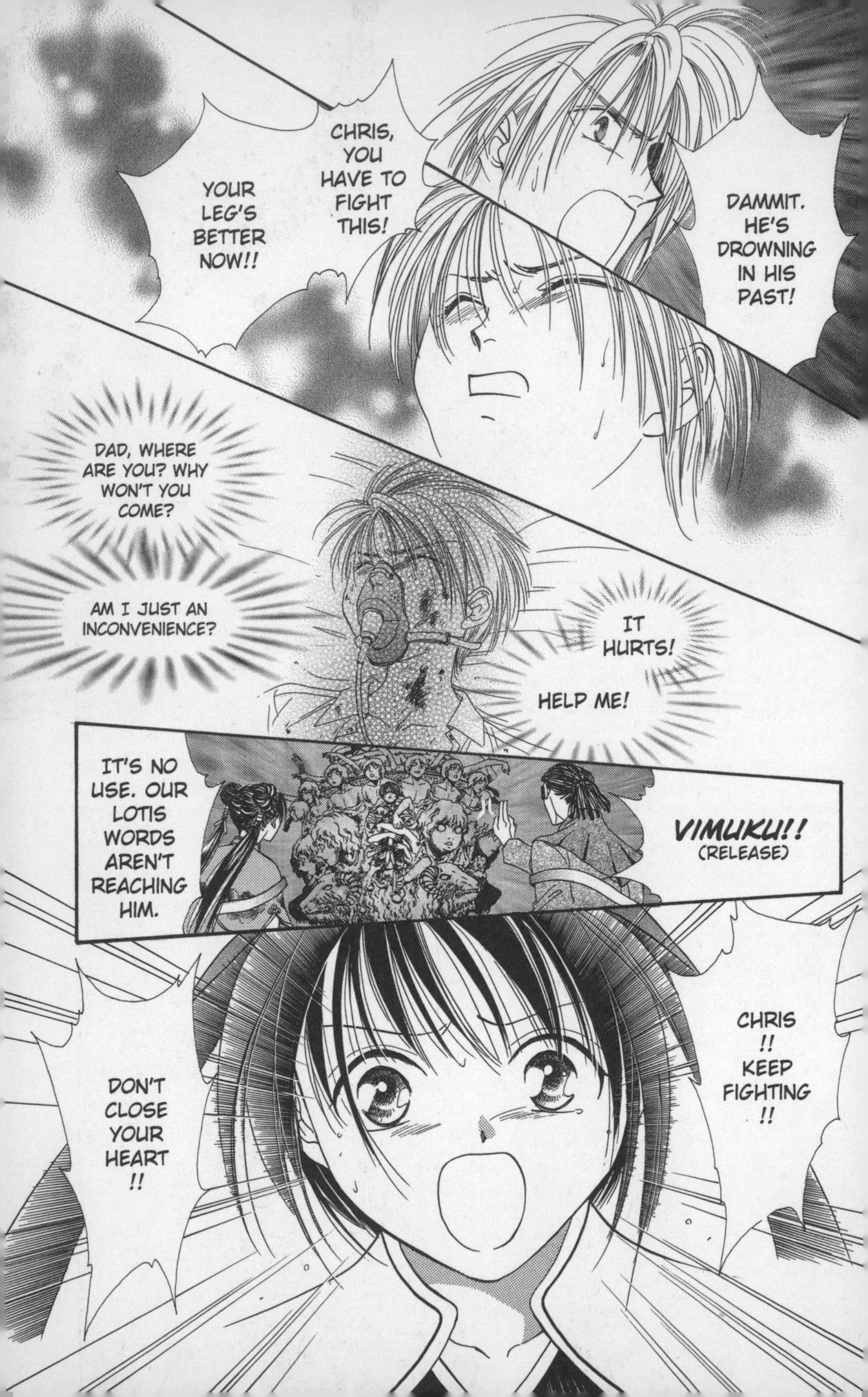
DAMMIT. HE'S DROWNING IN HIS PAST!
CHRIS, YOU HAVE TO FIGHT THIS!
YOUR LEG'S BETTER NOW!!
IT HURTS!
HELP ME!
DAD, WHERE ARE YOU? WHY WON'T YOU COME?
AM I JUST AN INCONVENIENCE?
VIMUKU!! (RELEASE)
IT'S NO USE. OUR LOTIS WORDS AREN'T REACHING HIM.
CHRIS!! KEEP FIGHTING!!
DON'T CLOSE YOUR HEART!!

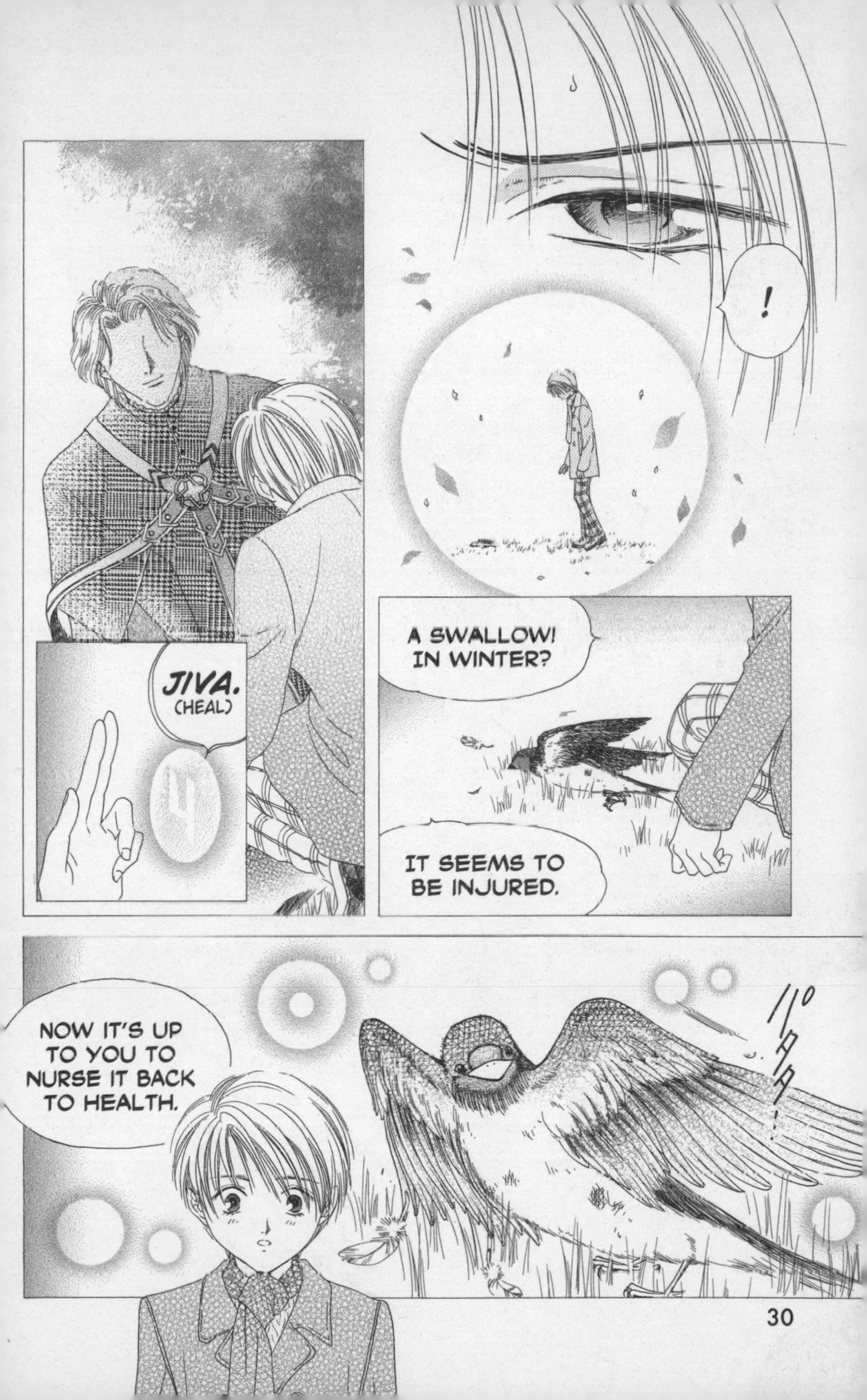
!
A SWALLOW! IN WINTER?
IT SEEMS TO BE INJURED.
JIVA.
(HEAL)
パタタ!
NOW IT'S UP TO YOU TO NURSE IT BACK TO HEALTH.

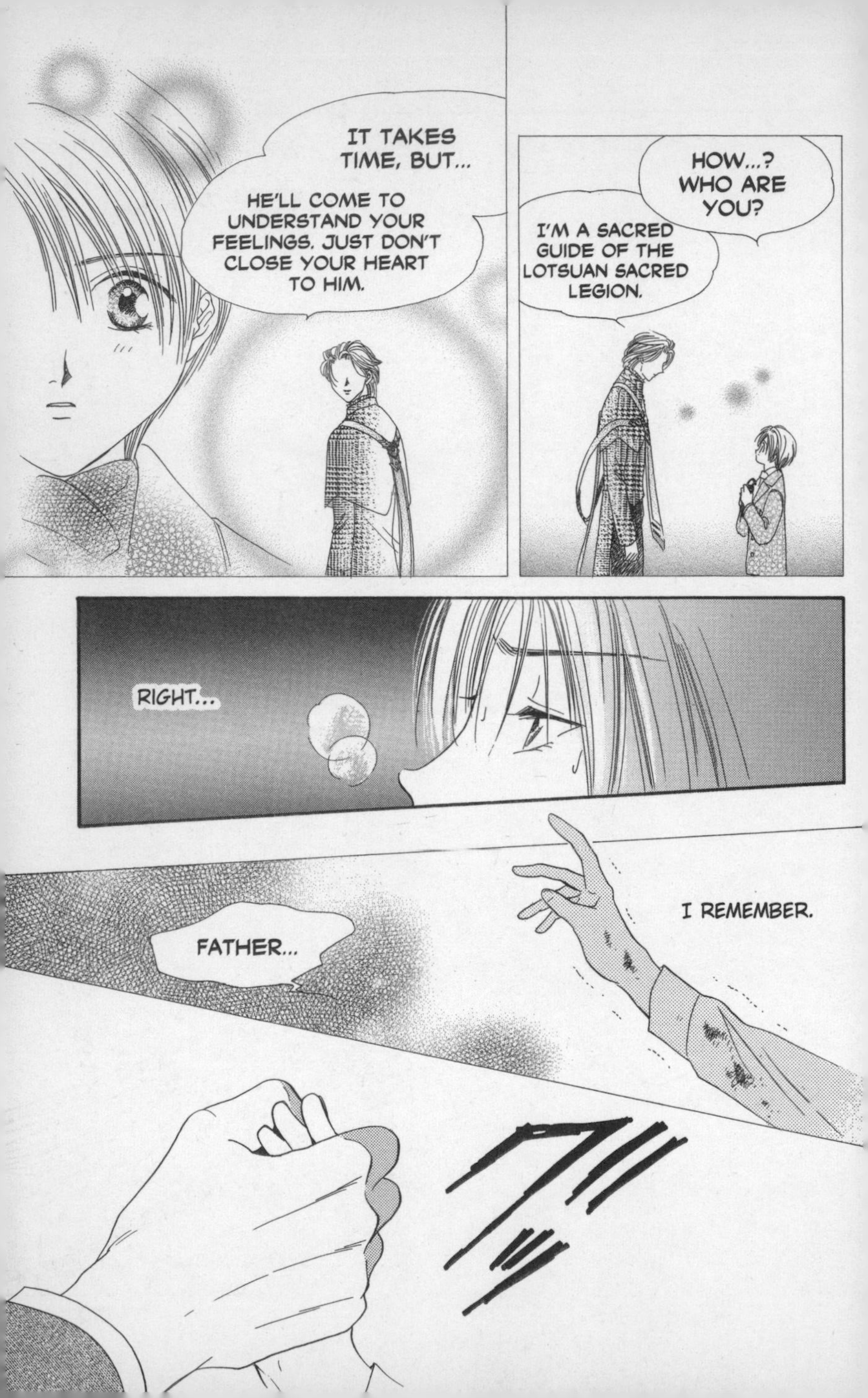
HOW...? WHO ARE YOU?
I'M A SACRED GUIDE OF THE LOTSUAN SACRED LEGION.
IT TAKES TIME, BUT...
HE'LL COME TO UNDERSTAND YOUR FEELINGS. JUST DON'T CLOSE YOUR HEART TO HIM.
RIGHT...
I REMEMBER.
FATHER...

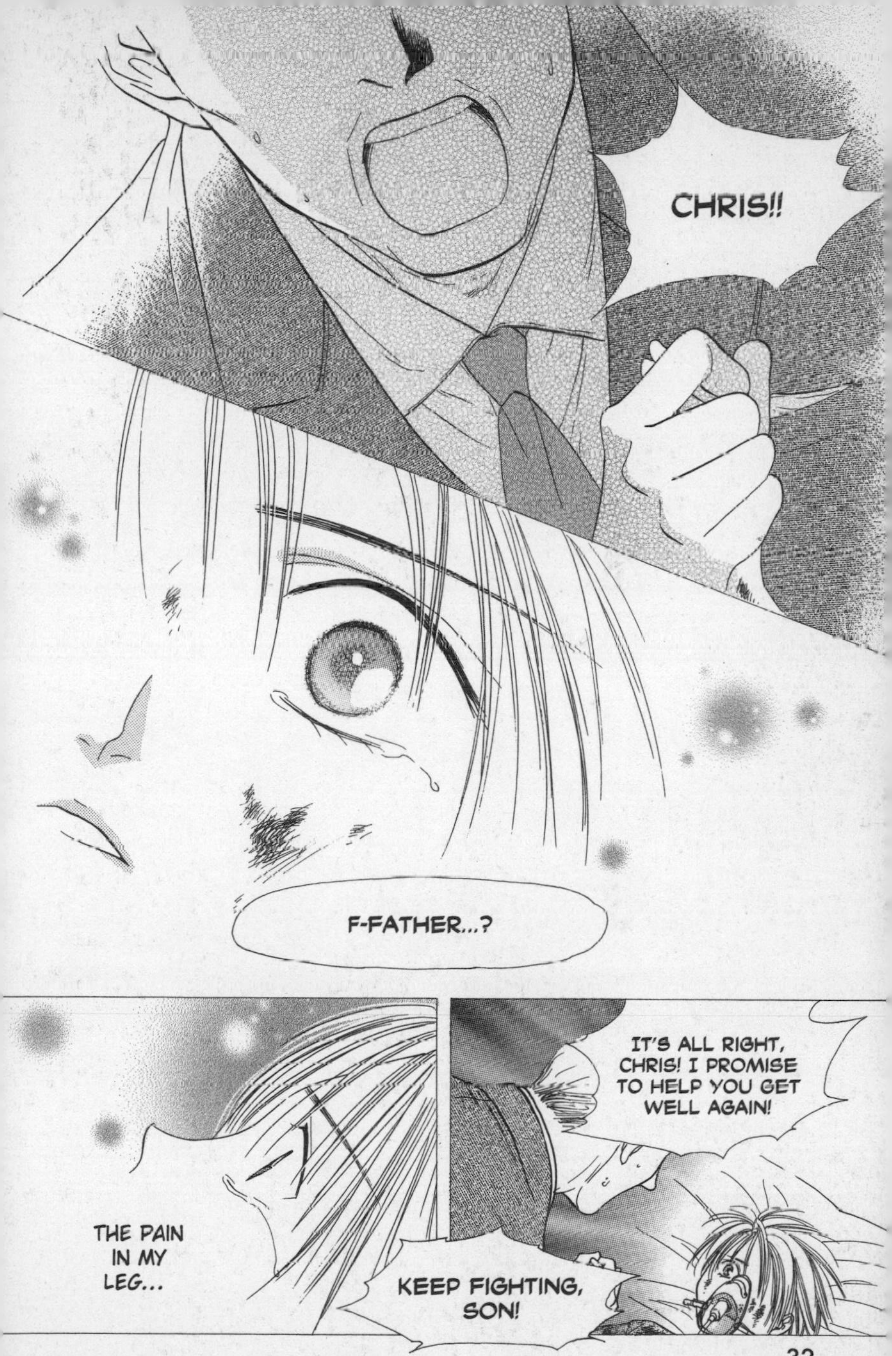
CHRIS!!
F-FATHER...?
IT'S ALL RIGHT, CHRIS! I PROMISE TO HELP YOU GET WELL AGAIN!
KEEP FIGHTING, SON!
THE PAIN IN MY LEG...

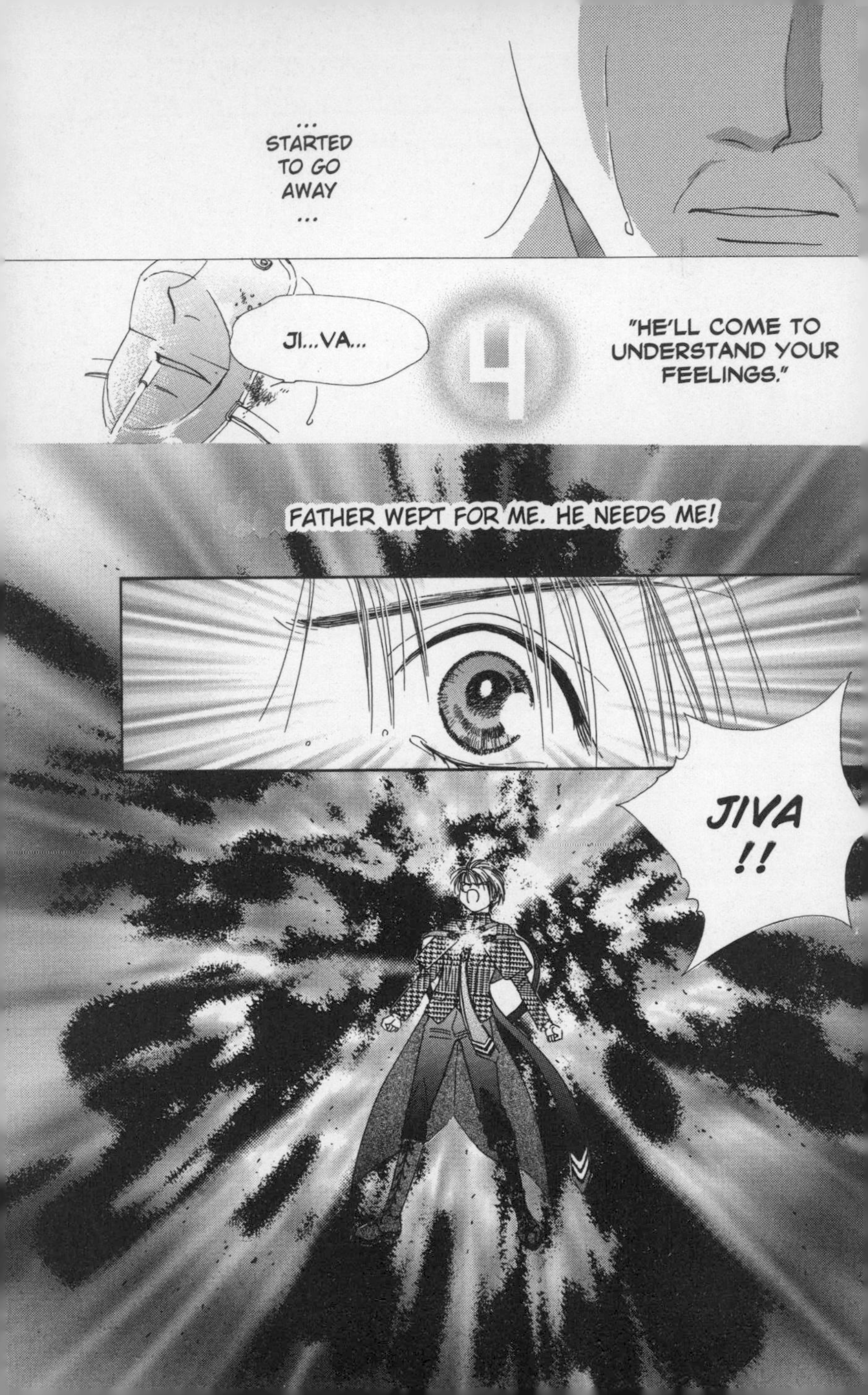
...
STARTED TO GO AWAY
...
"HE'LL COME TO UNDERSTAND YOUR FEELINGS."
4
JI...VA...
FATHER WEPT FOR ME. HE NEEDS ME!
JIVA !!

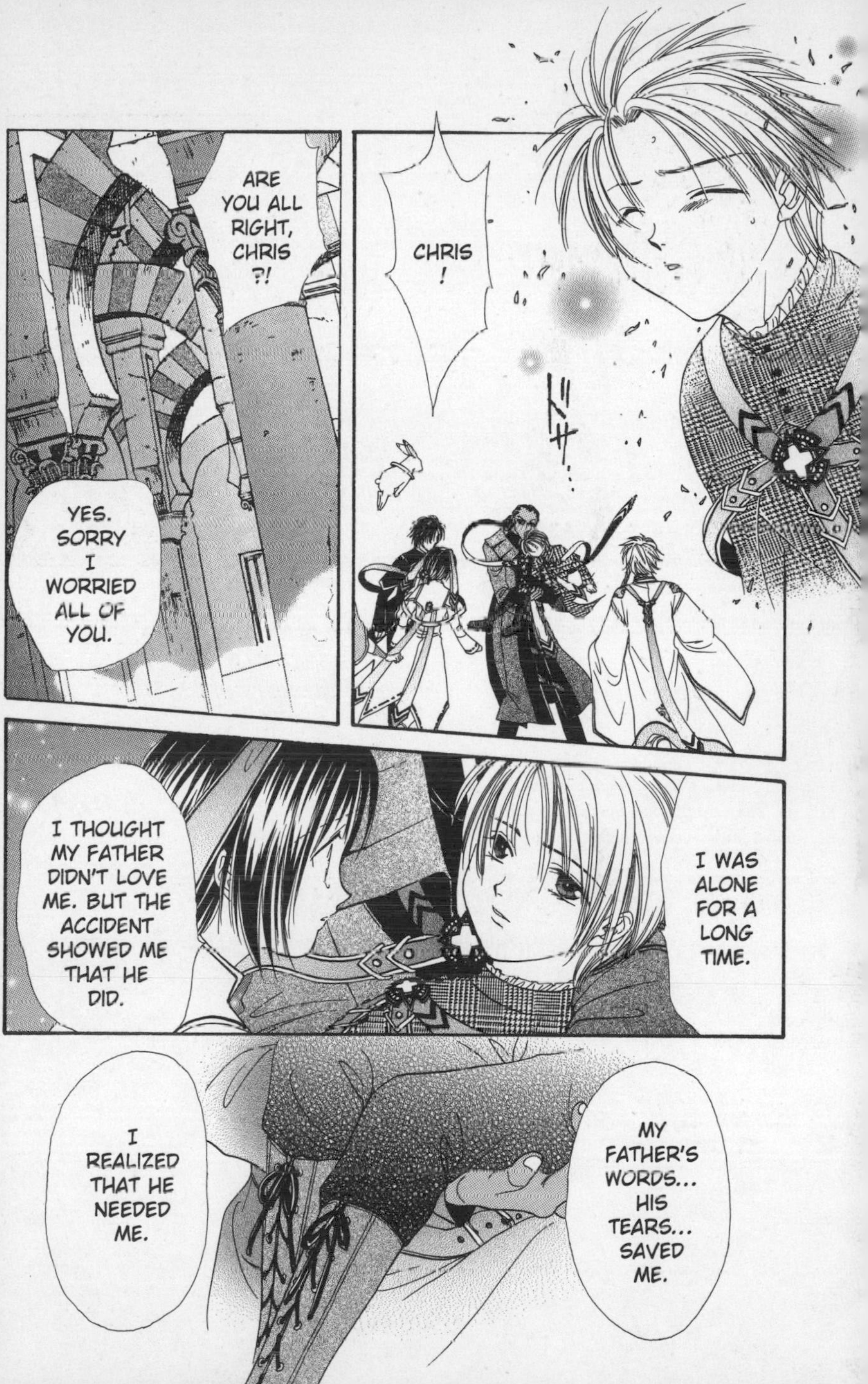
CHRIS!
ARE YOU ALL RIGHT, CHRIS?!
YES. SORRY I WORRIED ALL OF YOU.
I WAS ALONE FOR A LONG TIME.
I THOUGHT MY FATHER DIDN'T LOVE ME. BUT THE ACCIDENT SHOWED ME THAT HE DID.
MY FATHER'S WORDS... HIS TEARS... SAVED ME.
I REALIZED THAT HE NEEDED ME.

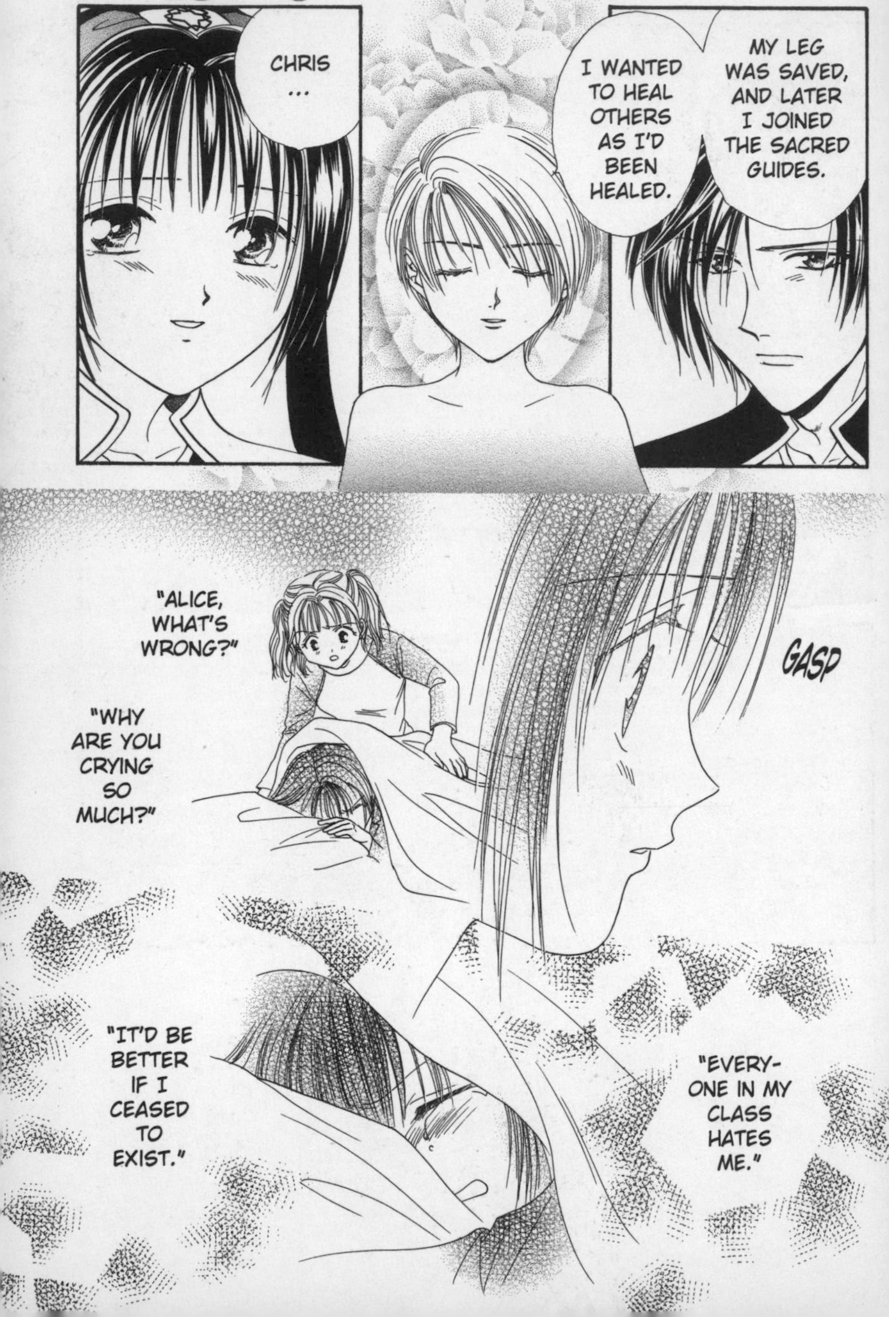
MY LEG WAS SAVED, AND LATER I JOINED THE SACRED GUIDES.
I WANTED TO HEAL OTHERS AS I'D BEEN HEALED.
CHRIS ...
GASP
"ALICE, WHAT'S WRONG?"
"WHY ARE YOU CRYING SO MUCH?"
"EVERY-ONE IN MY CLASS HATES ME."
"IT'D BE BETTER IF I CEASED TO EXIST."

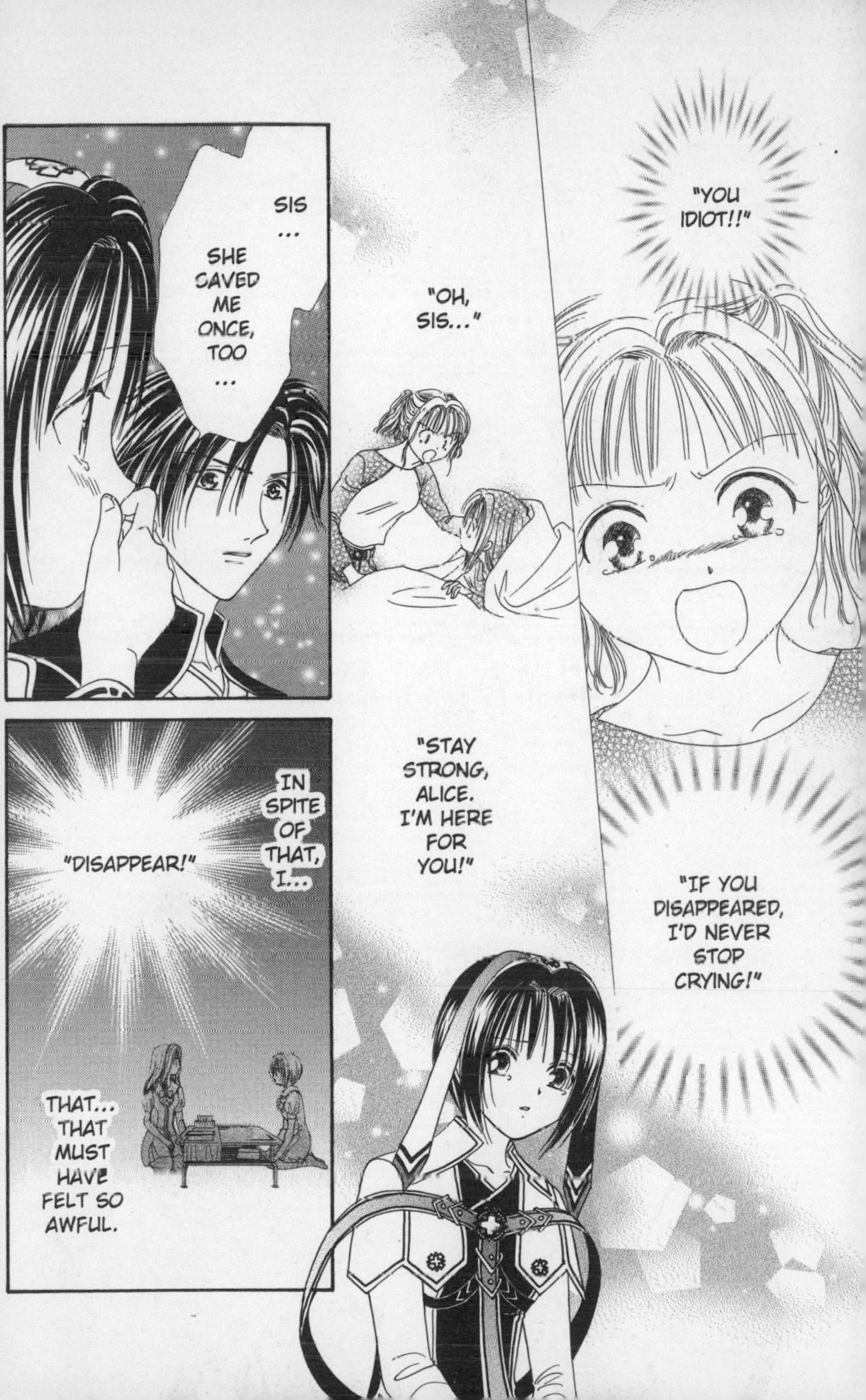
"YOU IDIOT!!"
"IF YOU DISAPPEARED, I'D NEVER STOP CRYING!"
"OH, SIS..."
"STAY STRONG, ALICE. I'M HERE FOR YOU!"
SIS ...
SHE SAVED ME ONCE, TOO ...
IN SPITE OF THAT, I...
"DISAPPEAR!"
THAT... THAT MUST HAVE FELT SO AWFUL.

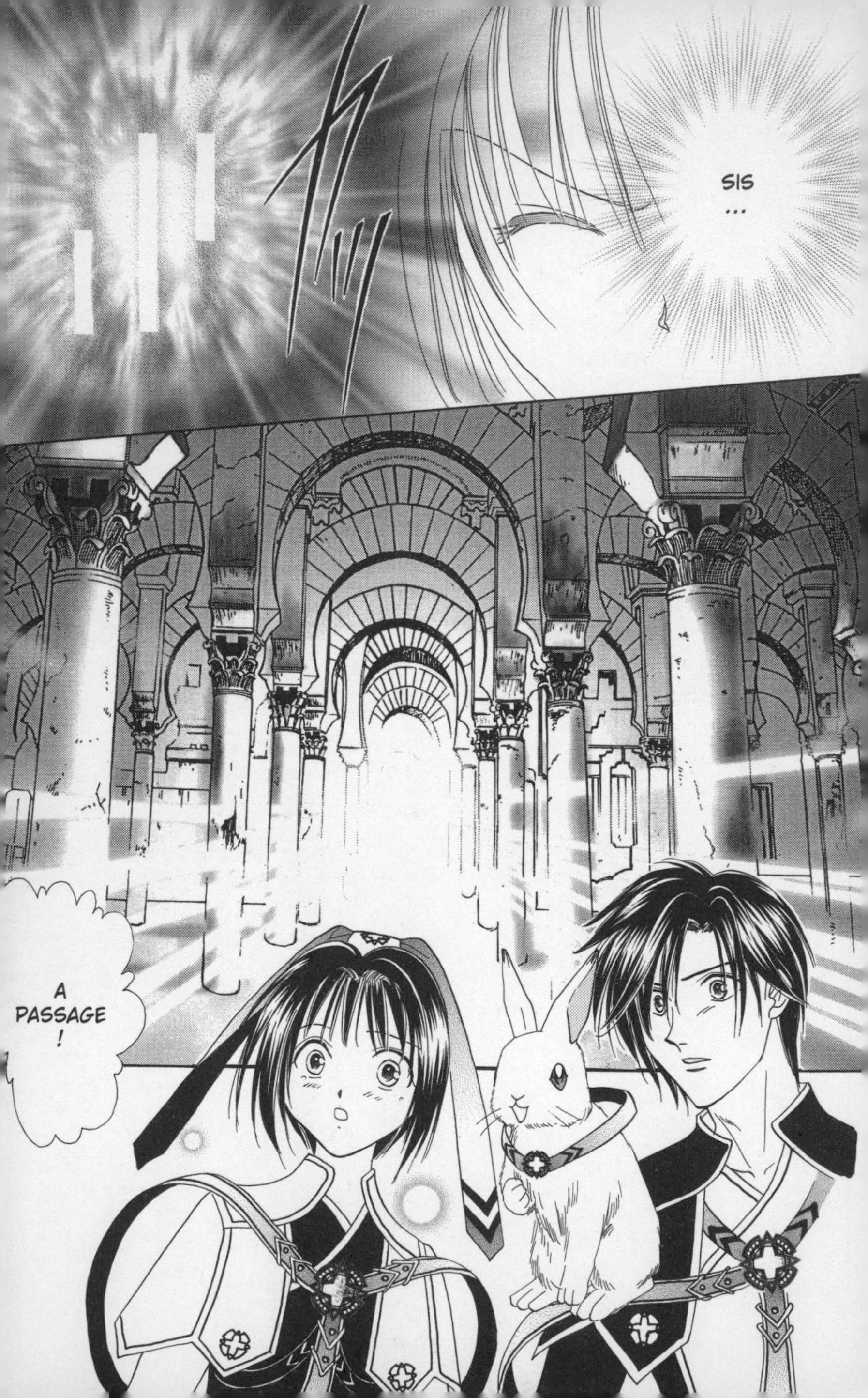
SIS
...
A
PASSAGE
!

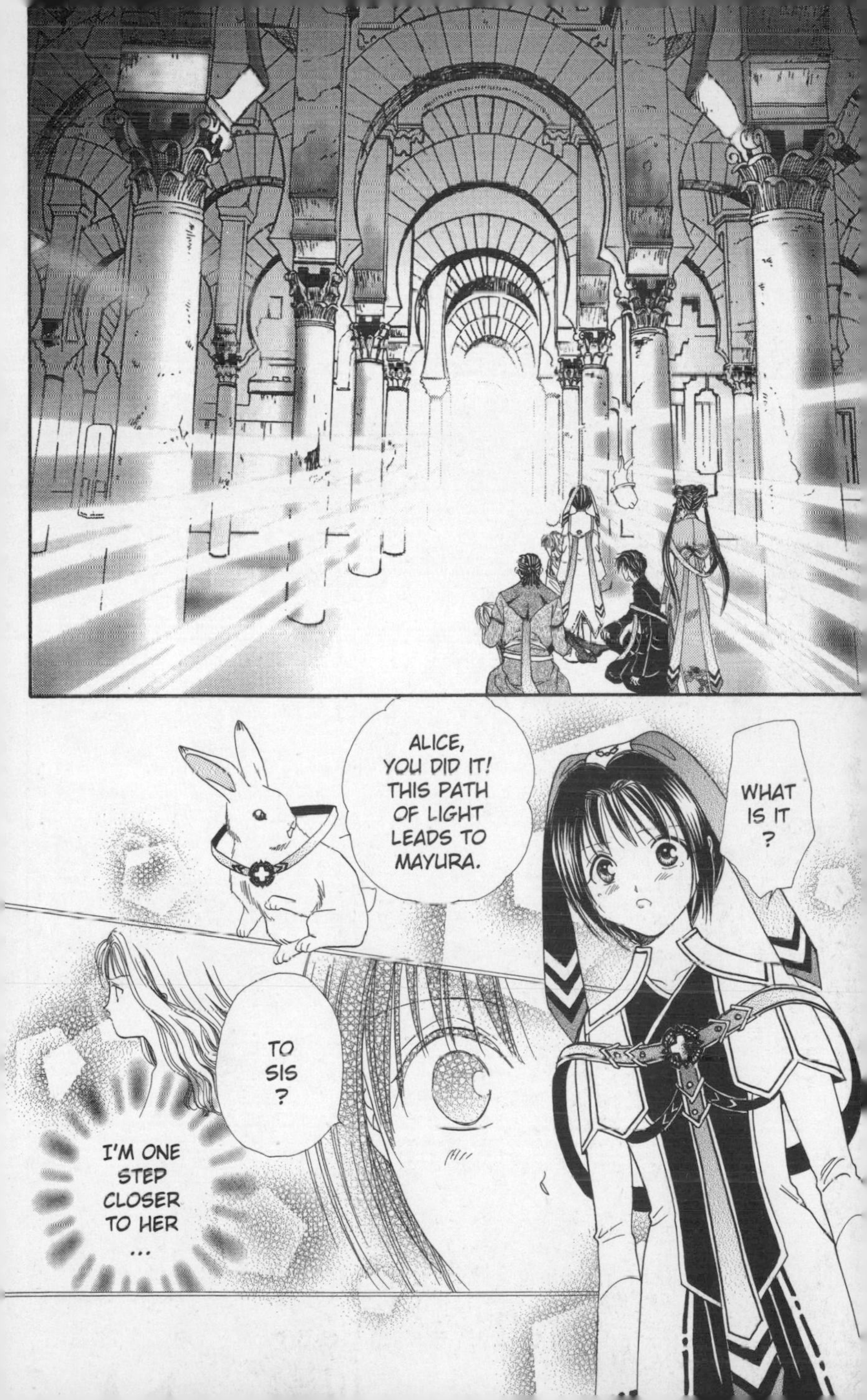
WHAT IS IT ?
ALICE, YOU DID IT! THIS PATH OF LIGHT LEADS TO MAYURA.
TO SIS ?
I'M ONE STEP CLOSER TO HER ...

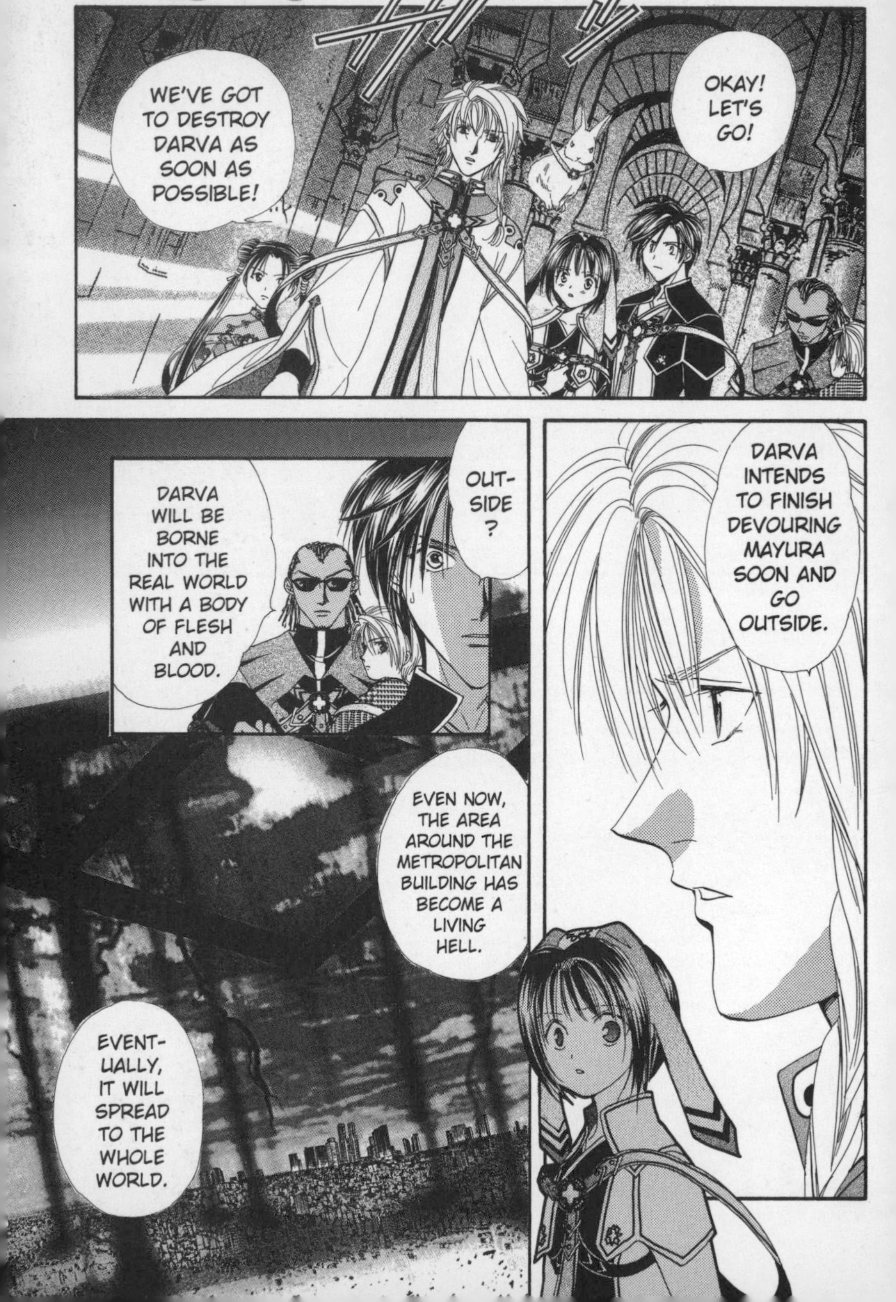
OKAY! LET'S GO!
WE'VE GOT TO DESTROY DARVA AS SOON AS POSSIBLE!
DARVA INTENDS TO FINISH DEVOURING MAYURA SOON AND GO OUTSIDE.
OUT-SIDE?
DARVA WILL BE BORNE INTO THE REAL WORLD WITH A BODY OF FLESH AND BLOOD.
EVEN NOW, THE AREA AROUND THE METROPOLITAN BUILDING HAS BECOME A LIVING HELL.
EVENT-UALLY, IT WILL SPREAD TO THE WHOLE WORLD.

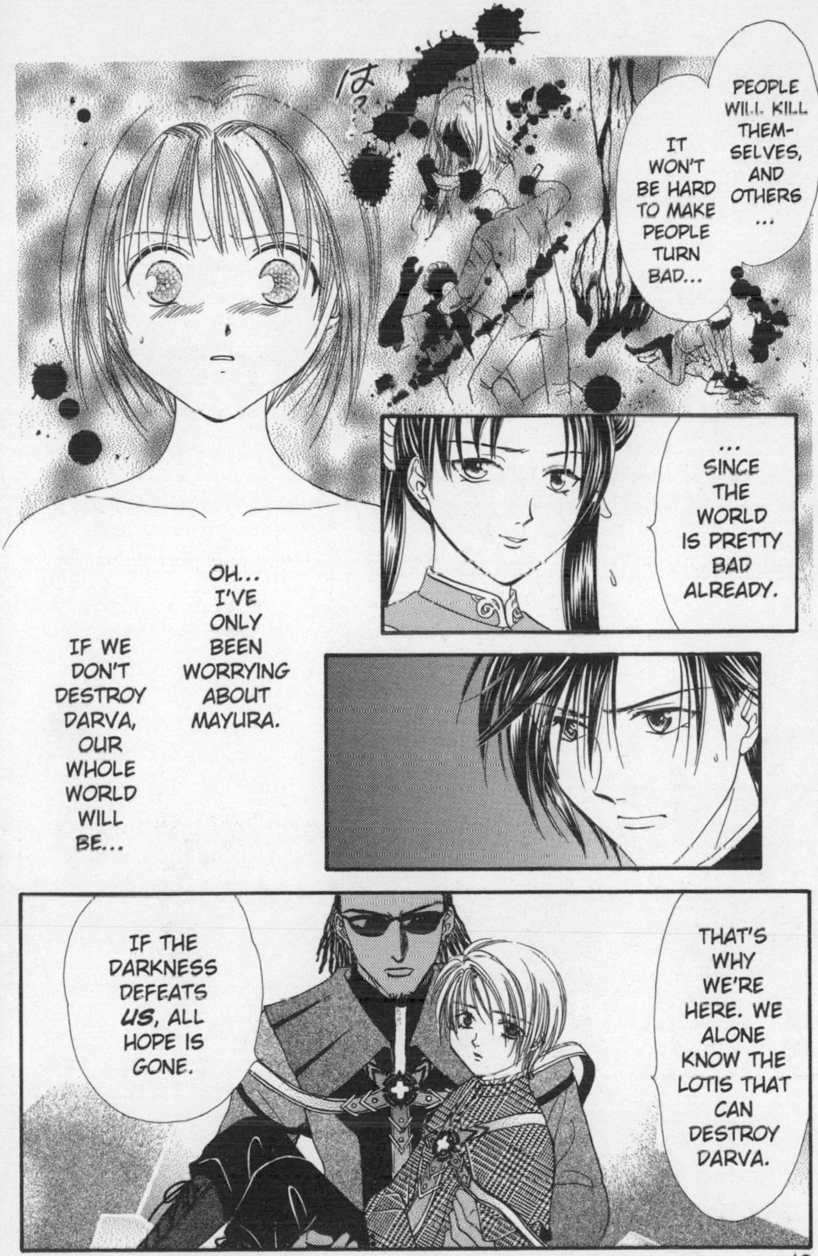

は
PEOPLE WILL KILL THEMSELVES, AND OTHERS...
IT WON'T BE HARD TO MAKE PEOPLE TURN BAD...
...SINCE THE WORLD IS PRETTY BAD ALREADY.
OH... I'VE ONLY BEEN WORRYING ABOUT MAYURA.
IF WE DON'T DESTROY DARVA, OUR WHOLE WORLD WILL BE...
THAT'S WHY WE'RE HERE. WE ALONE KNOW THE LOTIS THAT CAN DESTROY DARVA.
IF THE DARKNESS DEFEATS *US*, ALL HOPE IS GONE.

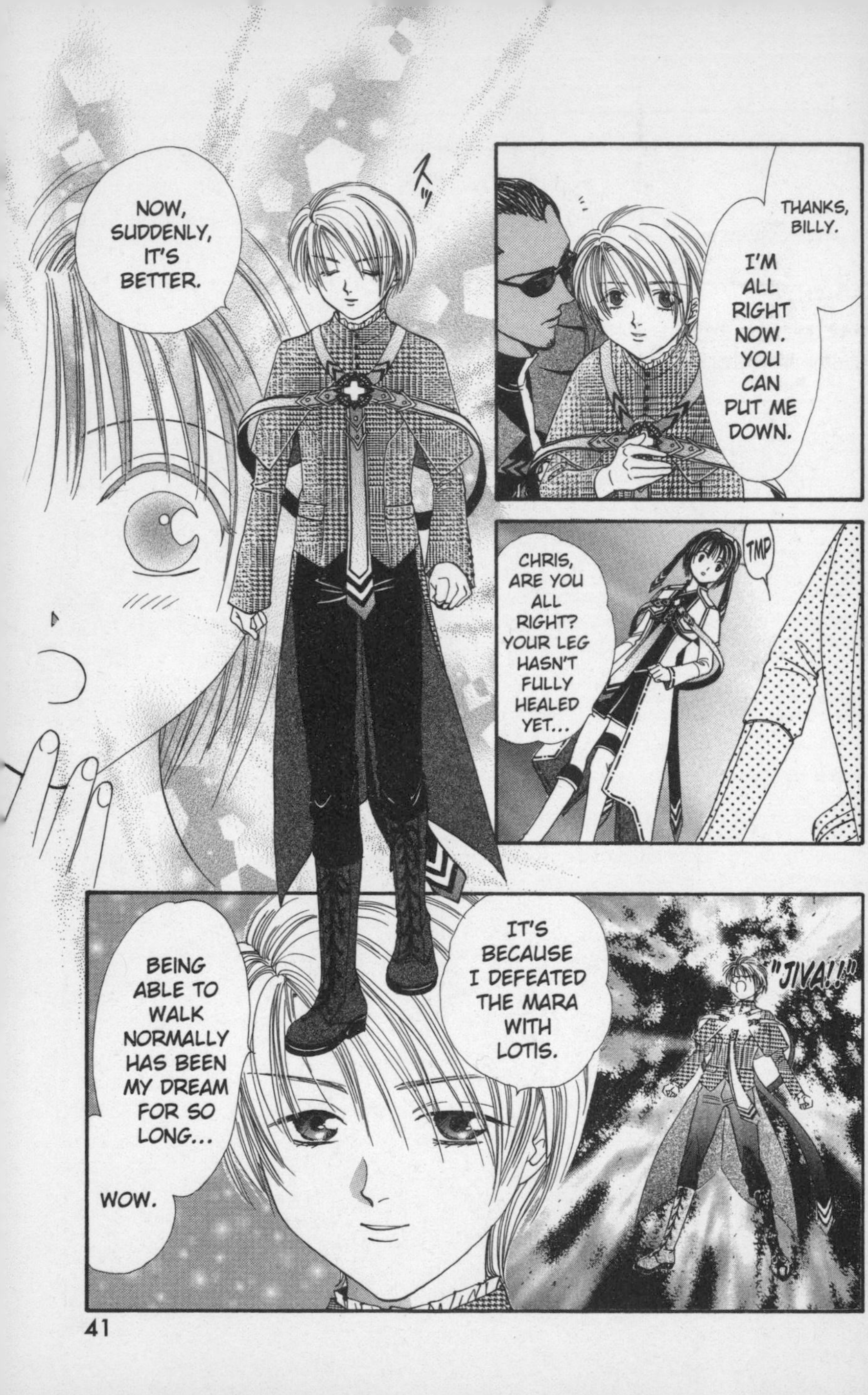
THANKS, BILLY.
I'M ALL RIGHT NOW. YOU CAN PUT ME DOWN.
TMP
CHRIS, ARE YOU ALL RIGHT? YOUR LEG HASN'T FULLY HEALED YET...
スッ
NOW, SUDDENLY, IT'S BETTER.
IT'S BECAUSE I DEFEATED THE MARA WITH LOTIS.
"JIVA!!"
BEING ABLE TO WALK NORMALLY HAS BEEN MY DREAM FOR SO LONG...
WOW.

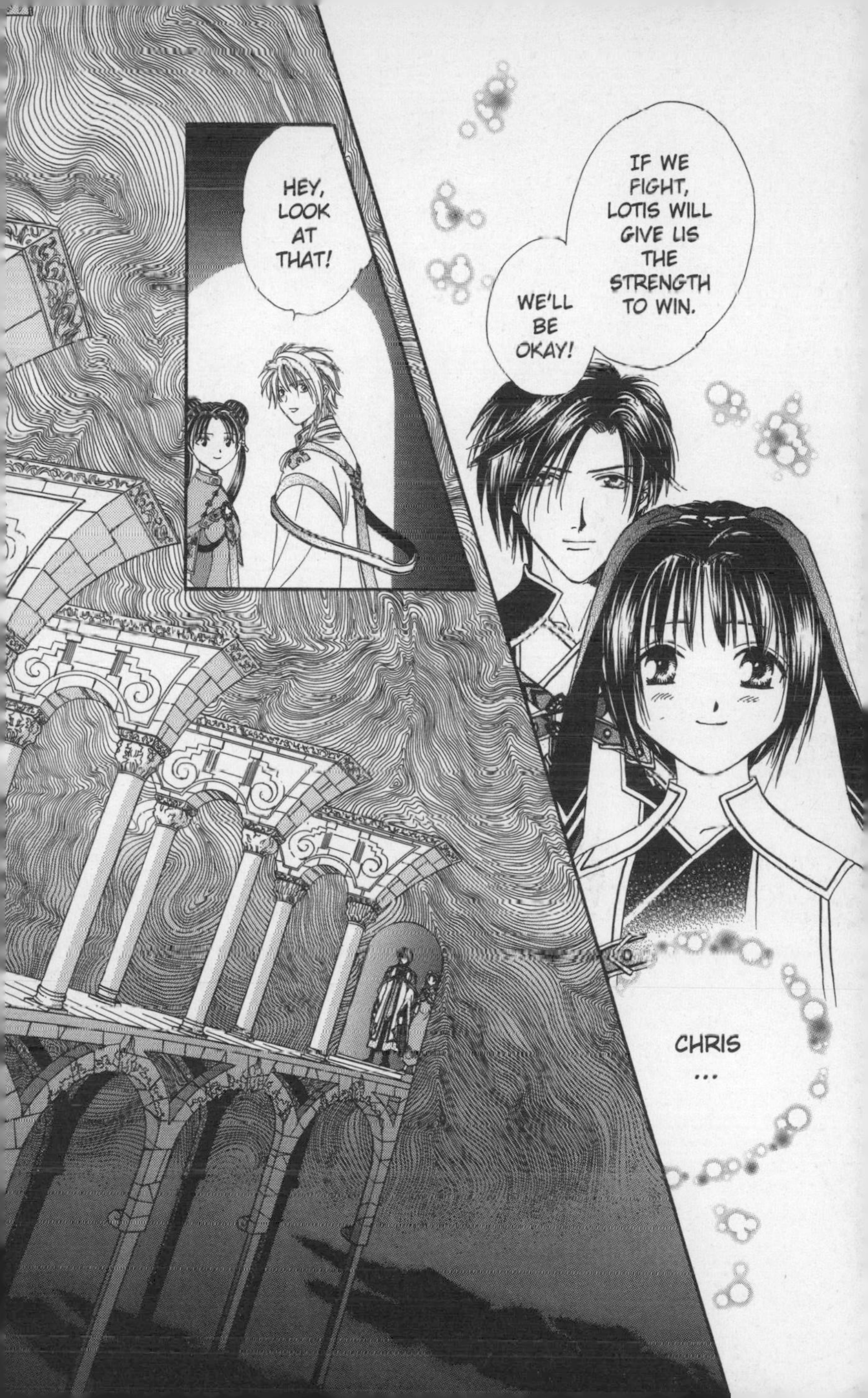
IF WE FIGHT, LOTIS WILL GIVE US THE STRENGTH TO WIN.
WE'LL BE OKAY!
CHRIS ...
HEY, LOOK AT THAT!

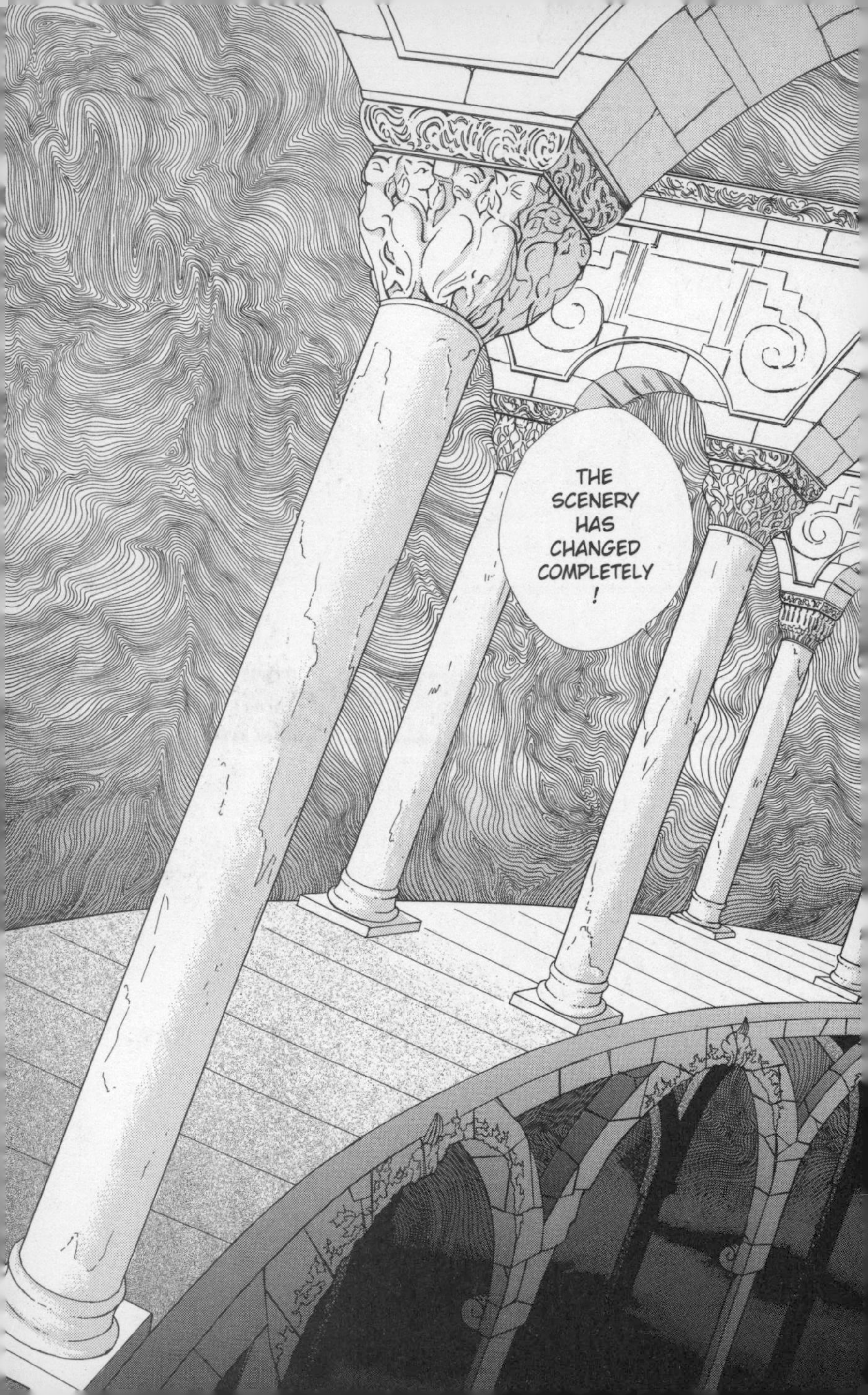
THE SCENERY HAS CHANGED COMPLETELY!

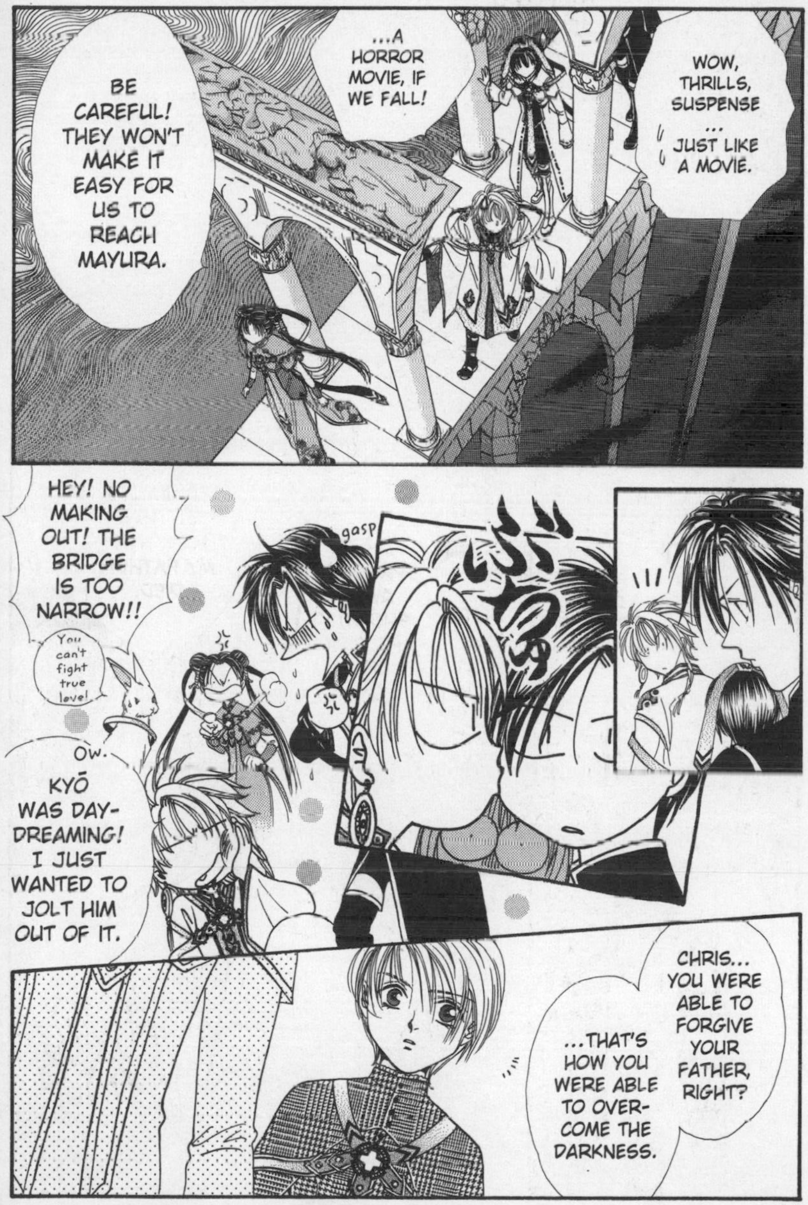
WOW, THRILLS, SUSPENSE ... JUST LIKE A MOVIE.
...A HORROR MOVIE, IF WE FALL!
BE CAREFUL! THEY WON'T MAKE IT EASY FOR US TO REACH MAYURA.
gasp
HEY! NO MAKING OUT! THE BRIDGE IS TOO NARROW!!
You can't fight true love!
OW. KYŌ WAS DAY-DREAMING! I JUST WANTED TO JOLT HIM OUT OF IT.
CHRIS... YOU WERE ABLE TO FORGIVE YOUR FATHER, RIGHT?
...THAT'S HOW YOU WERE ABLE TO OVERCOME THE DARKNESS.

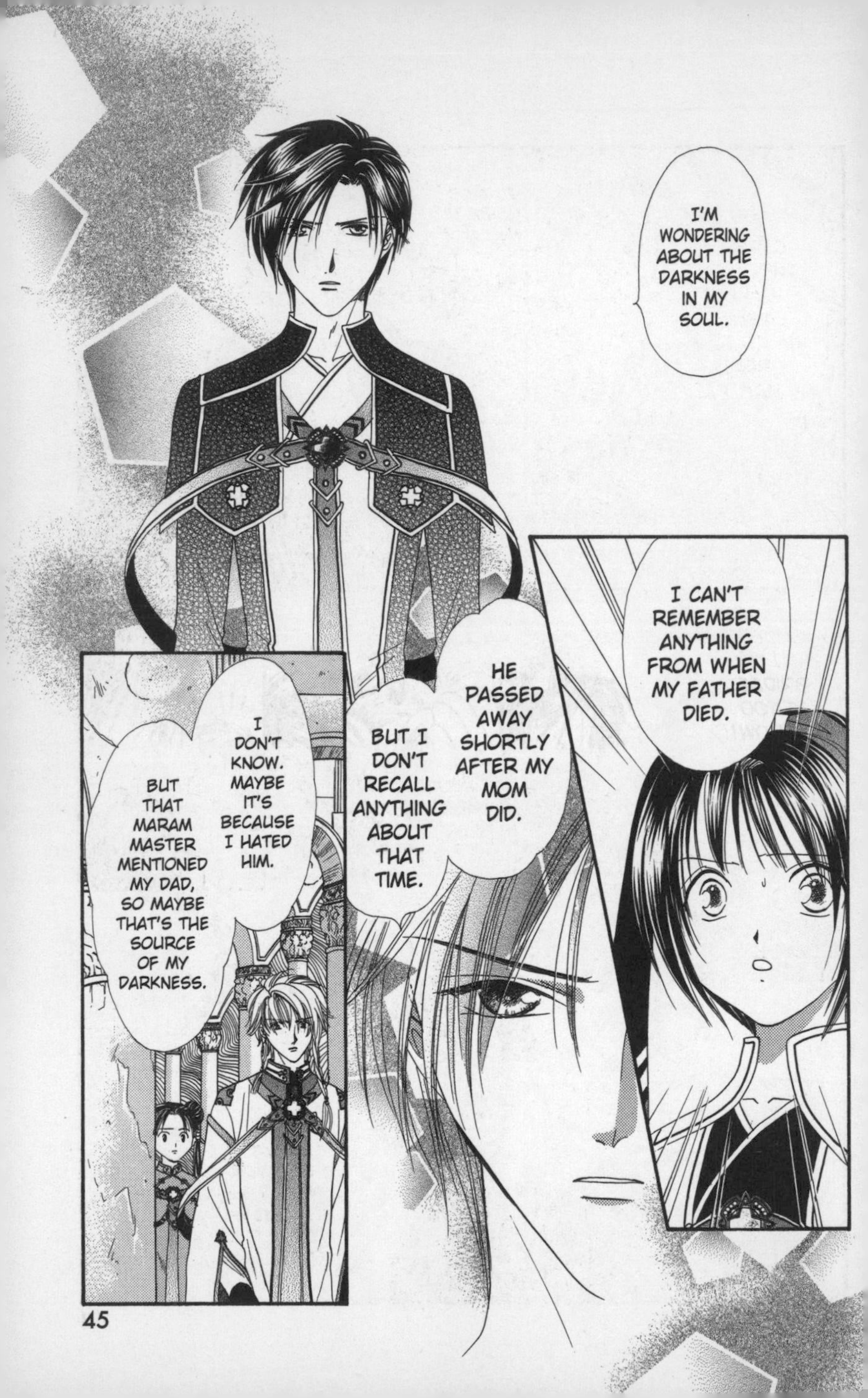
I'M WONDERING ABOUT THE DARKNESS IN MY SOUL.
I CAN'T REMEMBER ANYTHING FROM WHEN MY FATHER DIED.
HE PASSED AWAY SHORTLY AFTER MY MOM DID.
BUT I DON'T RECALL ANYTHING ABOUT THAT TIME.
I DON'T KNOW. MAYBE IT'S BECAUSE I HATED HIM.
BUT THAT MARAM MASTER MENTIONED MY DAD, SO MAYBE THAT'S THE SOURCE OF MY DARKNESS.

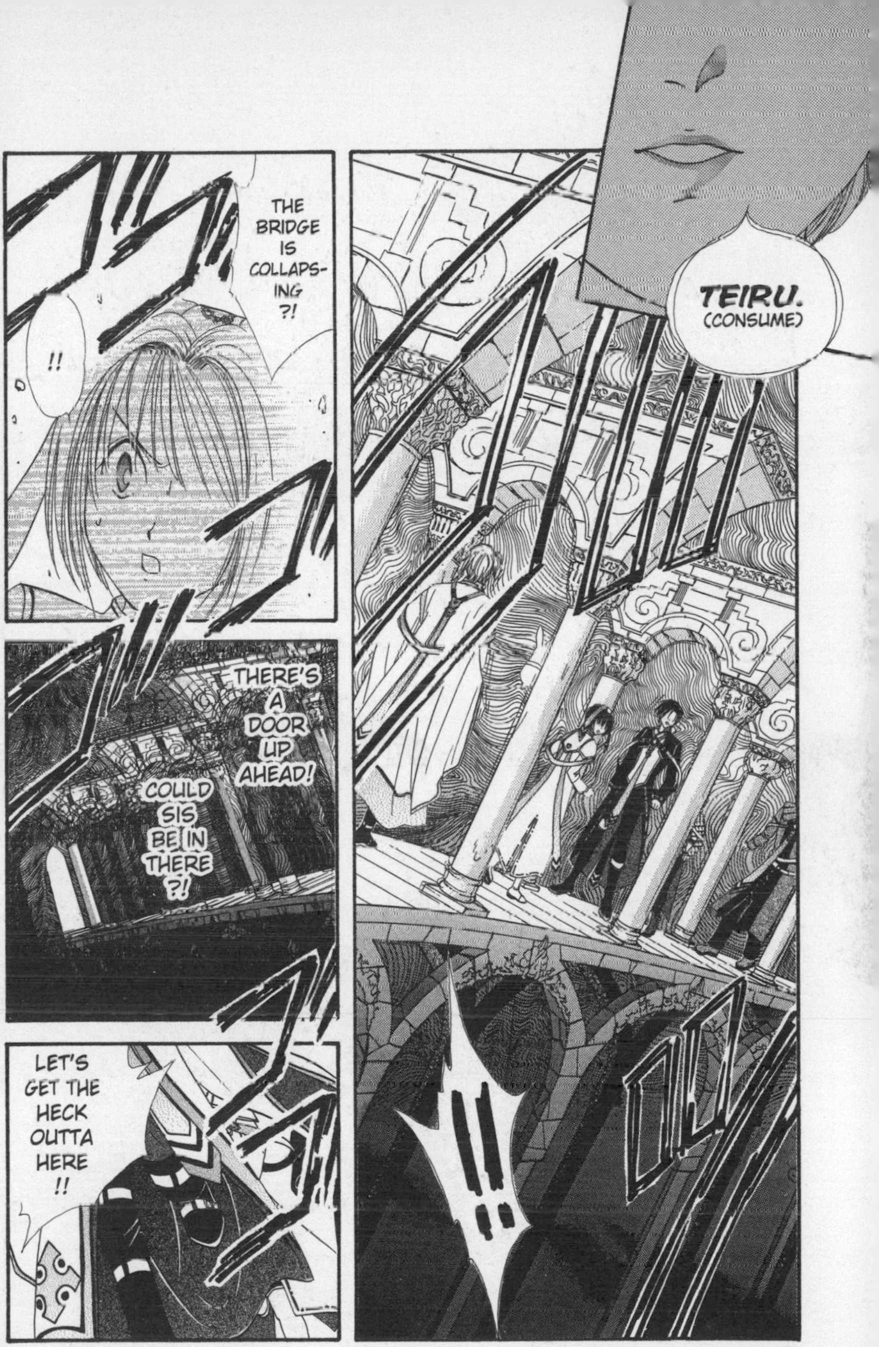
TEIRU.
(CONSUME)
!!
THE BRIDGE IS COLLAPSING?!
!!
THERE'S A DOOR UP AHEAD!
COULD SIS BE IN THERE?!
LET'S GET THE HECK OUTTA HERE!!

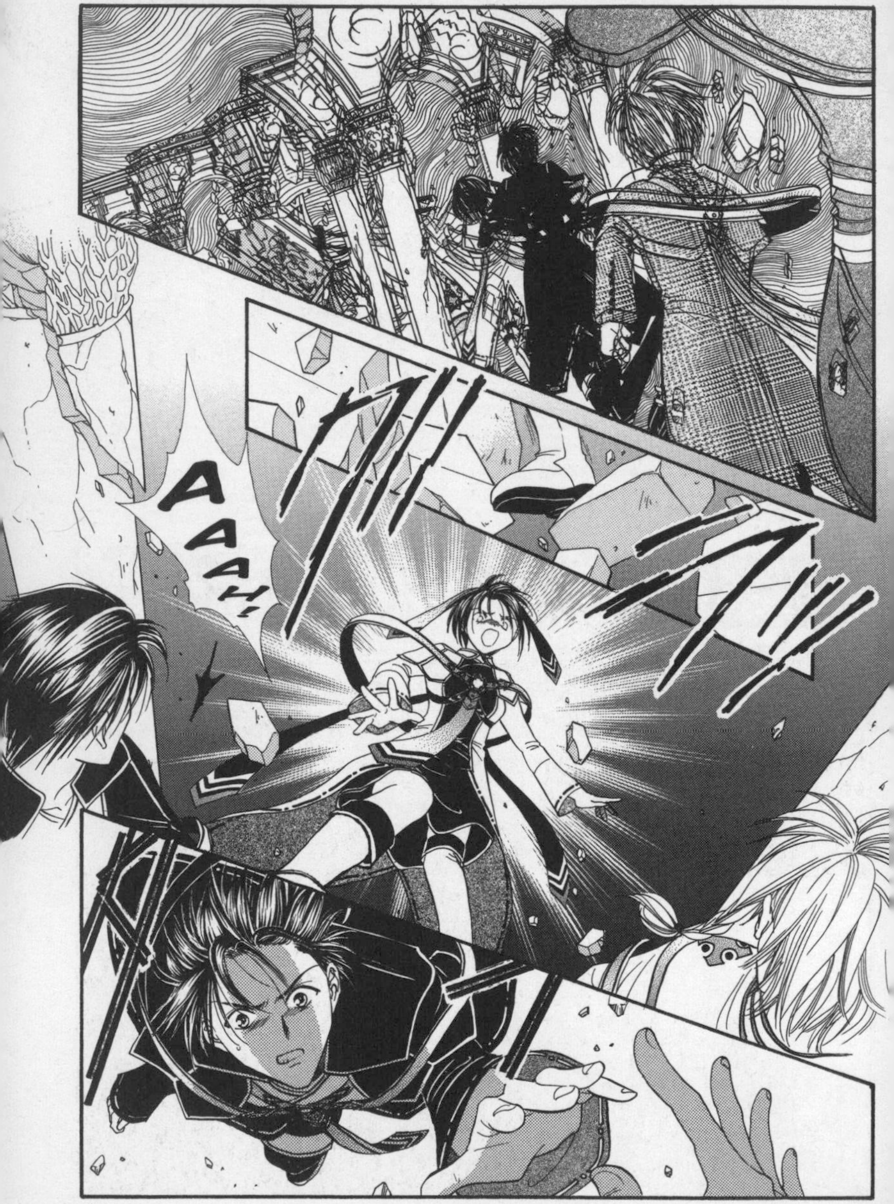
AAAAH!

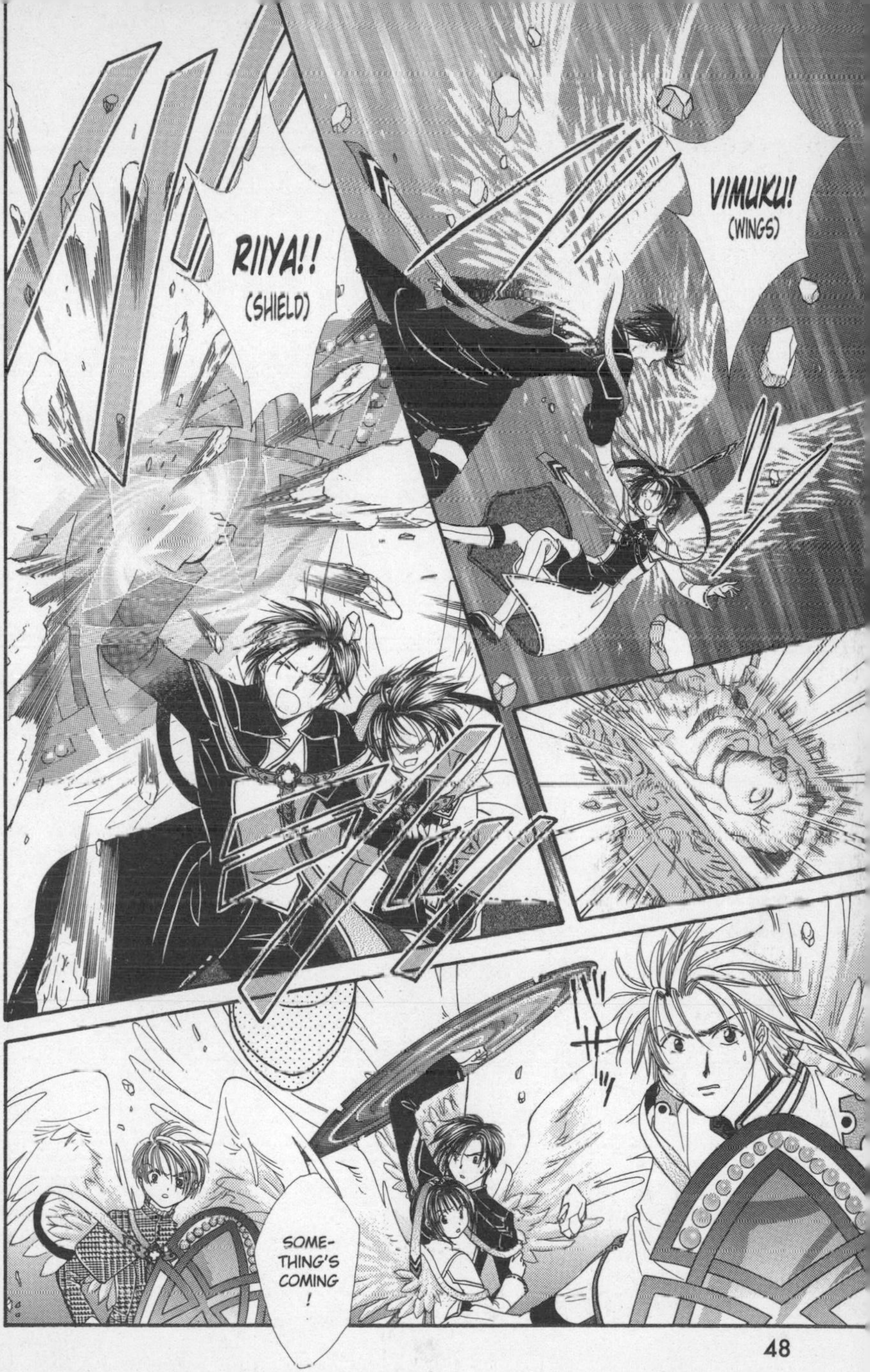
VIMUKU!
(WINGS)
RIIYA!!
(SHIELD)
SOME-THING'S COMING!

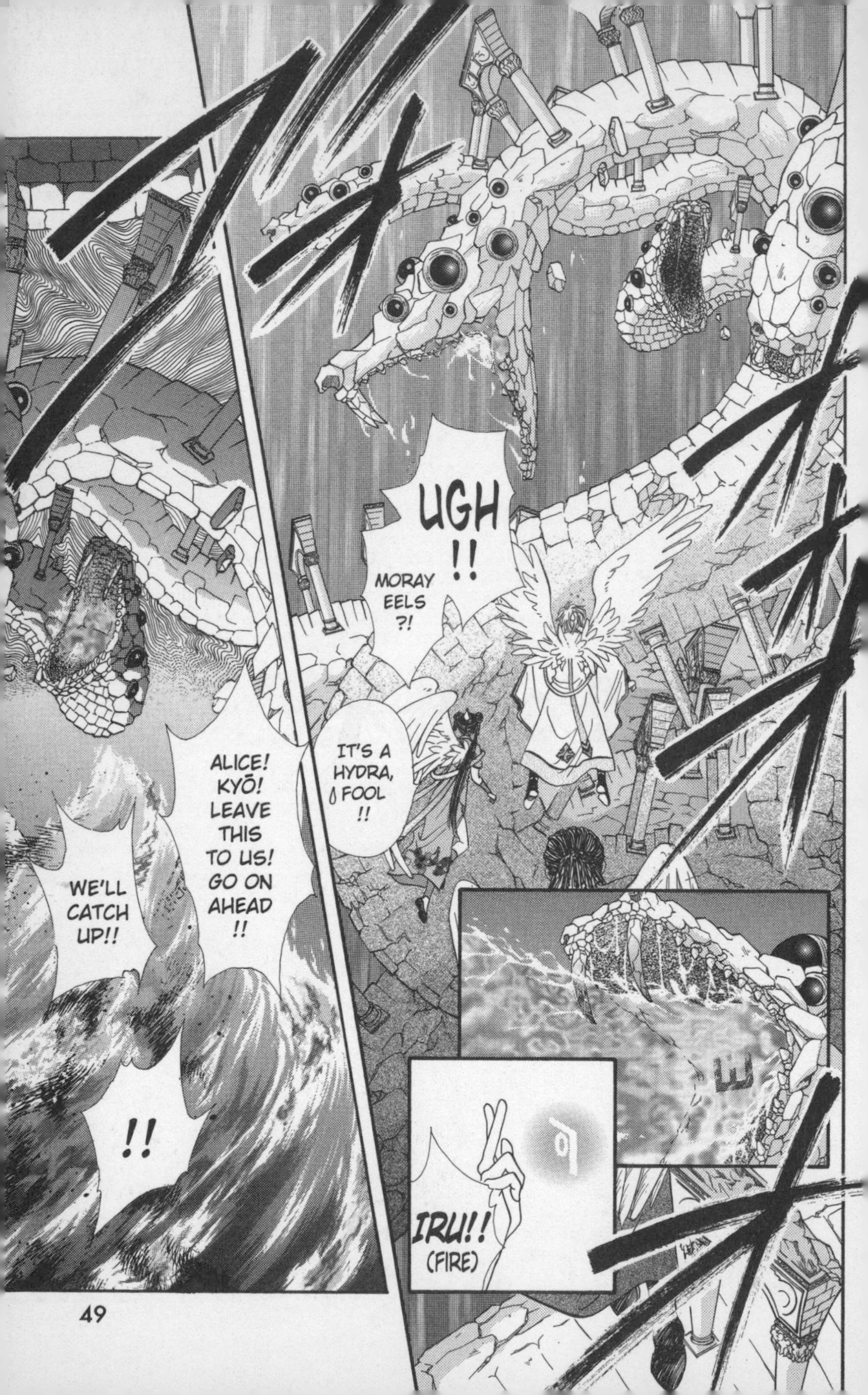
UGH!!
MORAY EELS?!
IT'S A HYDRA, FOOL!!
IRU!! (FIRE)
ALICE! KYŌ! LEAVE THIS TO US! GO ON AHEAD!!
WE'LL CATCH UP!!
!!

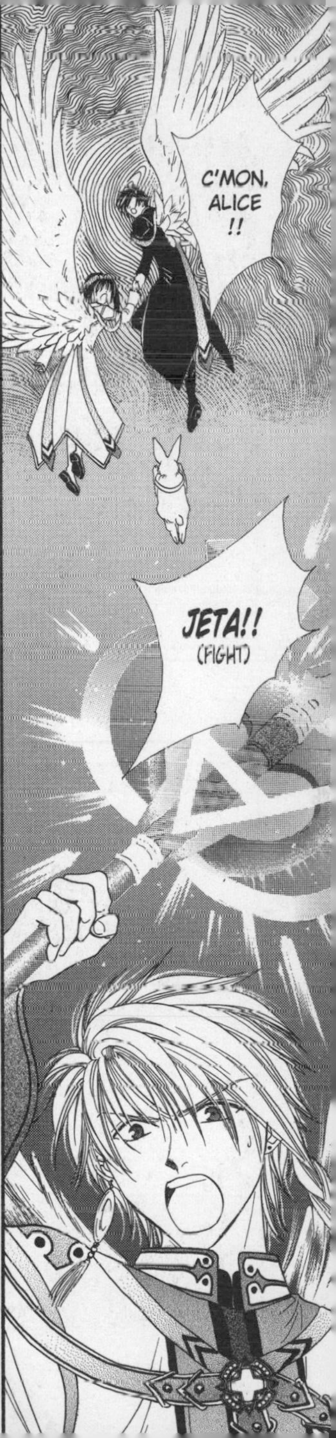
C'MON, ALICE !!
JETA!!
(FIGHT)
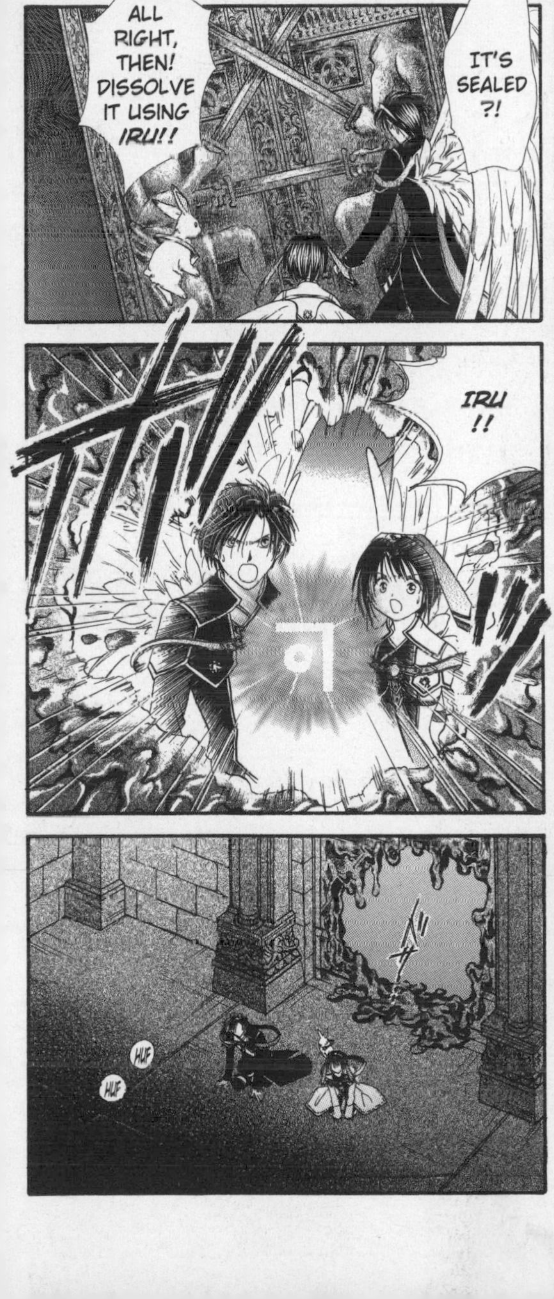
IT'S SEALED ?!
ALL RIGHT, THEN! DISSOLVE IT USING *IRU!!*
IRU !!
HUF
HUF

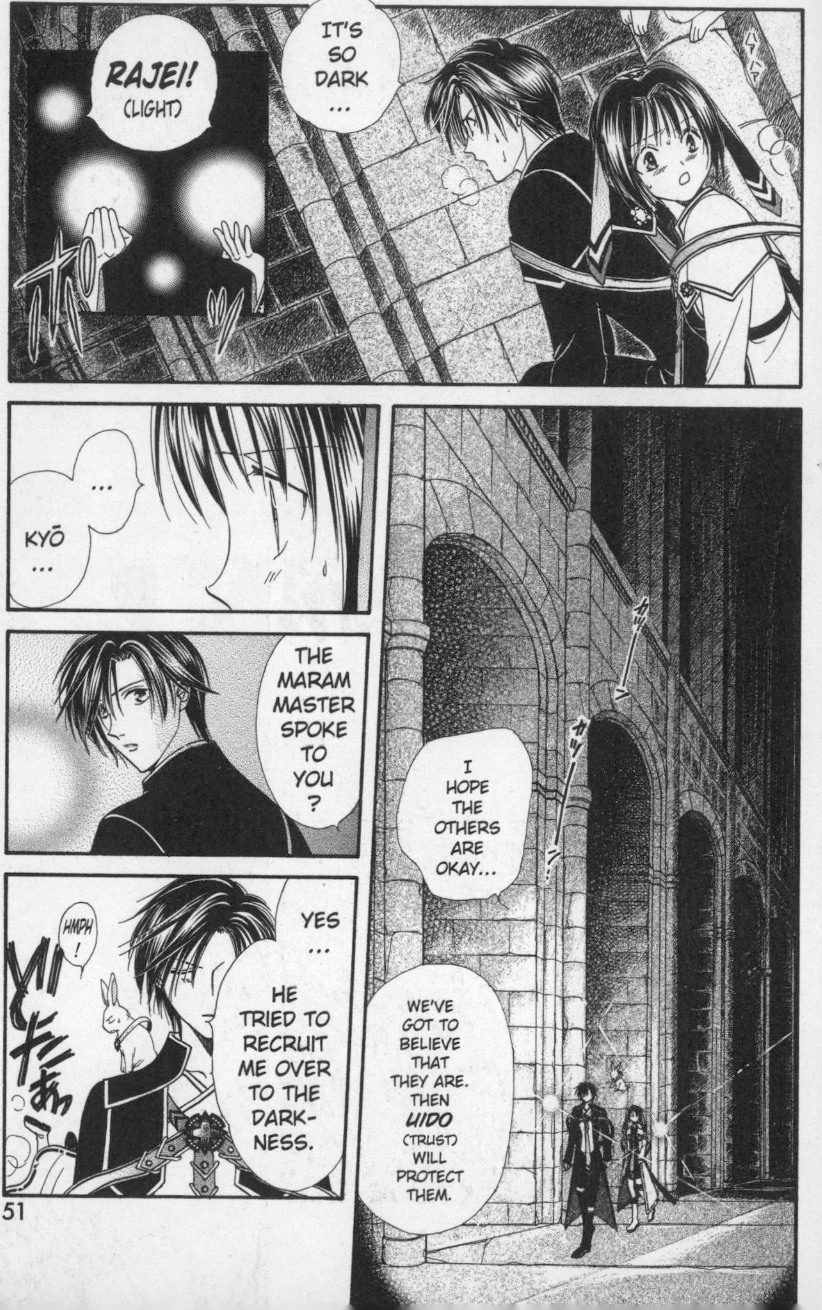
IT'S SO DARK ...
RAJEI! (LIGHT)
I HOPE THE OTHERS ARE OKAY...
WE'VE GOT TO BELIEVE THAT THEY ARE. THEN UIDO (TRUST) WILL PROTECT THEM.
...
KYŌ ...
THE MARAM MASTER SPOKE TO YOU?
YES ...
HE TRIED TO RECRUIT ME OVER TO THE DARK-NESS.
HMPH!

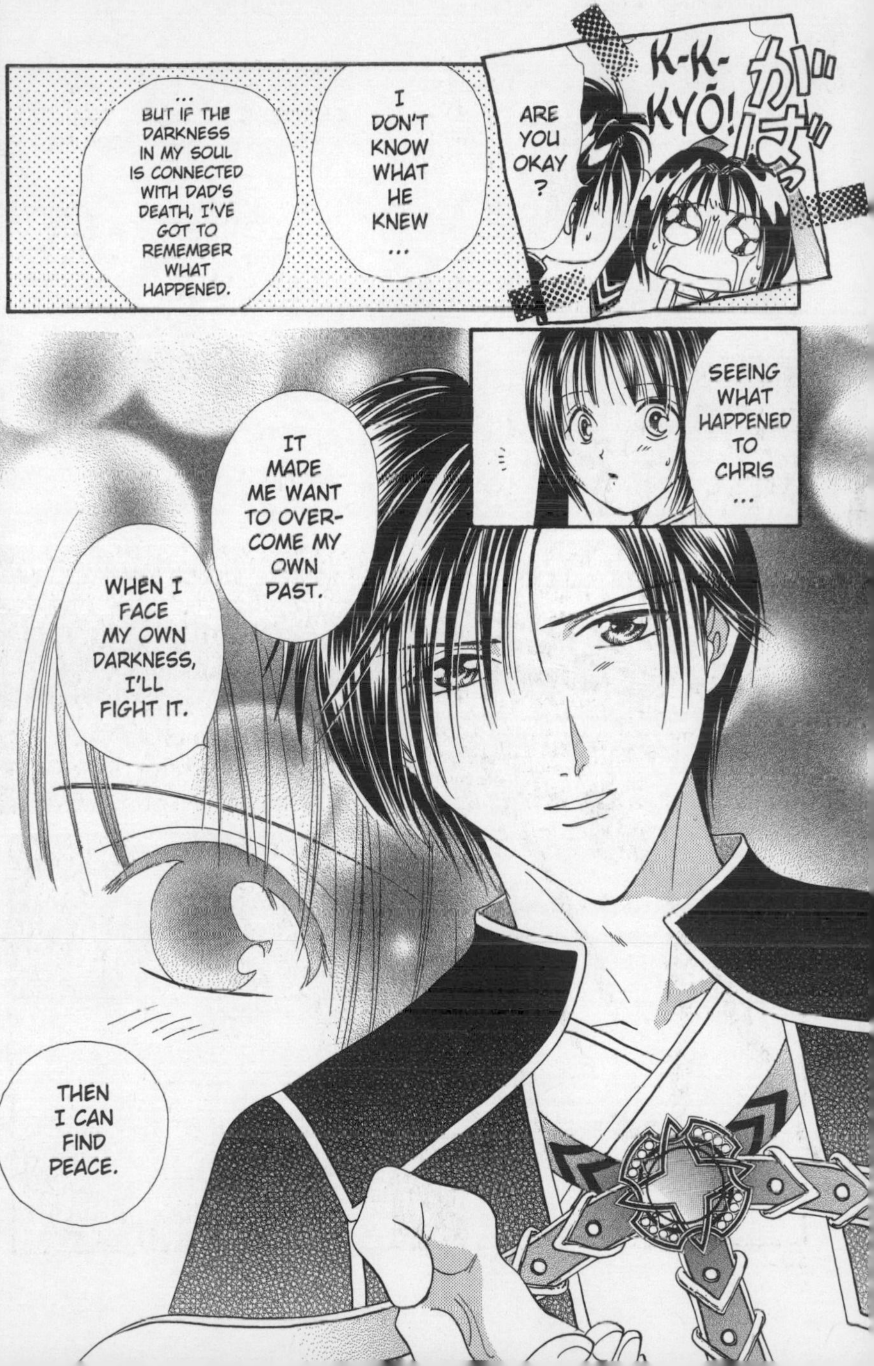
K-K-KYŌ!
がばっ
ARE YOU OKAY?
I DON'T KNOW WHAT HE KNEW...
...BUT IF THE DARKNESS IN MY SOUL IS CONNECTED WITH DAD'S DEATH, I'VE GOT TO REMEMBER WHAT HAPPENED.
SEEING WHAT HAPPENED TO CHRIS...
IT MADE ME WANT TO OVER-COME MY OWN PAST.
WHEN I FACE MY OWN DARKNESS, I'LL FIGHT IT.
THEN I CAN FIND PEACE.

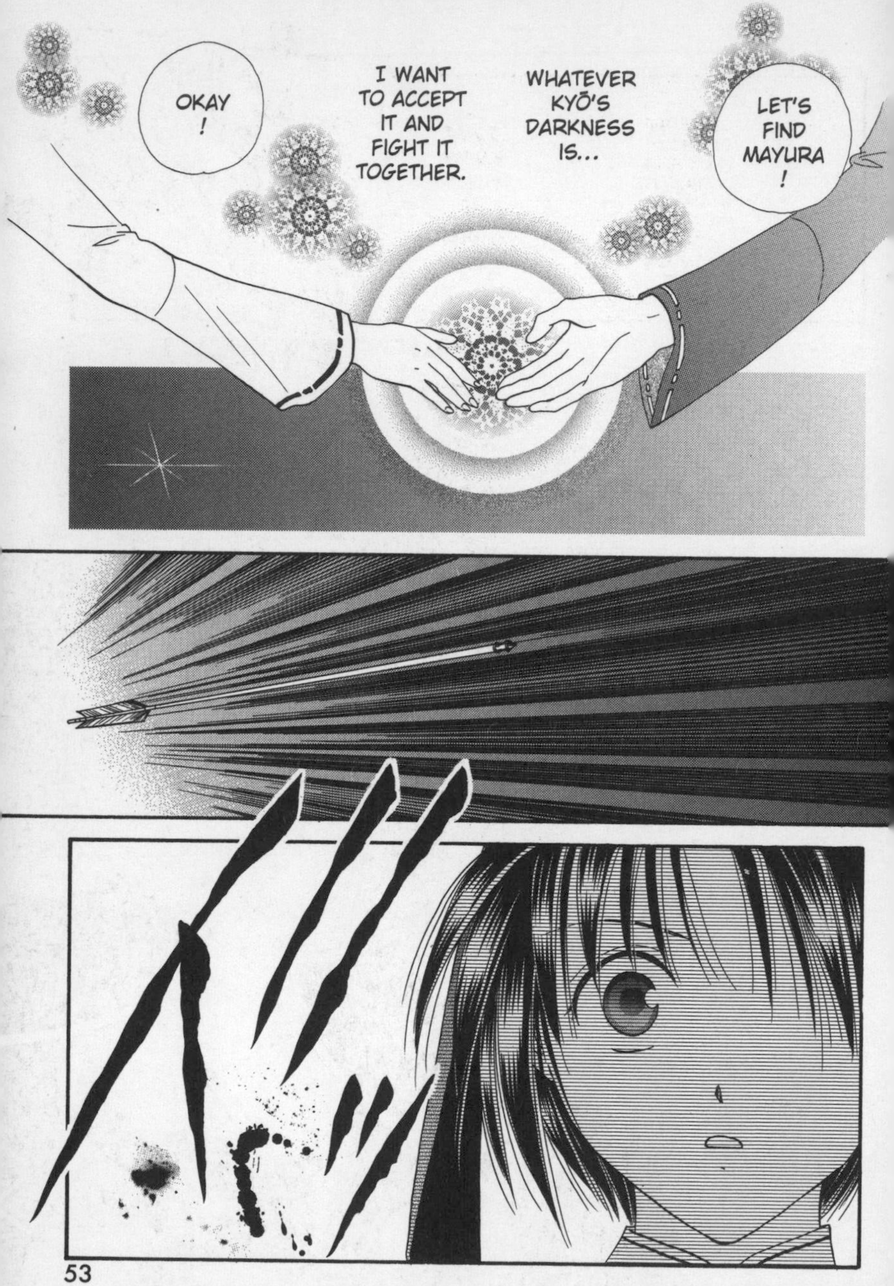
LET'S FIND MAYURA!
WHATEVER KYŌ'S DARKNESS IS...
I WANT TO ACCEPT IT AND FIGHT IT TOGETHER.
OKAY!

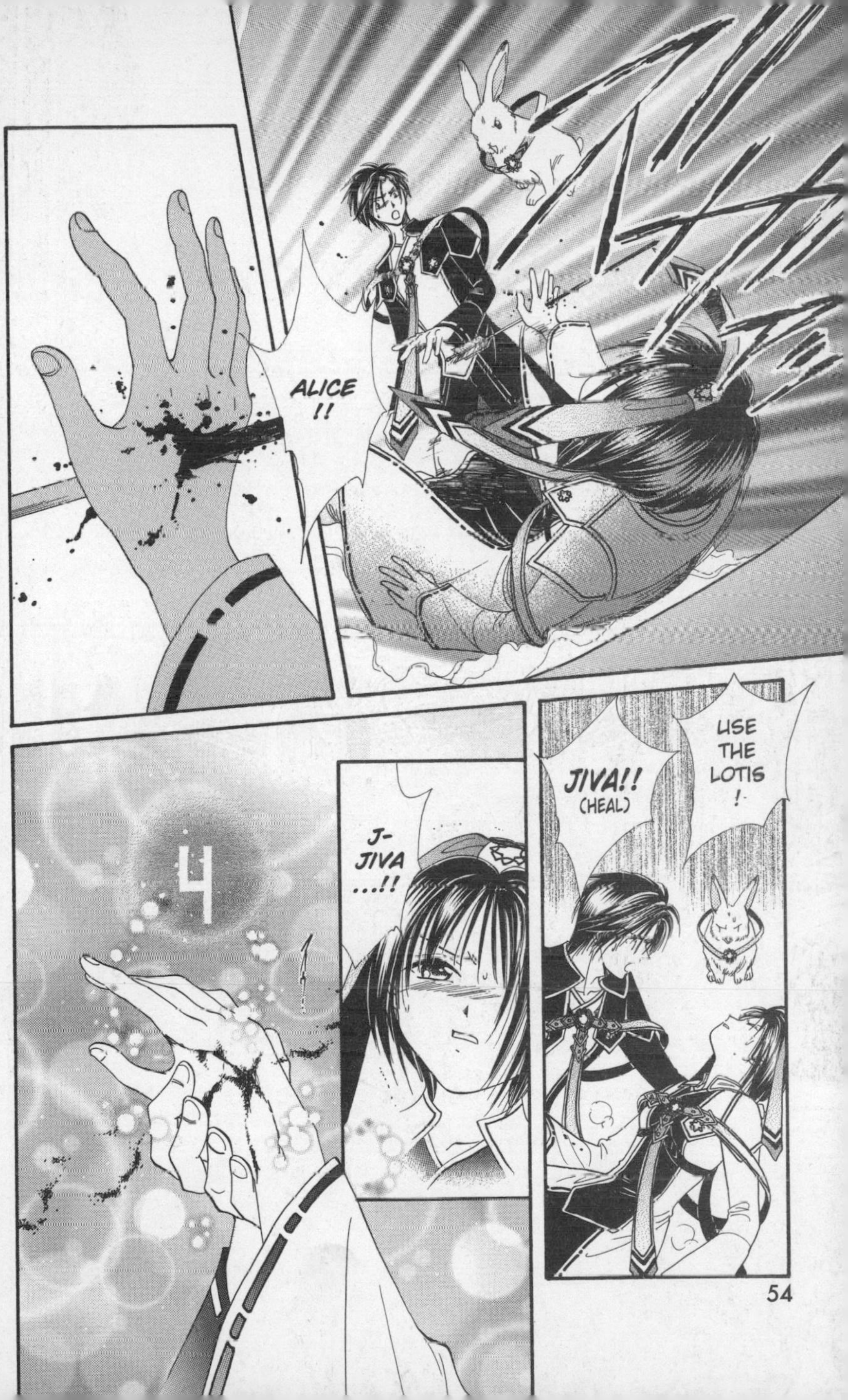
ALICE !!
USE THE LOTIS !
JIVA!! (HEAL)
J-JIVA ...!!

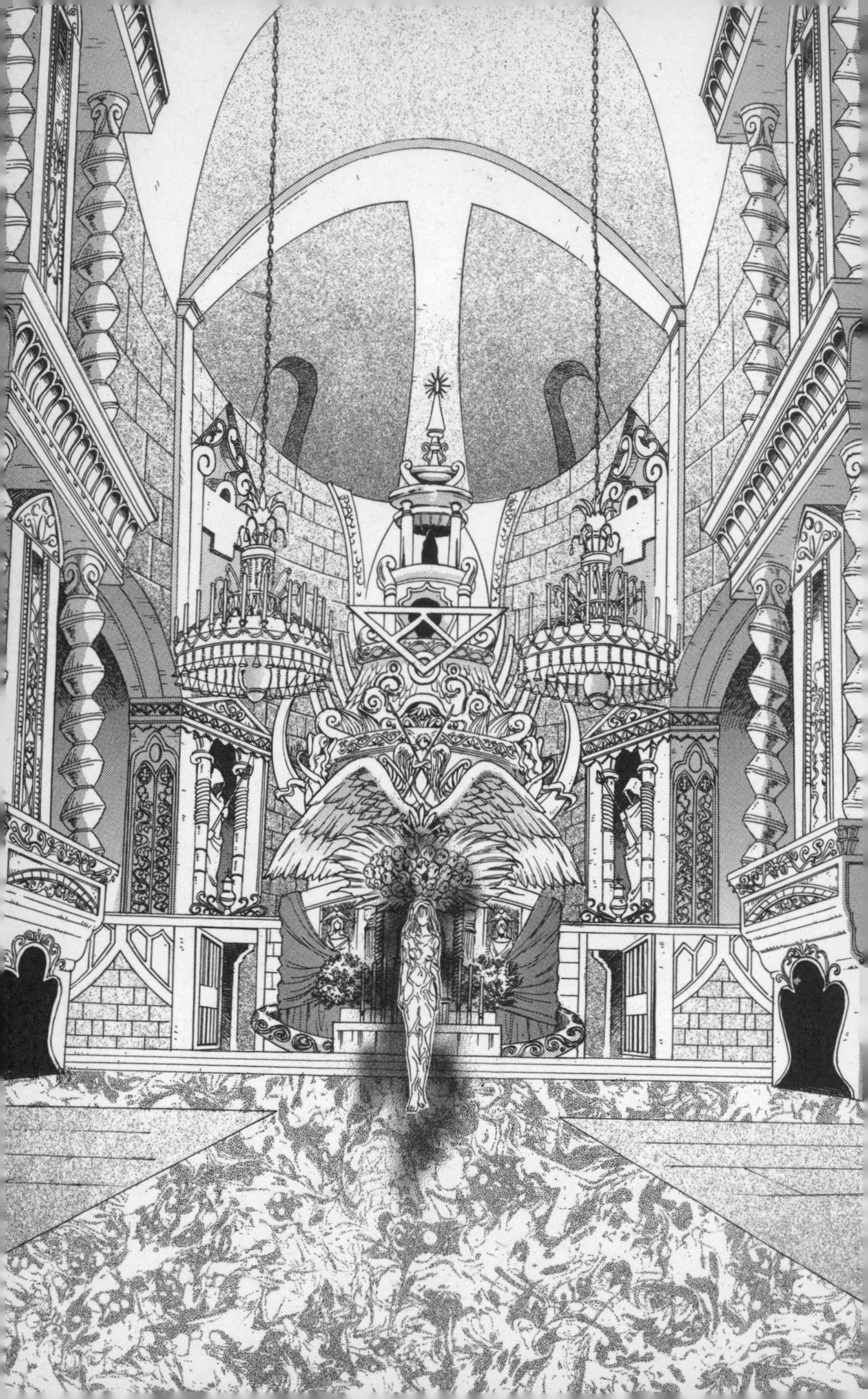

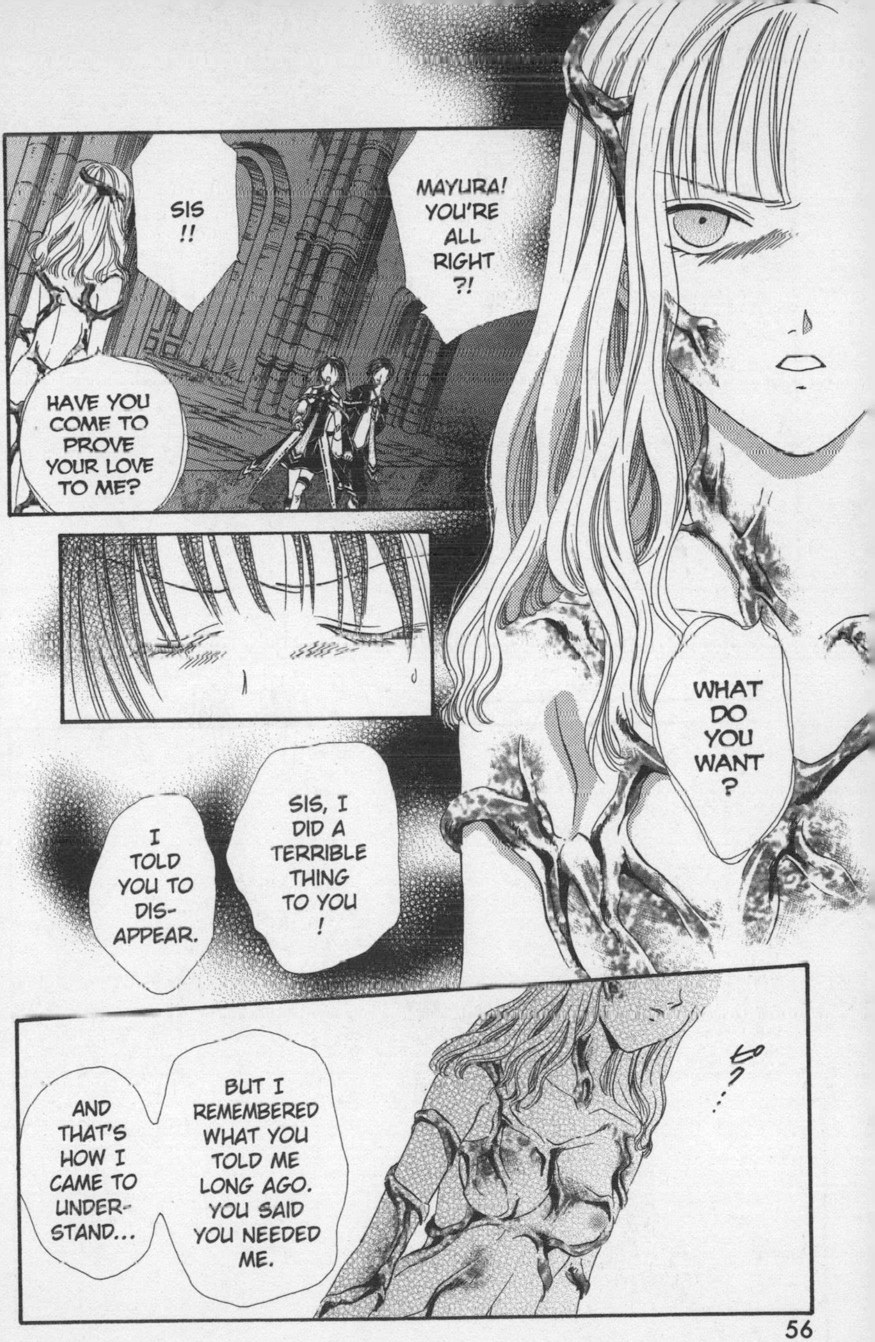
MAYURA! YOU'RE ALL RIGHT ?!
SIS !!
HAVE YOU COME TO PROVE YOUR LOVE TO ME?
WHAT DO YOU WANT ?
SIS, I DID A TERRIBLE THING TO YOU !
I TOLD YOU TO DIS-APPEAR.
BUT I REMEMBERED WHAT YOU TOLD ME LONG AGO. YOU SAID YOU NEEDED ME.
AND THAT'S HOW I CAME TO UNDER-STAND...

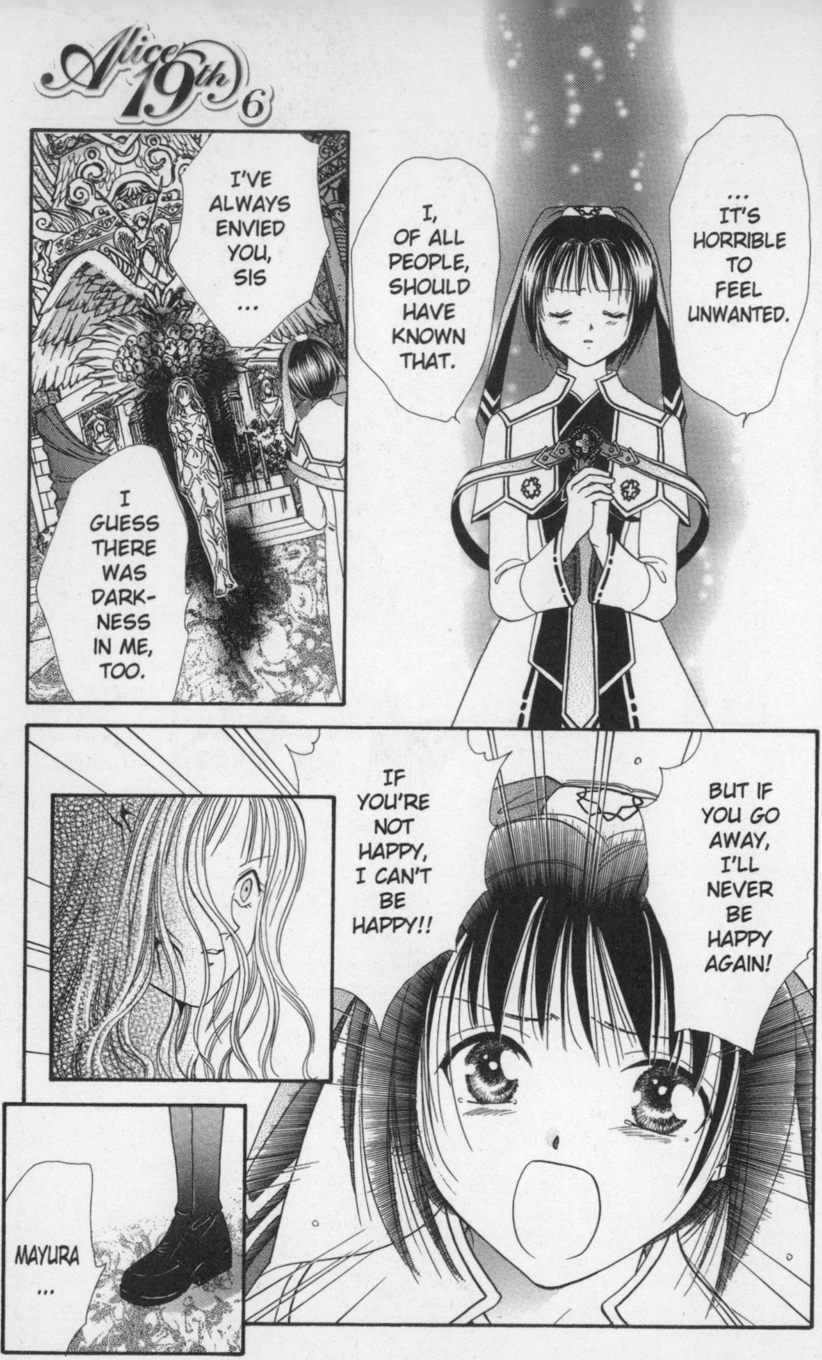
... IT'S HORRIBLE TO FEEL UNWANTED.
I, OF ALL PEOPLE, SHOULD HAVE KNOWN THAT.
I'VE ALWAYS ENVIED YOU, SIS ...
I GUESS THERE WAS DARKNESS IN ME, TOO.
BUT IF YOU GO AWAY, I'LL NEVER BE HAPPY AGAIN!
IF YOU'RE NOT HAPPY, I CAN'T BE HAPPY!!
MAYURA ...

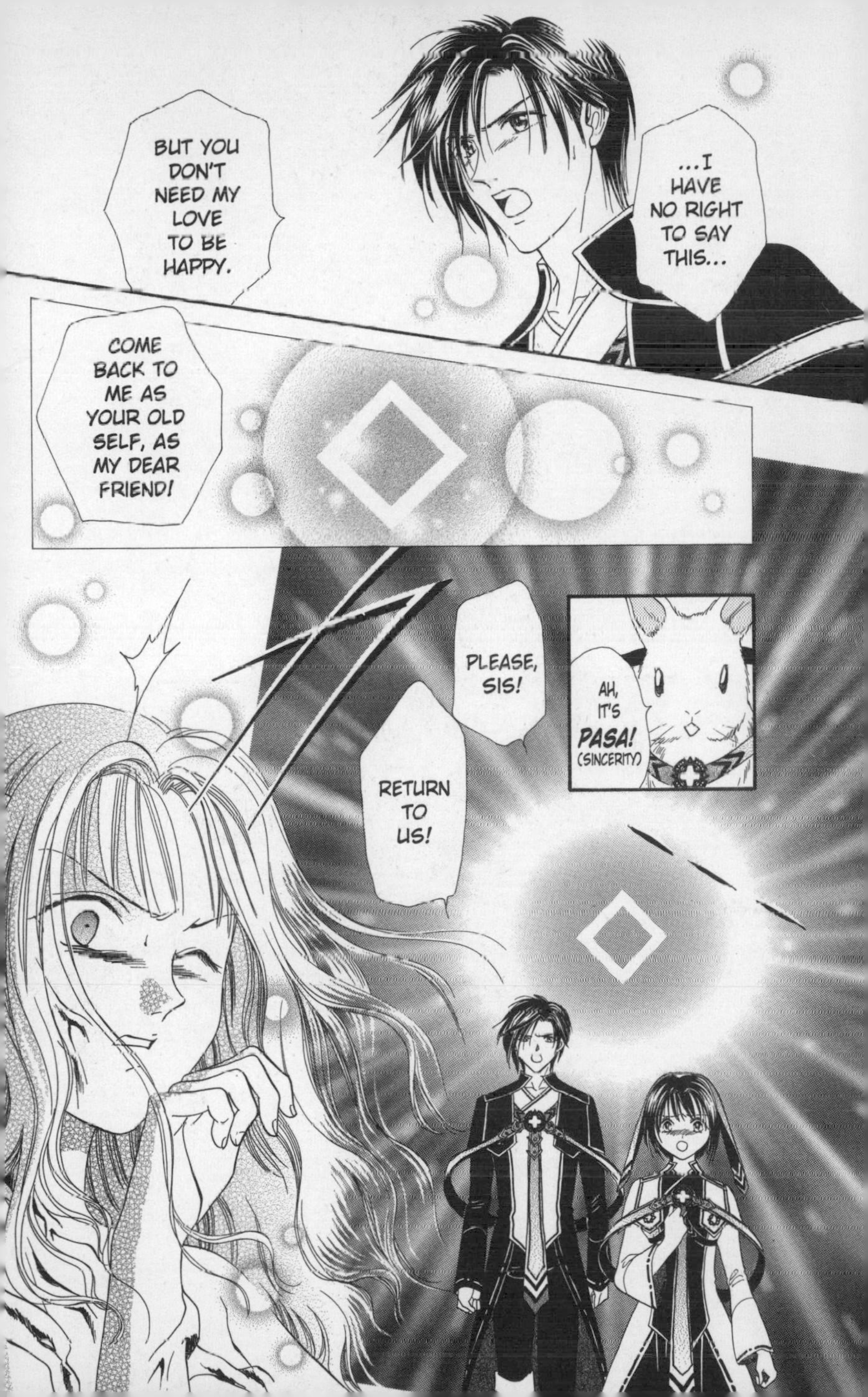
...I HAVE NO RIGHT TO SAY THIS...
BUT YOU DON'T NEED MY LOVE TO BE HAPPY.
COME BACK TO ME AS YOUR OLD SELF, AS MY DEAR FRIEND!
AH, IT'S PASA! (SINCERITY)
PLEASE, SIS!
RETURN TO US!

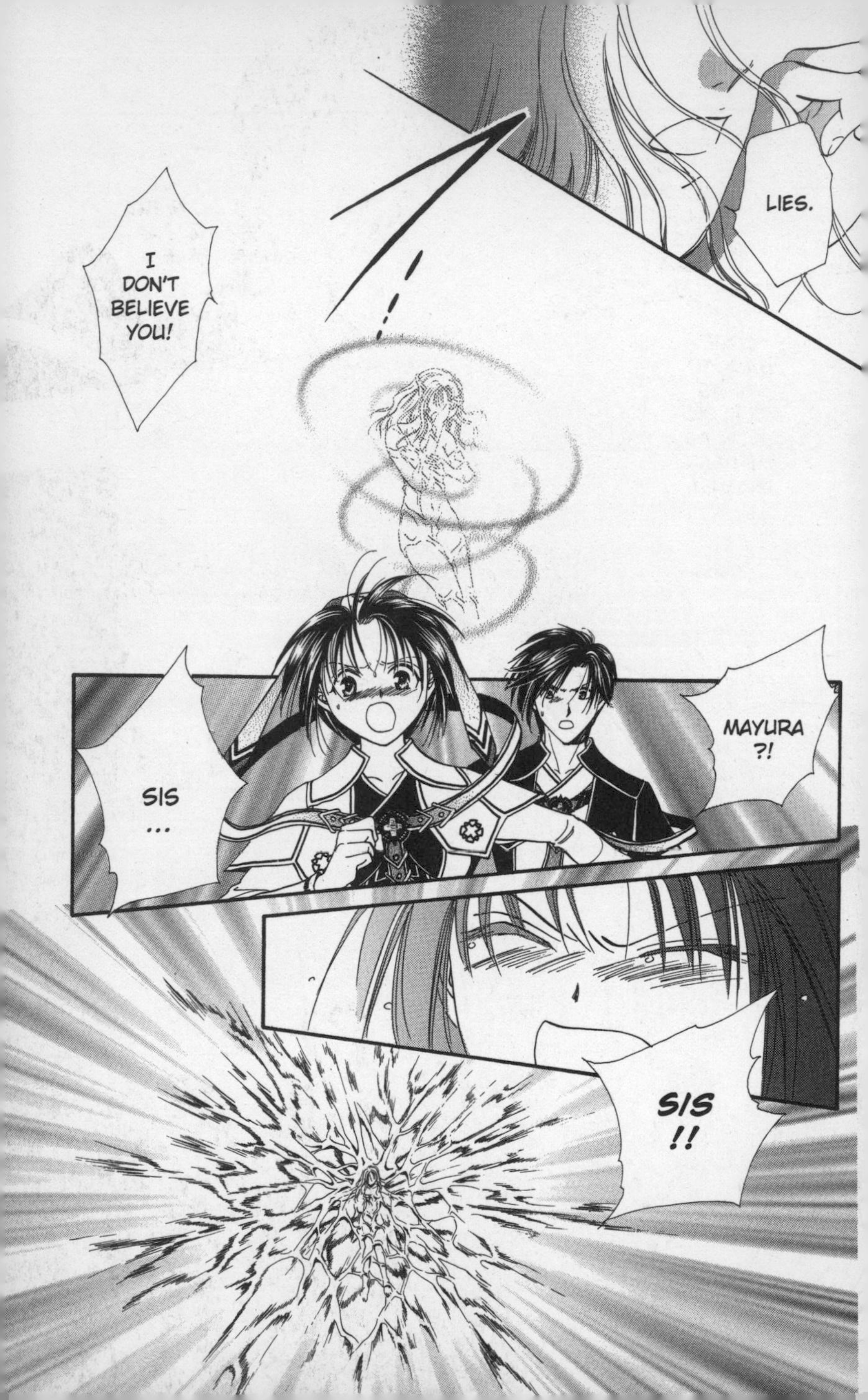
LIES.
I DON'T BELIEVE YOU!
MAYURA ?!
SIS ...
SIS !!

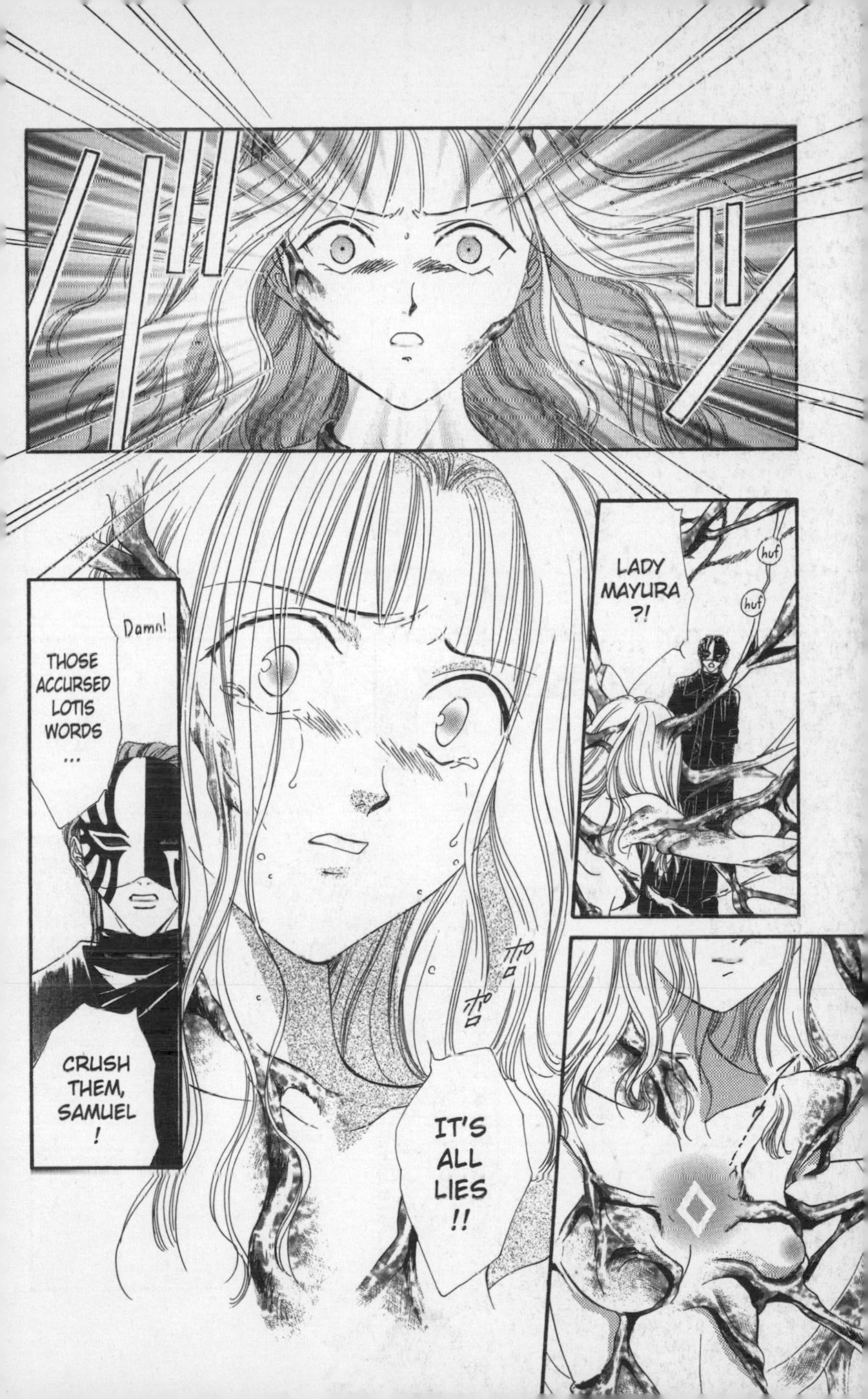

LADY MAYURA ?!
huf
huf
IT'S ALL LIES !!
Damn!
THOSE ACCURSED LOTIS WORDS ...
CRUSH THEM, SAMUEL !

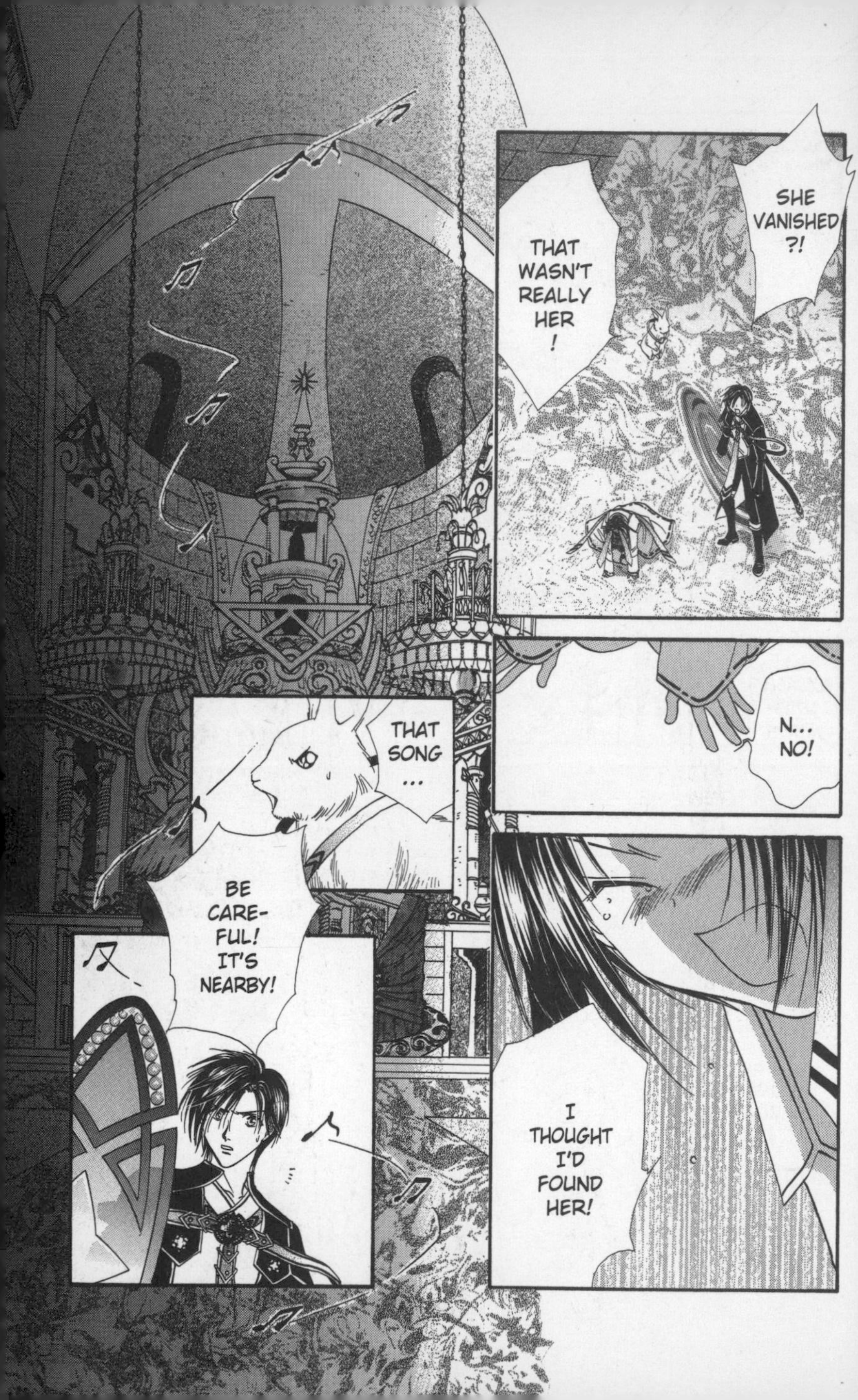
SHE VANISHED?!
THAT WASN'T REALLY HER!
N... NO!
THAT SONG...
I THOUGHT I'D FOUND HER!
BE CAREFUL! IT'S NEARBY!

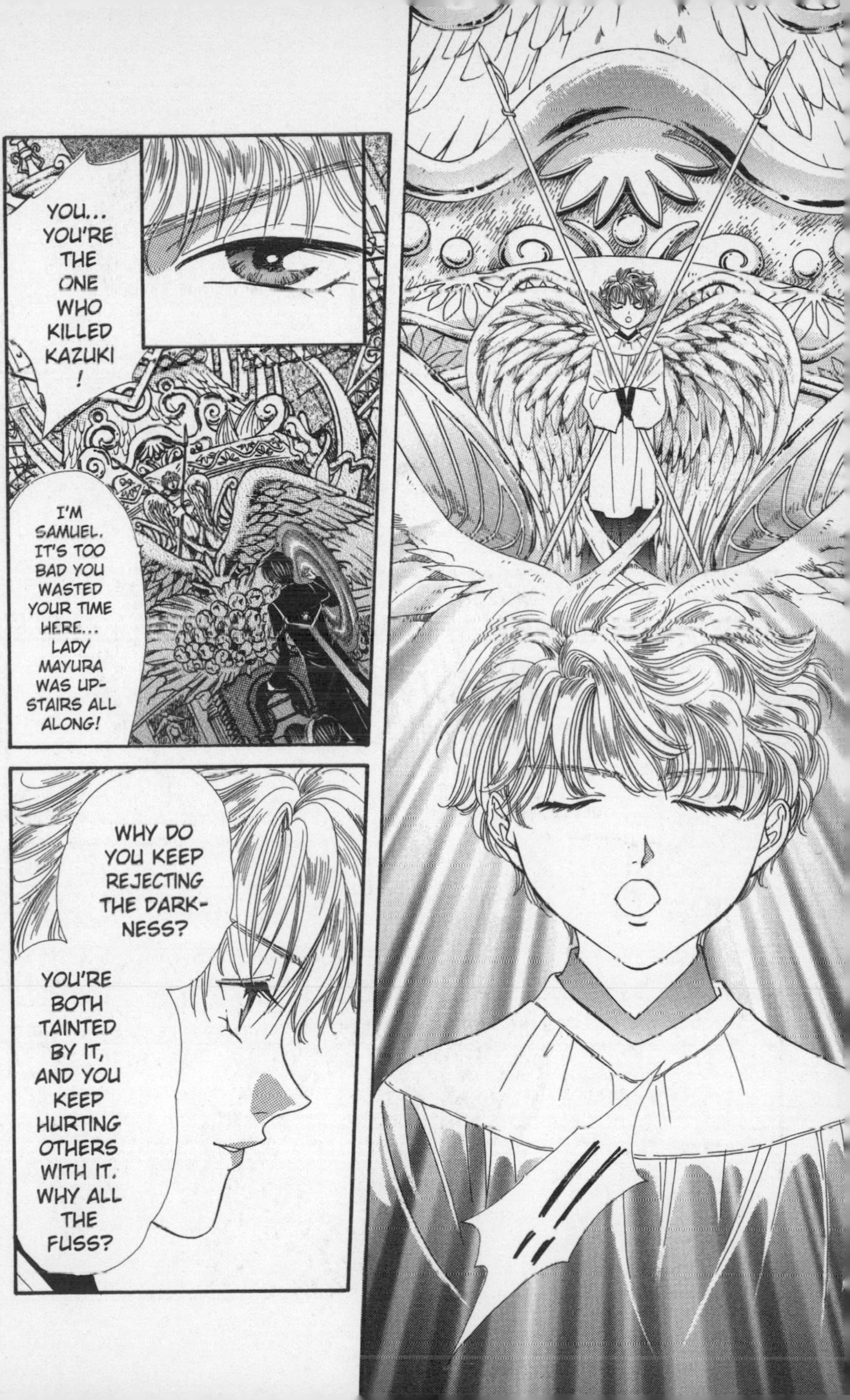
YOU... YOU'RE THE ONE WHO KILLED KAZUKI!
I'M SAMUEL. IT'S TOO BAD YOU WASTED YOUR TIME HERE... LADY MAYURA WAS UPSTAIRS ALL ALONG!
WHY DO YOU KEEP REJECTING THE DARKNESS?
YOU'RE BOTH TAINTED BY IT, AND YOU KEEP HURTING OTHERS WITH IT. WHY ALL THE FUSS?

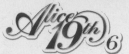

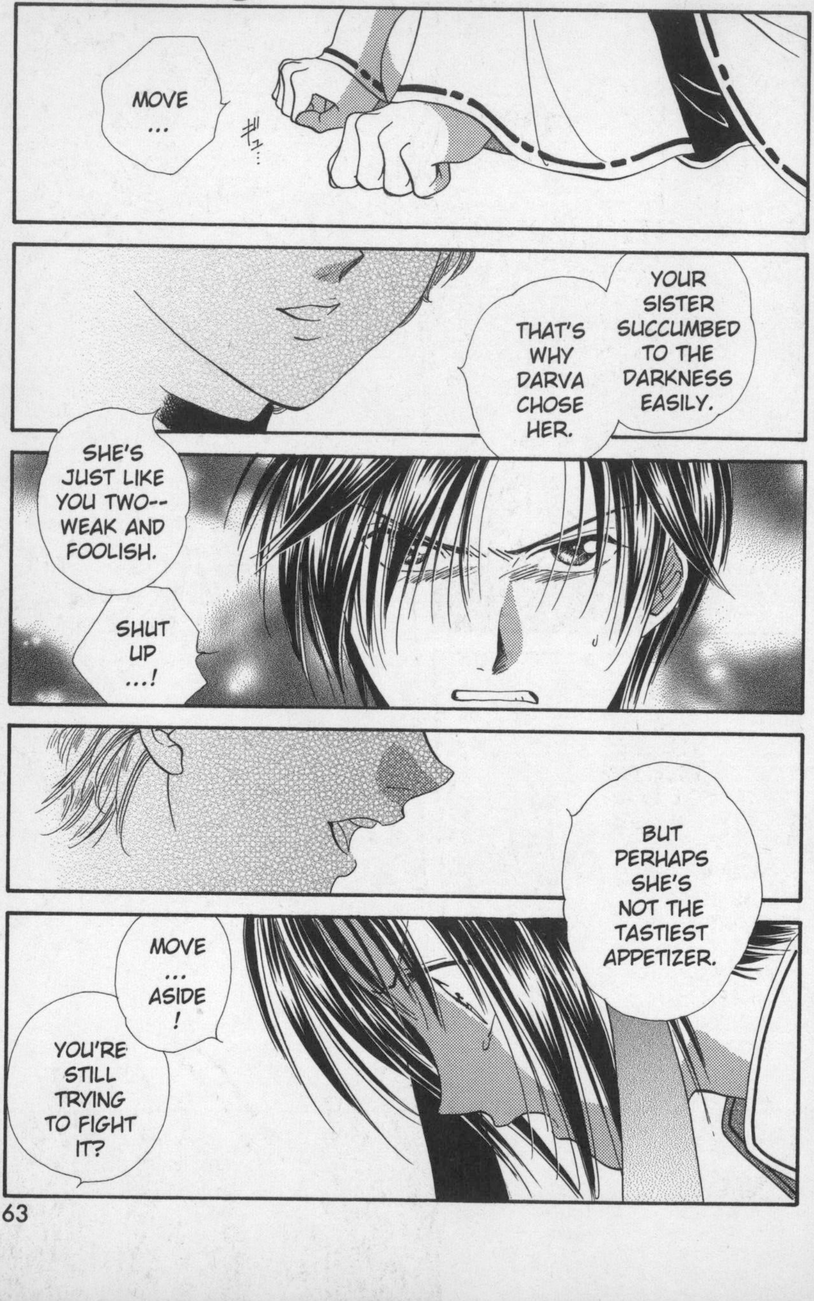
MOVE ...
ギュ…
YOUR SISTER SUCCUMBED TO THE DARKNESS EASILY.
THAT'S WHY DARVA CHOSE HER.
SHE'S JUST LIKE YOU TWO-- WEAK AND FOOLISH.
SHUT UP ...!
BUT PERHAPS SHE'S NOT THE TASTIEST APPETIZER.
MOVE ... ASIDE !
YOU'RE STILL TRYING TO FIGHT IT?

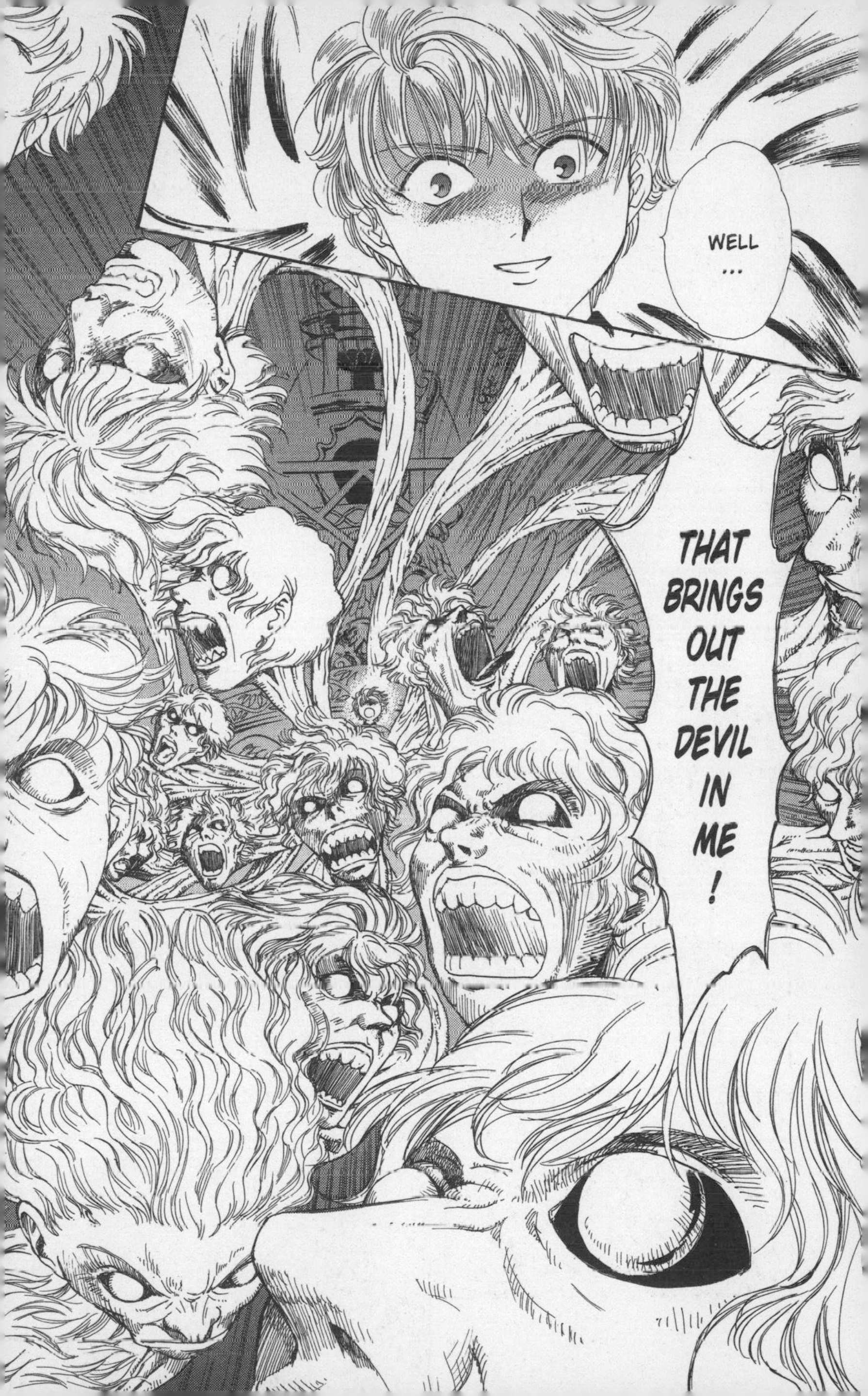
WELL ...
THAT BRINGS OUT THE DEVIL IN ME!

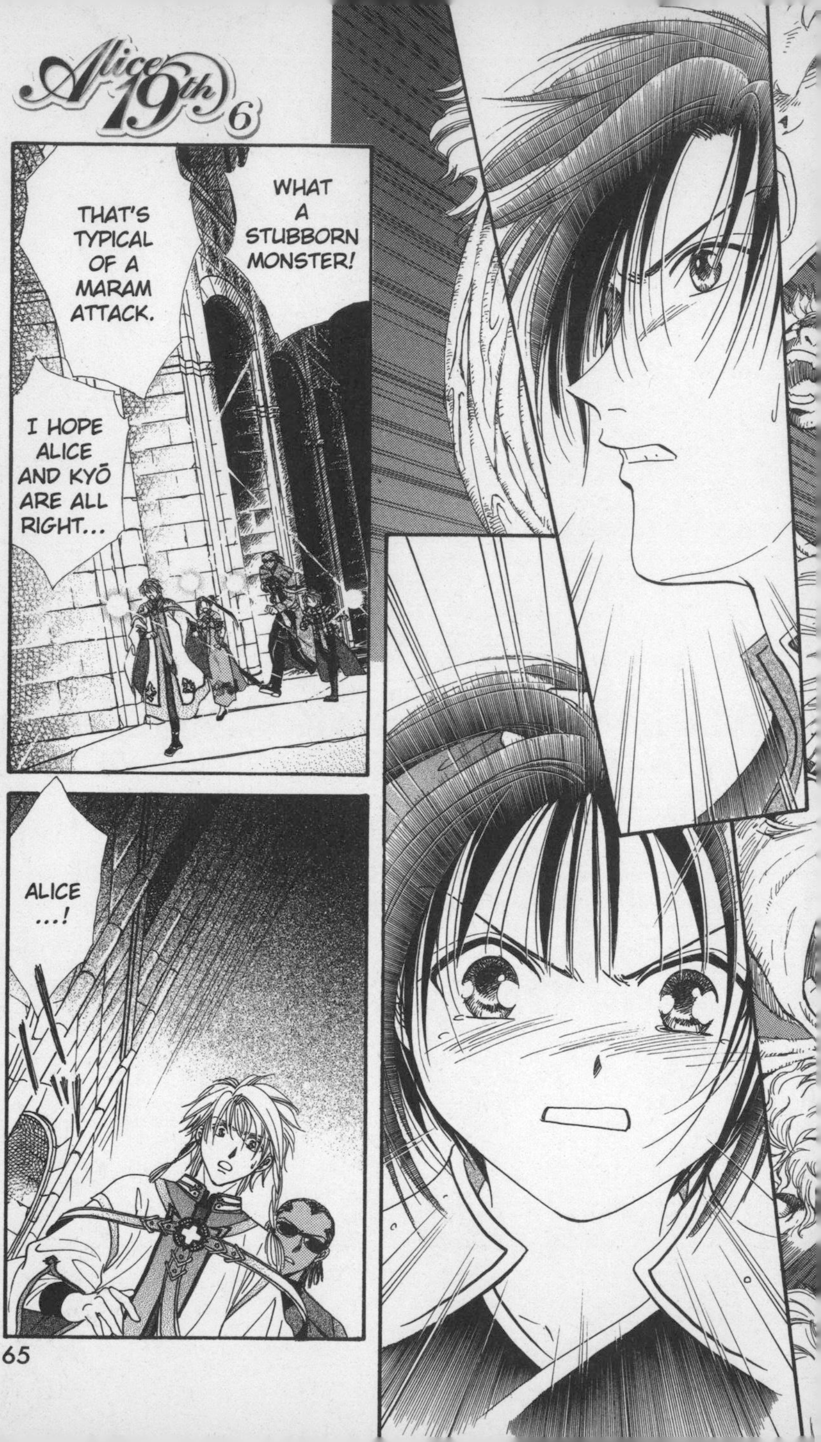
WHAT A STUBBORN MONSTER!
THAT'S TYPICAL OF A MARAM ATTACK.
I HOPE ALICE AND KYŌ ARE ALL RIGHT...
ALICE ...!

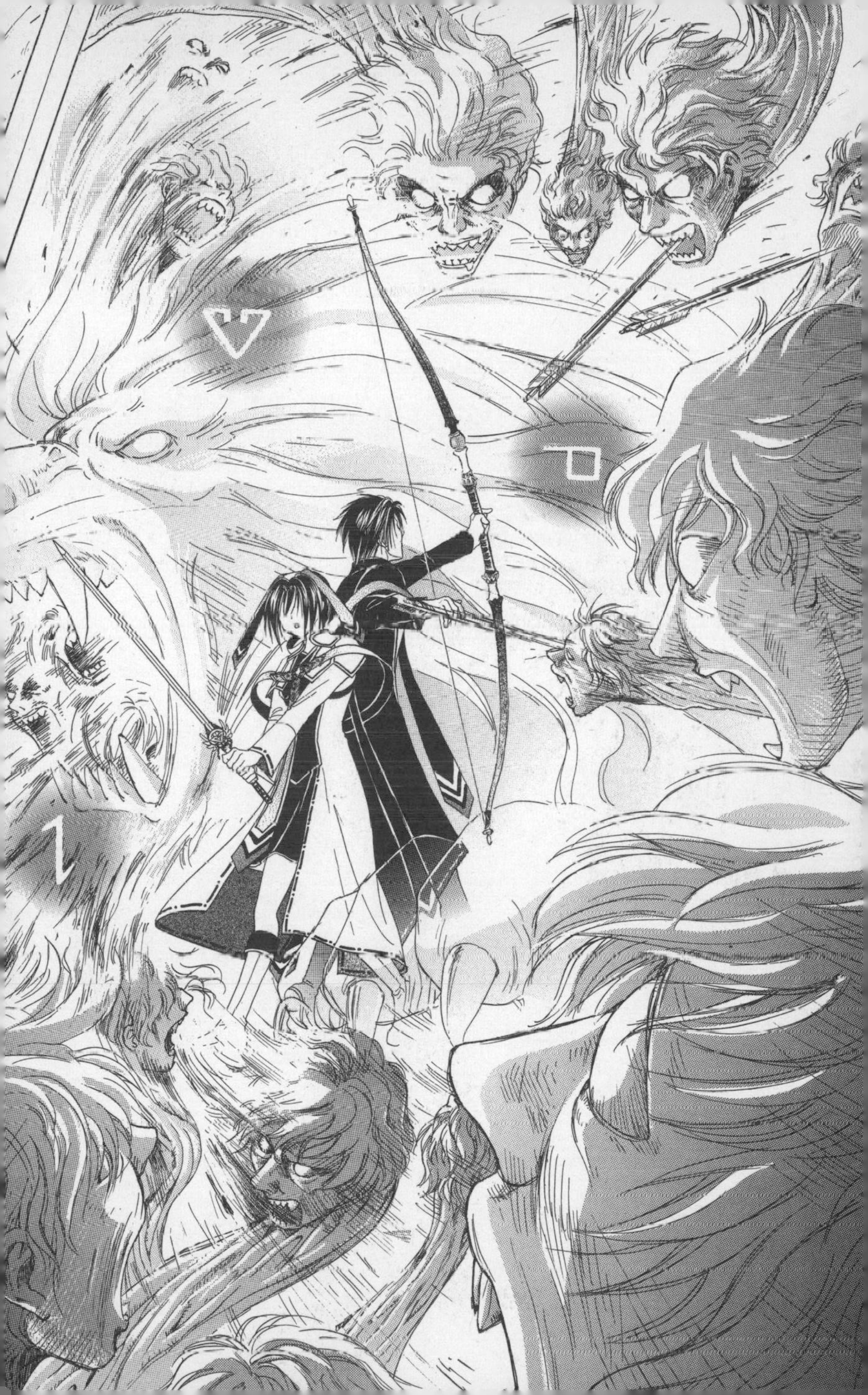

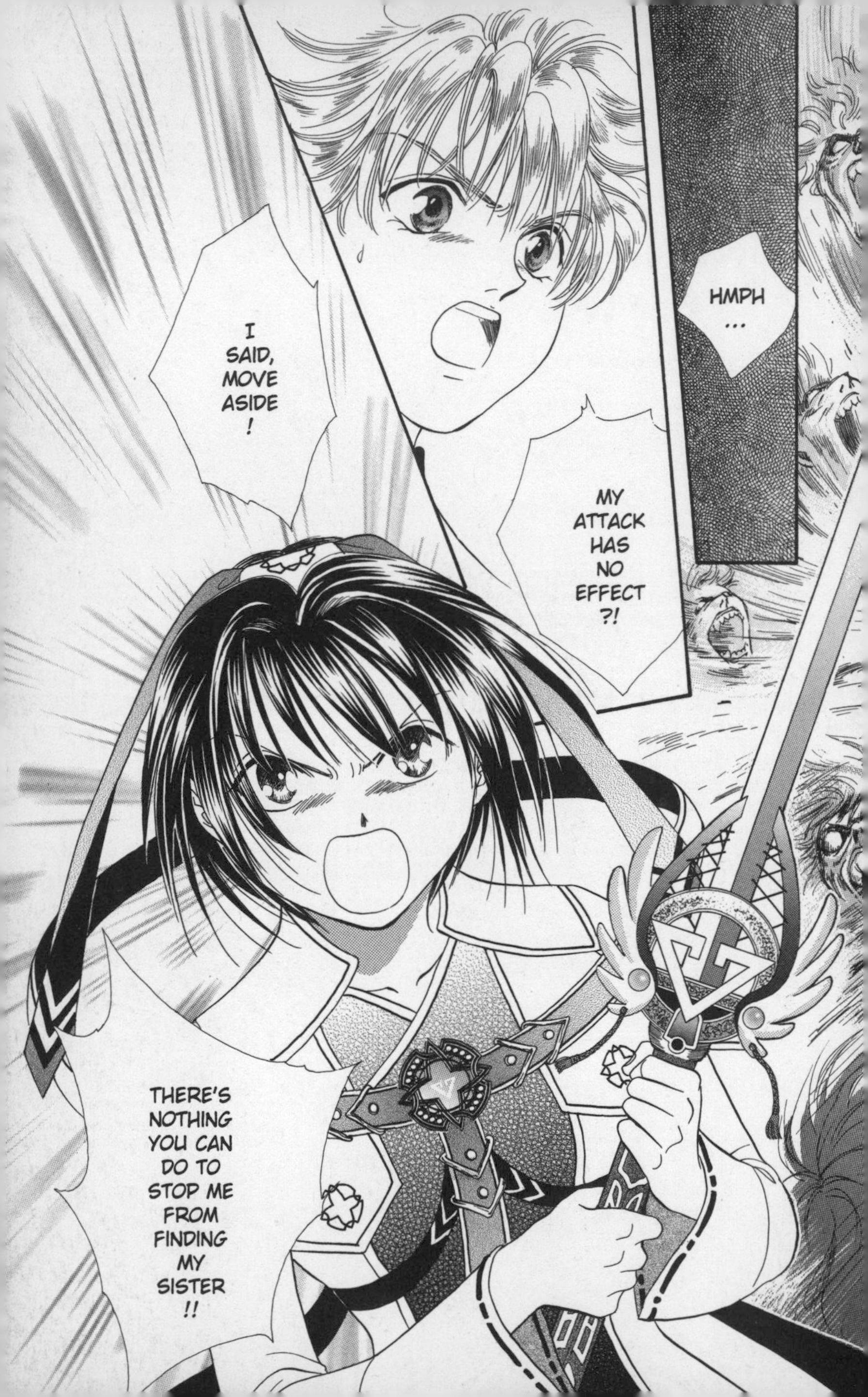
HMPH ...
I SAID, MOVE ASIDE !
MY ATTACK HAS NO EFFECT ?!
THERE'S NOTHING YOU CAN DO TO STOP ME FROM FINDING MY SISTER !!

* AGE: 13

* BLOOD TYPE: A

* ASTROLOGICAL SIGN: SCORPIO

* HEIGHT: JUST OVER 5 FEET

* BIRTHPLACE: ENGLAND

* THE 13TH HEIR TO THE
  HOUSE OF ROLAND

* A GIFTED YOUNG MAN,
  ALREADY IN COLLEGE.

* THOUGH WEALTHY, BRILLIANT, AND
  ARISTOCRATIC, OTHER BOYS ARE
  OFTEN ENVIOUS, AND HE HAS
  FEW FRIENDS TO CONFIDE IN.

* HIS MOTHER IS DECEASED. HE
  GAVE HIS MOTHER'S NAME TO A
  SWALLOW THAT HE FOUND AND
  SECRETLY ADOPTED.

* HE SEEMS COOL AND MATURE FOR
  HIS AGE, BUT HE HAS A FEROCIOUS
  SWEET TOOTH. WHEN SWEETS ARE
  PLACED BEFORE HIM, HE BEHAVES
  LIKE A CHILD. (OR PERHAPS THAT'S
  WHEN HIS TRUE CHARACTER
  ASSERTS ITSELF.)

* HOBBY: RIDING HORSES

* NEVER MISSES AFTERNOON TEA.

CHRISTOPHER WILLIAM ORSON ANDREW ROLAND

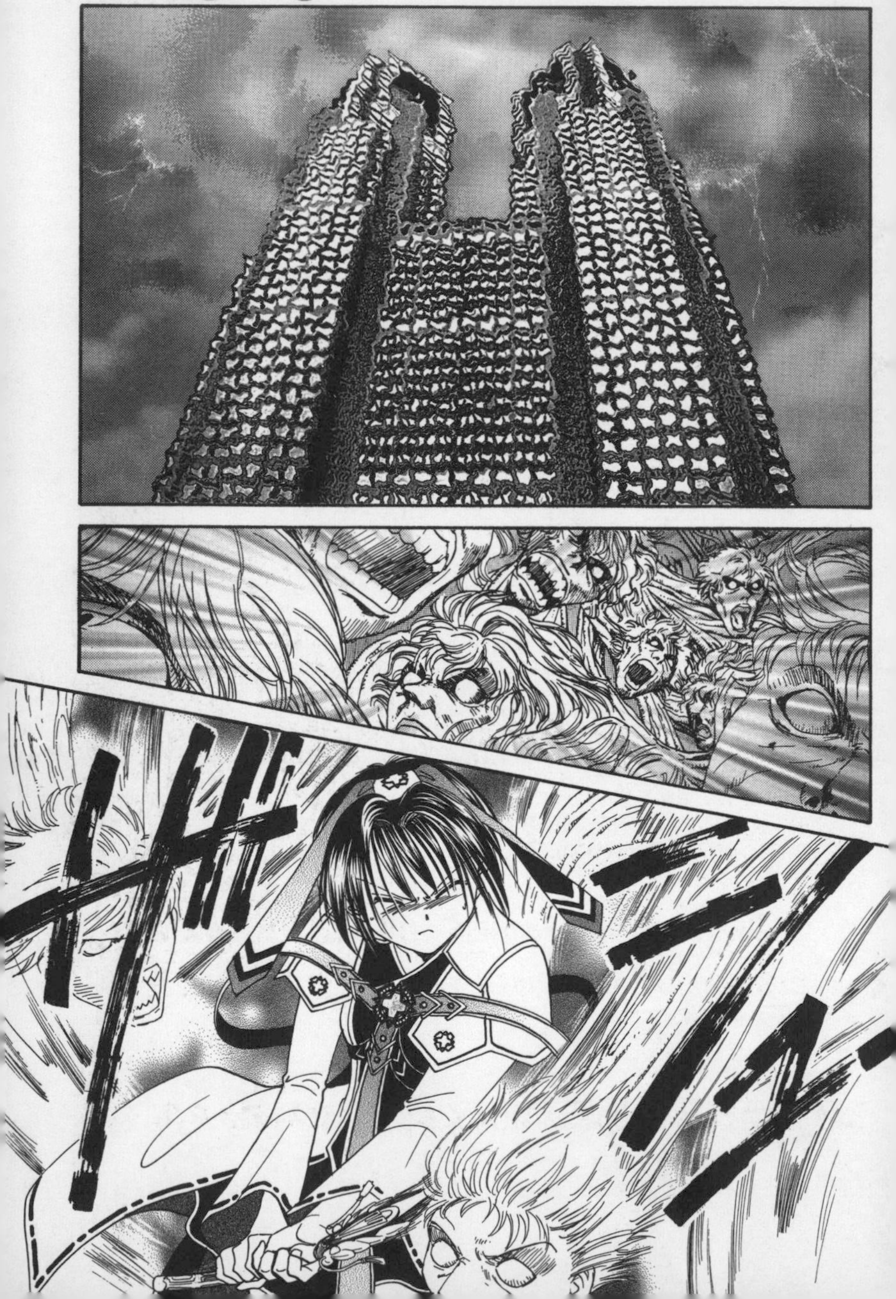

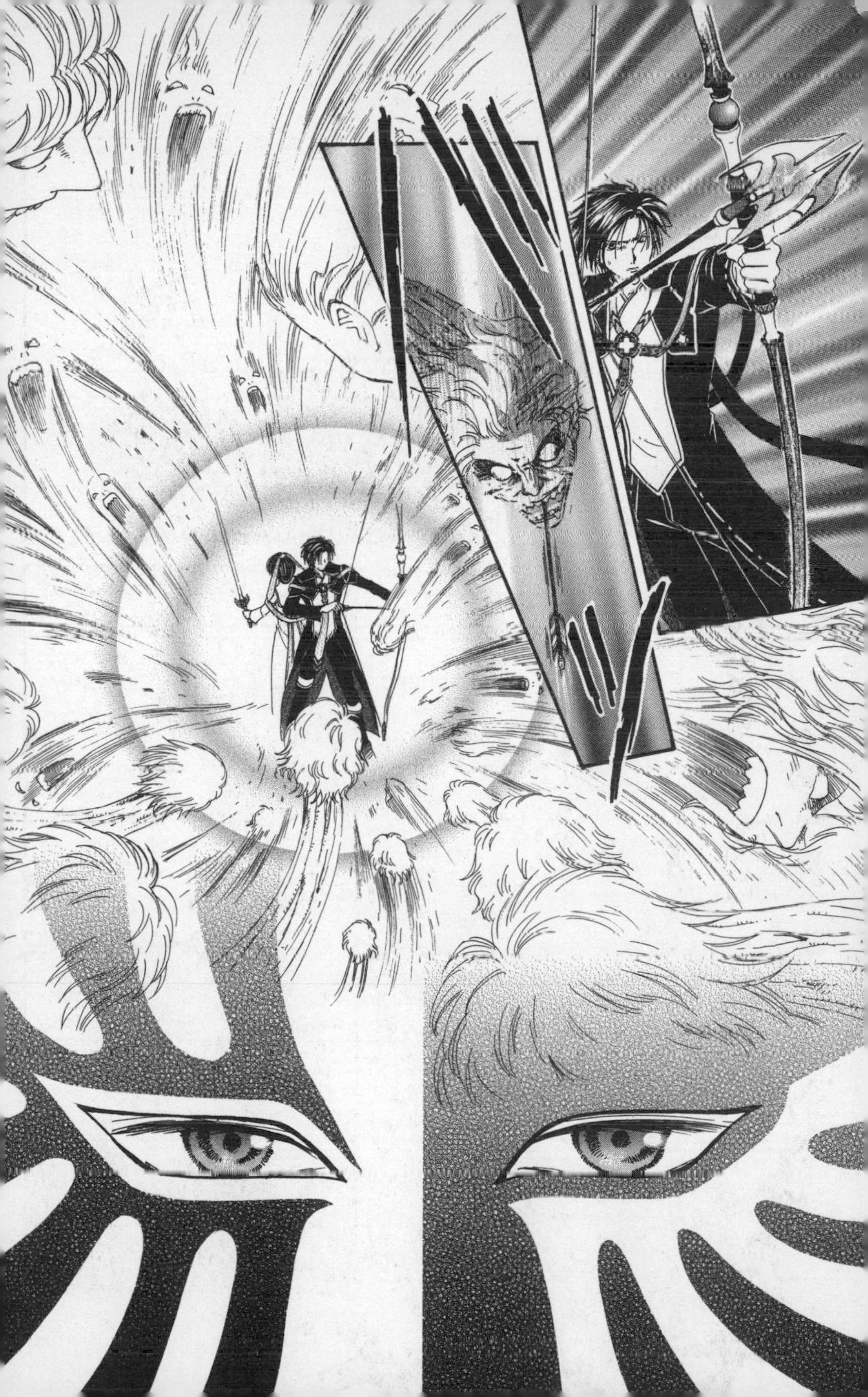

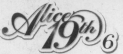

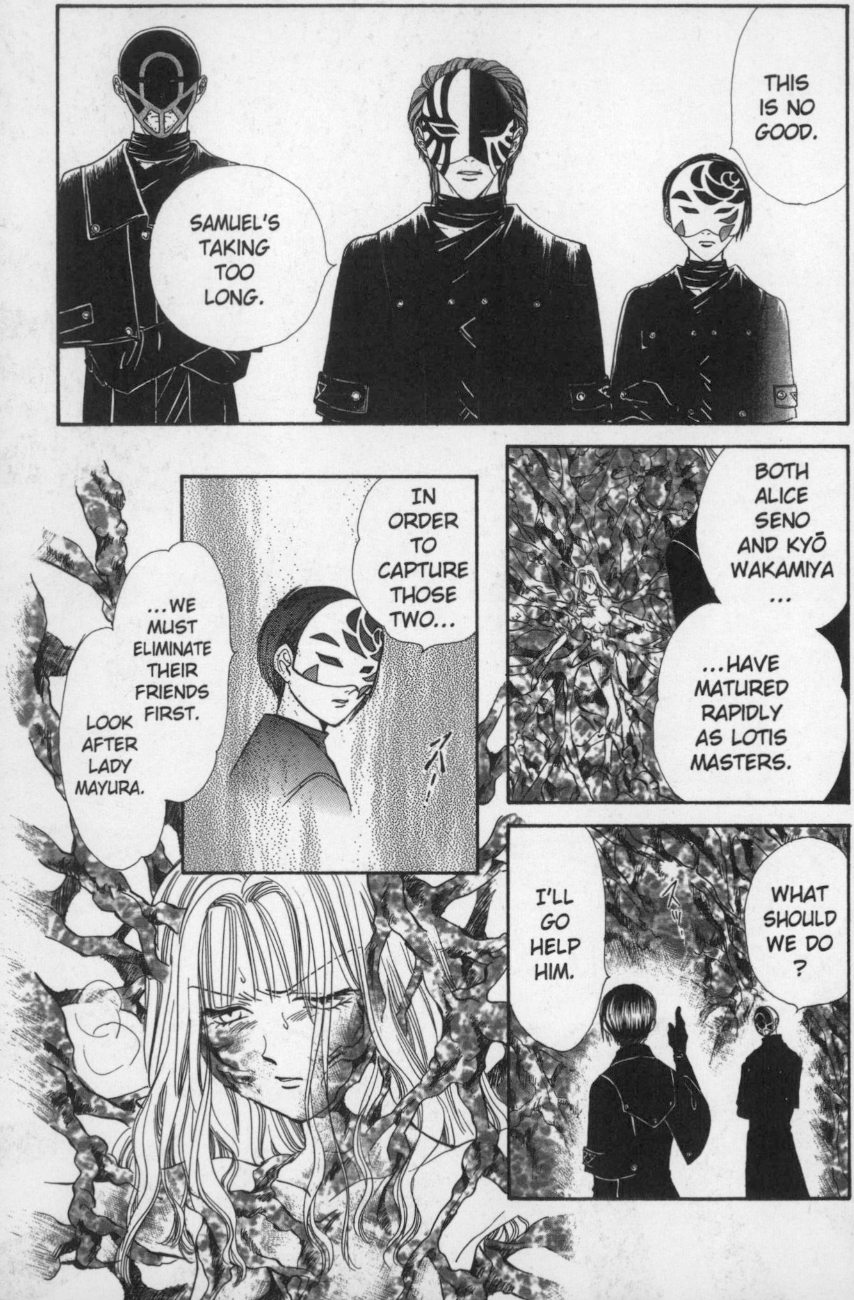
THIS IS NO GOOD.
SAMUEL'S TAKING TOO LONG.
BOTH ALICE SENO AND KYŌ WAKAMIYA...
...HAVE MATURED RAPIDLY AS LOTIS MASTERS.
WHAT SHOULD WE DO?
I'LL GO HELP HIM.
IN ORDER TO CAPTURE THOSE TWO...
...WE MUST ELIMINATE THEIR FRIENDS FIRST.
LOOK AFTER LADY MAYURA.

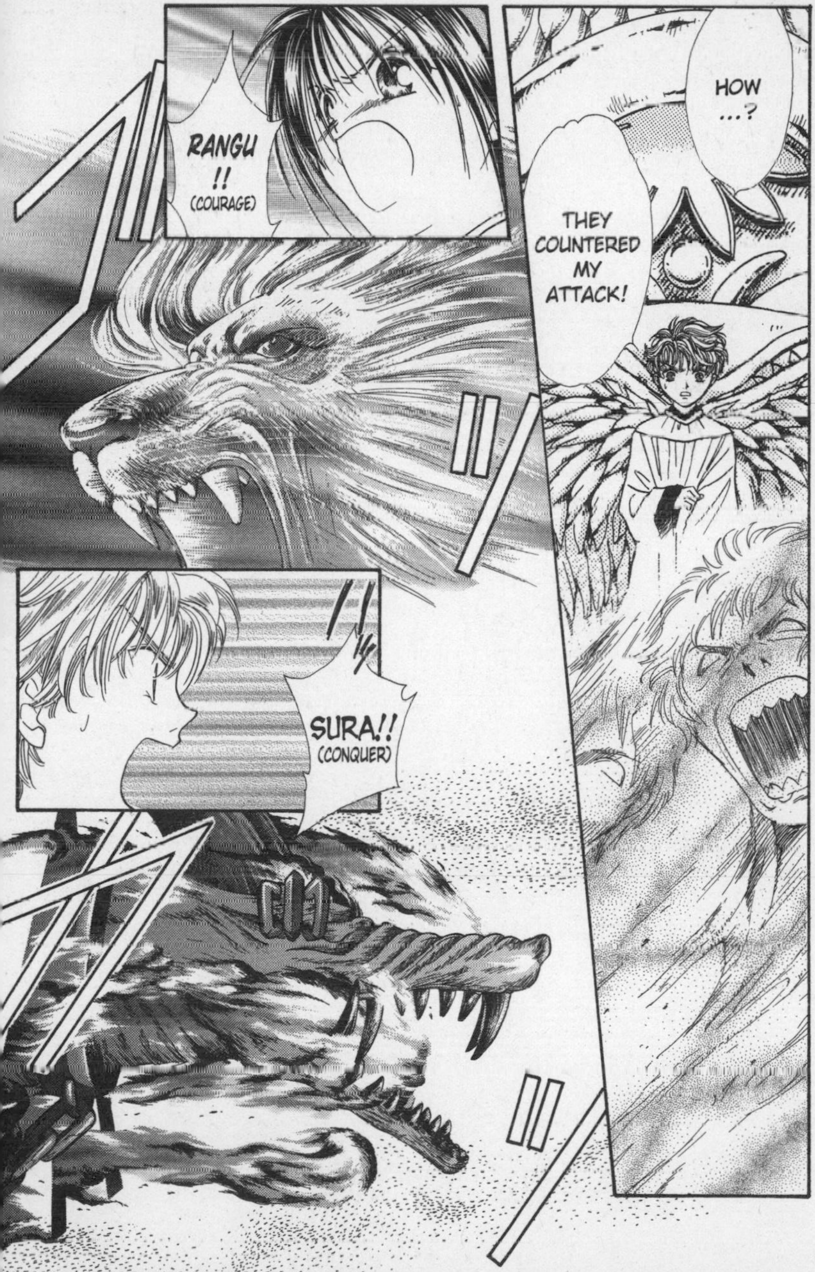
HOW ...?
THEY COUNTERED MY ATTACK!
RANGU !! (COURAGE)
SURA!! (CONQUER)

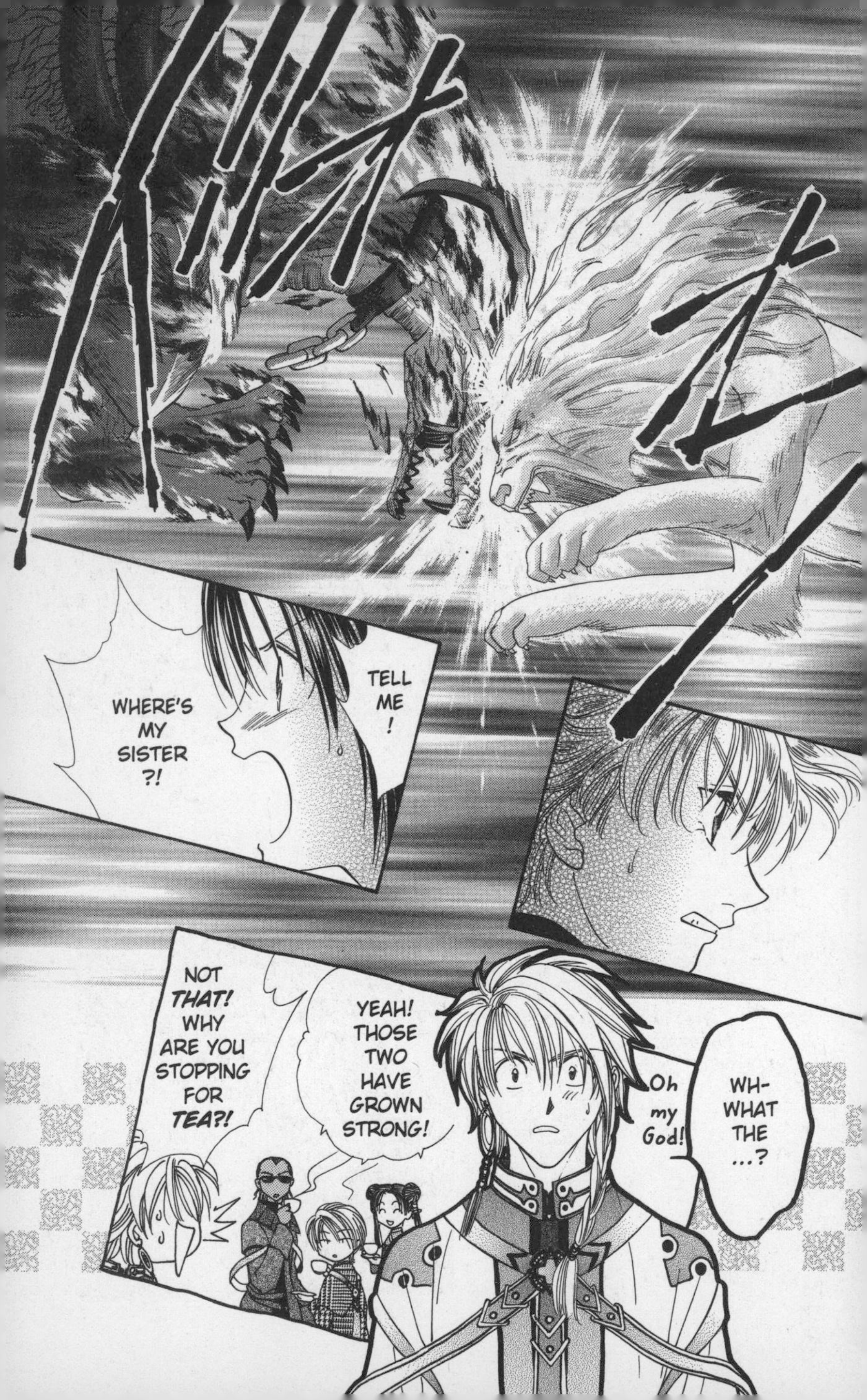
TELL ME!
WHERE'S MY SISTER?!
WH-WHAT THE...?
Oh my God!
YEAH! THOSE TWO HAVE GROWN STRONG!
NOT *THAT!* WHY ARE YOU STOPPING FOR *TEA?!*

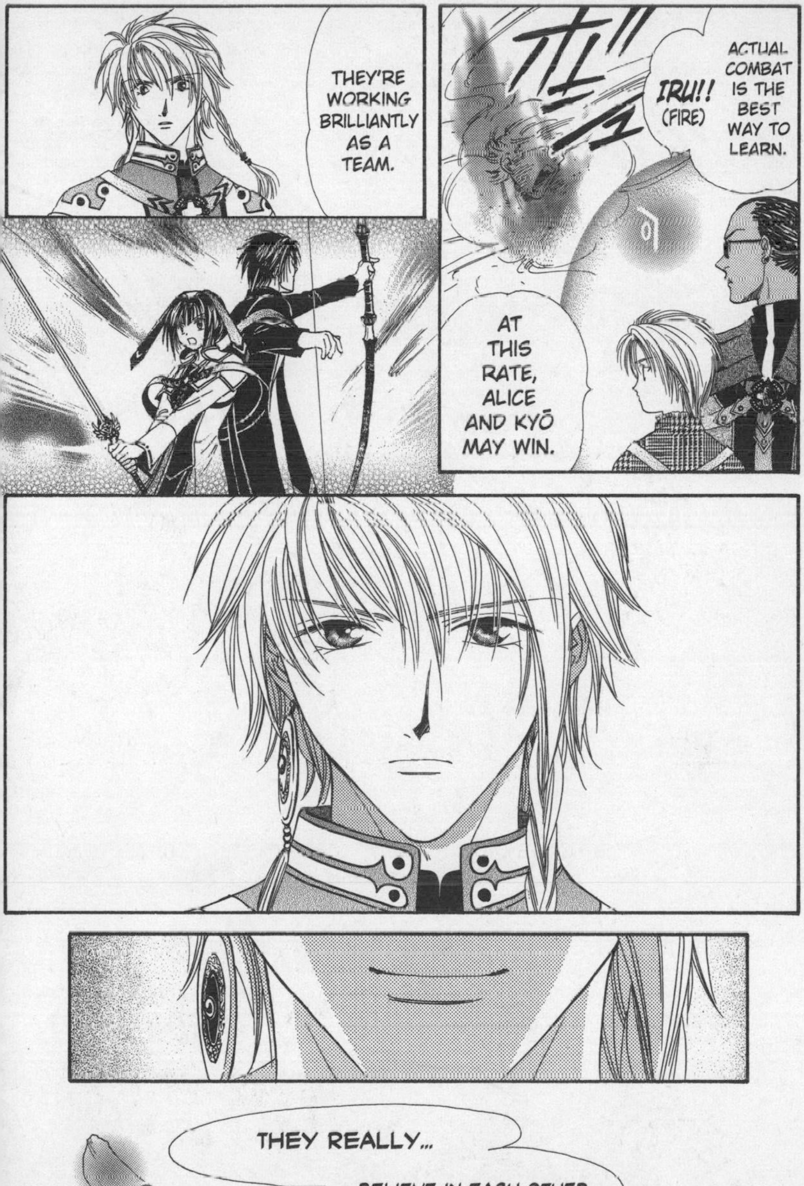
ACTUAL COMBAT IS THE BEST WAY TO LEARN.
IRU!! (FIRE)
AT THIS RATE, ALICE AND KYŌ MAY WIN.
THEY'RE WORKING BRILLIANTLY AS A TEAM.
THEY REALLY...
...BELIEVE IN EACH OTHER.

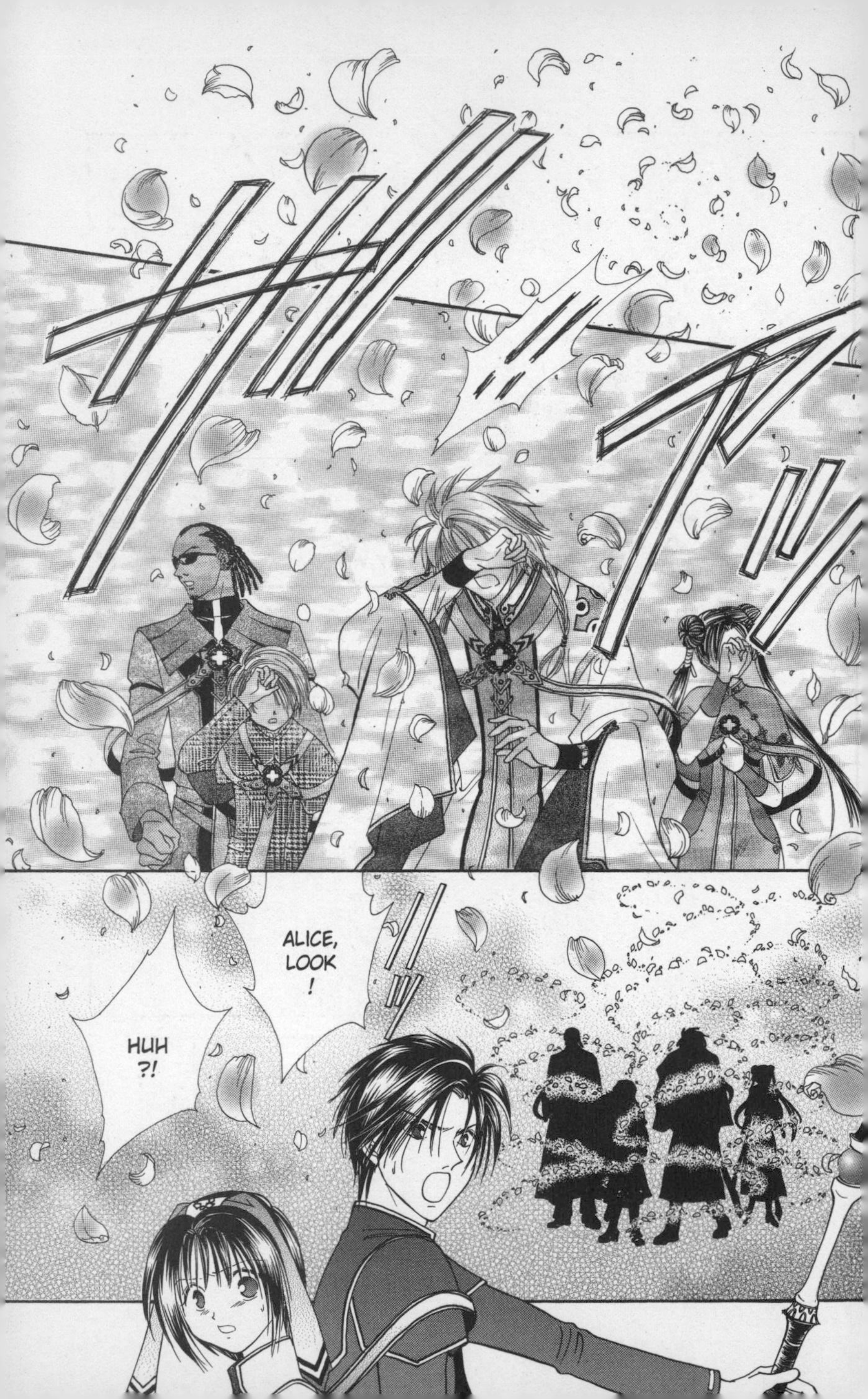
ALICE, LOOK!
HUH?!

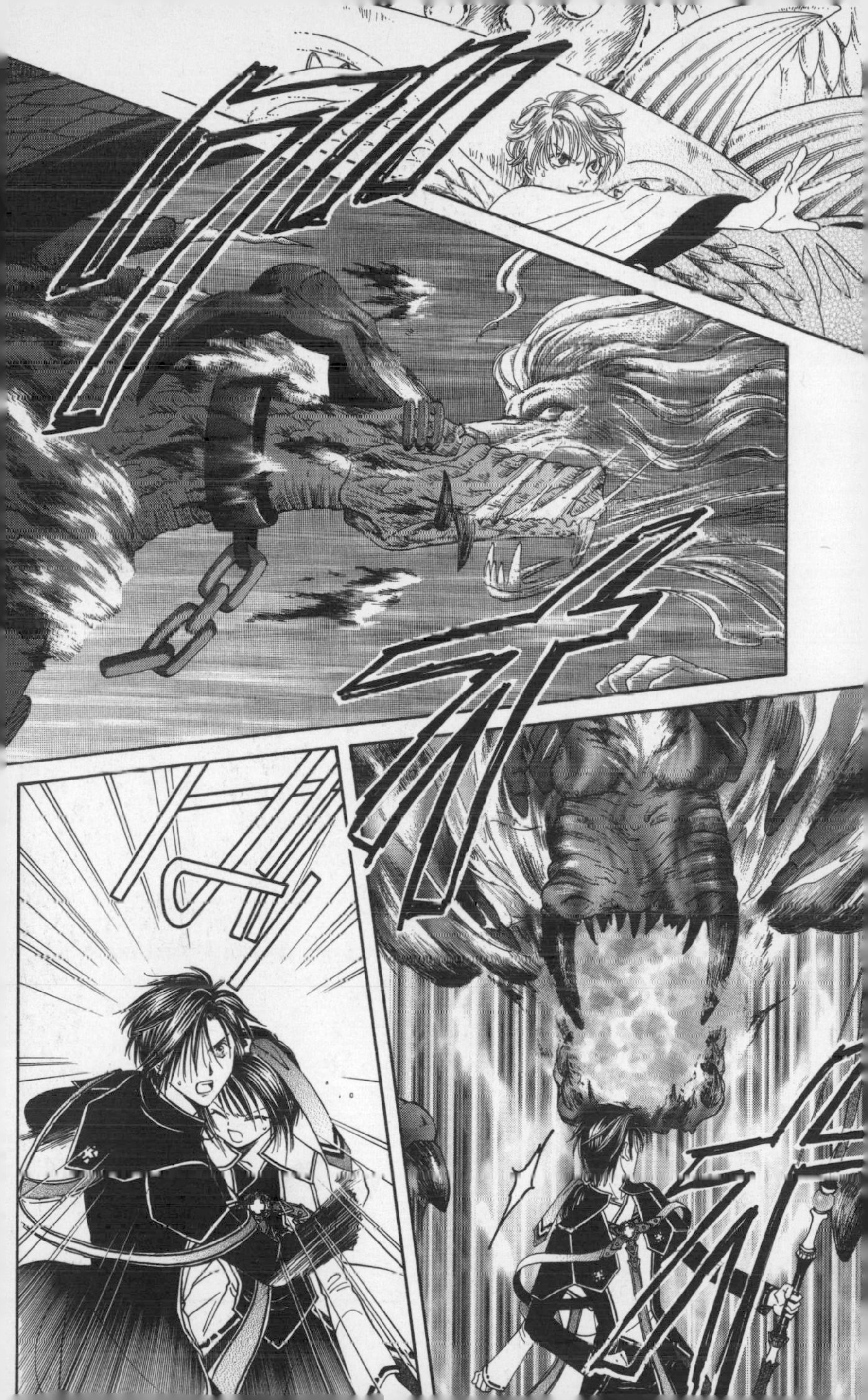

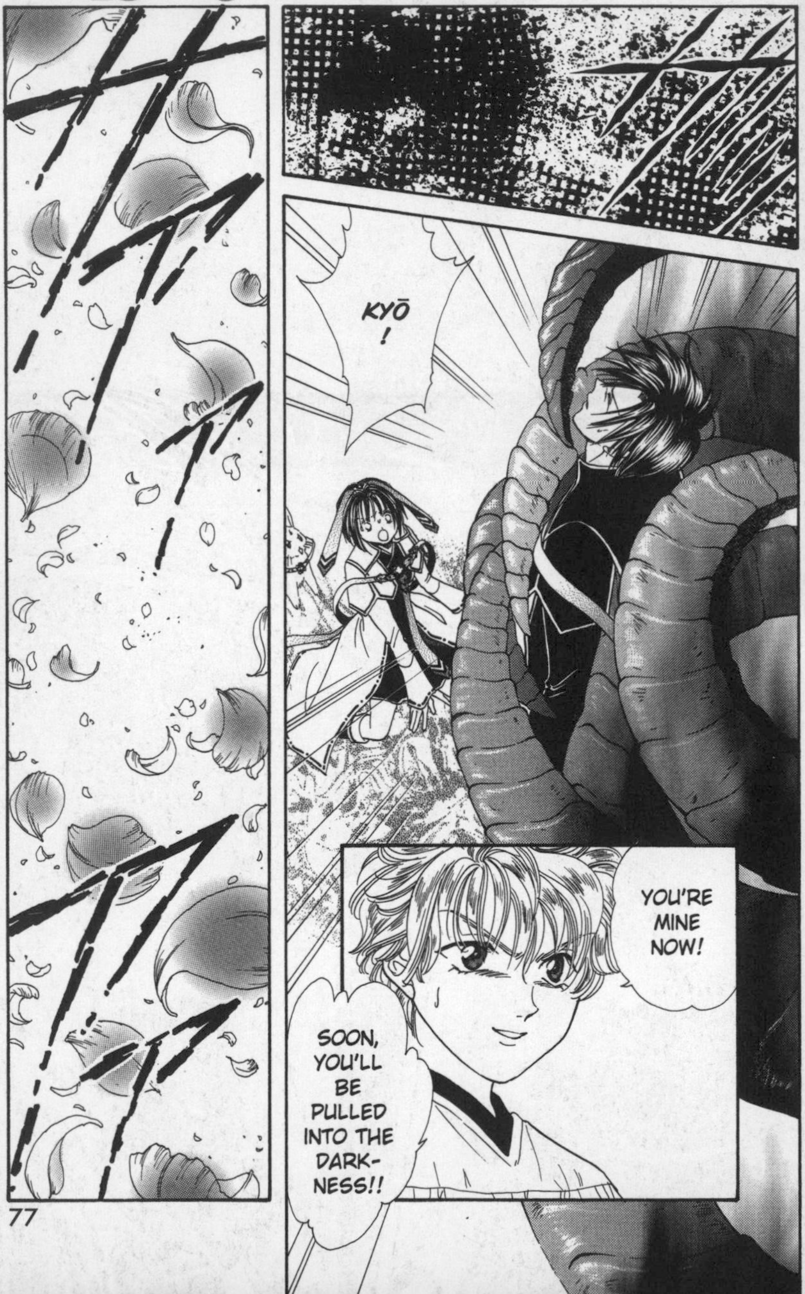
KYŌ!
YOU'RE MINE NOW!
SOON, YOU'LL BE PULLED INTO THE DARKNESS!!

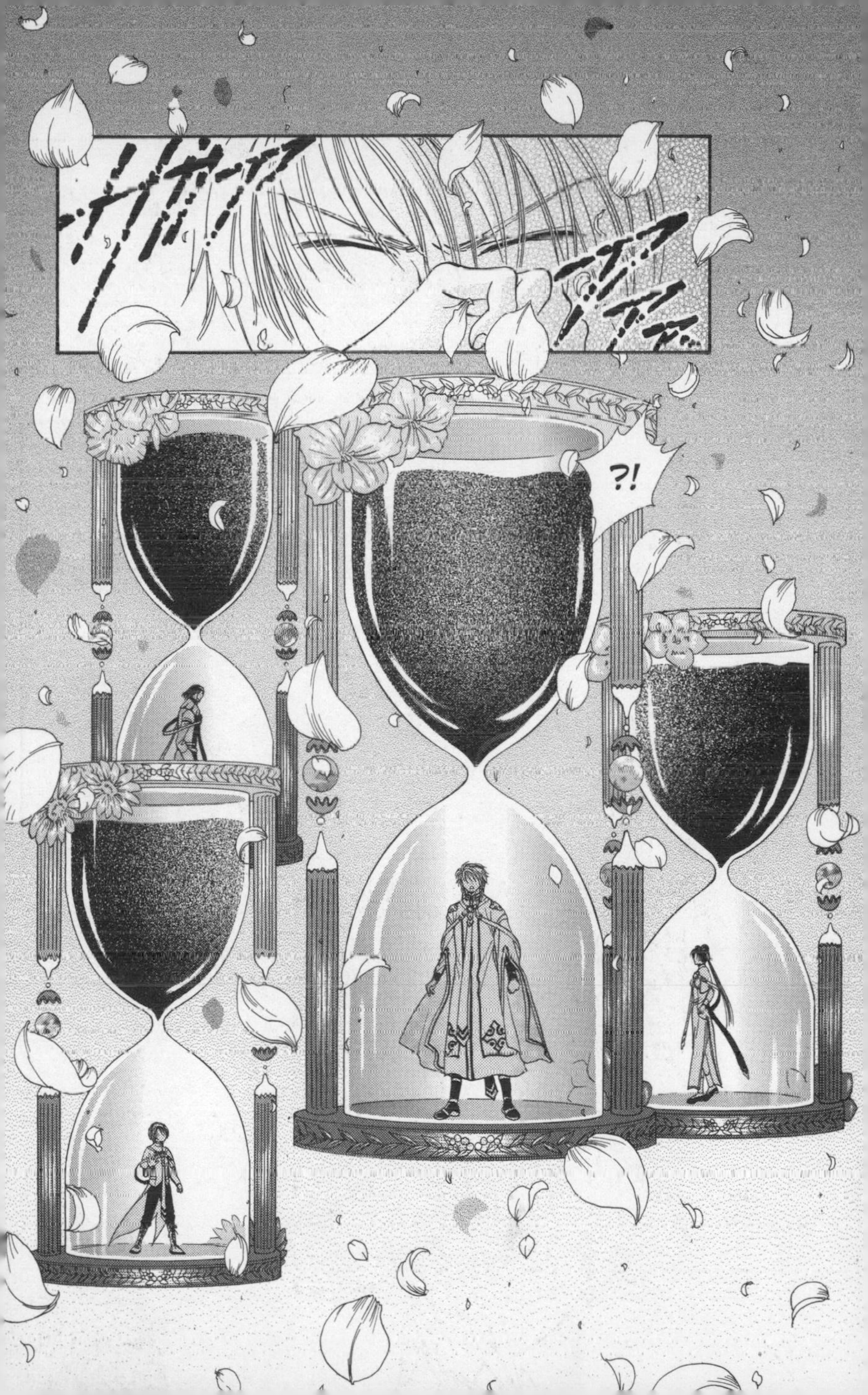
?!

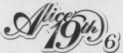

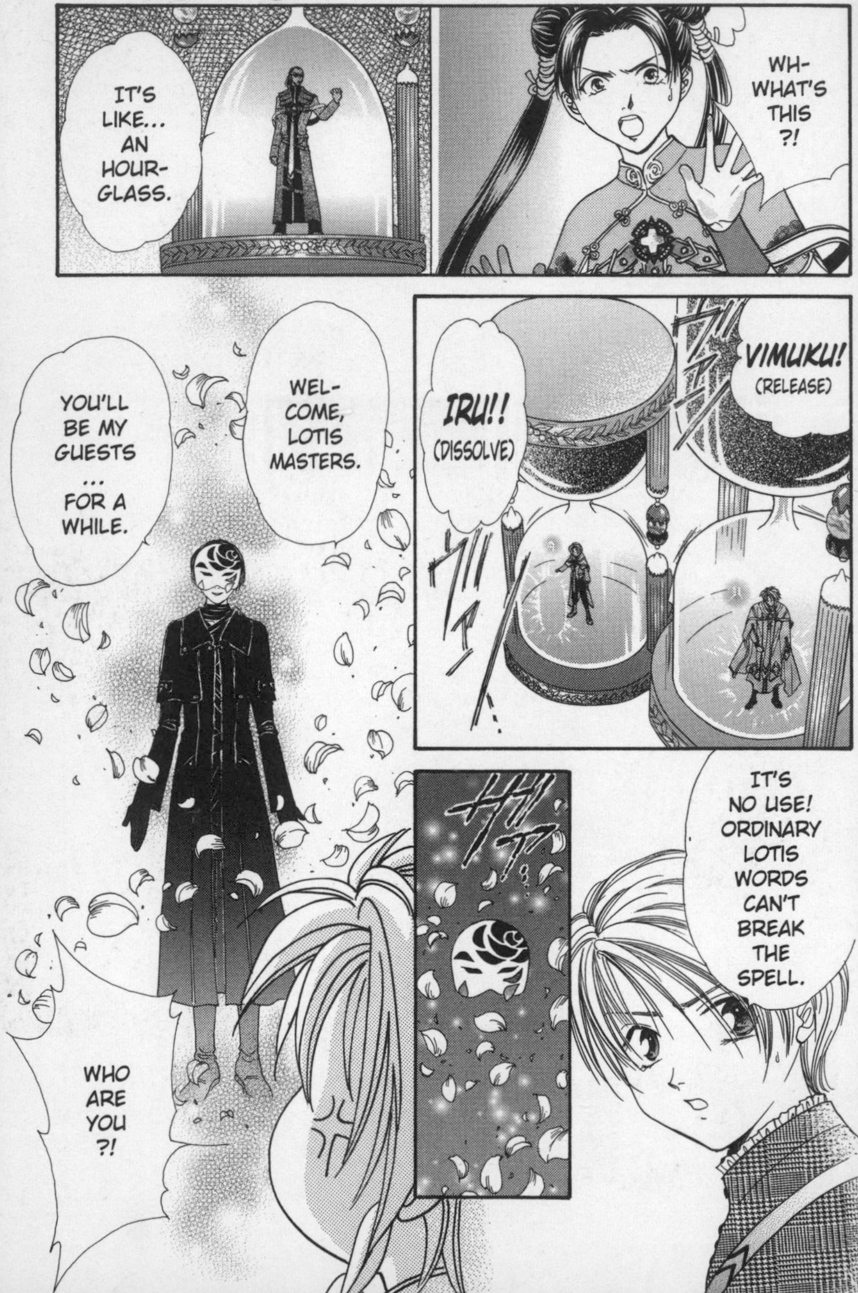
WH-WHAT'S THIS?!
IT'S LIKE... AN HOURGLASS.
VIMUKU! (RELEASE)
IRU!! (DISSOLVE)
WELCOME, LOTIS MASTERS.
YOU'LL BE MY GUESTS... FOR A WHILE.
IT'S NO USE! ORDINARY LOTIS WORDS CAN'T BREAK THE SPELL.
WHO ARE YOU?!

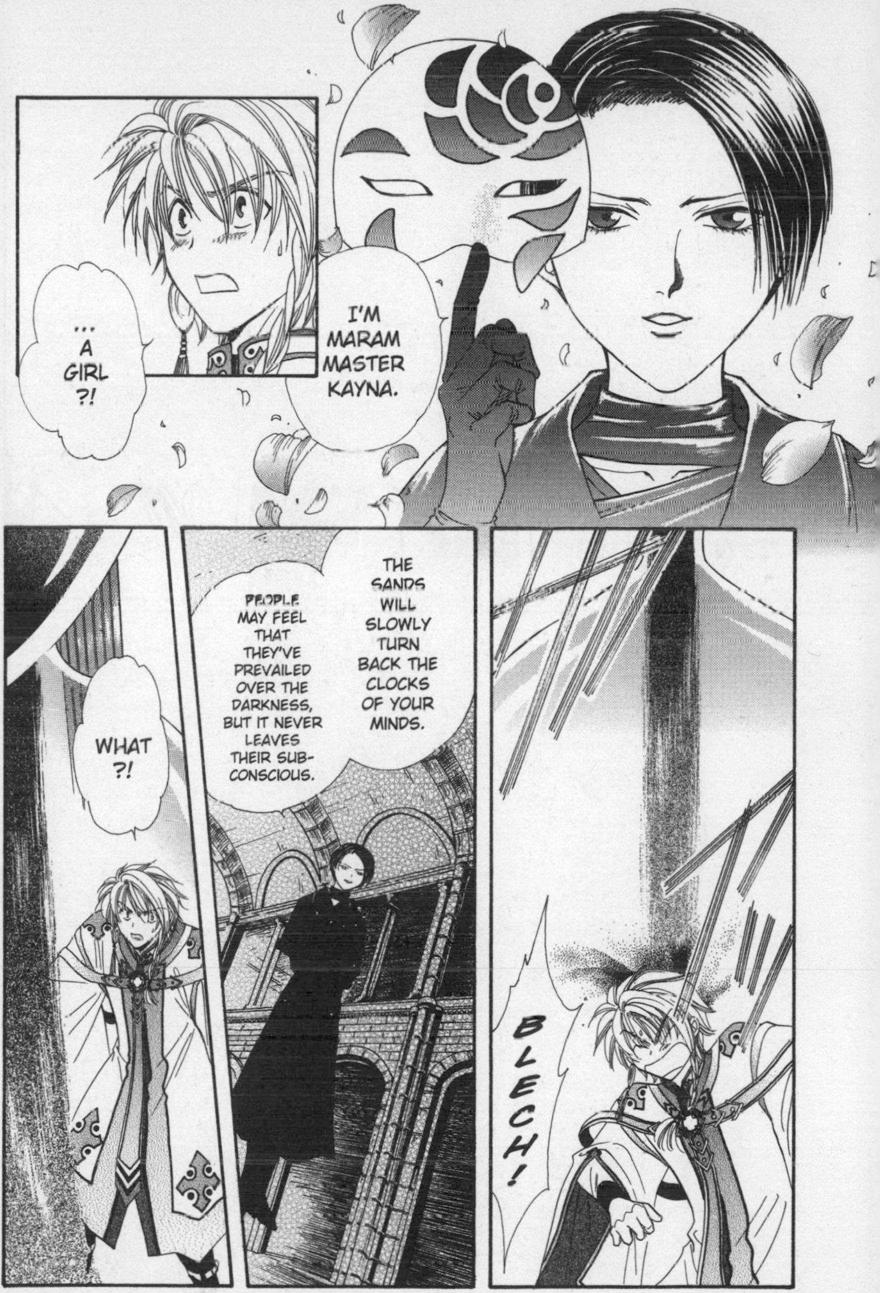
I'M MARAM MASTER KAYNA.
... A GIRL ?!
BLECH!
THE SANDS WILL SLOWLY TURN BACK THE CLOCKS OF YOUR MINDS.
PEOPLE MAY FEEL THAT THEY'VE PREVAILED OVER THE DARKNESS, BUT IT NEVER LEAVES THEIR SUB-CONSCIOUS.
WHAT ?!

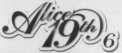

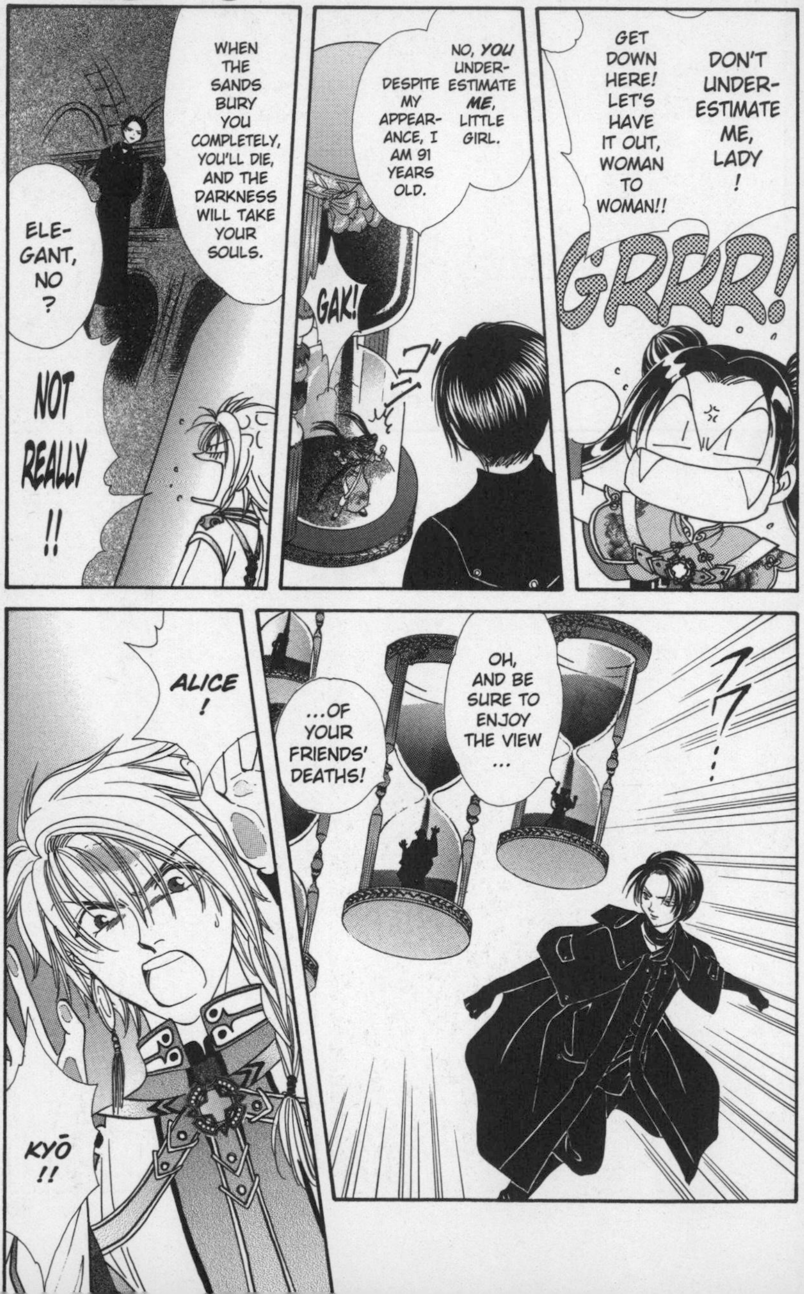
DON'T UNDER-ESTIMATE ME, LADY!
GET DOWN HERE! LET'S HAVE IT OUT, WOMAN TO WOMAN!!
GRRR!
NO, *YOU* UNDER-ESTIMATE *ME*, LITTLE GIRL.
DESPITE MY APPEARANCE, I AM 91 YEARS OLD.
GAK!
WHEN THE SANDS BURY YOU COMPLETELY, YOU'LL DIE, AND THE DARKNESS WILL TAKE YOUR SOULS.
ELEGANT, NO?
NOT REALLY!!
OH, AND BE SURE TO ENJOY THE VIEW ...
...OF YOUR FRIENDS' DEATHS!
ALICE!
KYŌ!!

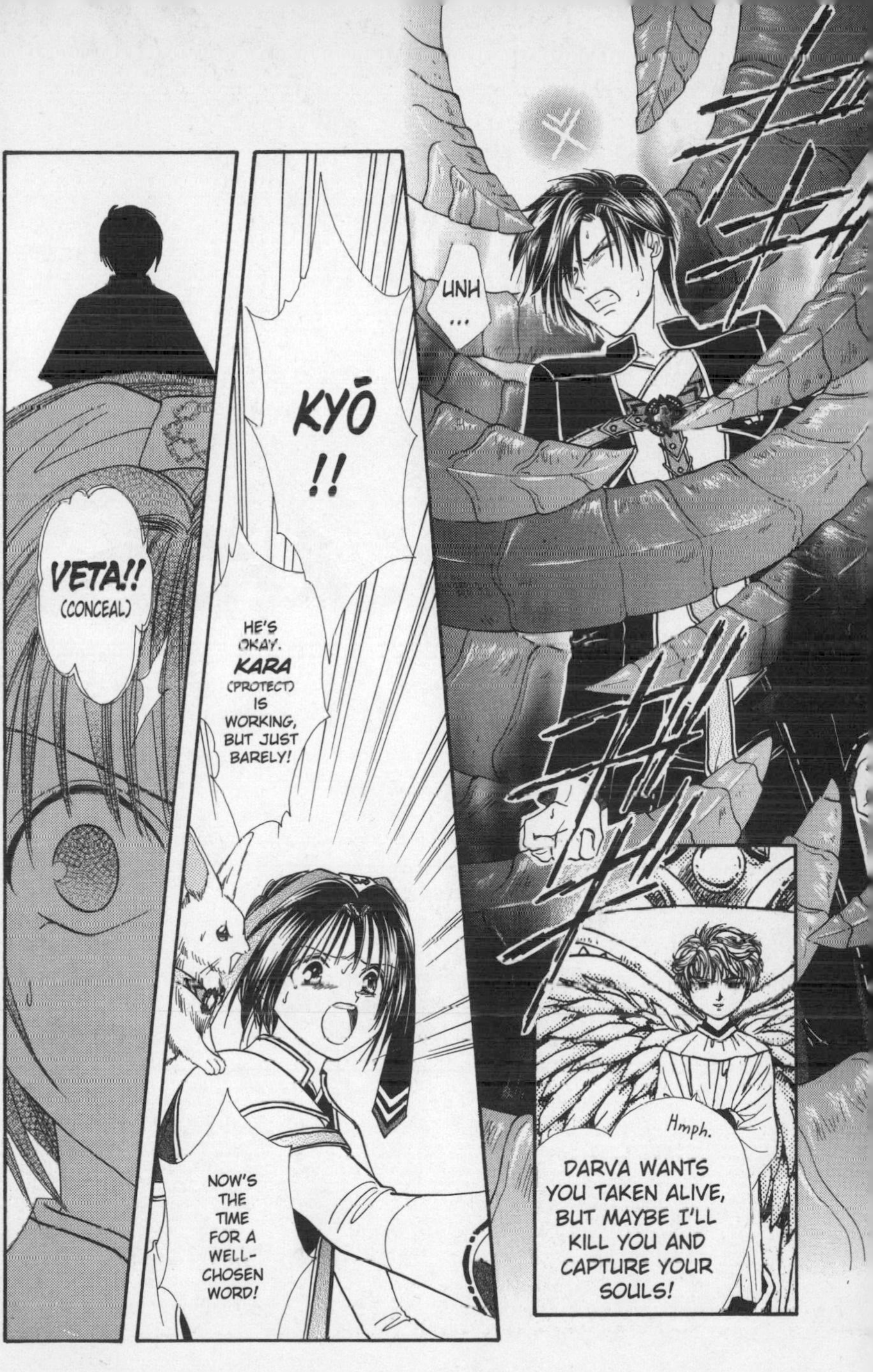
UNH ...
Hmph.
DARVA WANTS YOU TAKEN ALIVE, BUT MAYBE I'LL KILL YOU AND CAPTURE YOUR SOULS!
KYŌ !!
HE'S OKAY. KARA (PROTECT) IS WORKING, BUT JUST BARELY!
NOW'S THE TIME FOR A WELL-CHOSEN WORD!
VETA!! (CONCEAL)

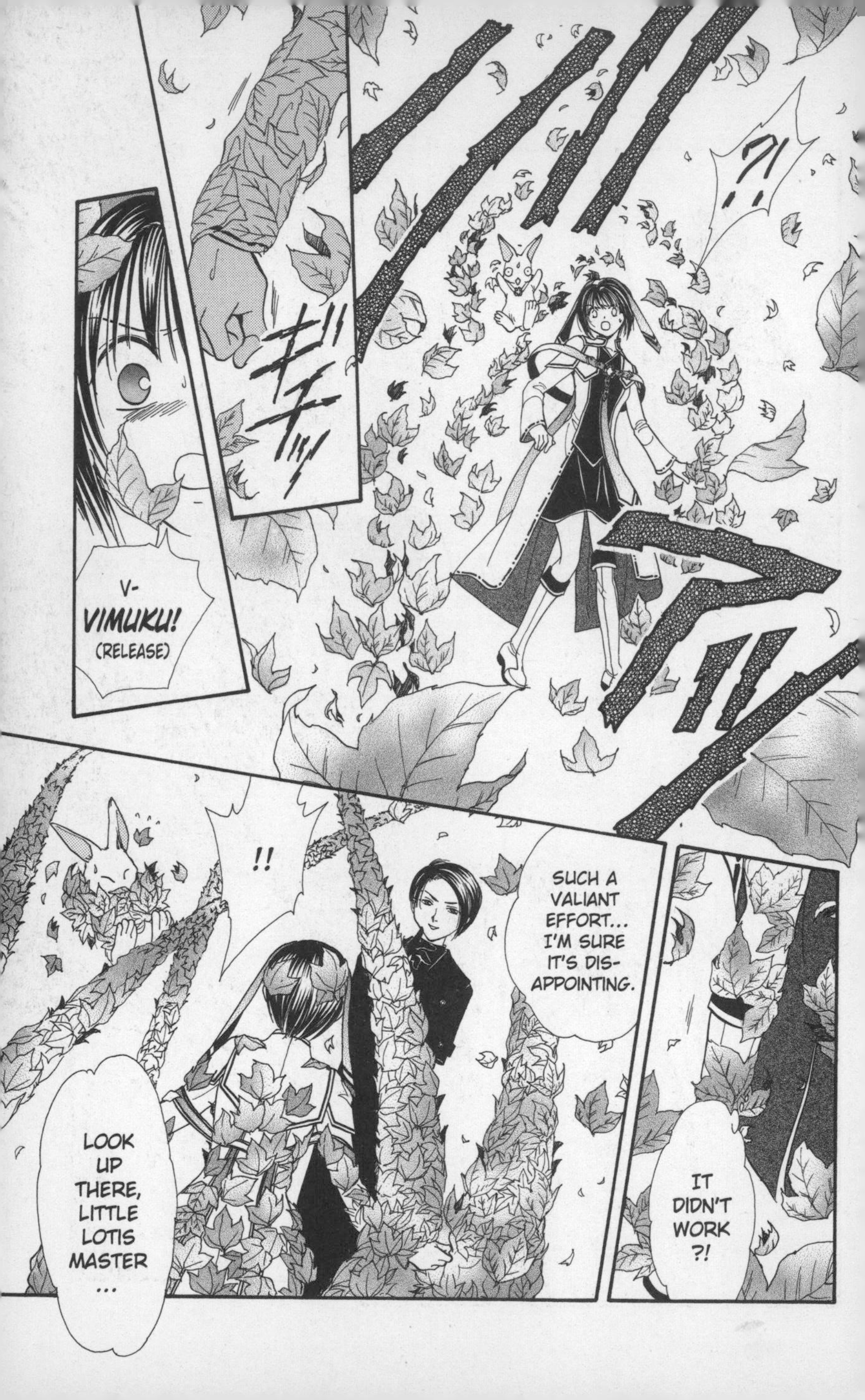
?!
V- VIMUKU! (RELEASE)
IT DIDN'T WORK ?!
SUCH A VALIANT EFFORT... I'M SURE IT'S DIS-APPOINTING.
!!
LOOK UP THERE, LITTLE LOTIS MASTER ...

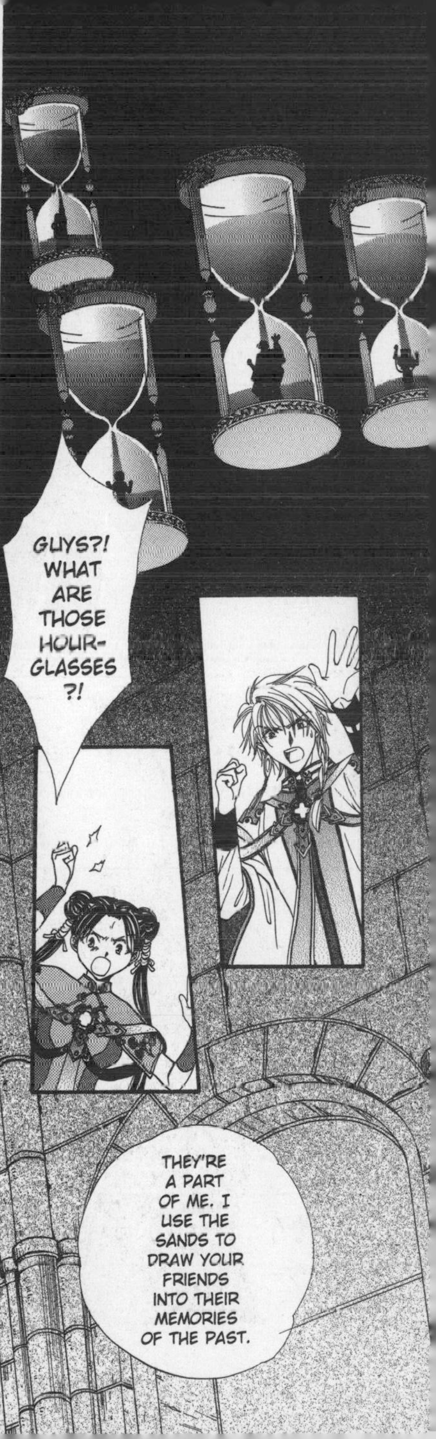
GUYS?! WHAT ARE THOSE HOUR-GLASSES?!
THEY'RE A PART OF ME. I USE THE SANDS TO DRAW YOUR FRIENDS INTO THEIR MEMORIES OF THE PAST.
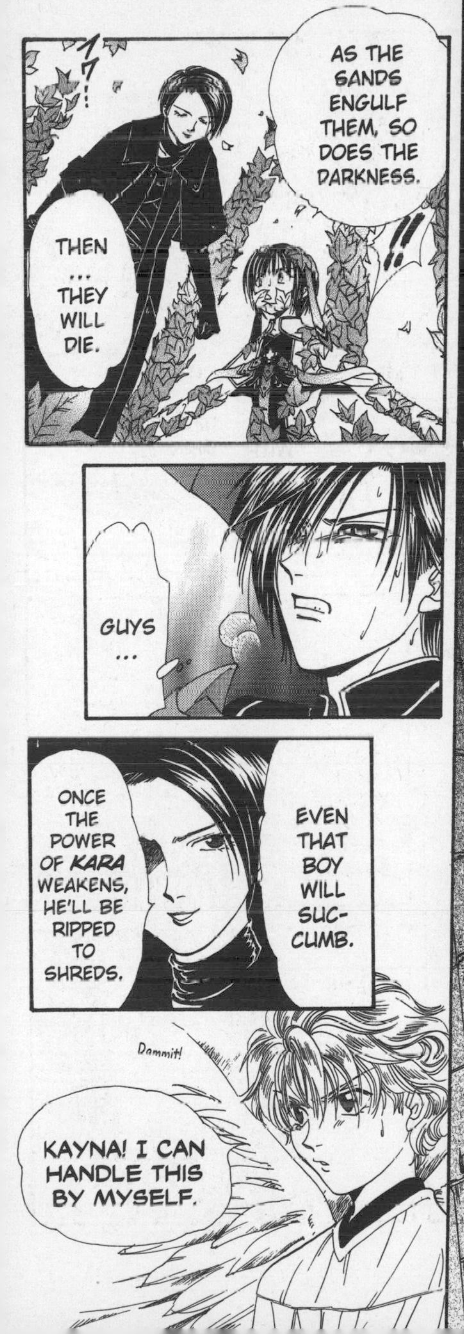
AS THE SANDS ENGULF THEM, SO DOES THE DARKNESS.
THEN ... THEY WILL DIE.
GUYS ...
EVEN THAT BOY WILL SUC-CUMB.
ONCE THE POWER OF *KARA* WEAKENS, HE'LL BE RIPPED TO SHREDS.
Dammit!
KAYNA! I CAN HANDLE THIS BY MYSELF.

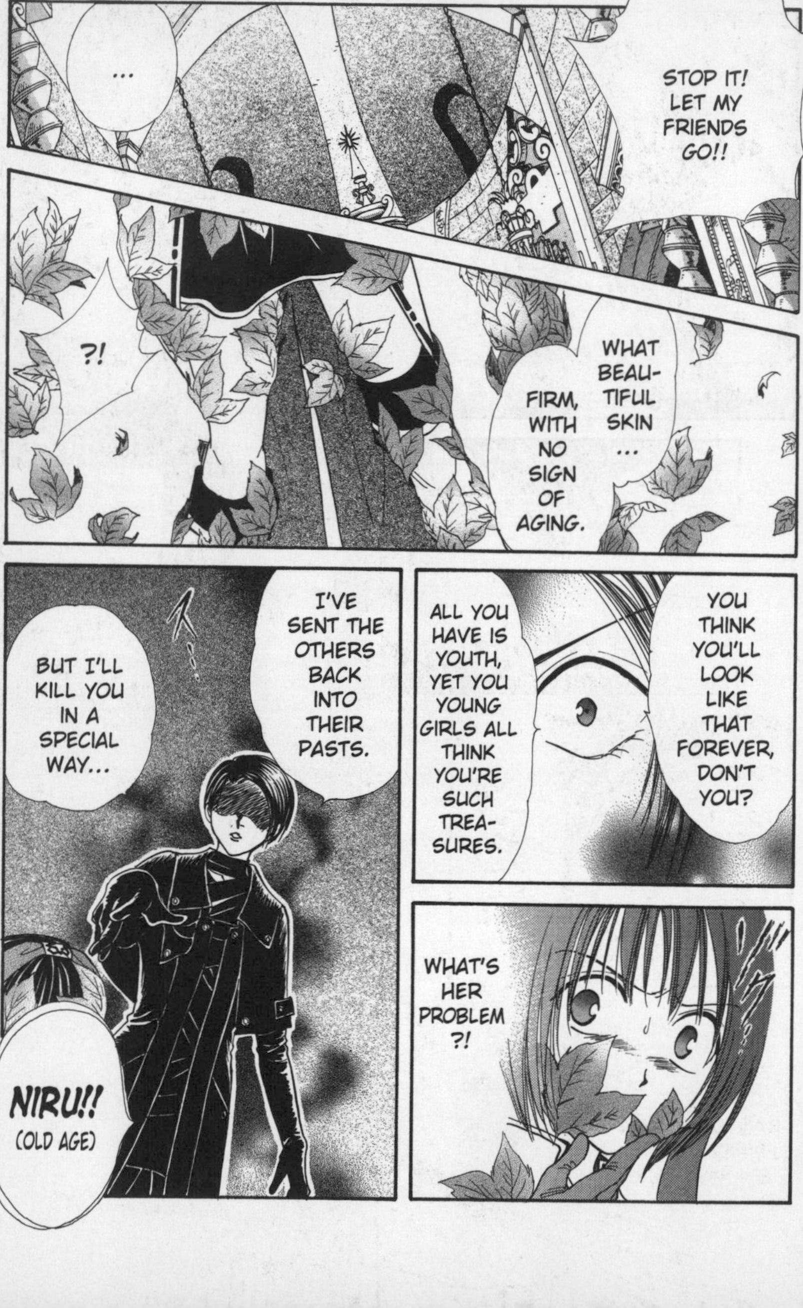
STOP IT! LET MY FRIENDS GO!!
...
WHAT BEAU-TIFUL SKIN...
FIRM, WITH NO SIGN OF AGING.
?!
YOU THINK YOU'LL LOOK LIKE THAT FOREVER, DON'T YOU?
ALL YOU HAVE IS YOUTH, YET YOU YOUNG GIRLS ALL THINK YOU'RE SUCH TREA-SURES.
WHAT'S HER PROBLEM ?!
I'VE SENT THE OTHERS BACK INTO THEIR PASTS.
BUT I'LL KILL YOU IN A SPECIAL WAY...
NIRU!!
(OLD AGE)

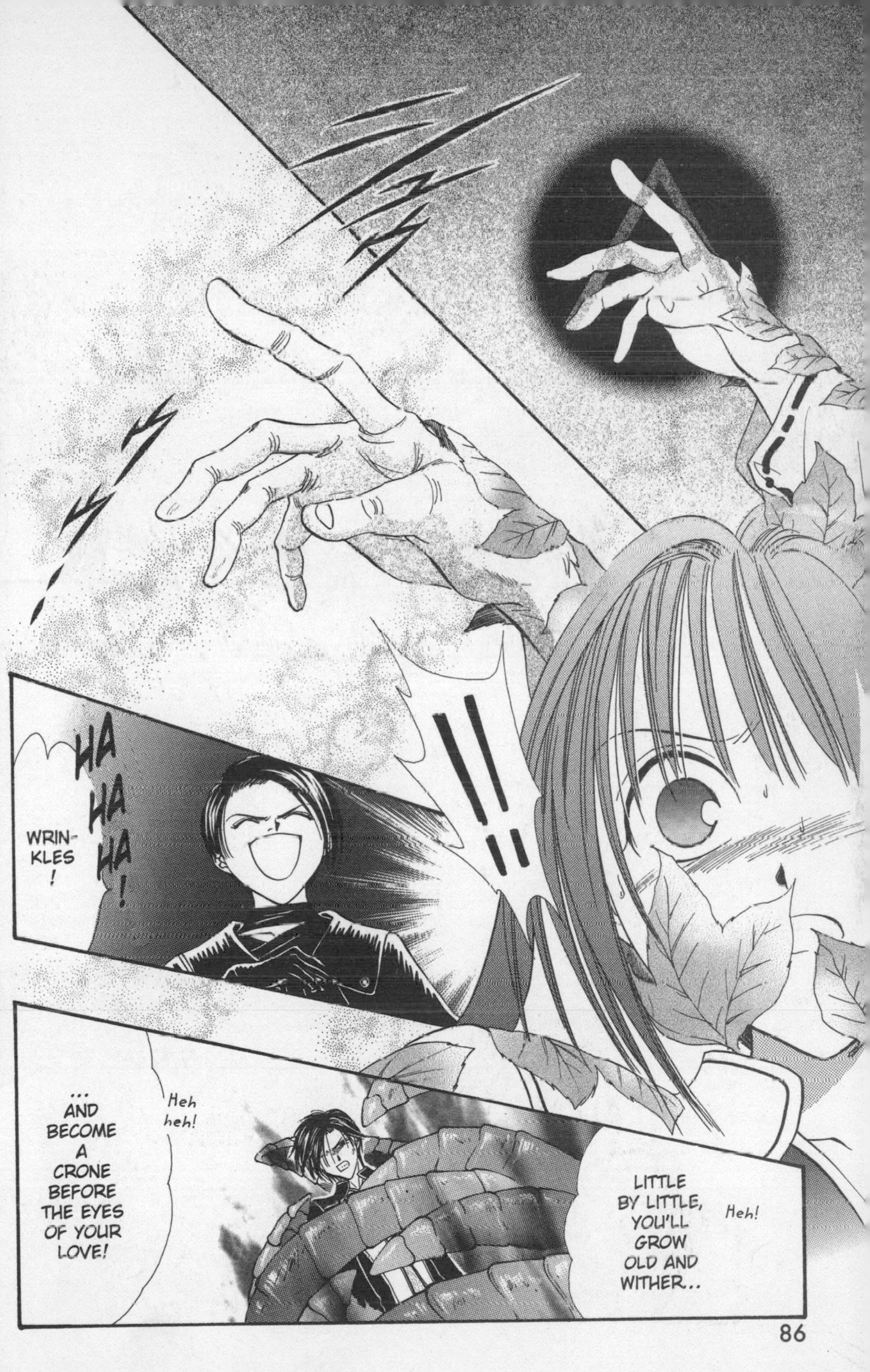
HA HA HA!
WRIN-KLES!
Heh!
LITTLE BY LITTLE, YOU'LL GROW OLD AND WITHER..
Heh heh!
... AND BECOME A CRONE BEFORE THE EYES OF YOUR LOVE!

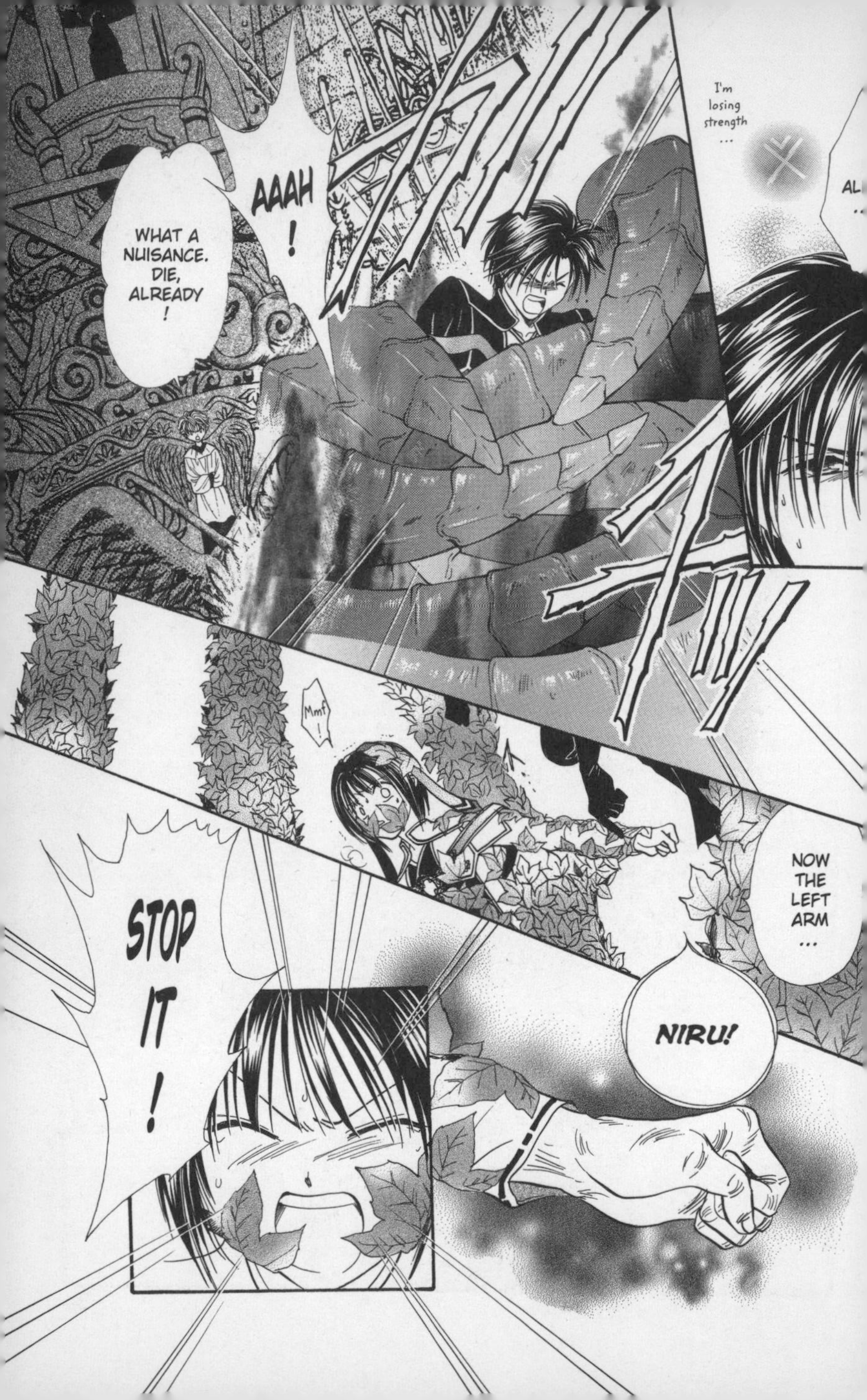

I'm losing strength ...
AL
AAAH!
WHAT A NUISANCE. DIE, ALREADY!
NOW THE LEFT ARM ...
Mmf!
NIRU!
STOP IT!

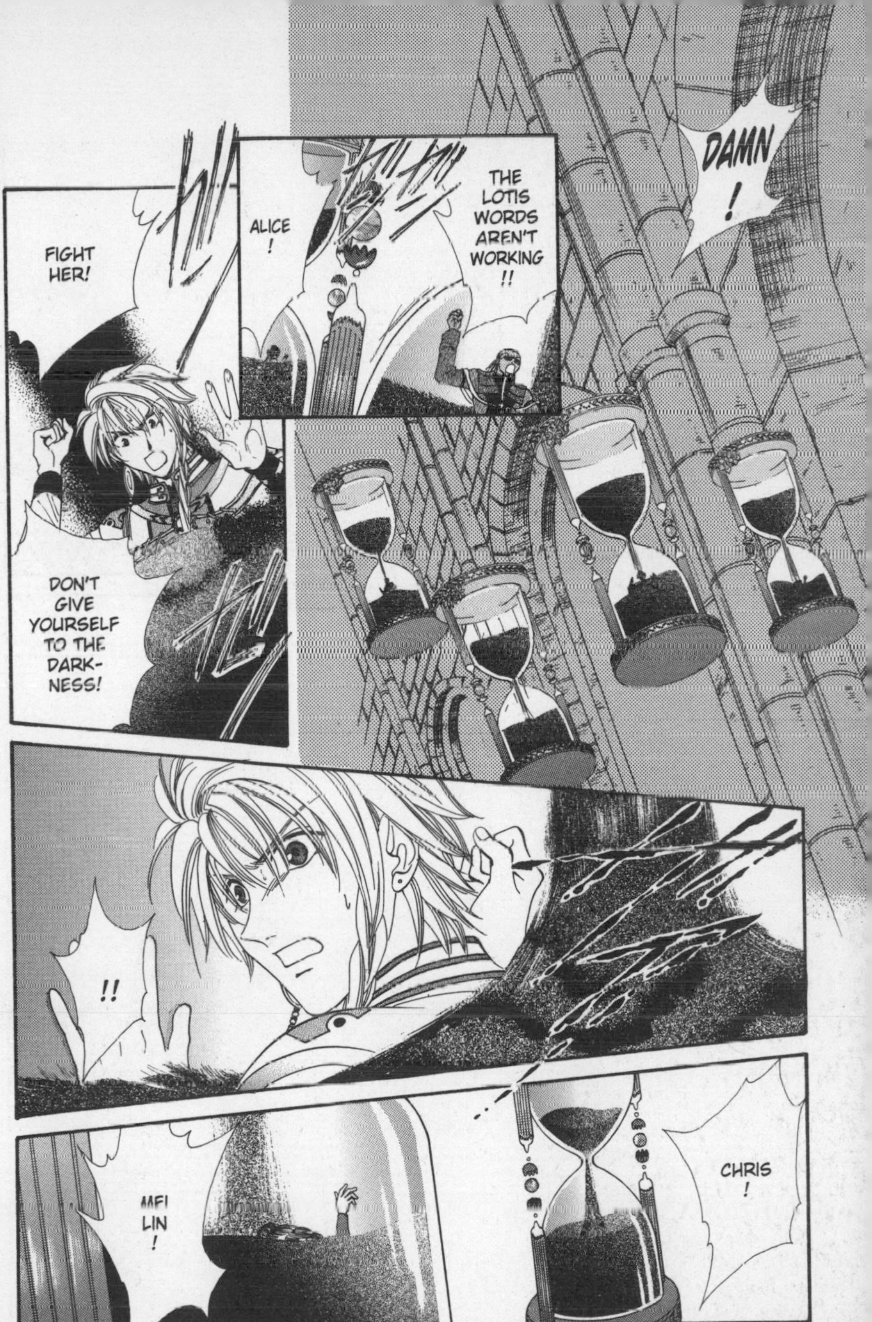
DAMN !
THE LOTIS WORDS AREN'T WORKING !!
ALICE !
FIGHT HER!
DON'T GIVE YOURSELF TO THE DARK-NESS!
!!
CHRIS !
MEI LIN !

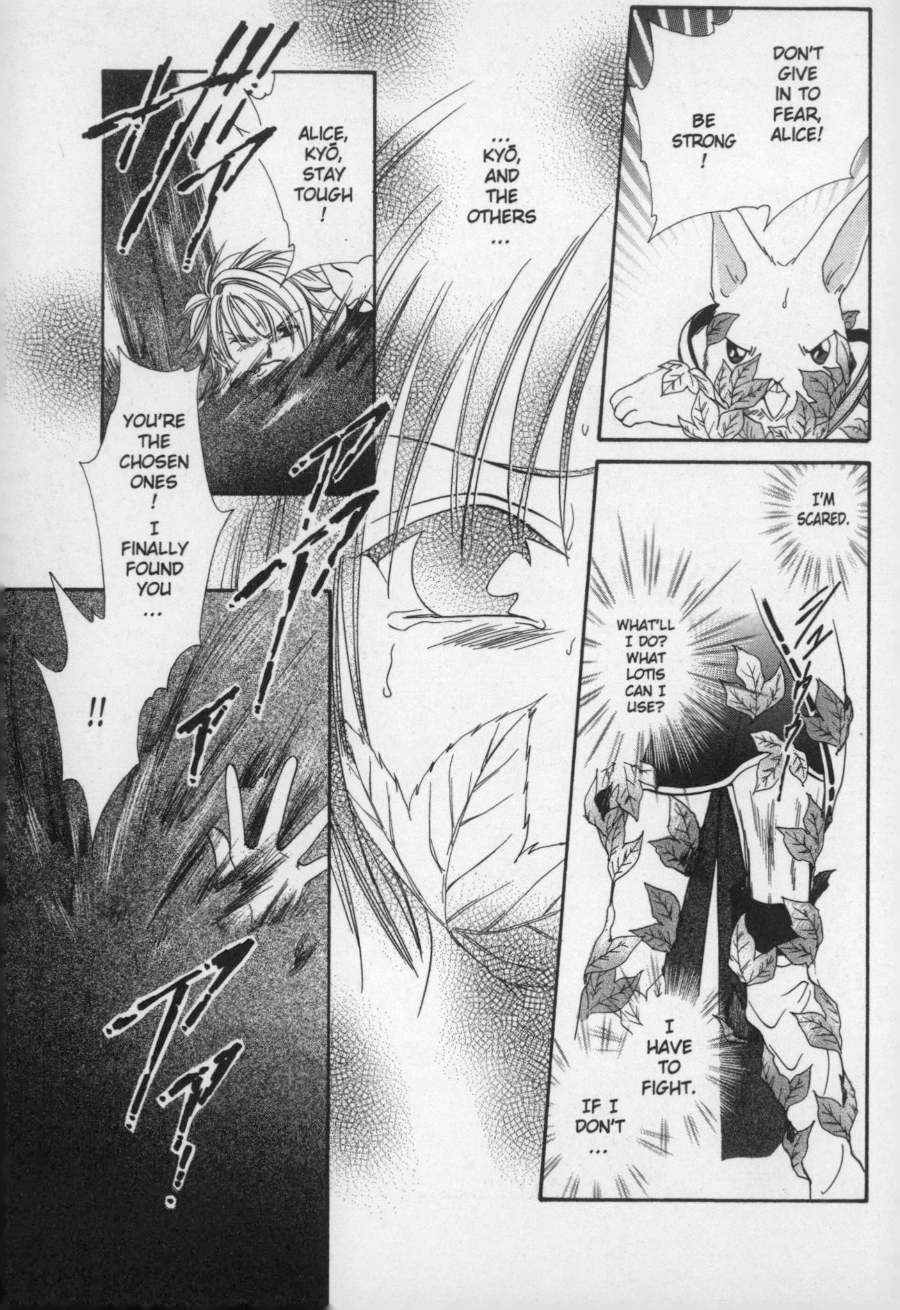
DON'T GIVE IN TO FEAR, ALICE!
BE STRONG!
I'M SCARED.
WHAT'LL I DO? WHAT LOTIS CAN I USE?
I HAVE TO FIGHT.
IF I DON'T...
...KYŌ, AND THE OTHERS...
ALICE, KYŌ, STAY TOUGH!
YOU'RE THE CHOSEN ONES!
I FINALLY FOUND YOU...
!!

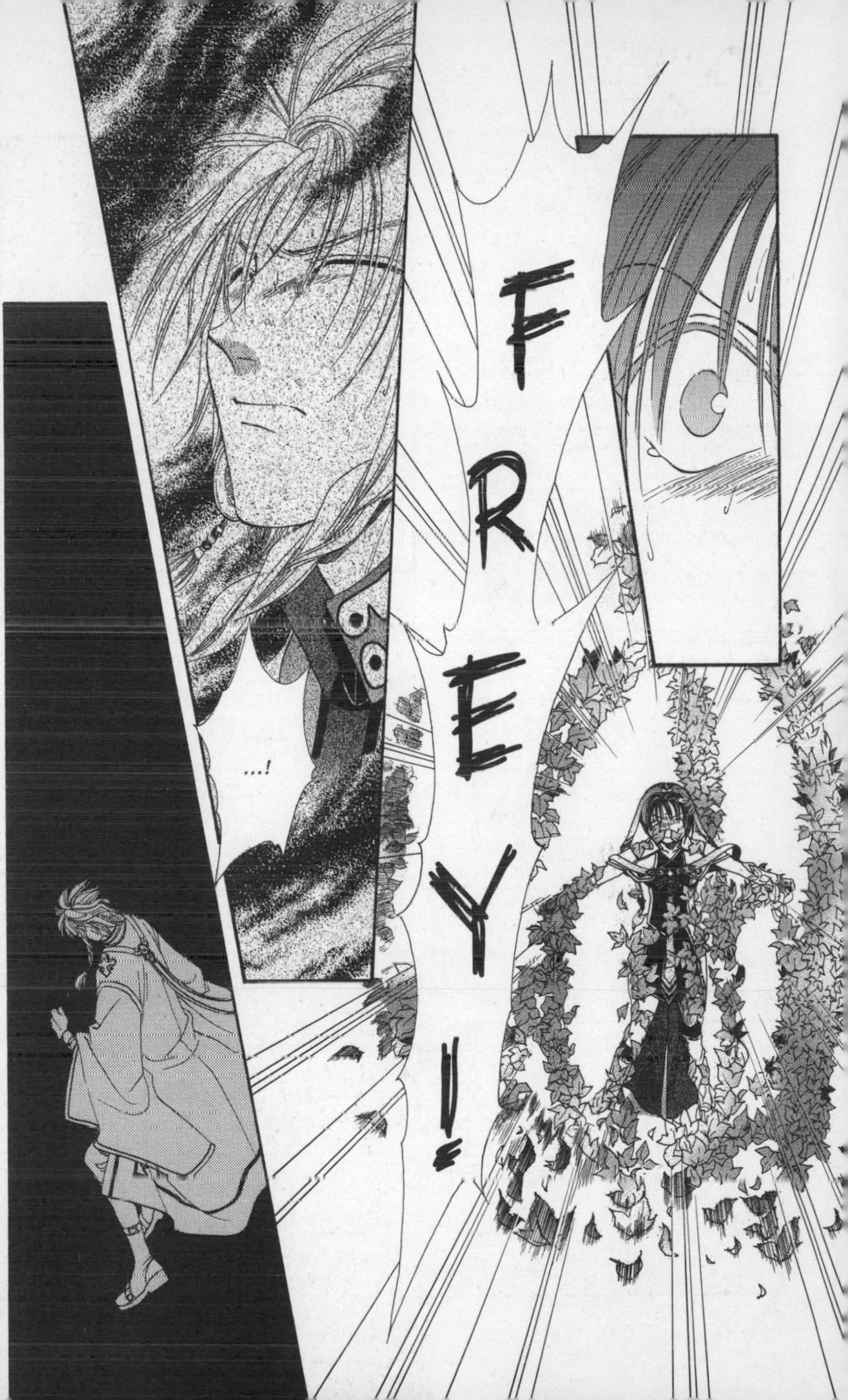
FREY!
...!

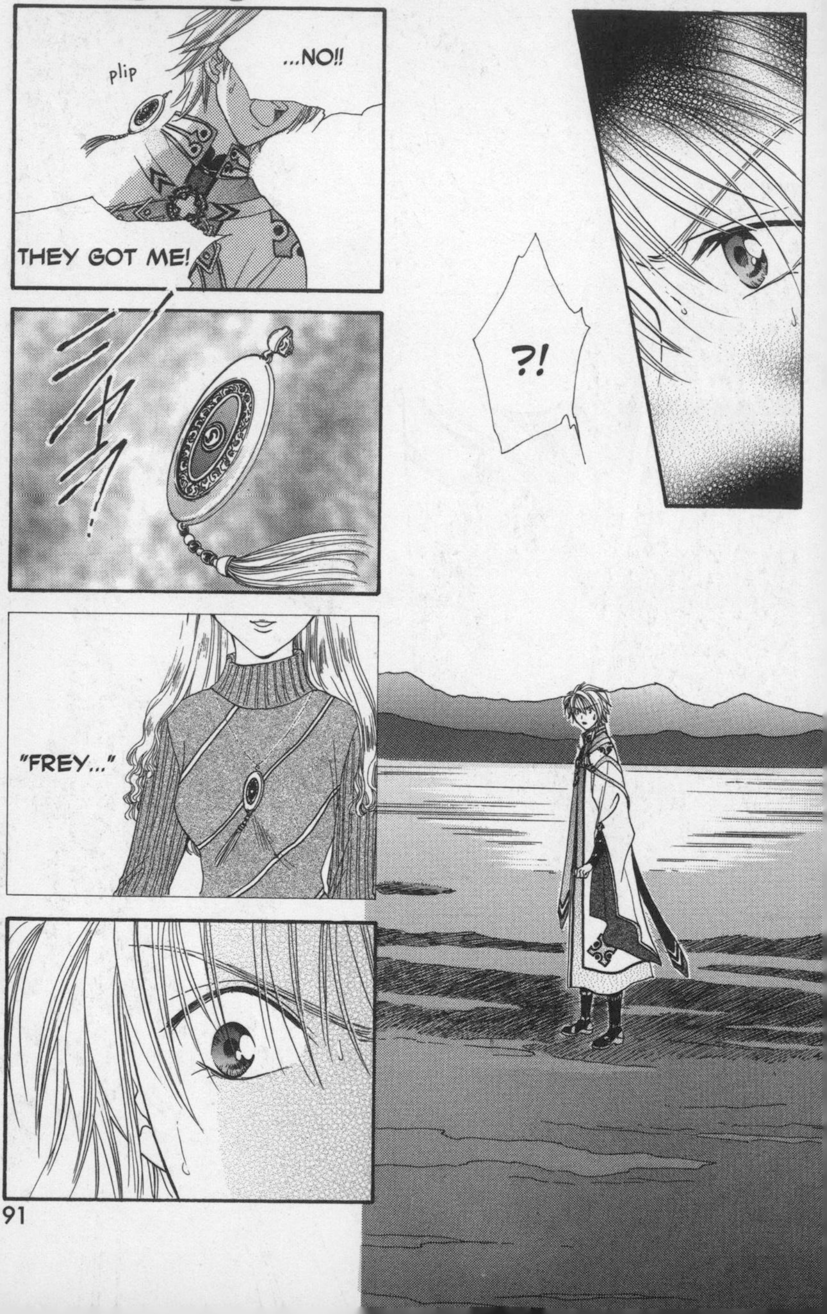
?!
...NO!!
plip
THEY GOT ME!
"FREY..."

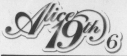

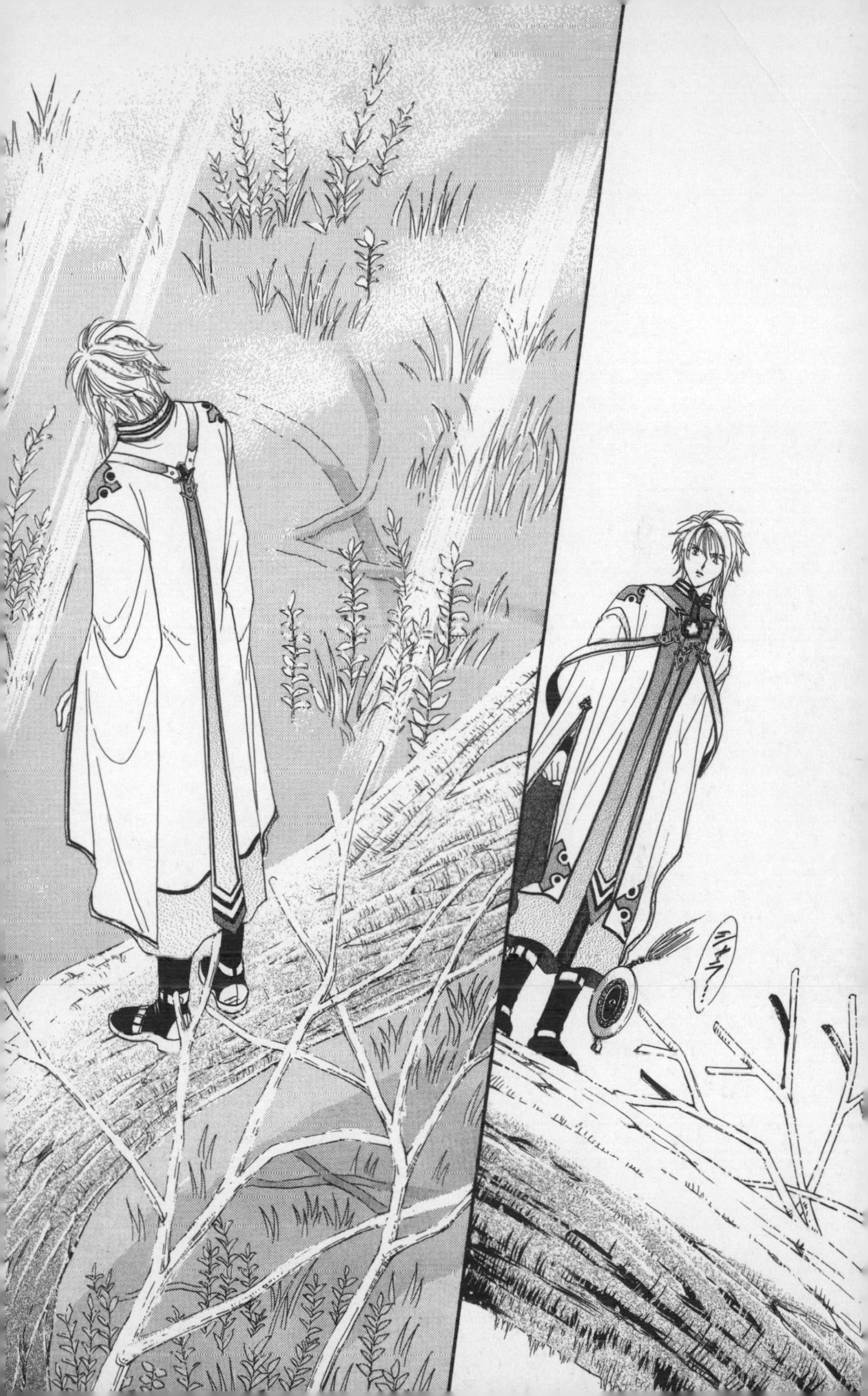
ジャン…

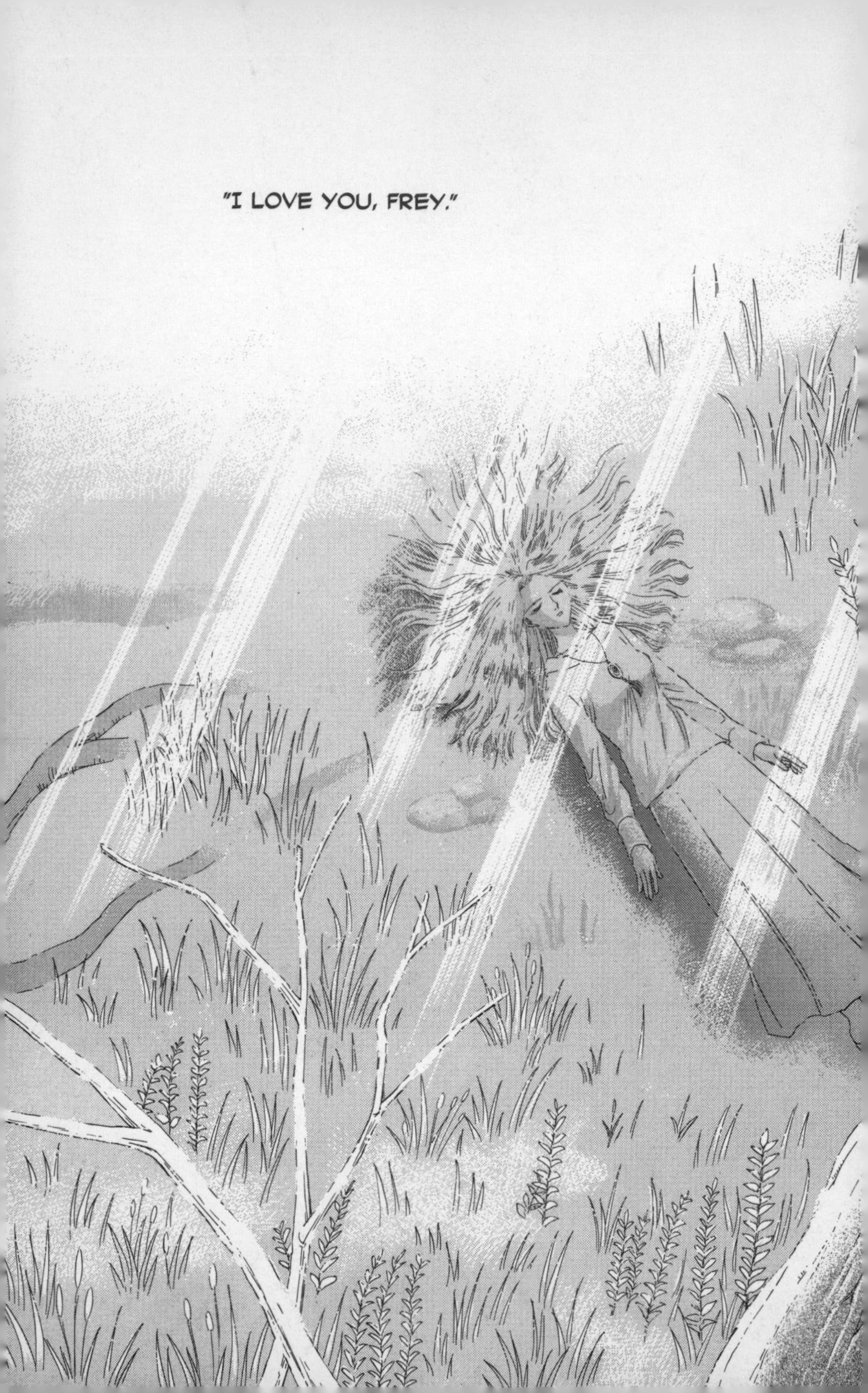
"I LOVE YOU, FREY."

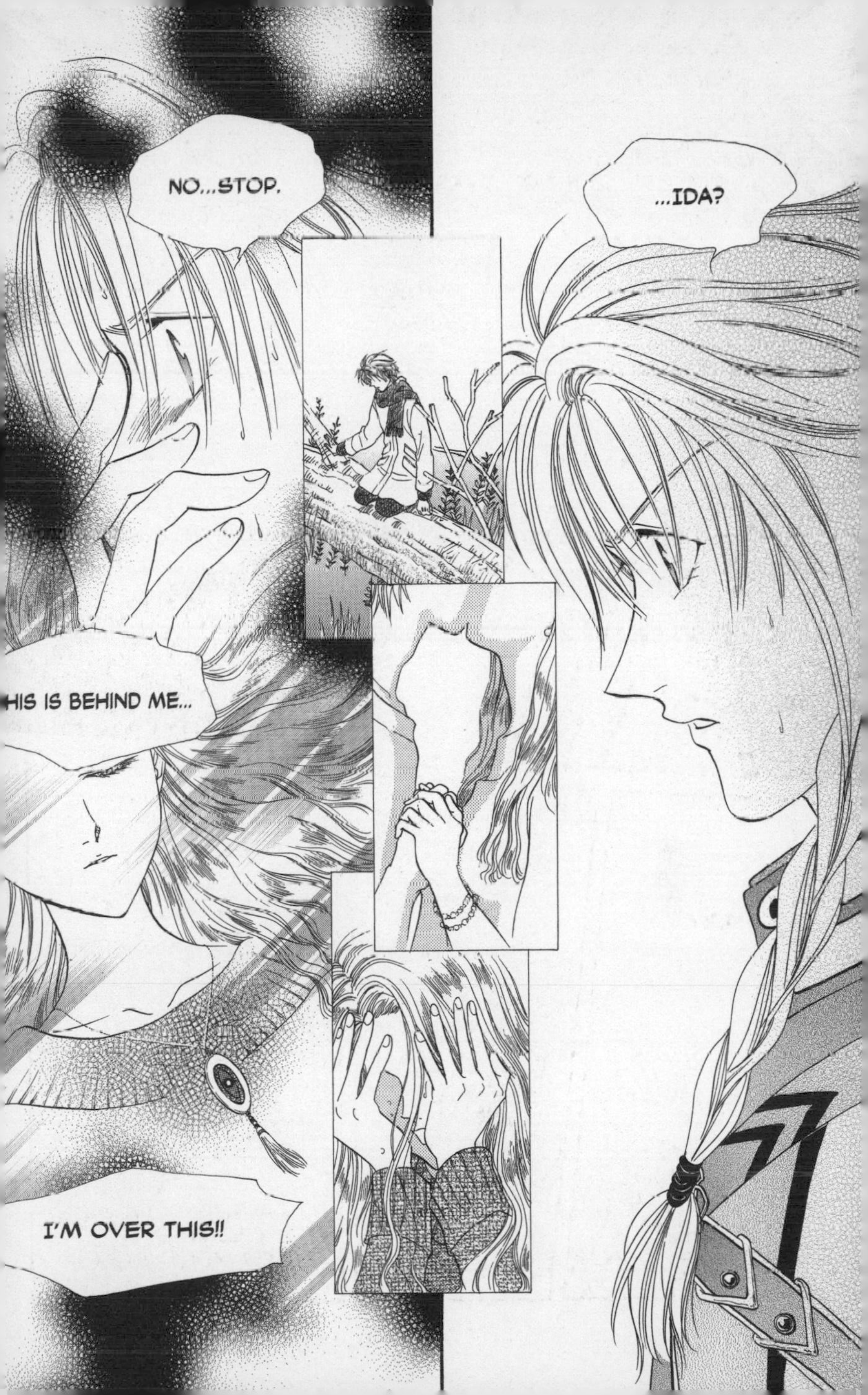
...IDA?
NO...STOP.
HIS IS BEHIND ME...
I'M OVER THIS!!

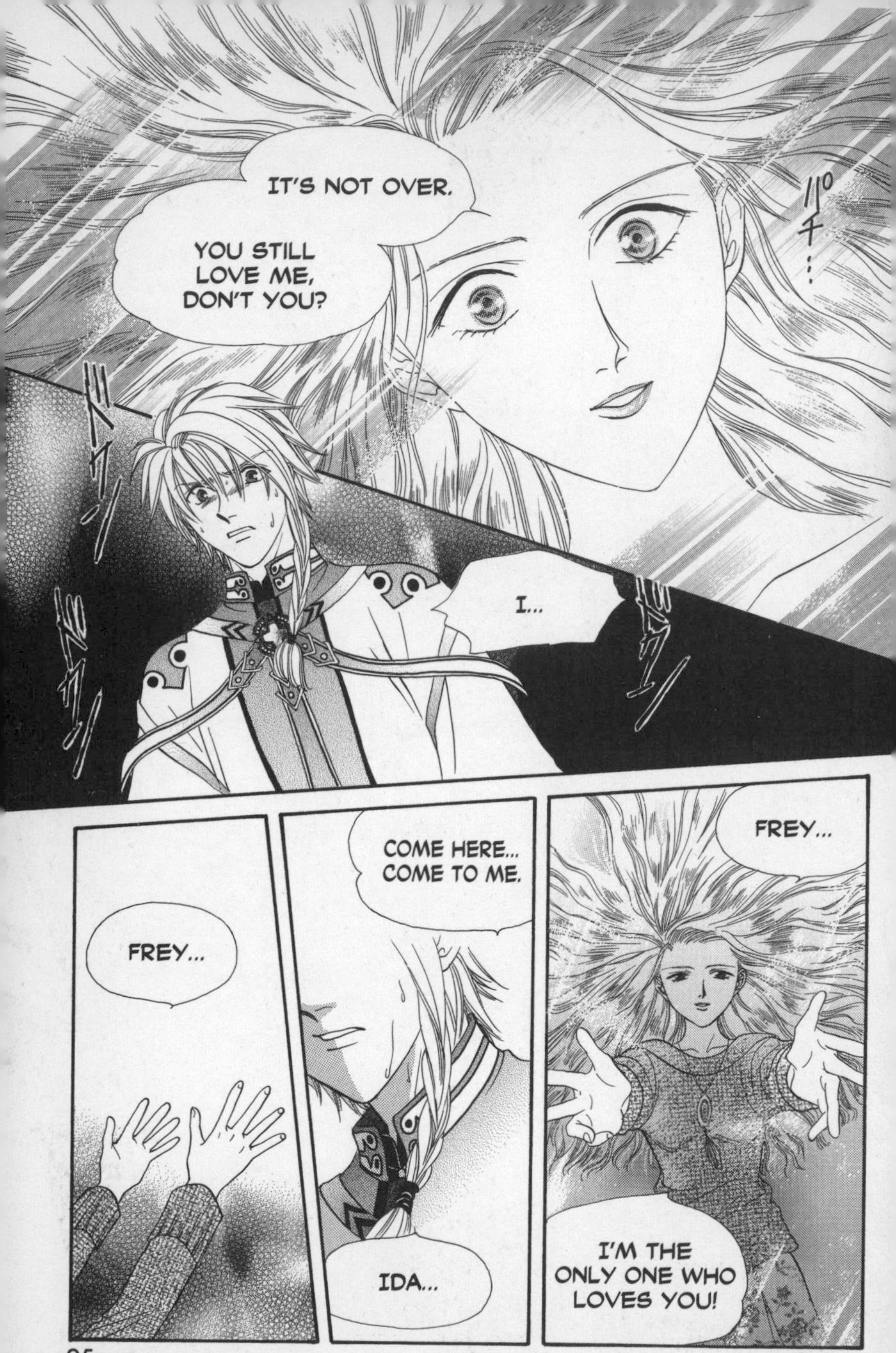

IT'S NOT OVER.
YOU STILL LOVE ME, DON'T YOU?
I...
FREY...
I'M THE ONLY ONE WHO LOVES YOU!
COME HERE... COME TO ME.
IDA...
FREY...

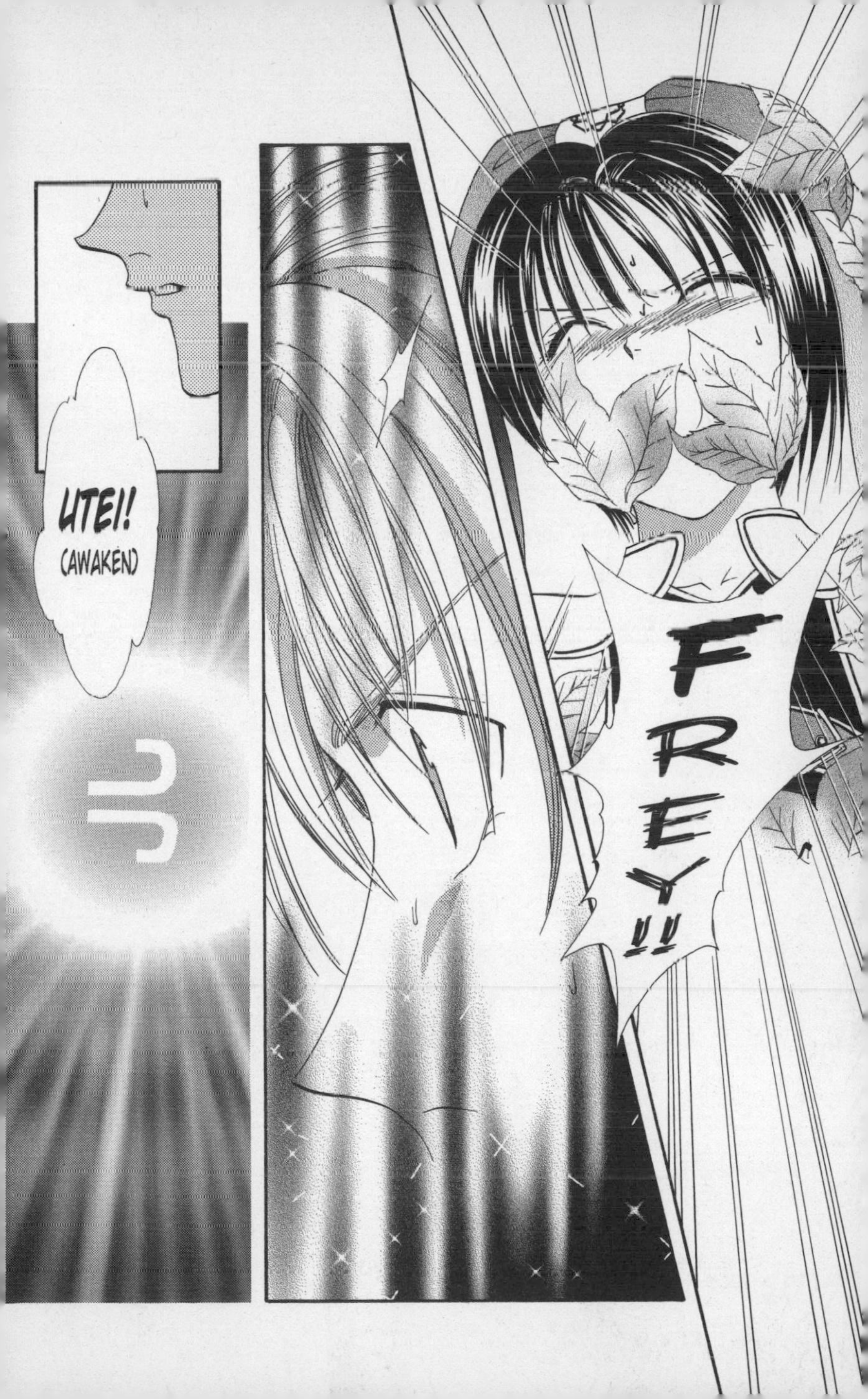
FREY!!
UTEI!
(AWAKEN)

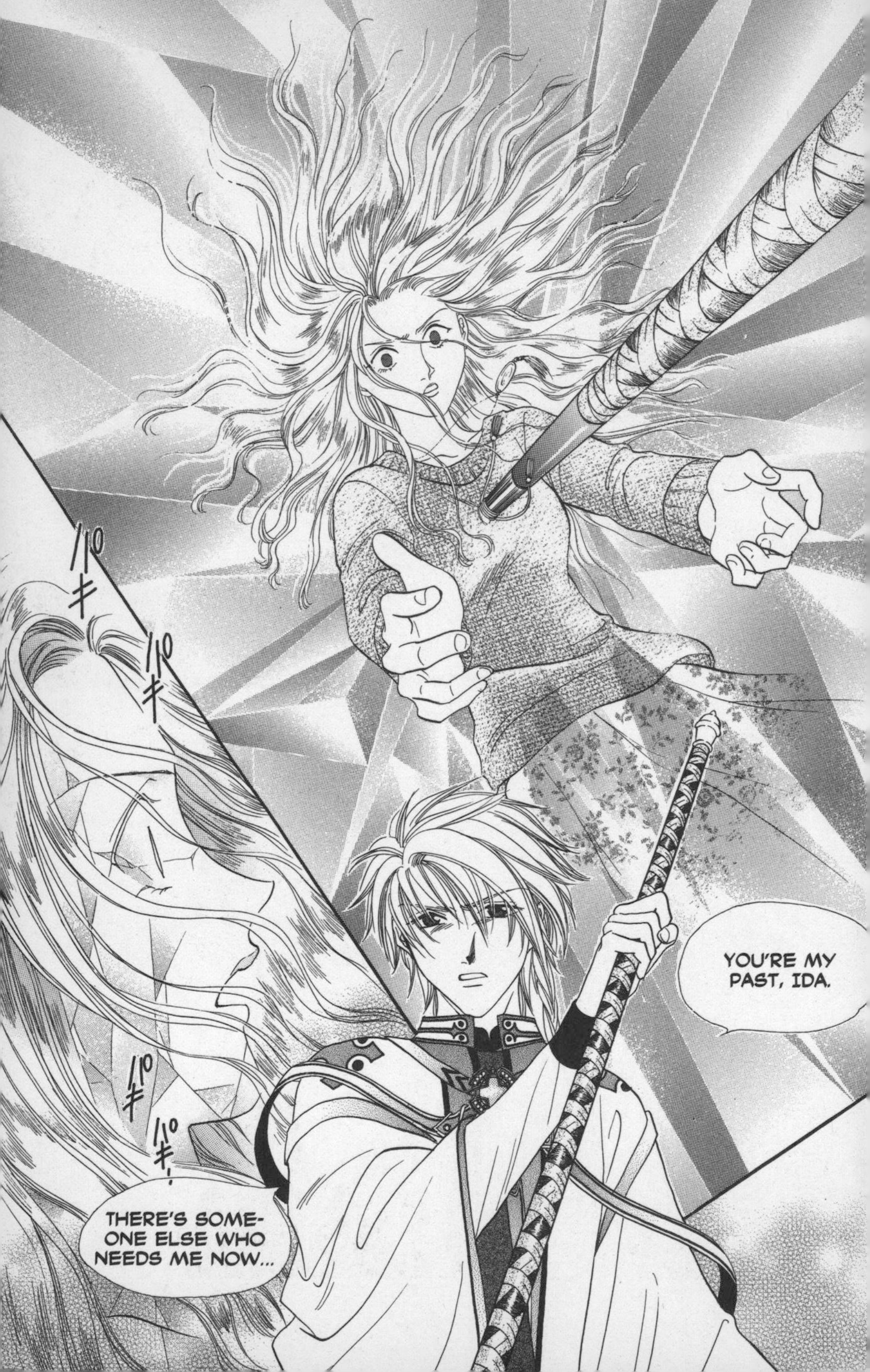
YOU'RE MY PAST, IDA.
パキ
パキ
パキ
パキ!
THERE'S SOME-ONE ELSE WHO NEEDS ME NOW...

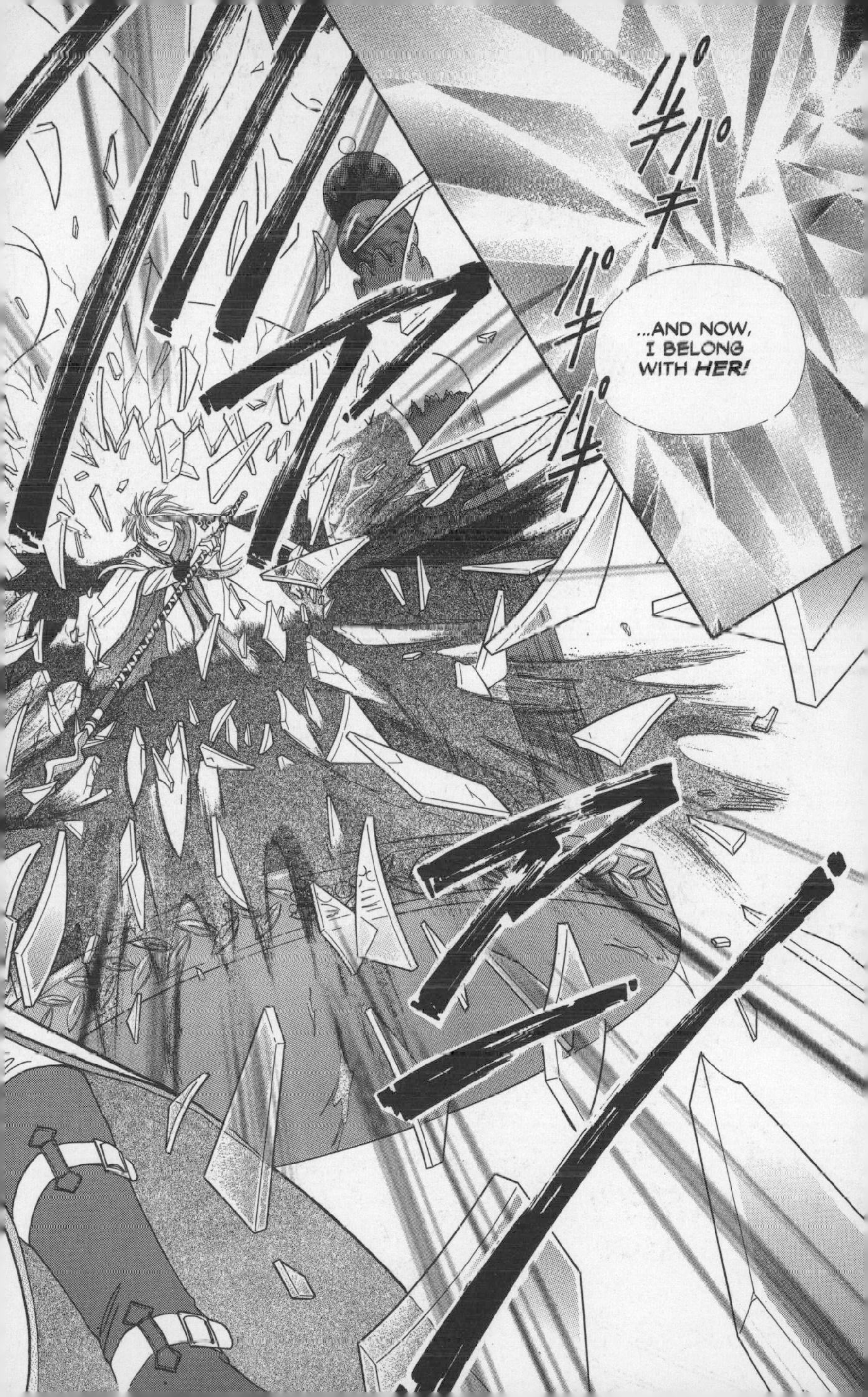

パキパキ
...AND NOW, I BELONG WITH HER!
パキパキ

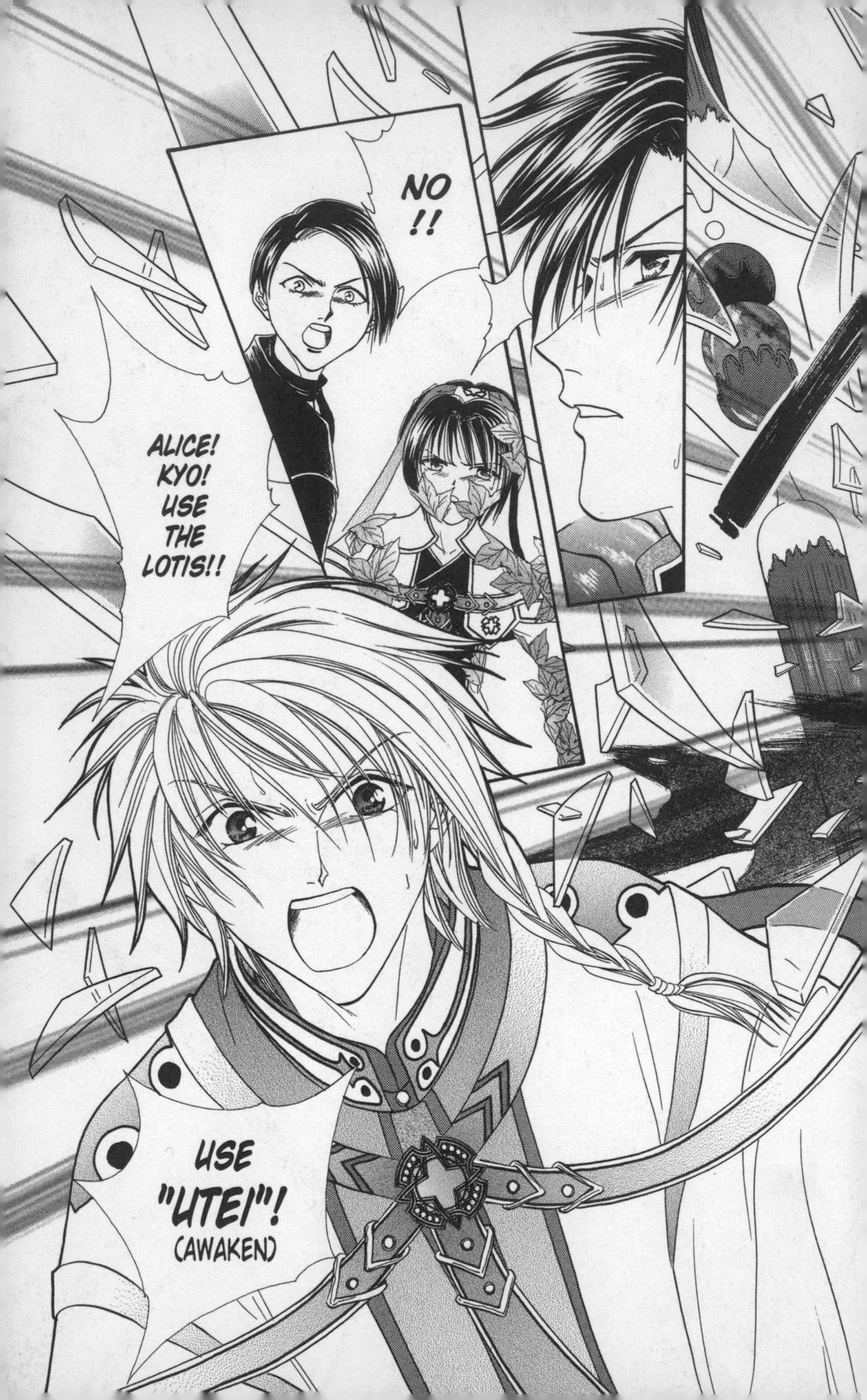
NO!!
ALICE! KYO! USE THE LOTIS!!
USE "UTEI"! (AWAKEN)

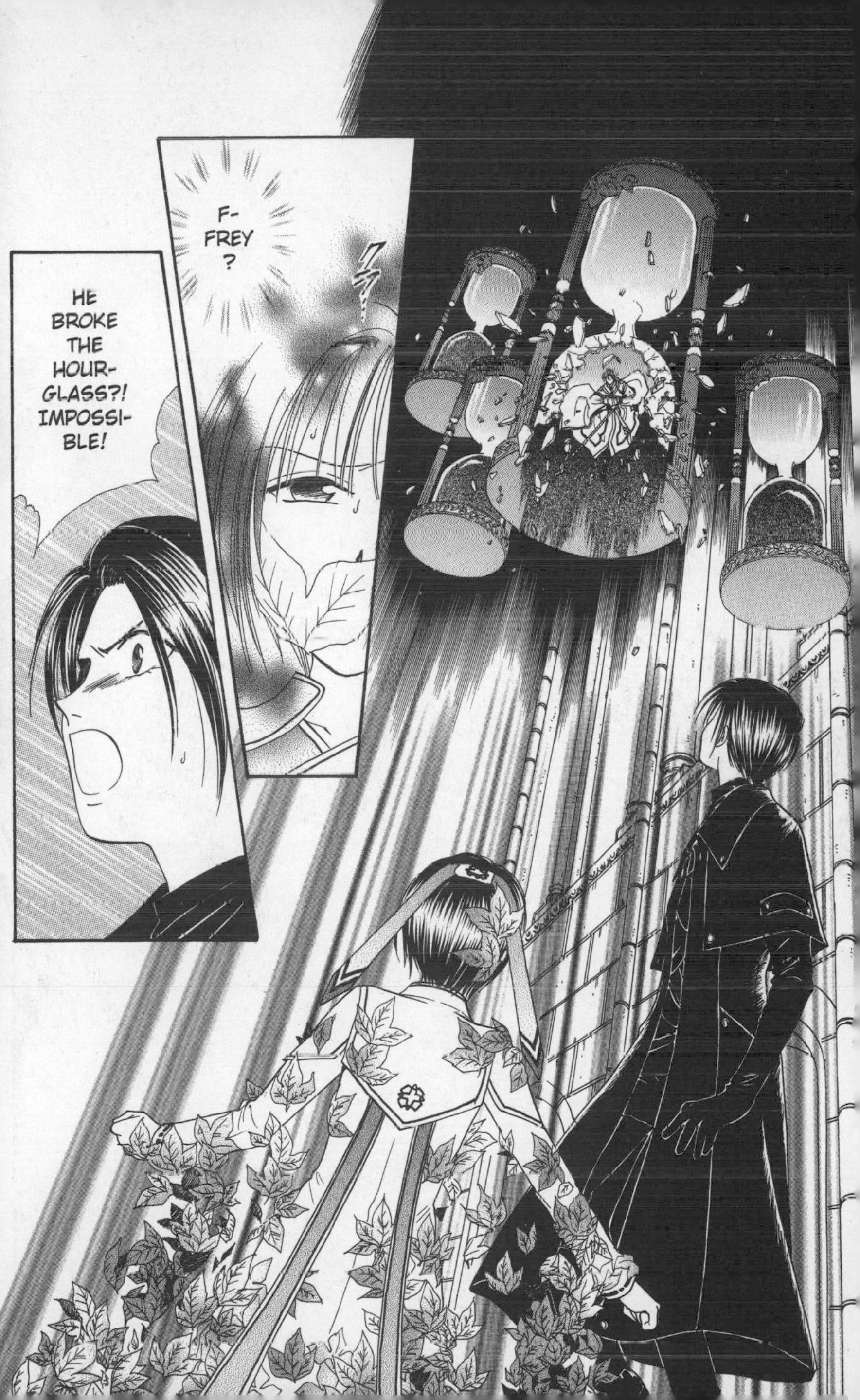
F-
FREY
?
HE
BROKE
THE
HOUR-
GLASS?!
IMPOSSI-
BLE!

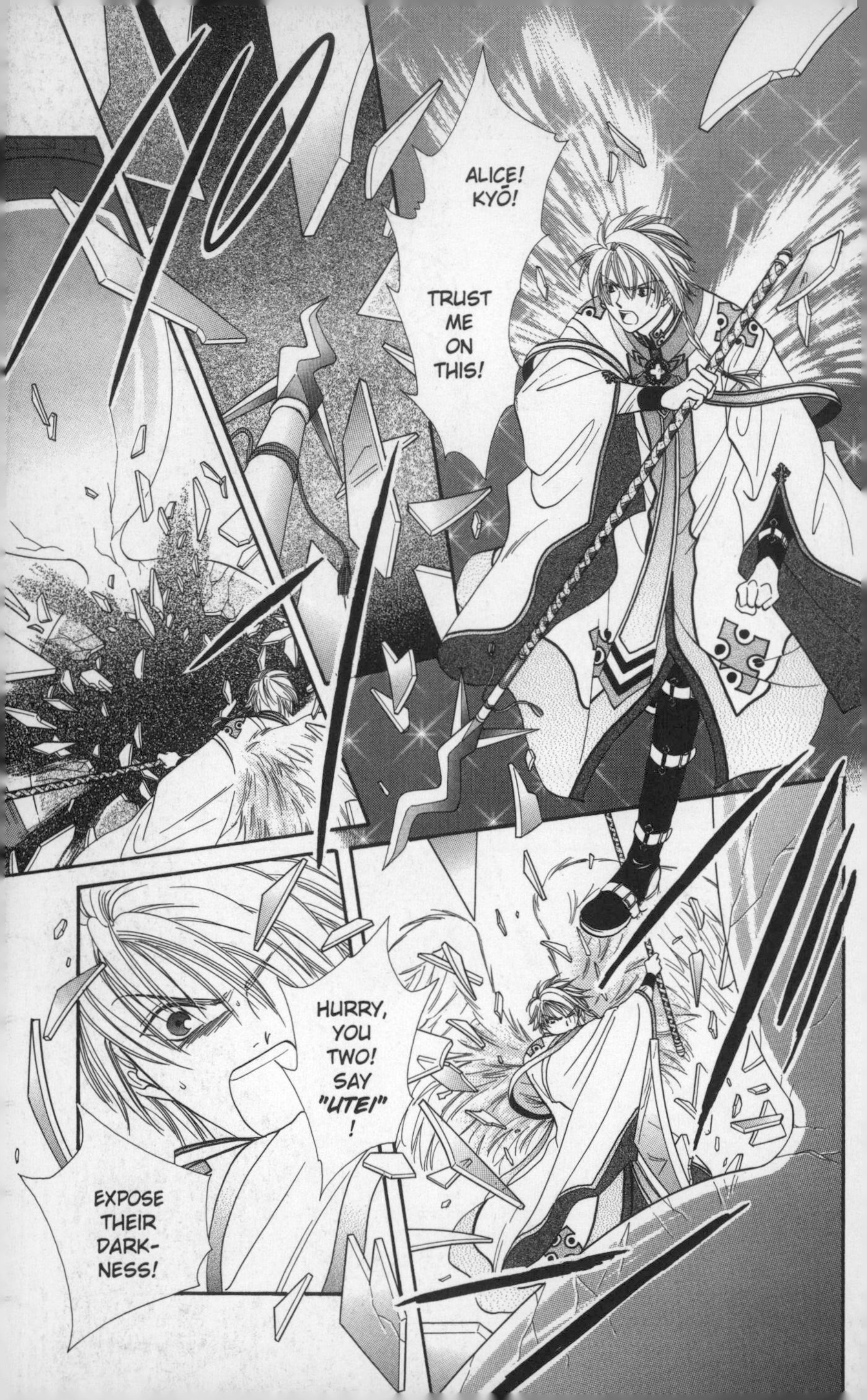
ALICE! KYŌ!
TRUST ME ON THIS!
HURRY, YOU TWO! SAY "UTEI"!
EXPOSE THEIR DARK-NESS!

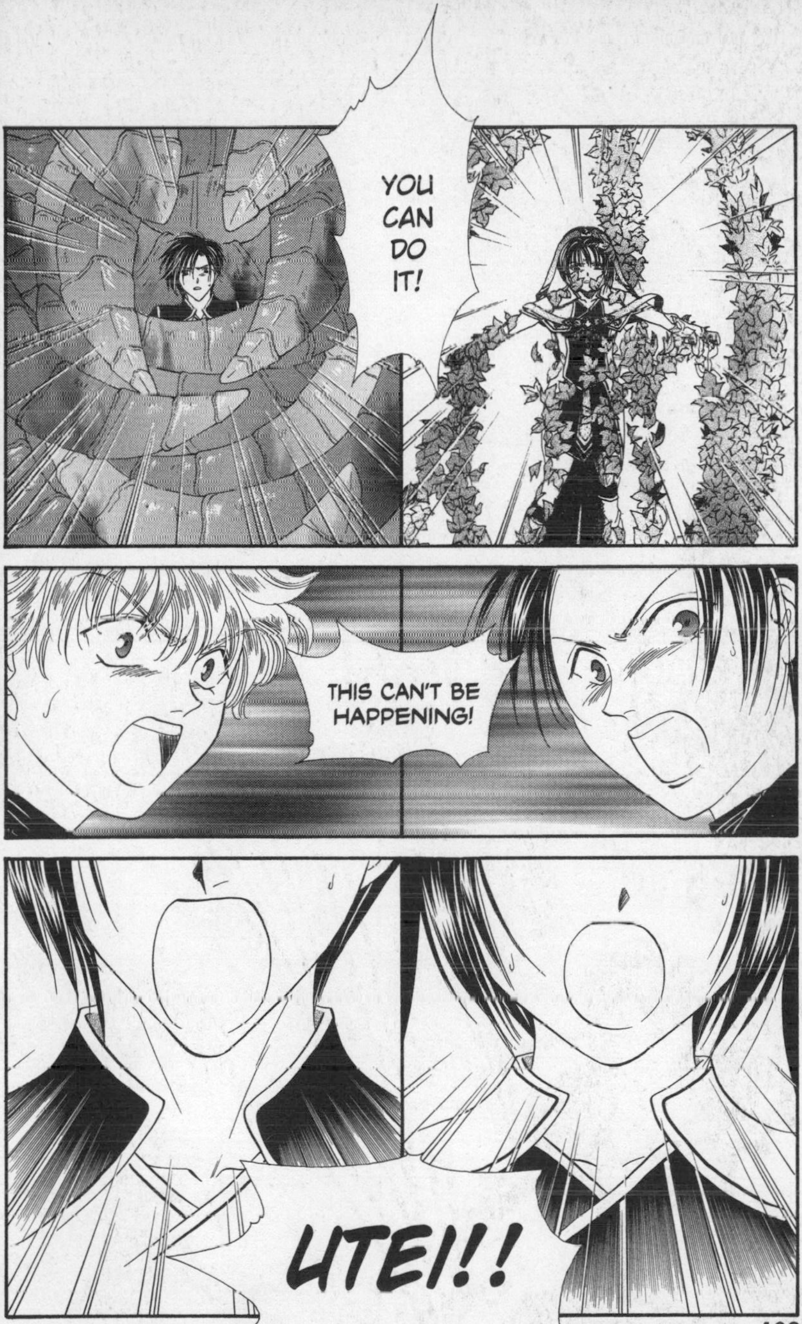
YOU CAN DO IT!
THIS CAN'T BE HAPPENING!
UTEI!!

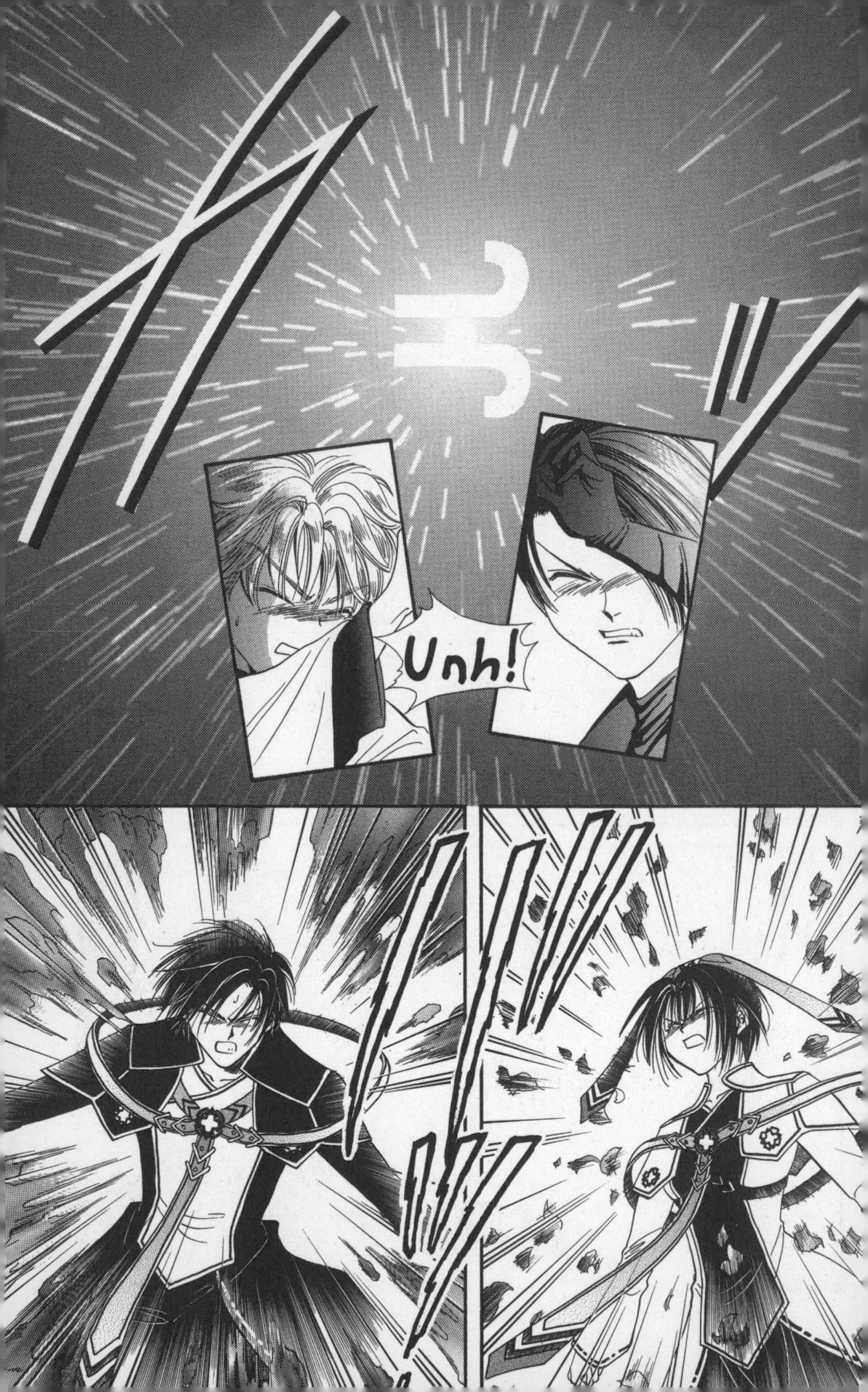
Unh!

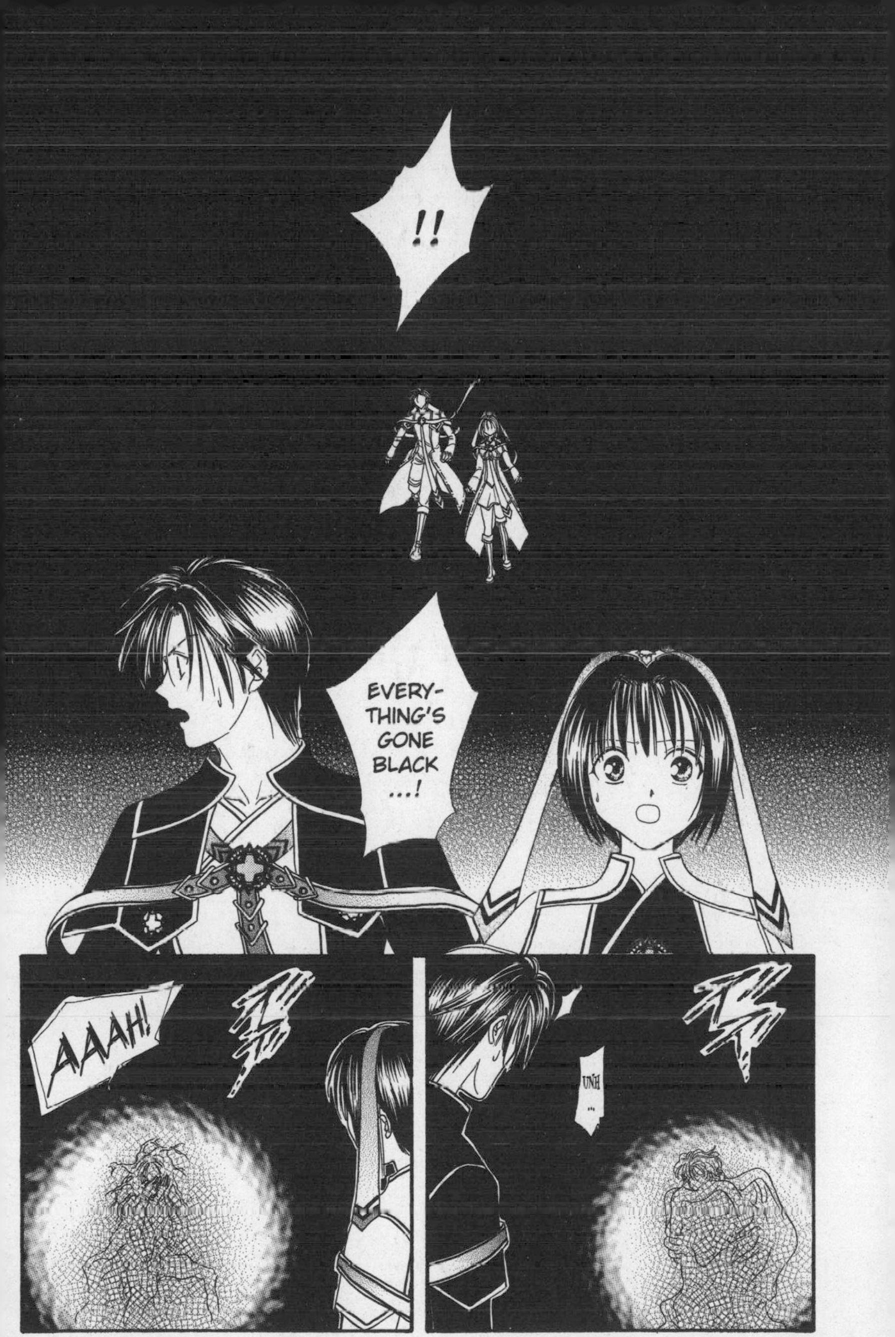
!!
EVERY-THING'S GONE BLACK ...!
UNH ...
AAAH!

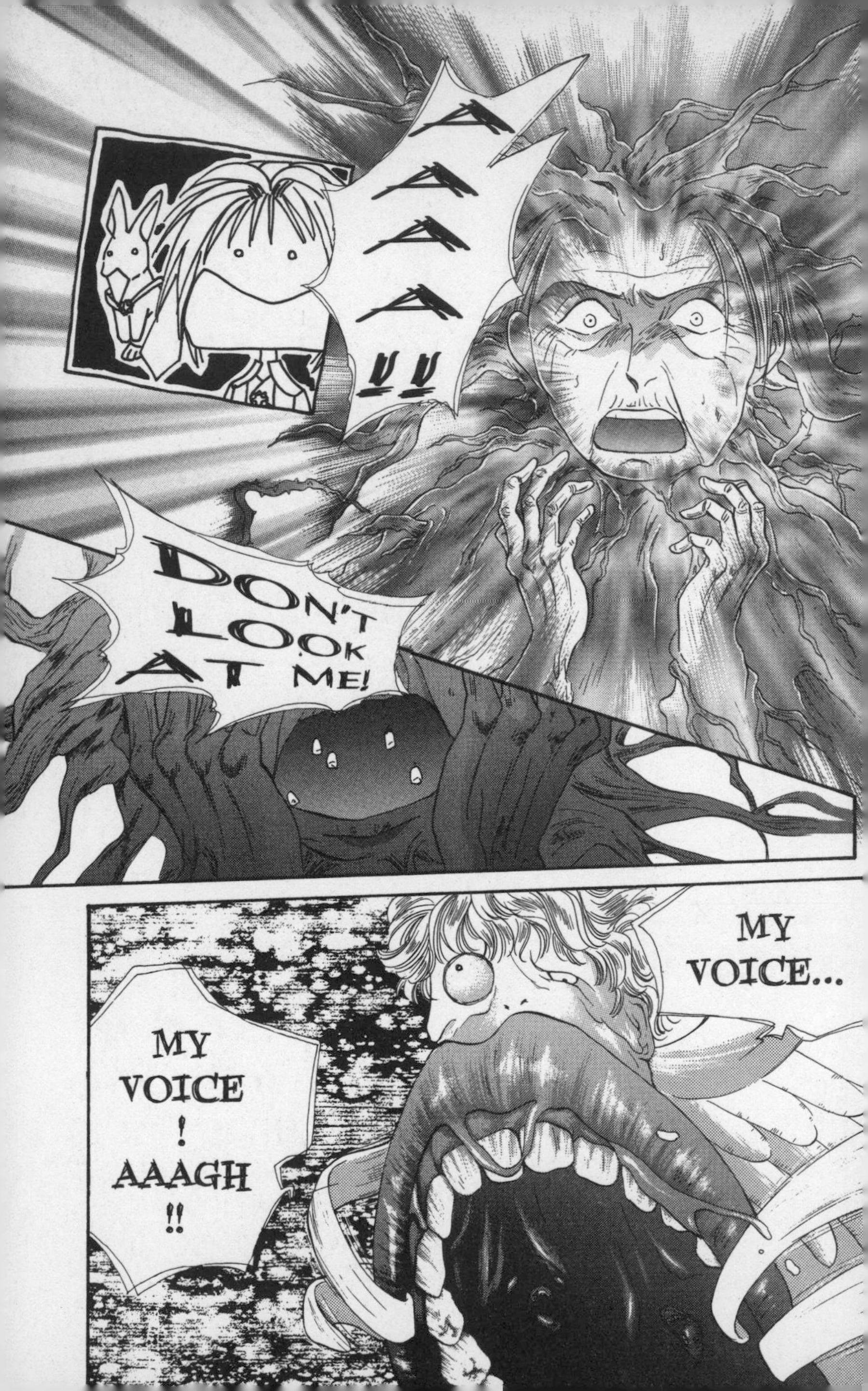
AAAAAA
DON'T LOOK AT ME!
MY VOICE...
MY VOICE! AAAGH!!

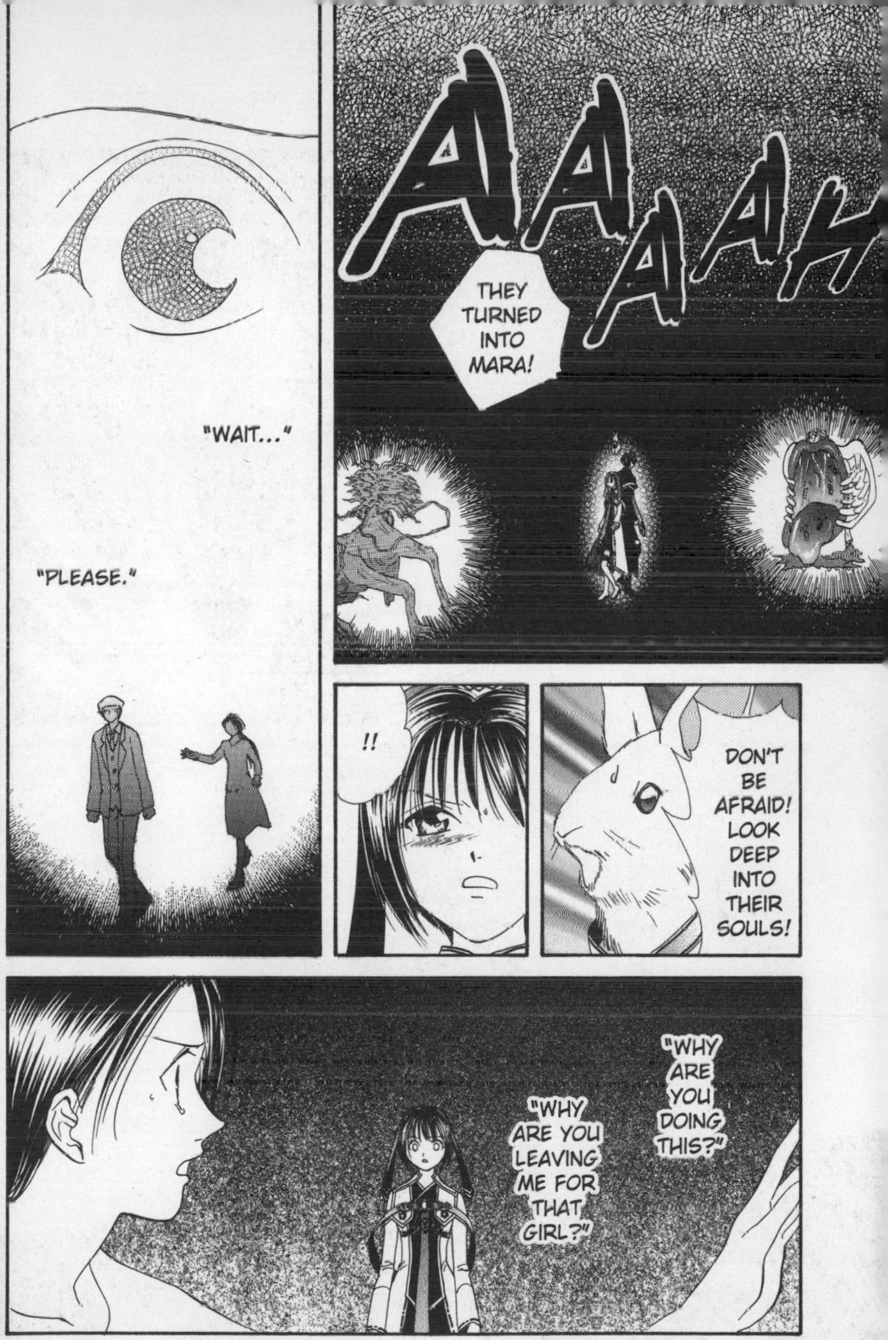
AAAAAAH
THEY TURNED INTO MARA!
DON'T BE AFRAID! LOOK DEEP INTO THEIR SOULS!
!!
"WAIT..."
"PLEASE."
"WHY ARE YOU DOING THIS?"
"WHY ARE YOU LEAVING ME FOR THAT GIRL?"

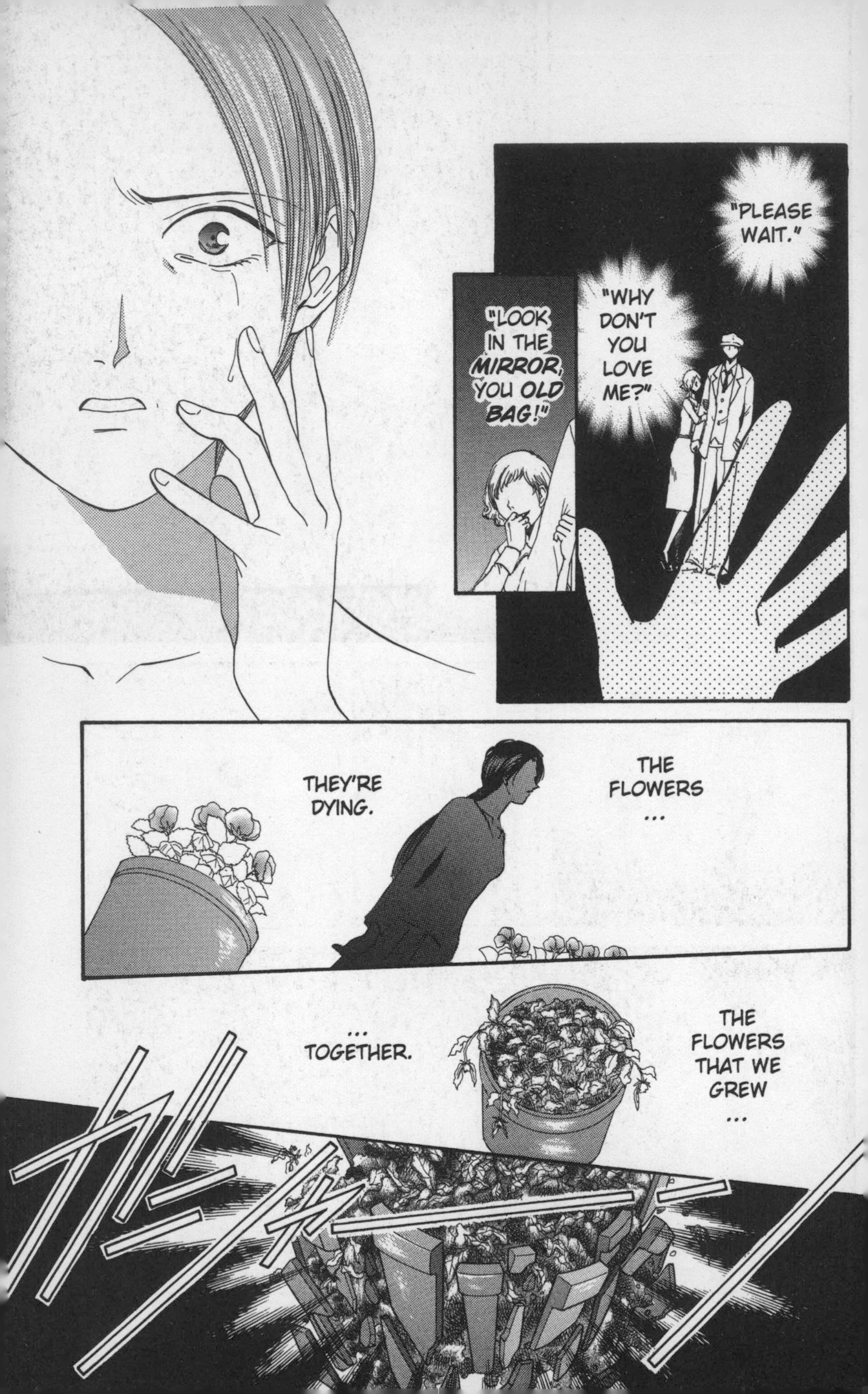
"PLEASE WAIT."
"WHY DON'T YOU LOVE ME?"
"LOOK IN THE MIRROR, YOU OLD BAG!"
THE FLOWERS ...
THEY'RE DYING.
THE FLOWERS THAT WE GREW ...
... TOGETHER.

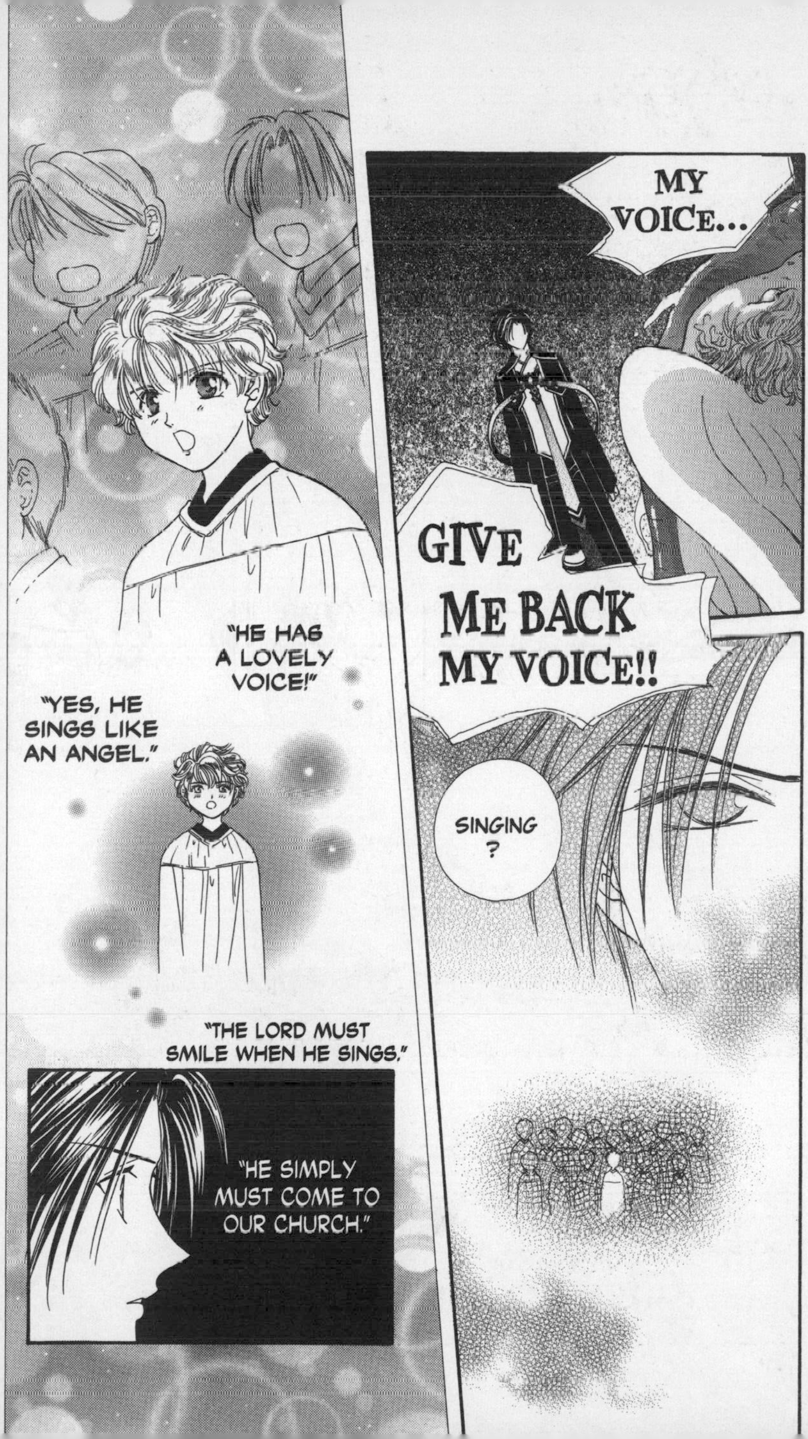
MY VOICE...
GIVE ME BACK MY VOICE!!
SINGING?
"HE HAS A LOVELY VOICE!"
"YES, HE SINGS LIKE AN ANGEL."
"THE LORD MUST SMILE WHEN HE SINGS."
"HE SIMPLY MUST COME TO OUR CHURCH."

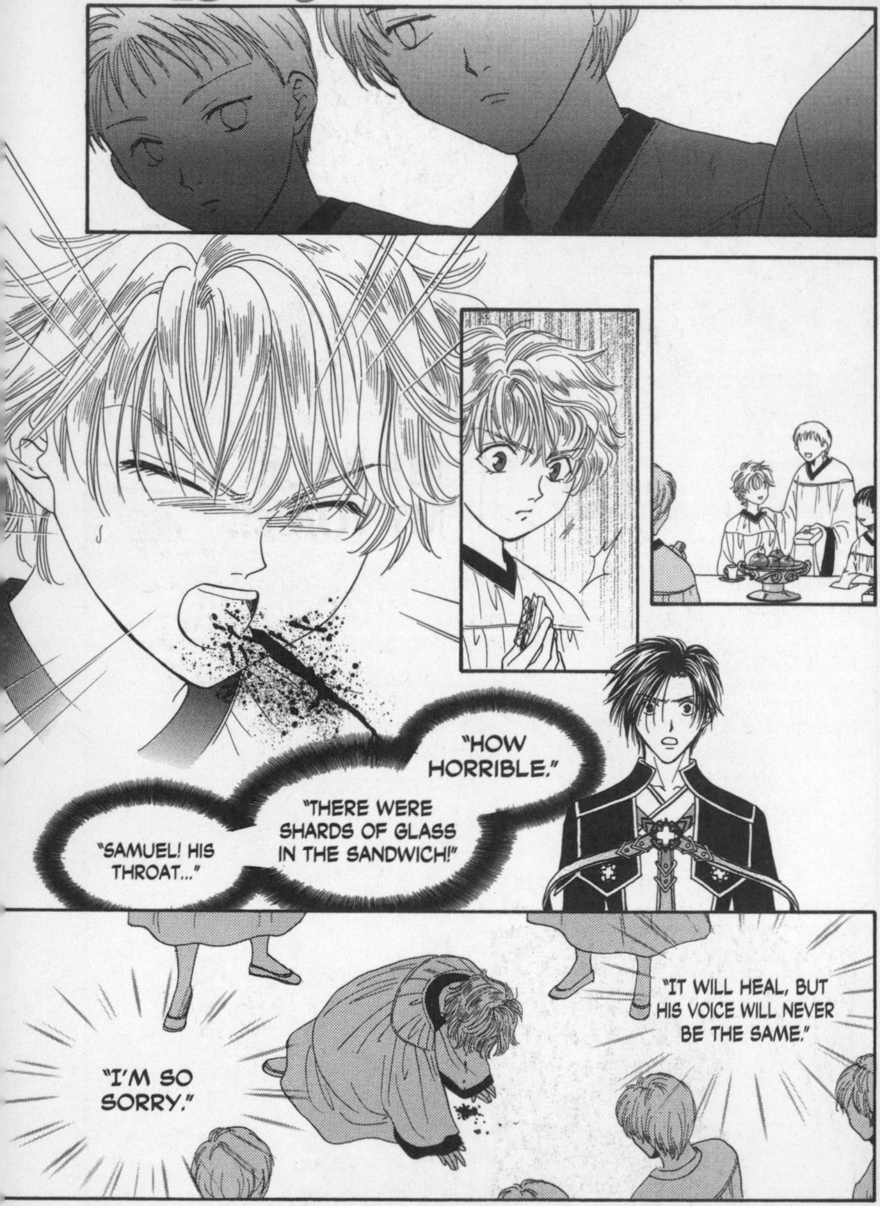
"HOW HORRIBLE."
"THERE WERE SHARDS OF GLASS IN THE SANDWICH!"
"SAMUEL! HIS THROAT..."
"IT WILL HEAL, BUT HIS VOICE WILL NEVER BE THE SAME."
"I'M SO SORRY."

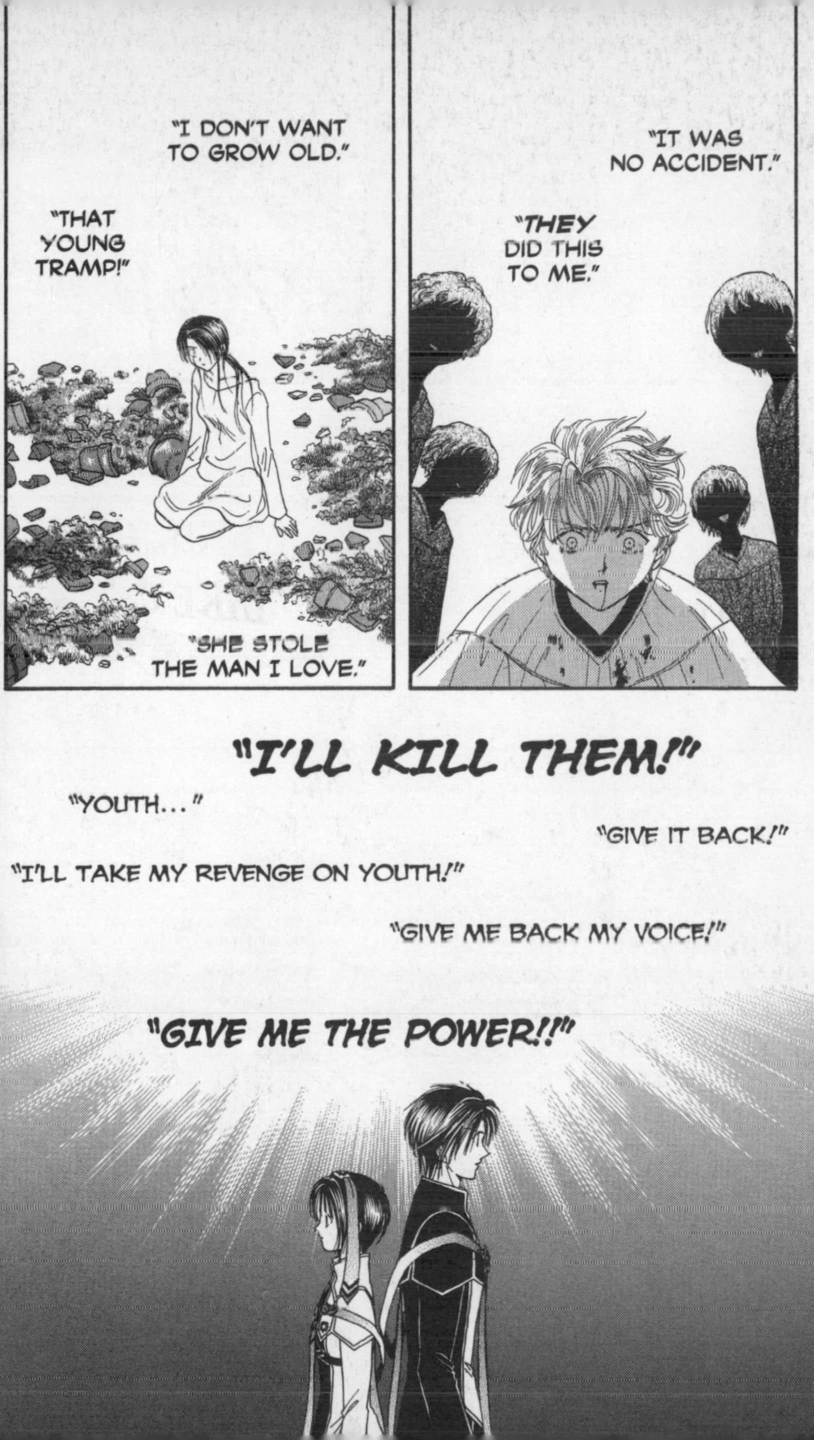
"IT WAS NO ACCIDENT."
"THEY DID THIS TO ME."
"I DON'T WANT TO GROW OLD."
"THAT YOUNG TRAMP!"
"SHE STOLE THE MAN I LOVE."
"I'LL KILL THEM!"
"YOUTH..."
"GIVE IT BACK!"
"I'LL TAKE MY REVENGE ON YOUTH!"
"GIVE ME BACK MY VOICE!"
"GIVE ME THE POWER!!"

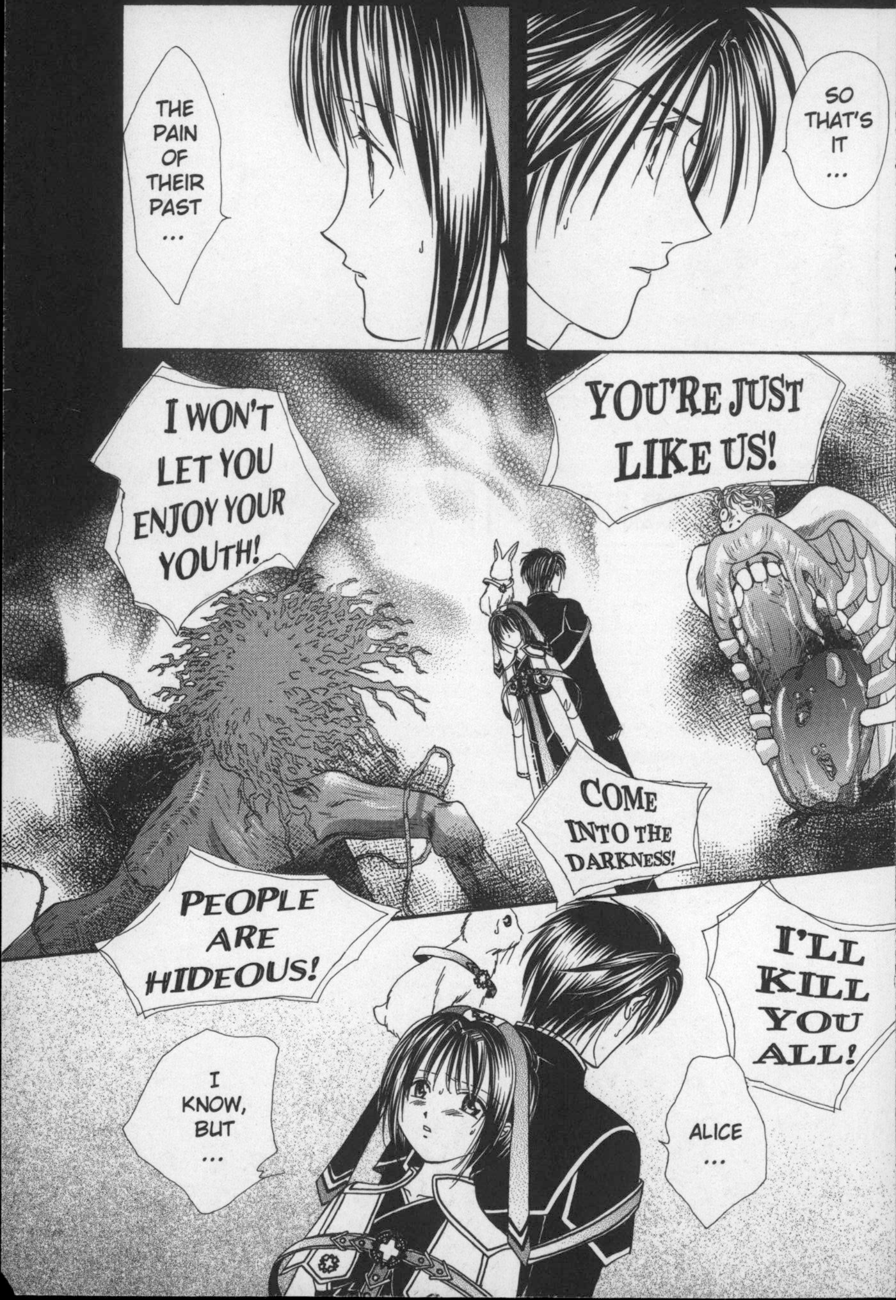
SO THAT'S IT ...
THE PAIN OF THEIR PAST ...
YOU'RE JUST LIKE US!
I WON'T LET YOU ENJOY YOUR YOUTH!
COME INTO THE DARKNESS!
PEOPLE ARE HIDEOUS!
I'LL KILL YOU ALL!
ALICE ...
I KNOW, BUT ...

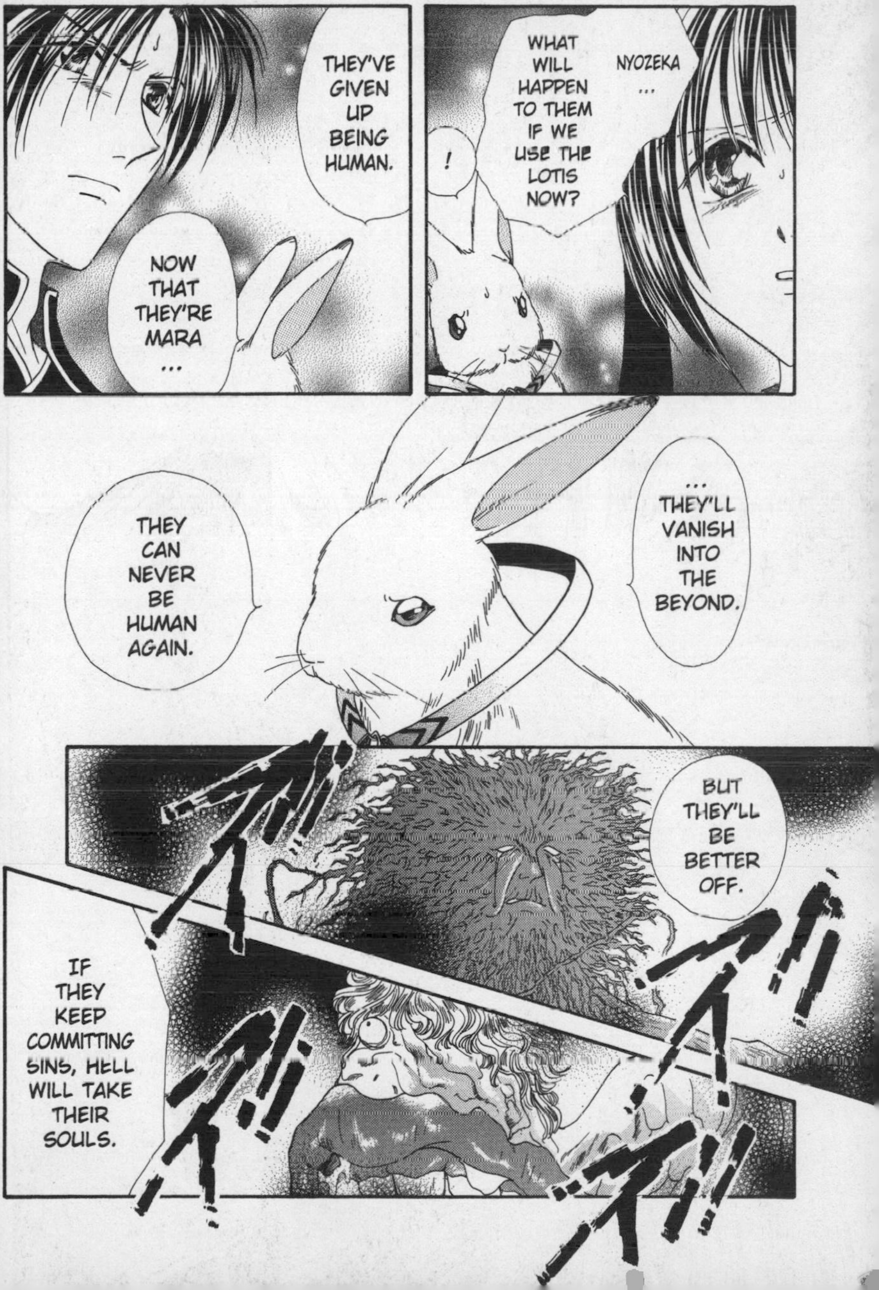
NYOZEKA ...
WHAT WILL HAPPEN TO THEM IF WE USE THE LOTIS NOW?
!
THEY'VE GIVEN UP BEING HUMAN.
NOW THAT THEY'RE MARA ...
... THEY'LL VANISH INTO THE BEYOND.
THEY CAN NEVER BE HUMAN AGAIN.
BUT THEY'LL BE BETTER OFF.
IF THEY KEEP COMMITTING SINS, HELL WILL TAKE THEIR SOULS.

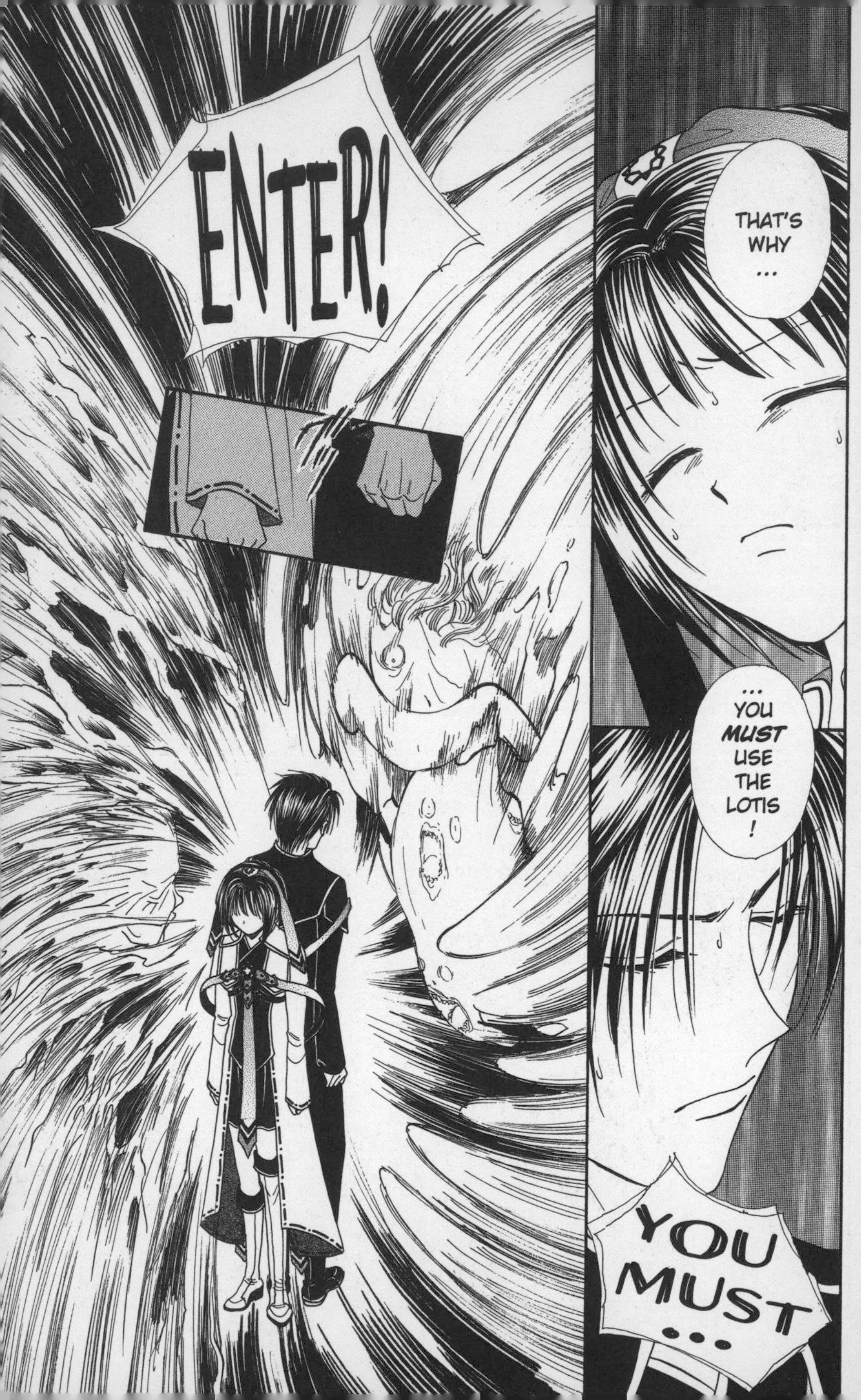
THAT'S WHY ...
... YOU MUST USE THE LOTIS !
YOU MUST ...
ENTER!

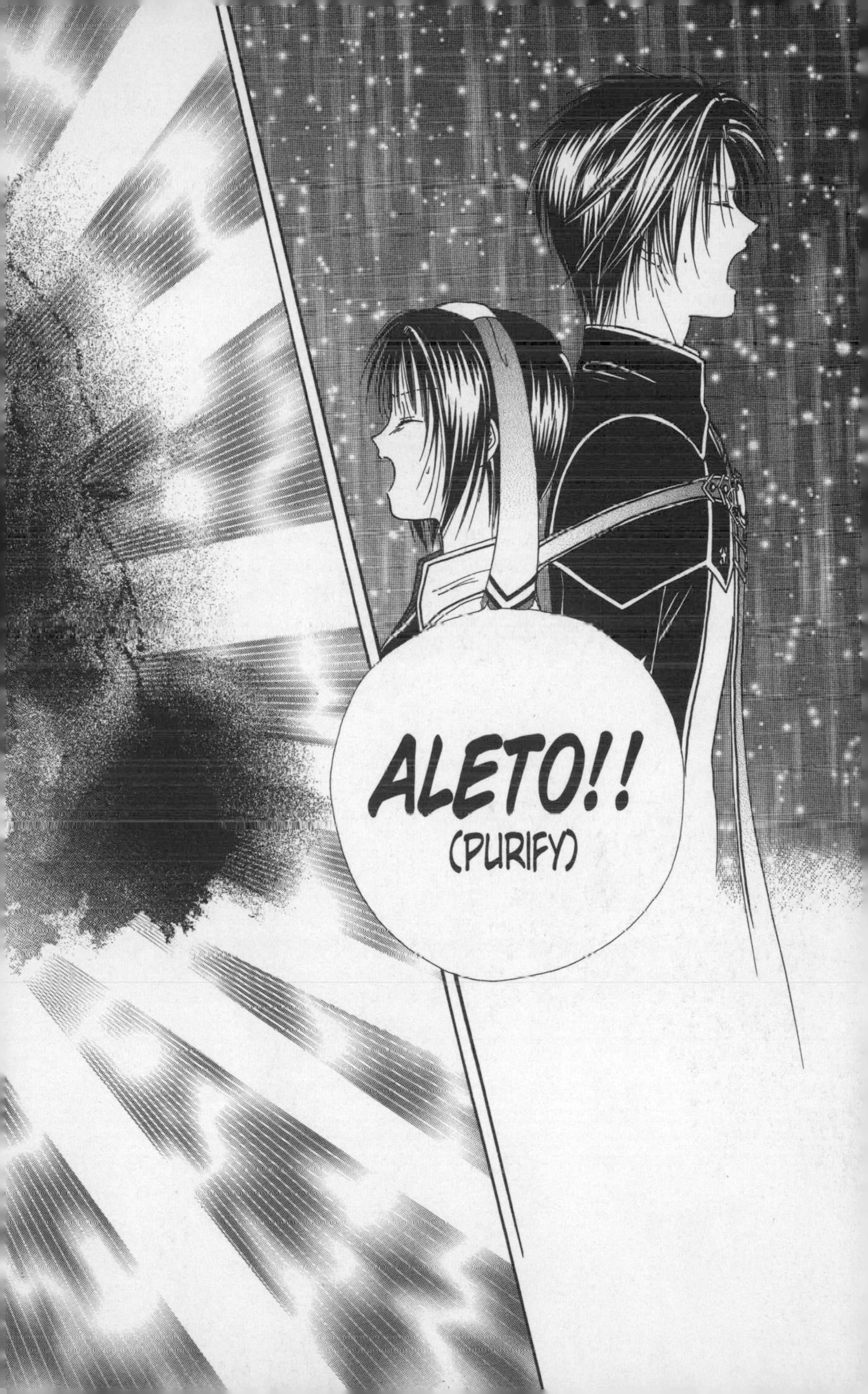
ALETO!!
(PURIFY)

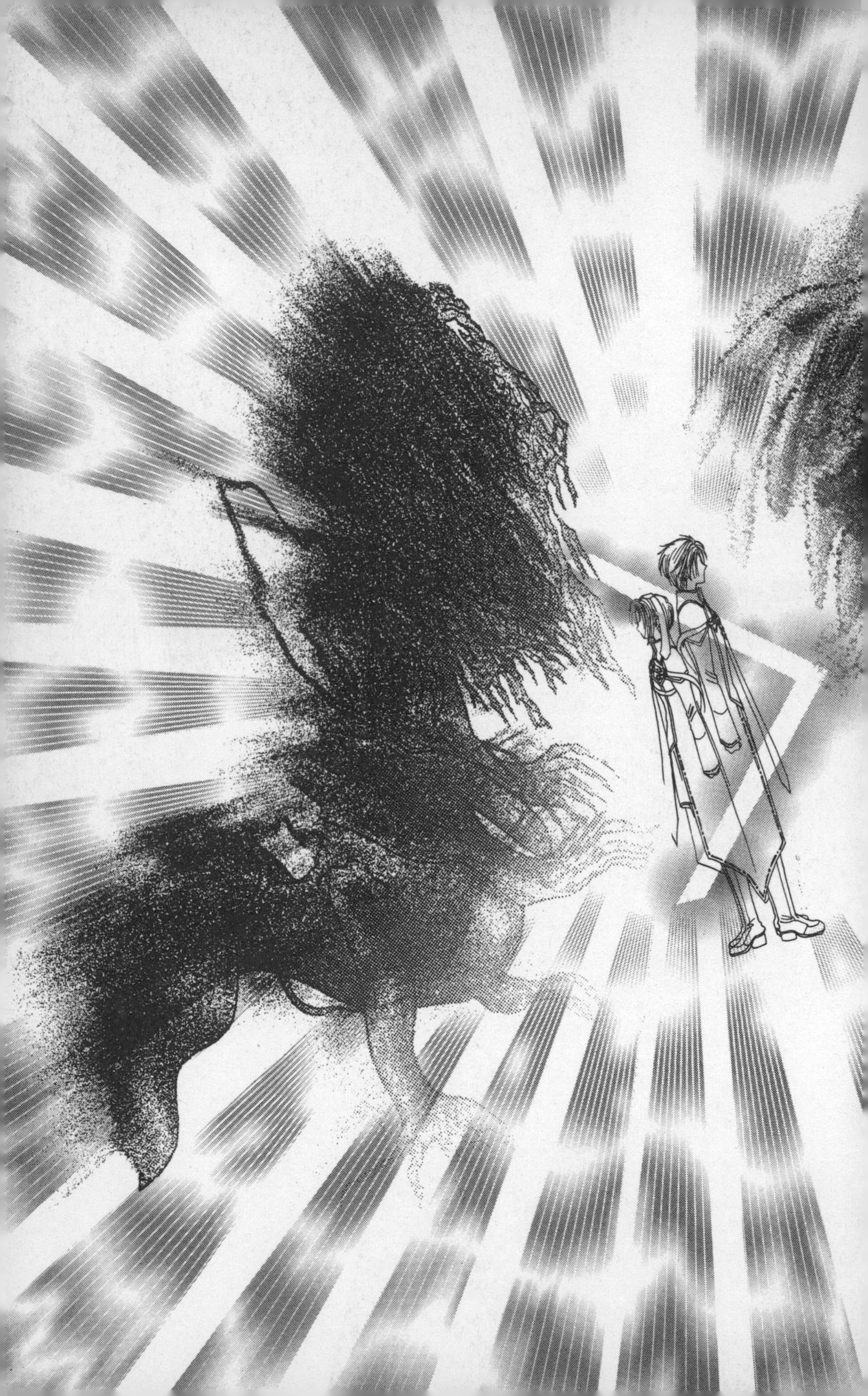

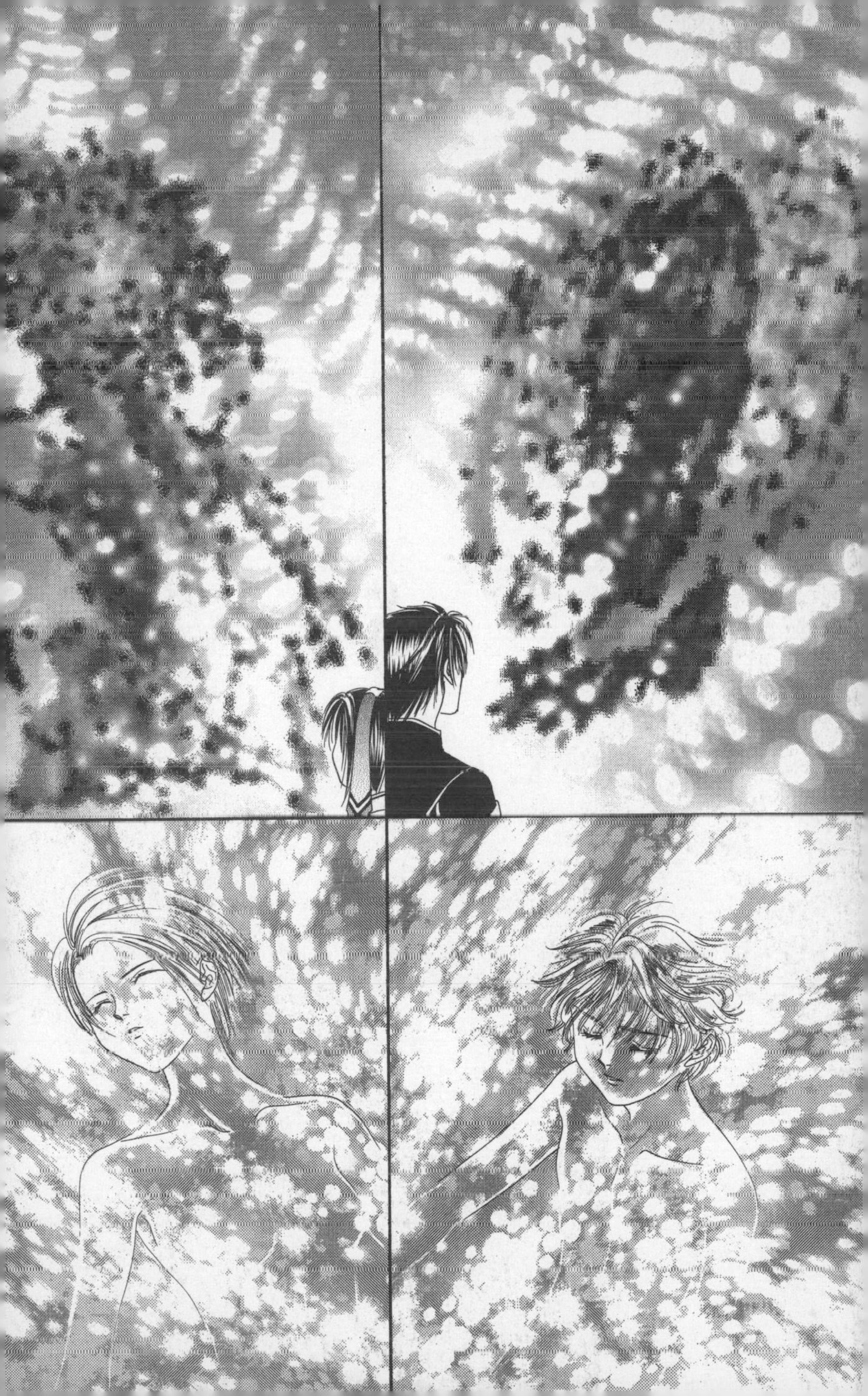

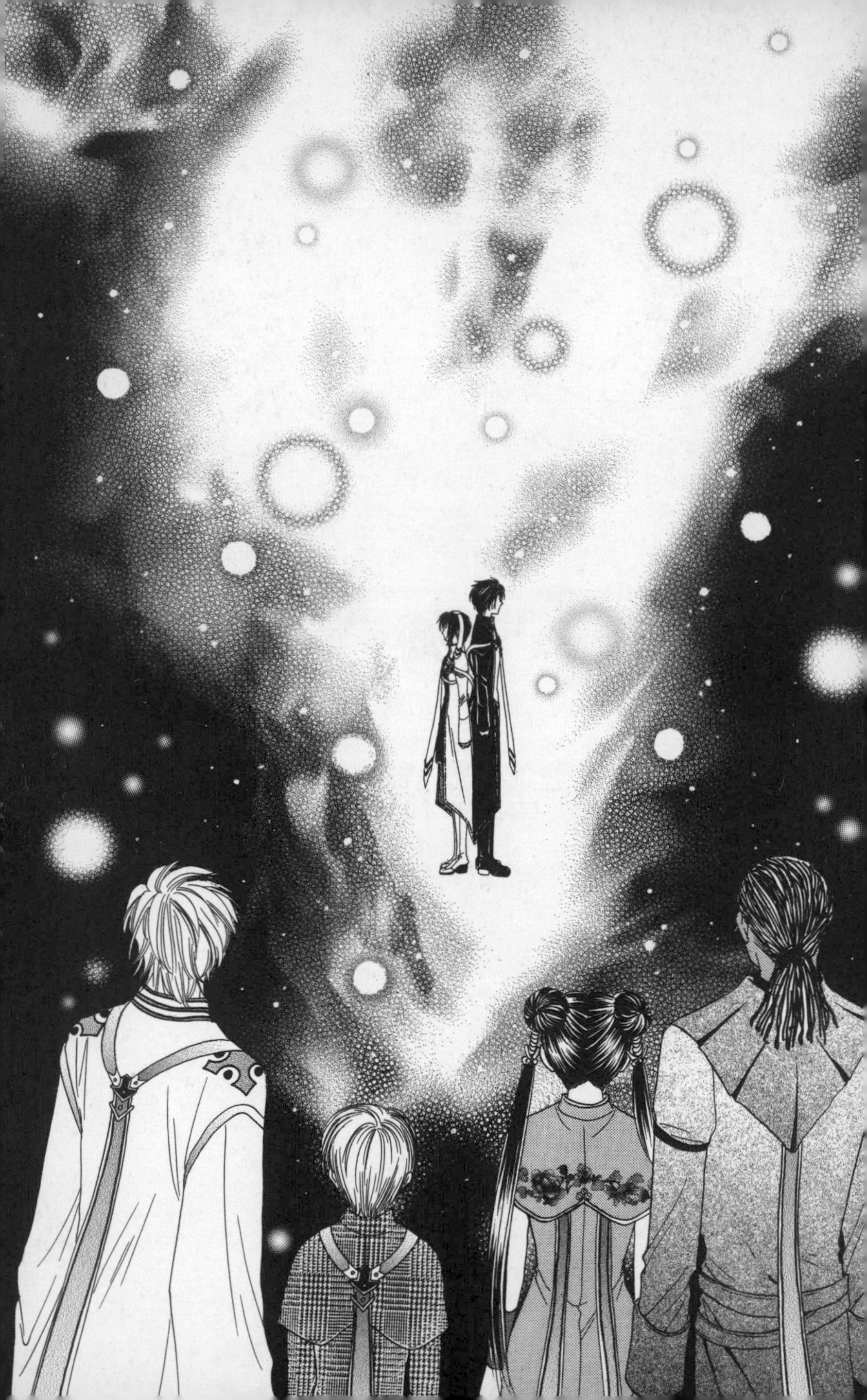

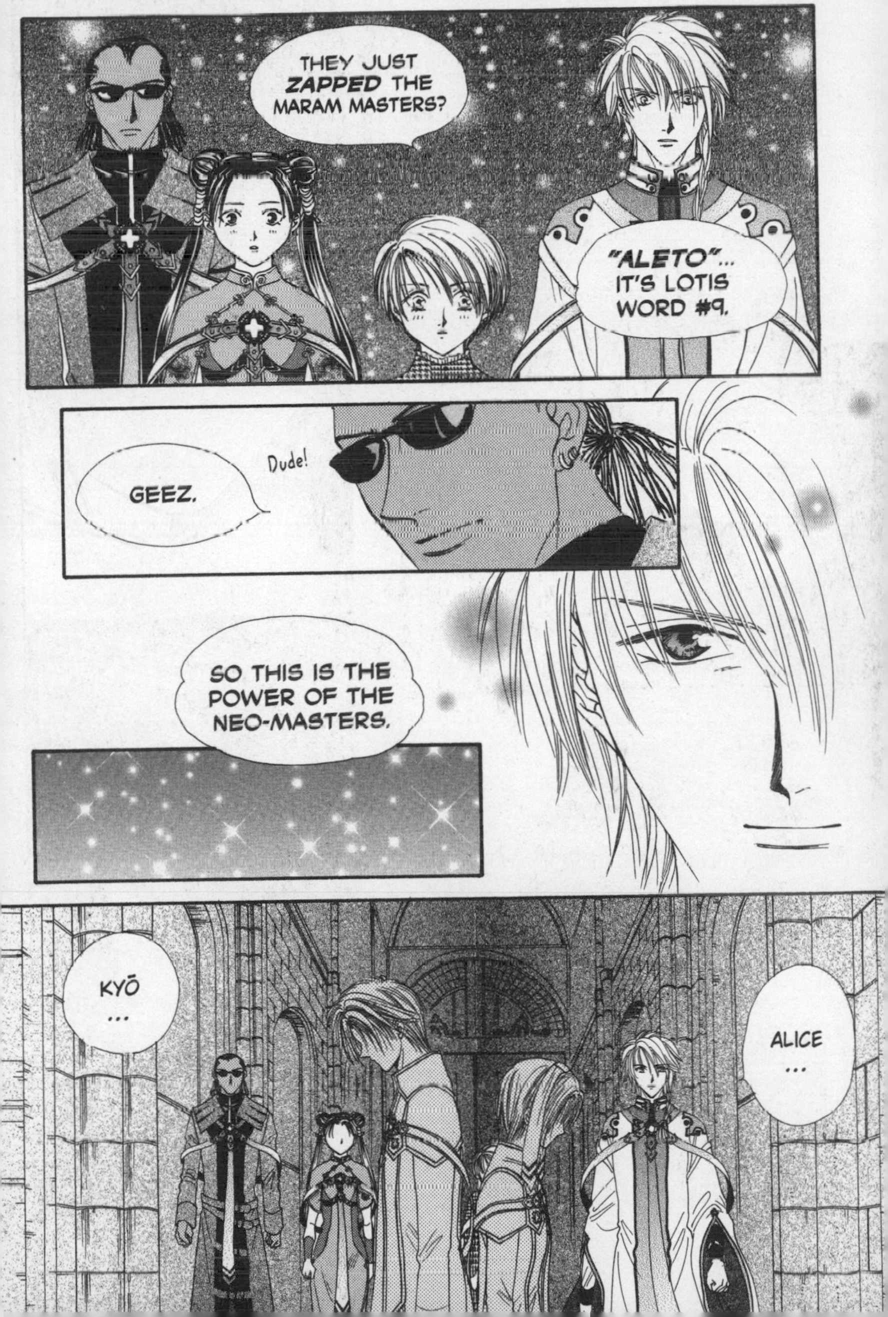
THEY JUST *ZAPPED* THE MARAM MASTERS?
"ALETO"... IT'S LOTIS WORD #9.
Dude!
GEEZ.
SO THIS IS THE POWER OF THE NEO-MASTERS.
ALICE ...
KYŌ ...

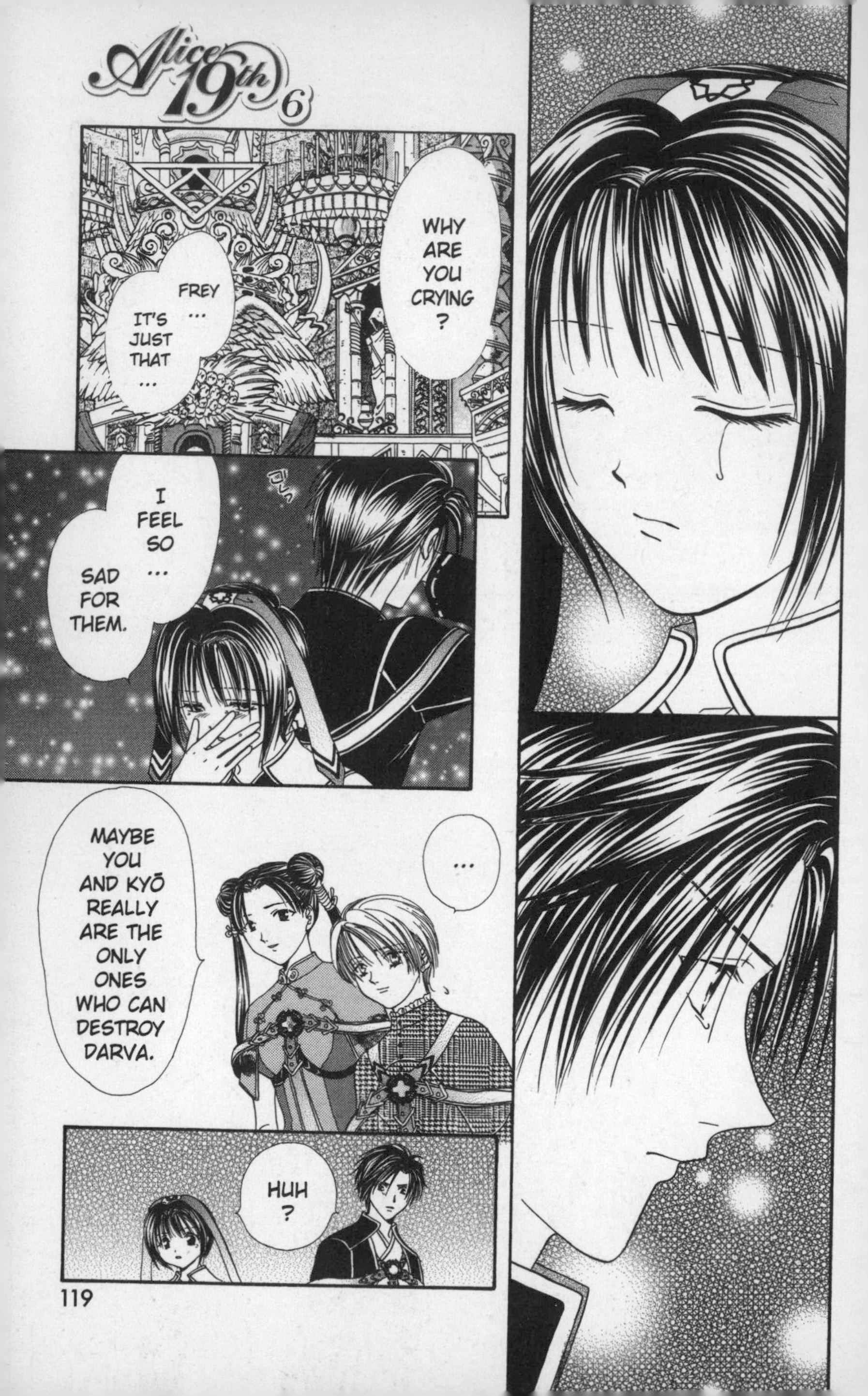
WHY ARE YOU CRYING?
FREY... IT'S JUST THAT...
I FEEL SO... SAD FOR THEM.
...
MAYBE YOU AND KYŌ REALLY ARE THE ONLY ONES WHO CAN DESTROY DARVA.
HUH?

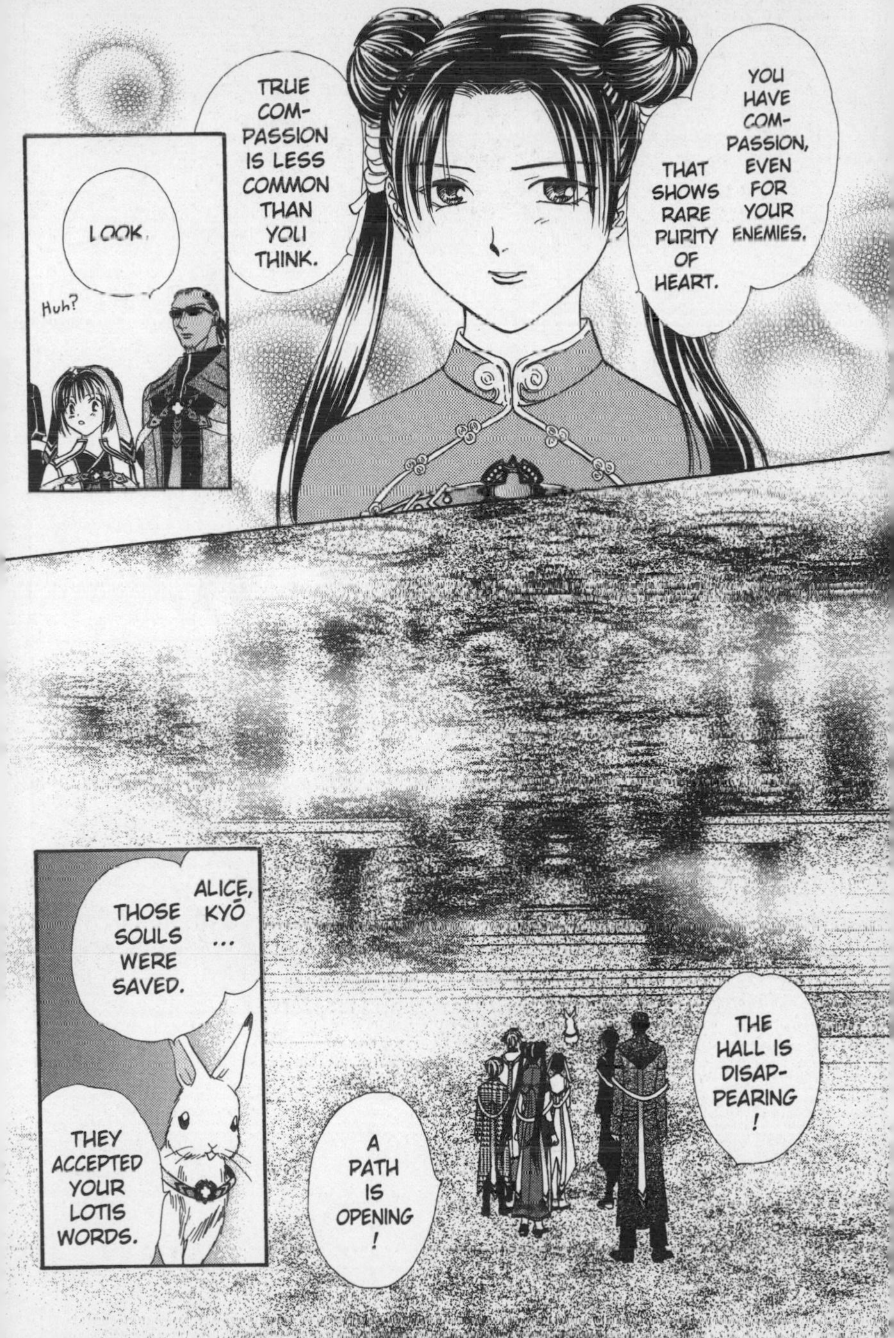
YOU HAVE COM-PASSION, EVEN FOR YOUR ENEMIES.
THAT SHOWS RARE PURITY OF HEART.
TRUE COM-PASSION IS LESS COMMON THAN YOU THINK.
LOOK.
Huh?
THE HALL IS DISAP-PEARING!
A PATH IS OPENING!
ALICE, KYŌ...
THOSE SOULS WERE SAVED.
THEY ACCEPTED YOUR LOTIS WORDS.

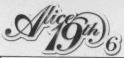

Wow, we're up to volume 6 of Alice 19th--at last!
Our story is nearing its climax. There's been a lot of trouble with the Real World, but the world of the Metropolitan Building was also rough.
No, I'm talking about the drawings. (Smile)
My assistants are working hard, so we're getting by somehow.
It's kind of a relief to know that all this hard work will soon be over. (Wry smile)
The hardest part is that all the characters change into costumes from their home countries. It was really difficult to remember that.
When my assistants heard that all the costumes would change, they asked me, "Why are you trying to kill us?!"
After all this time, I finally realized something.
I love costumes. Not wearing them, I just really love designing all kinds of costumes. ^^
I was short on time for this series, so I just dashed off some designs. It's really difficult.
That's why I'm thrilled when I see CosPlaying fans dressed as my characters. People say they love the uniforms I create, but it might be nice to draw real, ordinary uniforms sometimes. Maybe in my next series.
When I pick out my own clothes, I like things that are different...a little unusual.
I have to hunt around to find stuff like that, though.

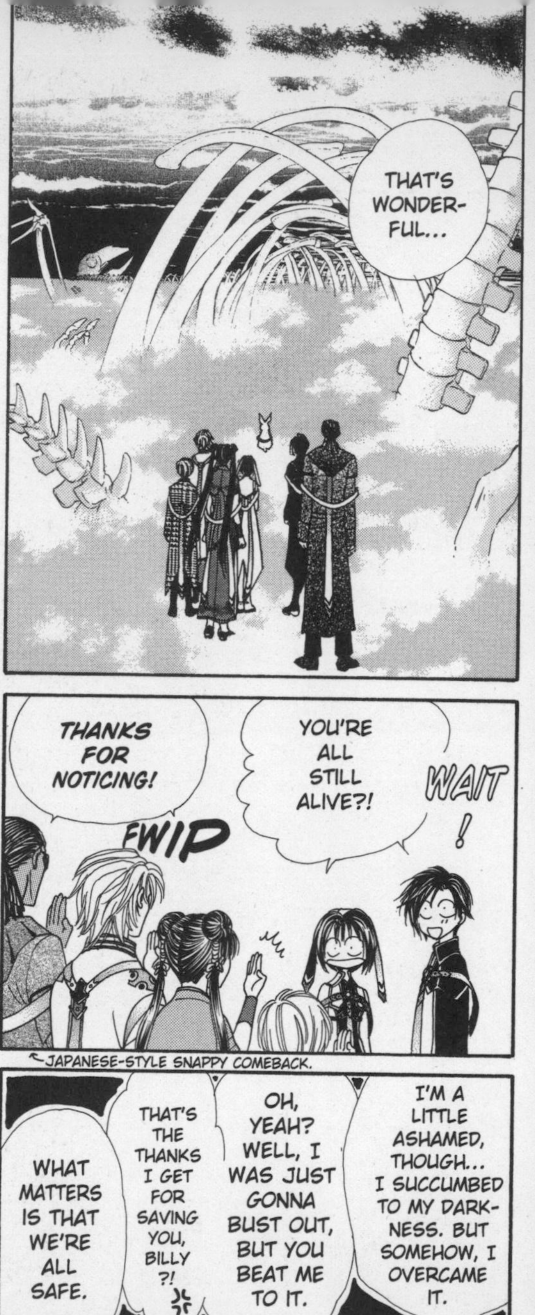
THAT'S WONDERFUL...
WAIT!
YOU'RE ALL STILL ALIVE?!
FWIP
THANKS FOR NOTICING!
←JAPANESE-STYLE SNAPPY COMEBACK.
I'M A LITTLE ASHAMED, THOUGH... I SUCCUMBED TO MY DARKNESS. BUT SOMEHOW, I OVERCAME IT.
OH, YEAH? WELL, I WAS JUST GONNA BUST OUT, BUT YOU BEAT ME TO IT.
THAT'S THE THANKS I GET FOR SAVING YOU, BILLY?!
WHAT MATTERS IS THAT WE'RE ALL SAFE.

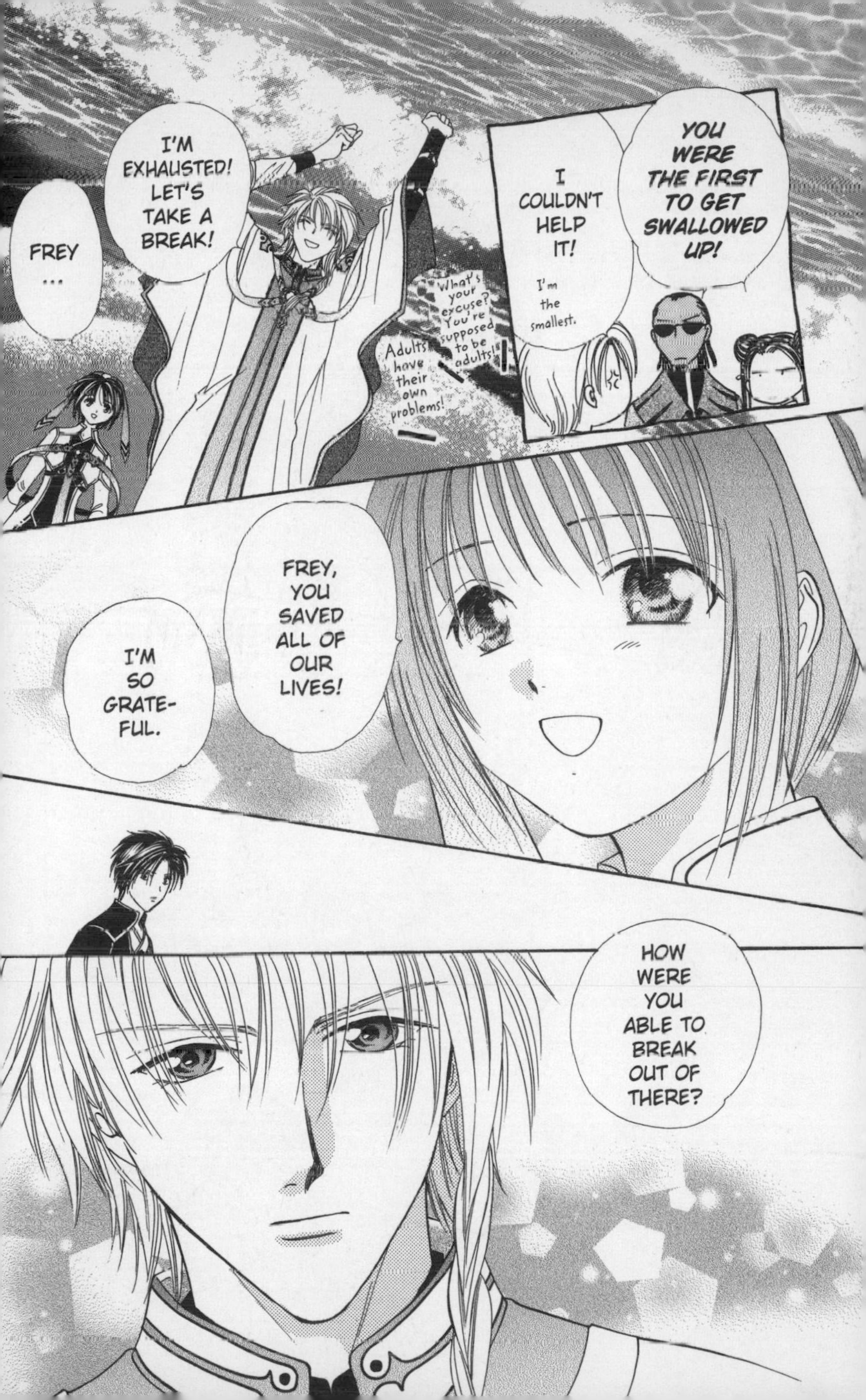
YOU WERE THE FIRST TO GET SWALLOWED UP!
I COULDN'T HELP IT!
I'm the smallest.
What's your excuse? You're supposed to be adults!
Adults have their own problems!
I'M EXHAUSTED! LET'S TAKE A BREAK!
FREY ...
FREY, YOU SAVED ALL OF OUR LIVES!
I'M SO GRATE-FUL.
HOW WERE YOU ABLE TO BREAK OUT OF THERE?

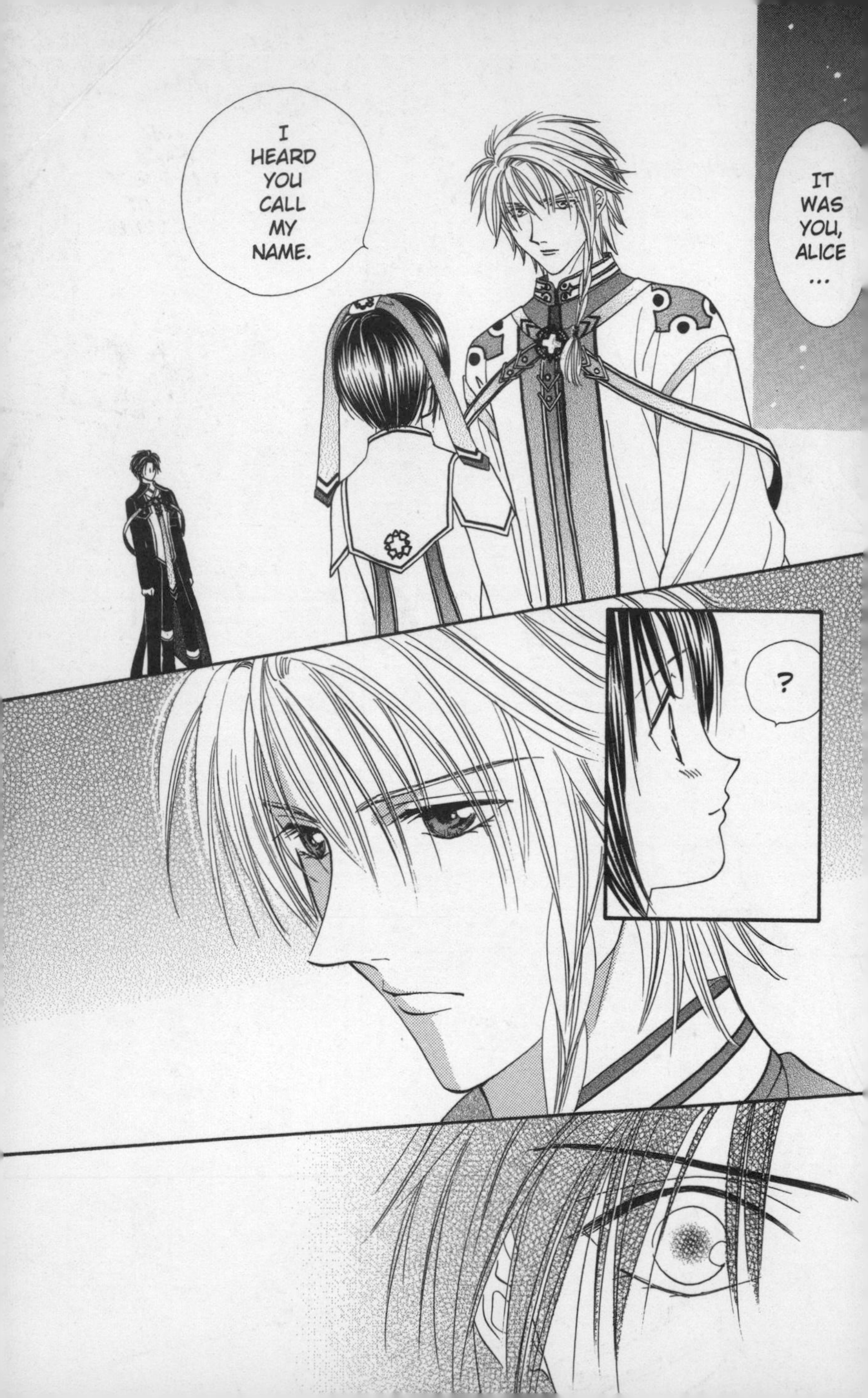
IT WAS YOU, ALICE ...
I HEARD YOU CALL MY NAME.
?

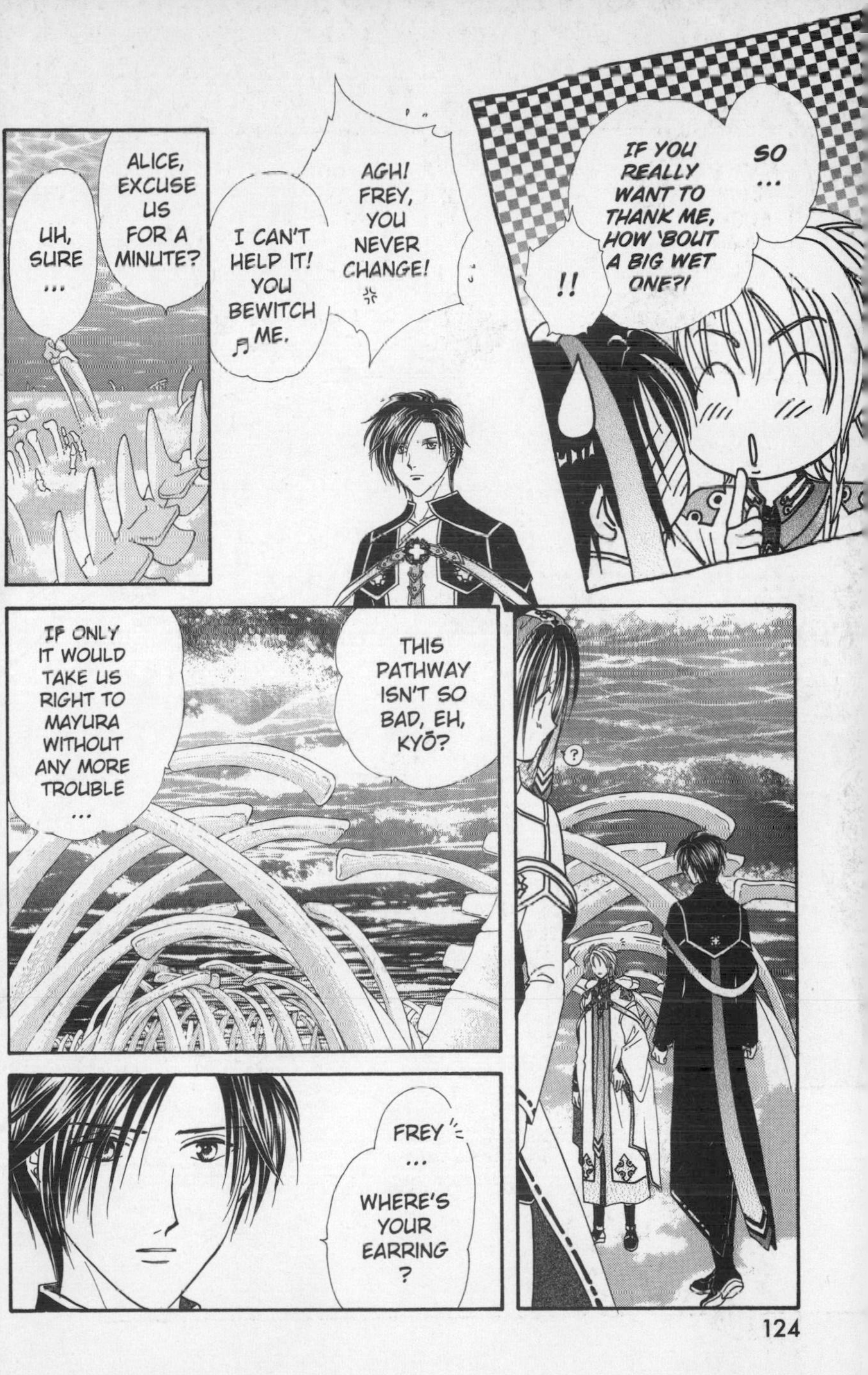
SO ...
IF YOU REALLY WANT TO THANK ME, HOW 'BOUT A BIG WET ONE?!
!!
AGH! FREY, YOU NEVER CHANGE!
I CAN'T HELP IT! YOU BEWITCH ME.
ALICE, EXCUSE US FOR A MINUTE?
UH, SURE ...
?
THIS PATHWAY ISN'T SO BAD, EH, KYŌ?
IF ONLY IT WOULD TAKE US RIGHT TO MAYURA WITHOUT ANY MORE TROUBLE ...
FREY ...
WHERE'S YOUR EARRING ?

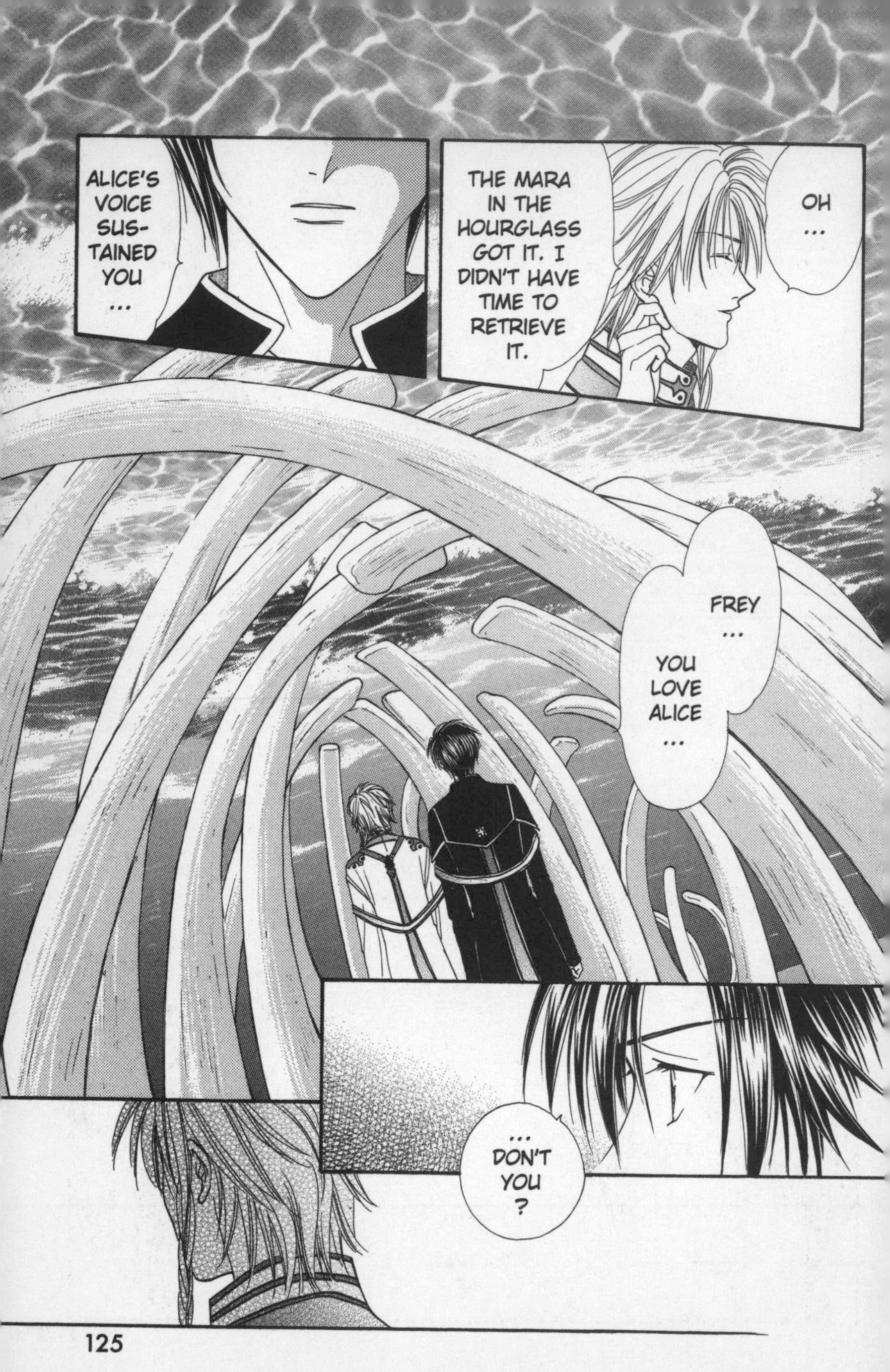
OH ...
THE MARA IN THE HOURGLASS GOT IT. I DIDN'T HAVE TIME TO RETRIEVE IT.
ALICE'S VOICE SUS-TAINED YOU ...
FREY ... YOU LOVE ALICE ...
... DON'T YOU ?

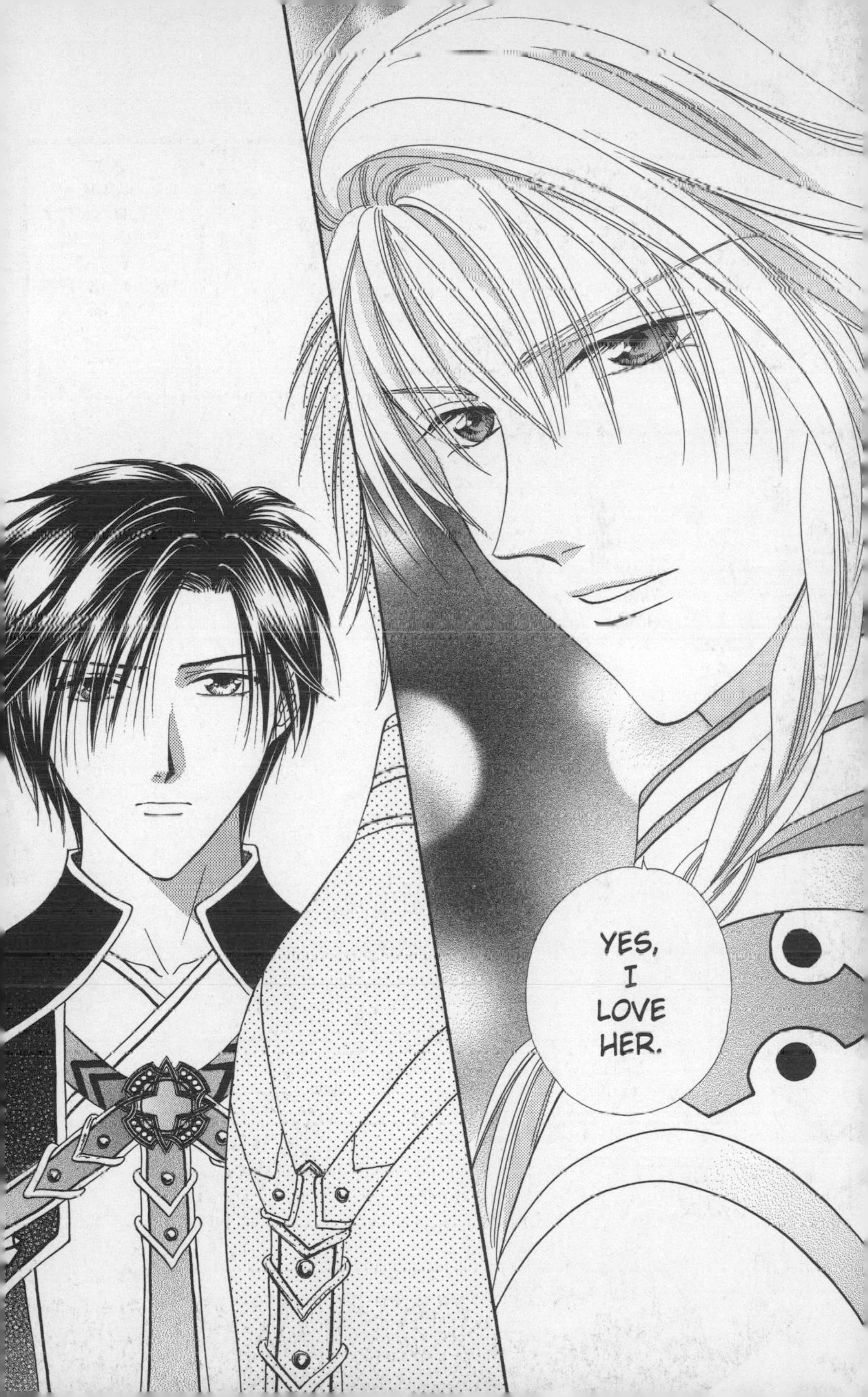
YES, I LOVE HER.

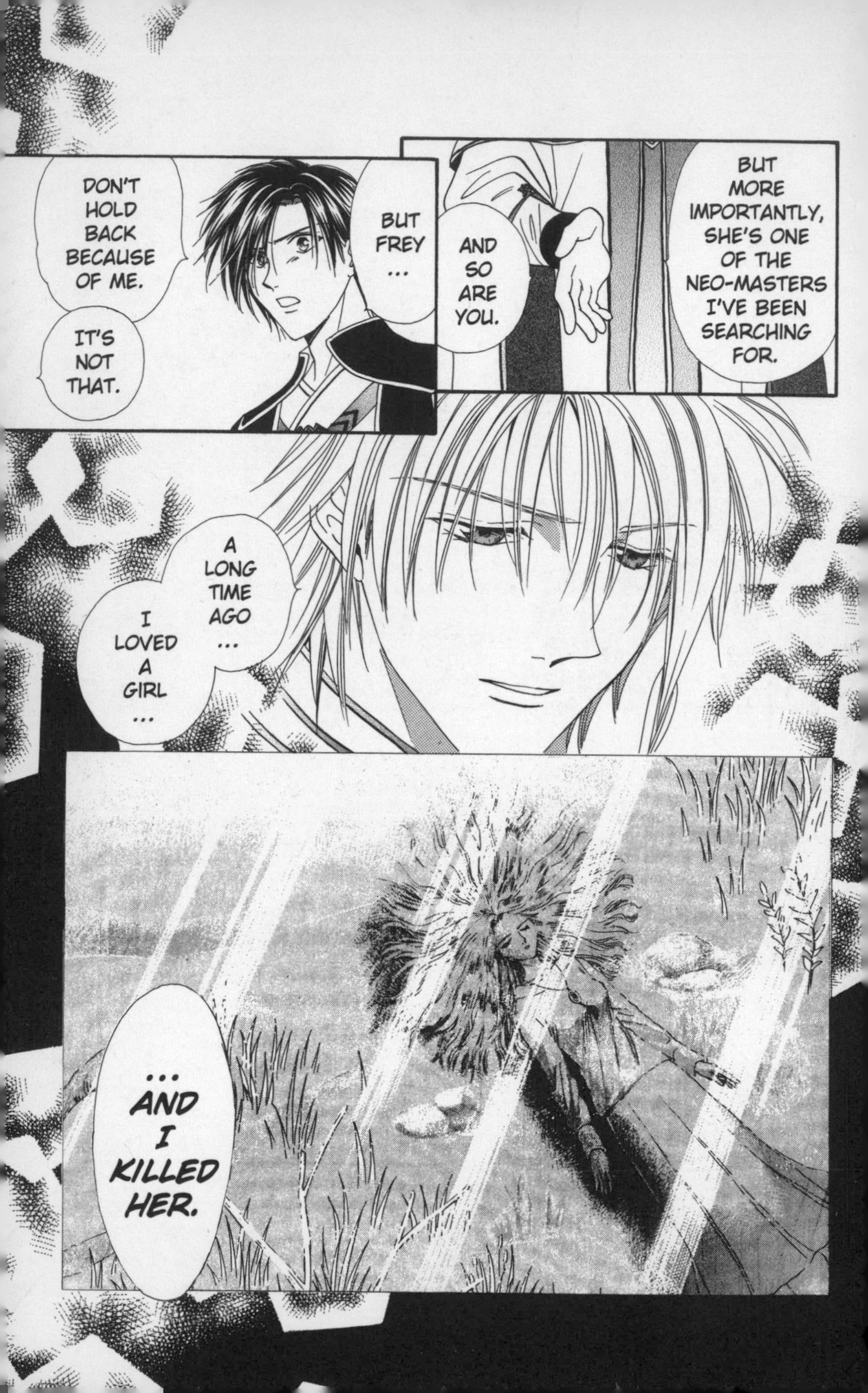
BUT MORE IMPORTANTLY, SHE'S ONE OF THE NEO-MASTERS I'VE BEEN SEARCHING FOR.
AND SO ARE YOU.
BUT FREY ...
DON'T HOLD BACK BECAUSE OF ME.
IT'S NOT THAT.
A LONG TIME AGO ...
I LOVED A GIRL ...
... AND I KILLED HER.

- AGE: 28

- BLOOD TYPE: B

- SIGN: LEO

- HEIGHT: 6' 4"

- BIRTHPLACE: U.S.A.

- GREW UP IN THE PROJECTS, SO HE USES ROUGH LANGUAGE. QUICK TO FIGHT, BUT KIND-HEARTED. LOOKS AFTER OTHERS. LIKES KIDS.

- ENGAGED TO BE MARRIED.

- LIKES MUSIC. PLAYS THE SAXOPHONE.

- OCCUPATION: POSTAL WORKER

BILLY MACDOWELL

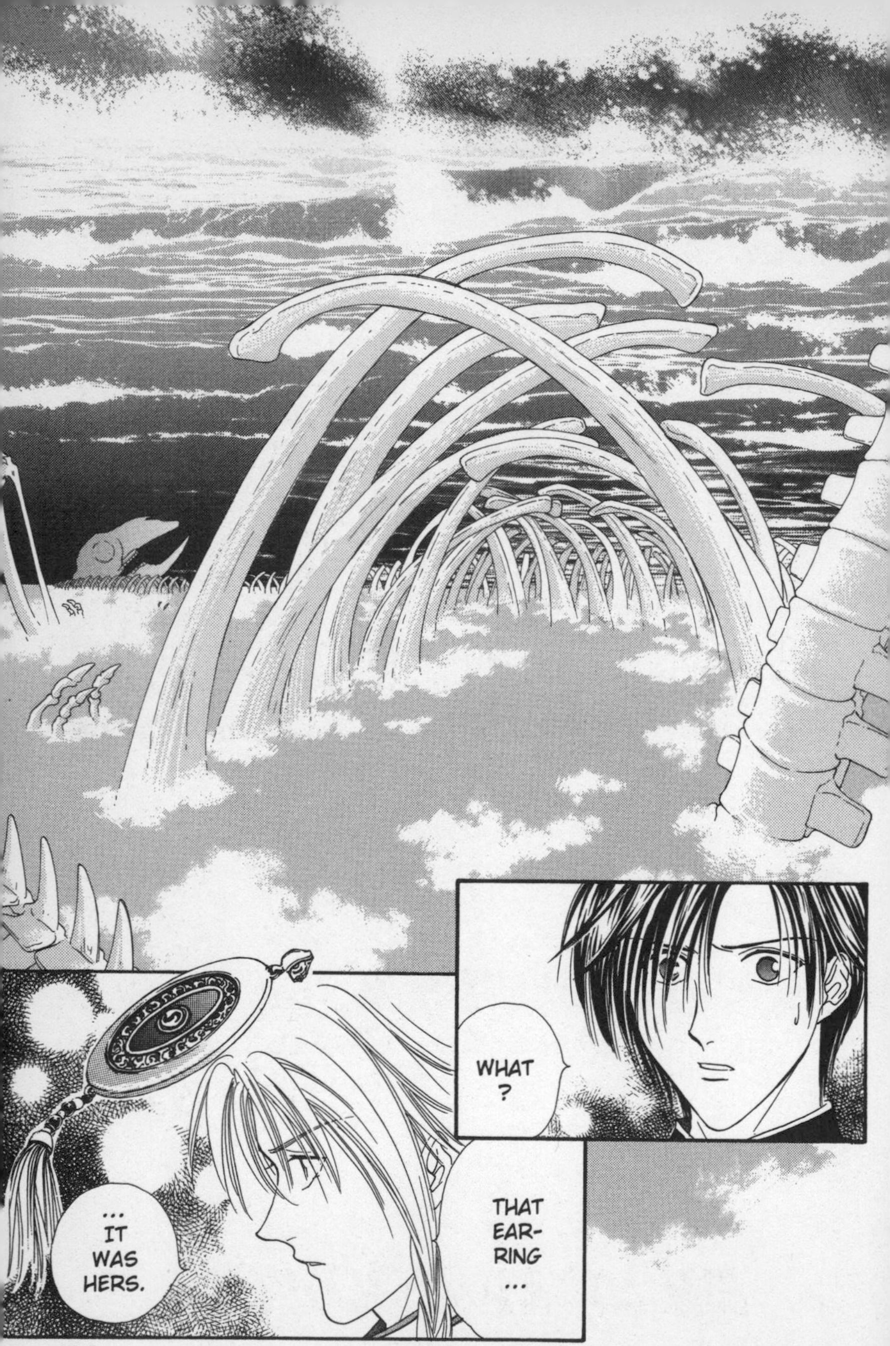
WHAT ?
THAT EAR-RING ...
... IT WAS HERS.

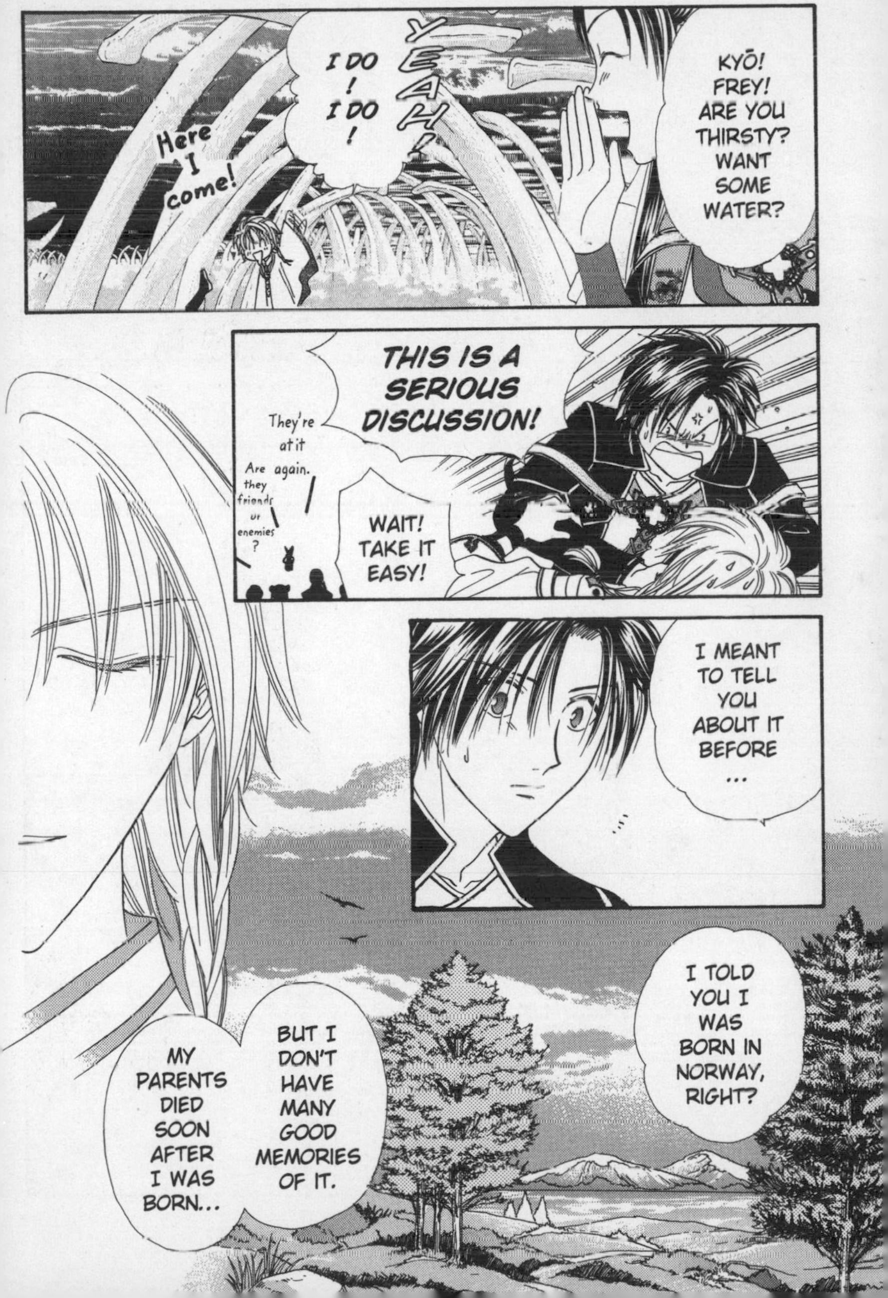
KYŌ! FREY! ARE YOU THIRSTY? WANT SOME WATER?
YEAH!
I DO! I DO!
Here I come!
THIS IS A SERIOUS DISCUSSION!
WAIT! TAKE IT EASY!
They're at it again.
Are they friends or enemies?
I MEANT TO TELL YOU ABOUT IT BEFORE ...
I TOLD YOU I WAS BORN IN NORWAY, RIGHT?
BUT I DON'T HAVE MANY GOOD MEMORIES OF IT.
MY PARENTS DIED SOON AFTER I WAS BORN...

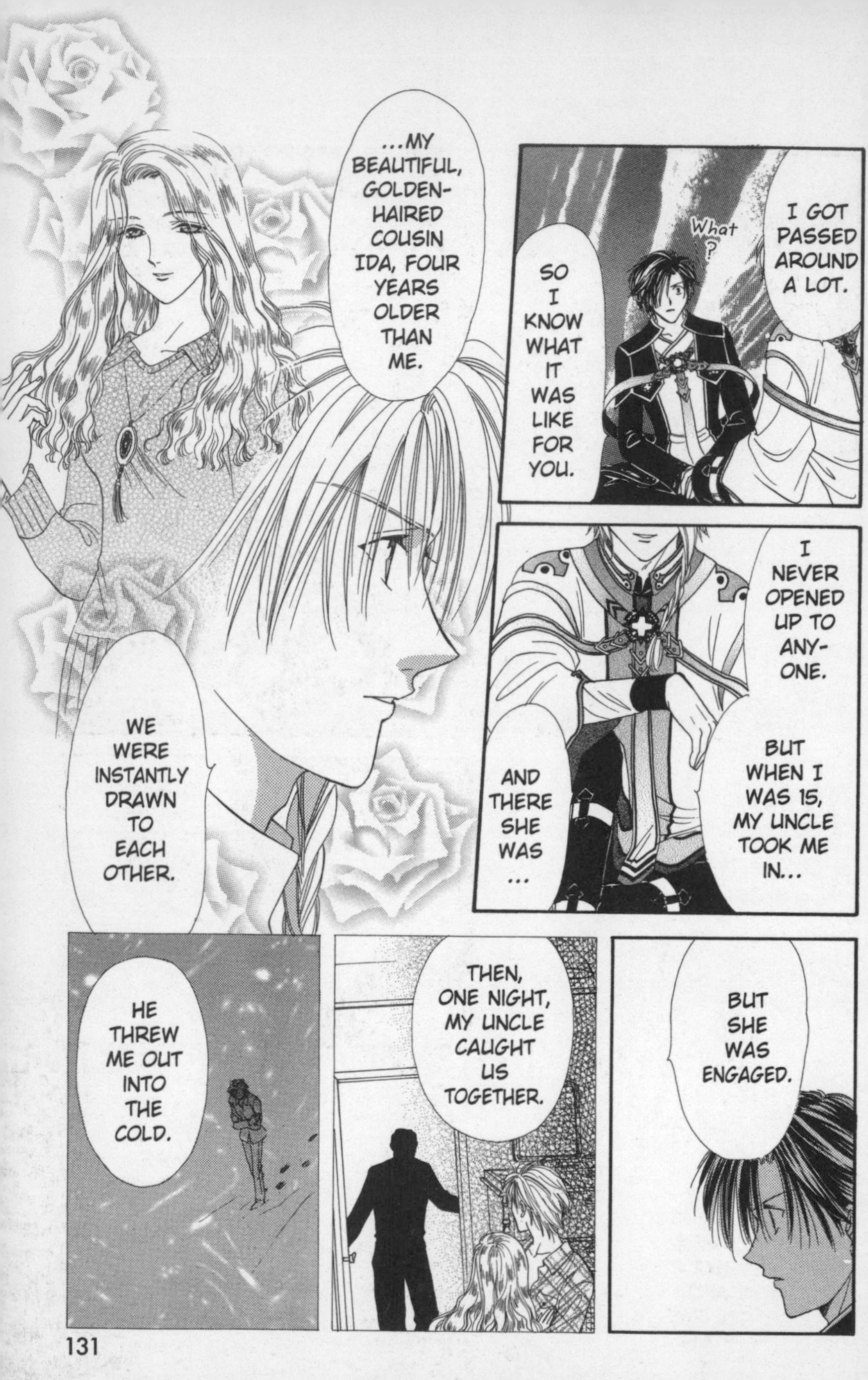
I GOT PASSED AROUND A LOT.
What ?
SO I KNOW WHAT IT WAS LIKE FOR YOU.
I NEVER OPENED UP TO ANY-ONE.
BUT WHEN I WAS 15, MY UNCLE TOOK ME IN...
AND THERE SHE WAS...
...MY BEAUTIFUL, GOLDEN-HAIRED COUSIN IDA, FOUR YEARS OLDER THAN ME.
WE WERE INSTANTLY DRAWN TO EACH OTHER.
BUT SHE WAS ENGAGED.
THEN, ONE NIGHT, MY UNCLE CAUGHT US TOGETHER.
HE THREW ME OUT INTO THE COLD.

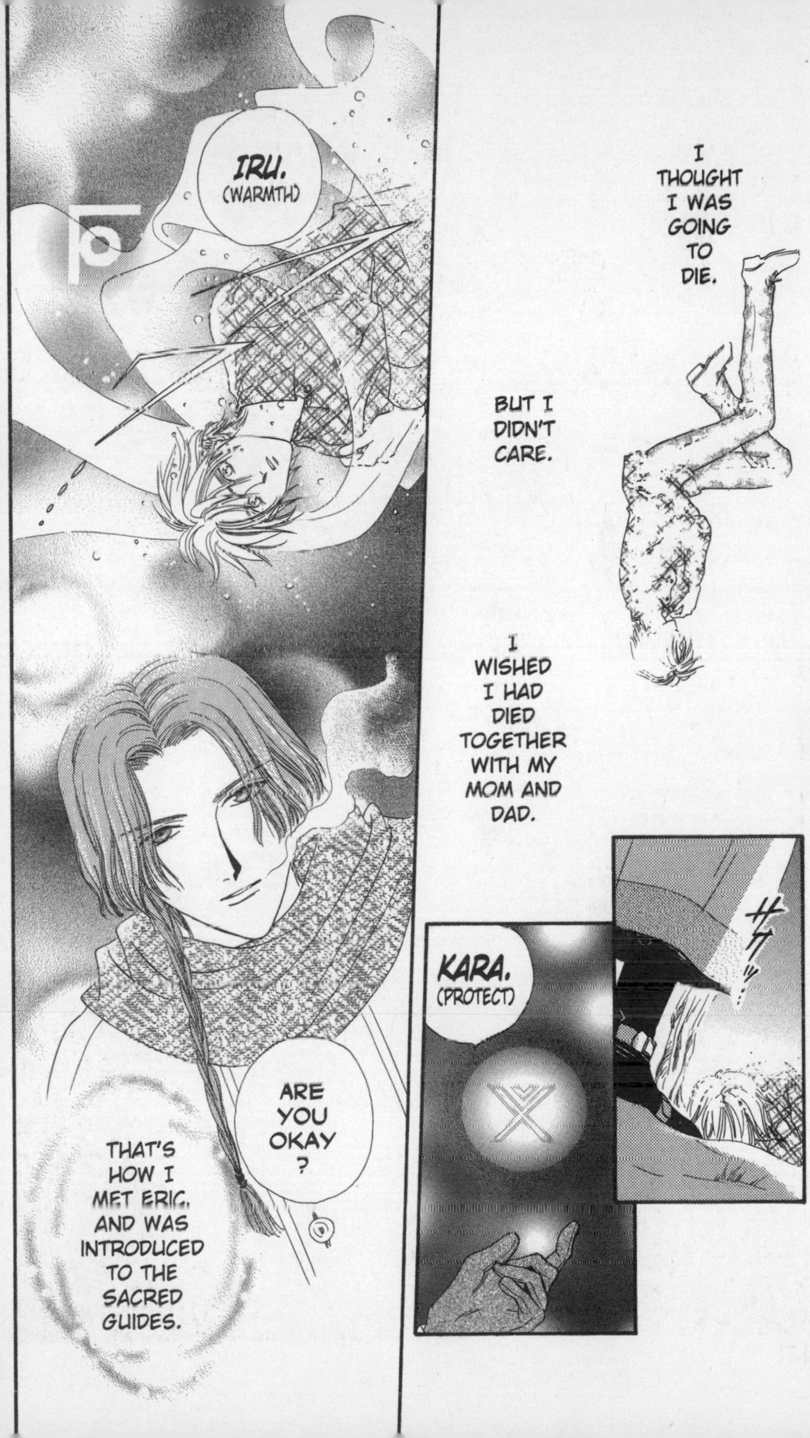
I THOUGHT I WAS GOING TO DIE.
BUT I DIDN'T CARE.
I WISHED I HAD DIED TOGETHER WITH MY MOM AND DAD.
ハッ!!
KARA. (PROTECT)
IRU. (WARMTH)
ARE YOU OKAY ?
THAT'S HOW I MET ERIC, AND WAS INTRODUCED TO THE SACRED GUIDES.

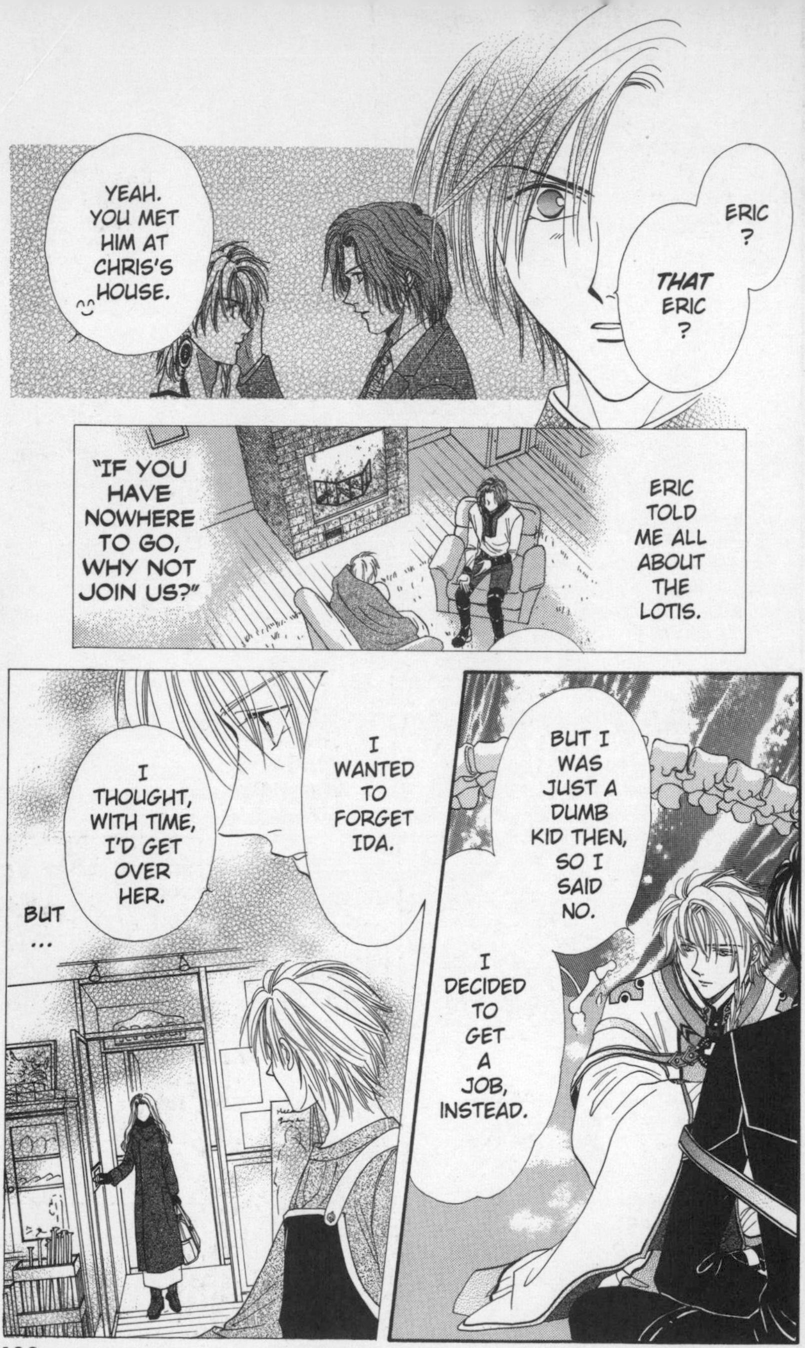
ERIC?
THAT ERIC?
YEAH. YOU MET HIM AT CHRIS'S HOUSE.
ERIC TOLD ME ALL ABOUT THE LOTIS.
"IF YOU HAVE NOWHERE TO GO, WHY NOT JOIN US?"
BUT I WAS JUST A DUMB KID THEN, SO I SAID NO.
I DECIDED TO GET A JOB, INSTEAD.
I WANTED TO FORGET IDA.
I THOUGHT, WITH TIME, I'D GET OVER HER.
BUT ...

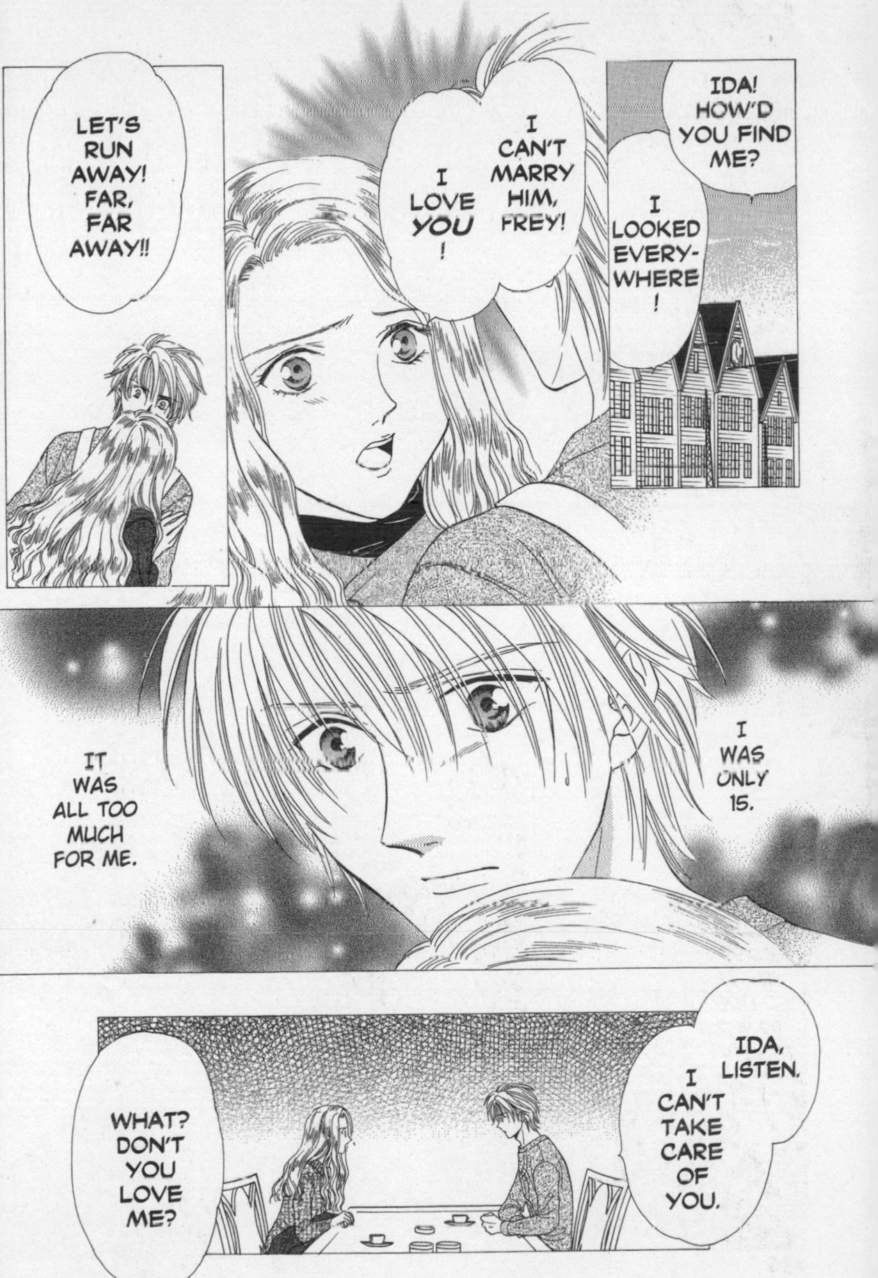
IDA! HOW'D YOU FIND ME?
I LOOKED EVERYWHERE!
I CAN'T MARRY HIM, FREY!
I LOVE YOU!
LET'S RUN AWAY! FAR, FAR AWAY!!
I WAS ONLY 15.
IT WAS ALL TOO MUCH FOR ME.
IDA, LISTEN.
I CAN'T TAKE CARE OF YOU.
WHAT? DON'T YOU LOVE ME?

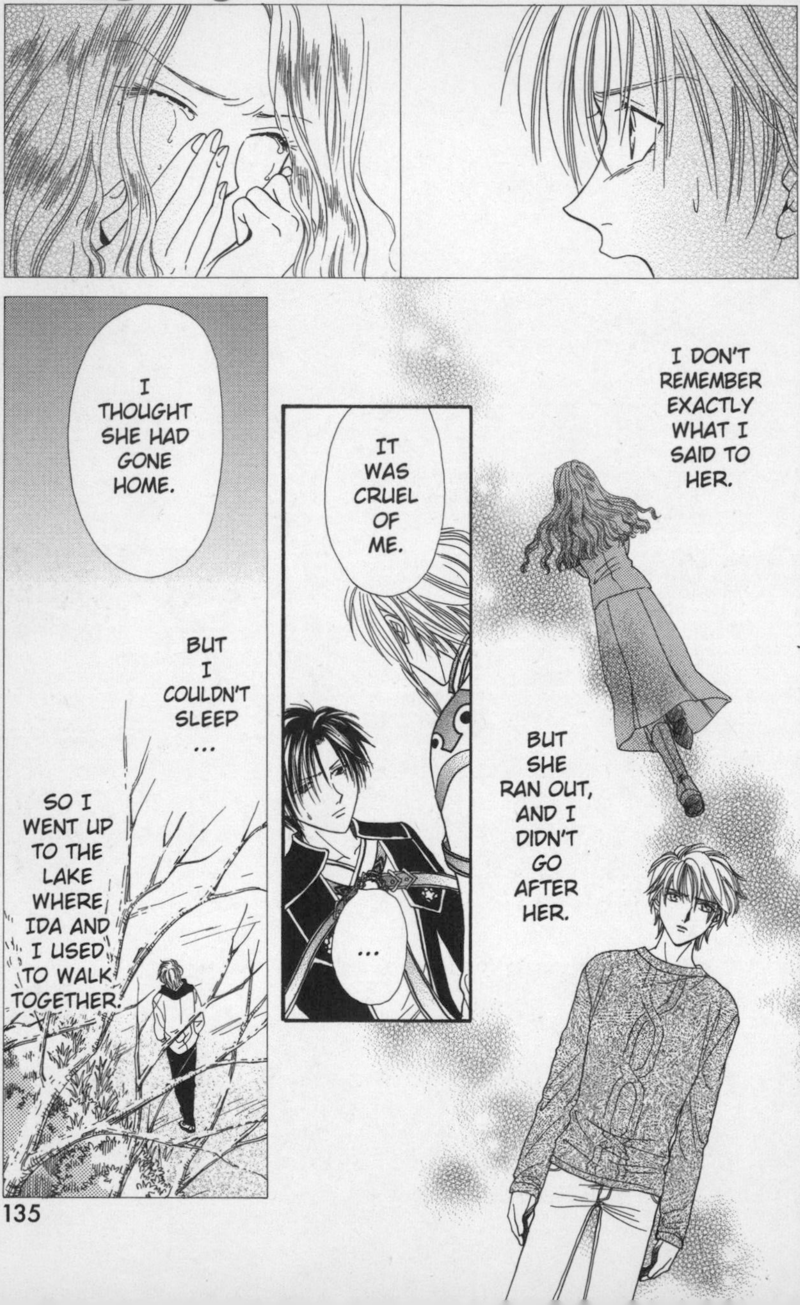
I DON'T REMEMBER EXACTLY WHAT I SAID TO HER.
BUT SHE RAN OUT, AND I DIDN'T GO AFTER HER.
IT WAS CRUEL OF ME.
...
I THOUGHT SHE HAD GONE HOME.
BUT I COULDN'T SLEEP ...
SO I WENT UP TO THE LAKE WHERE IDA AND I USED TO WALK TOGETHER.

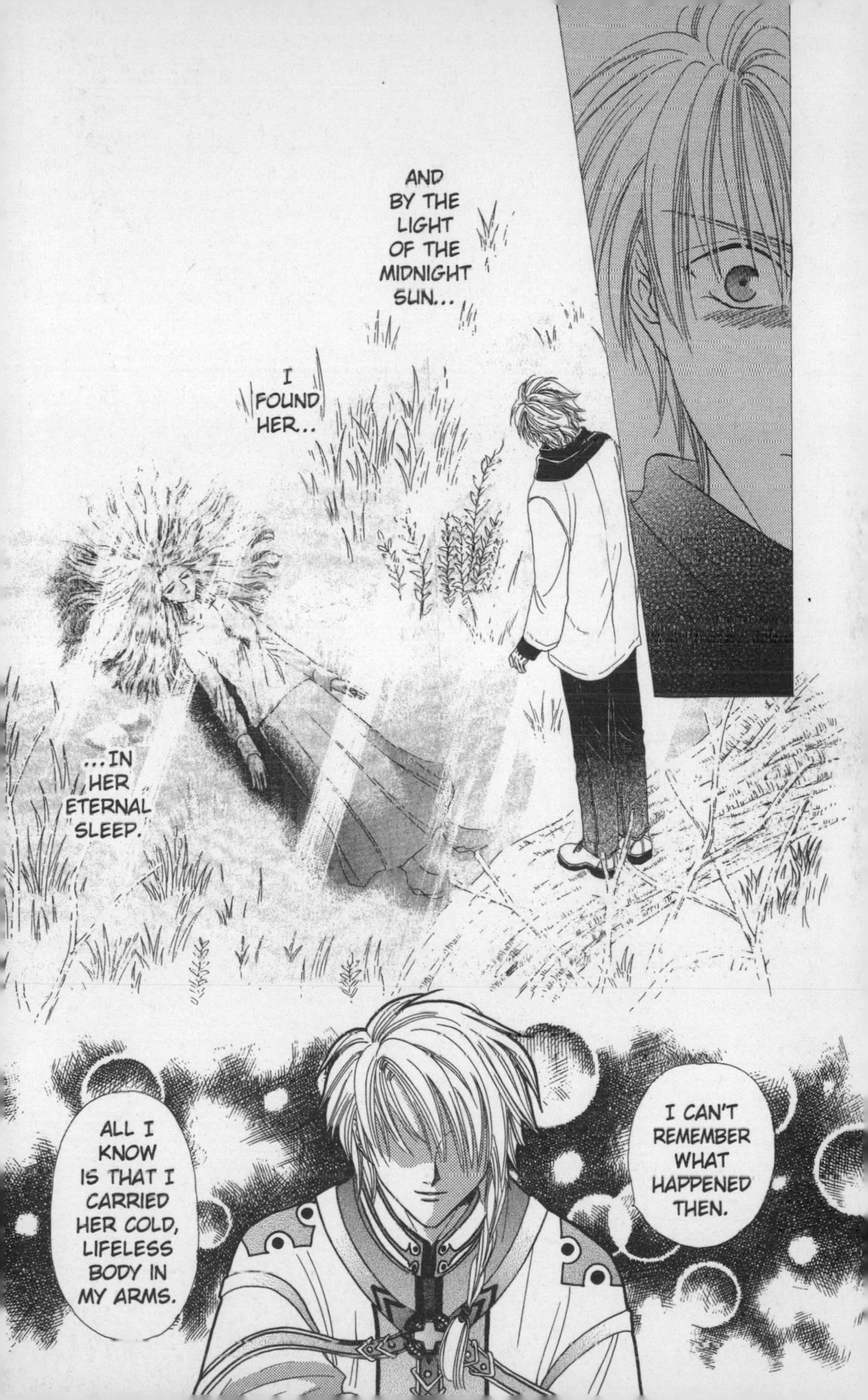
AND BY THE LIGHT OF THE MIDNIGHT SUN...
I FOUND HER..
...IN HER ETERNAL SLEEP.
I CAN'T REMEMBER WHAT HAPPENED THEN.
ALL I KNOW IS THAT I CARRIED HER COLD, LIFELESS BODY IN MY ARMS.

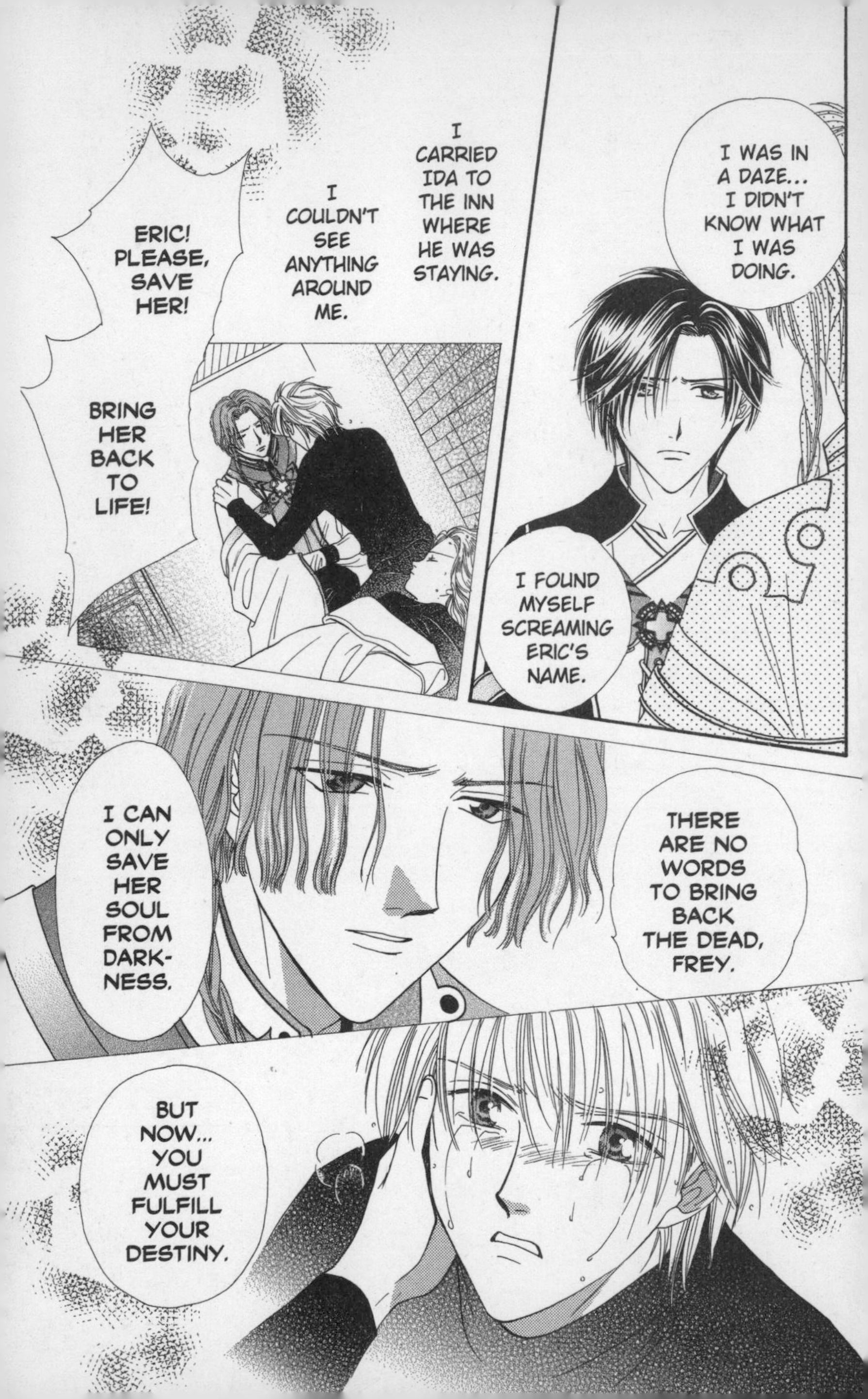
I WAS IN A DAZE... I DIDN'T KNOW WHAT I WAS DOING.
I FOUND MYSELF SCREAMING ERIC'S NAME.
I CARRIED IDA TO THE INN WHERE HE WAS STAYING.
I COULDN'T SEE ANYTHING AROUND ME.
ERIC! PLEASE, SAVE HER!
BRING HER BACK TO LIFE!
THERE ARE NO WORDS TO BRING BACK THE DEAD, FREY.
I CAN ONLY SAVE HER SOUL FROM DARK-NESS.
BUT NOW... YOU MUST FULFILL YOUR DESTINY.

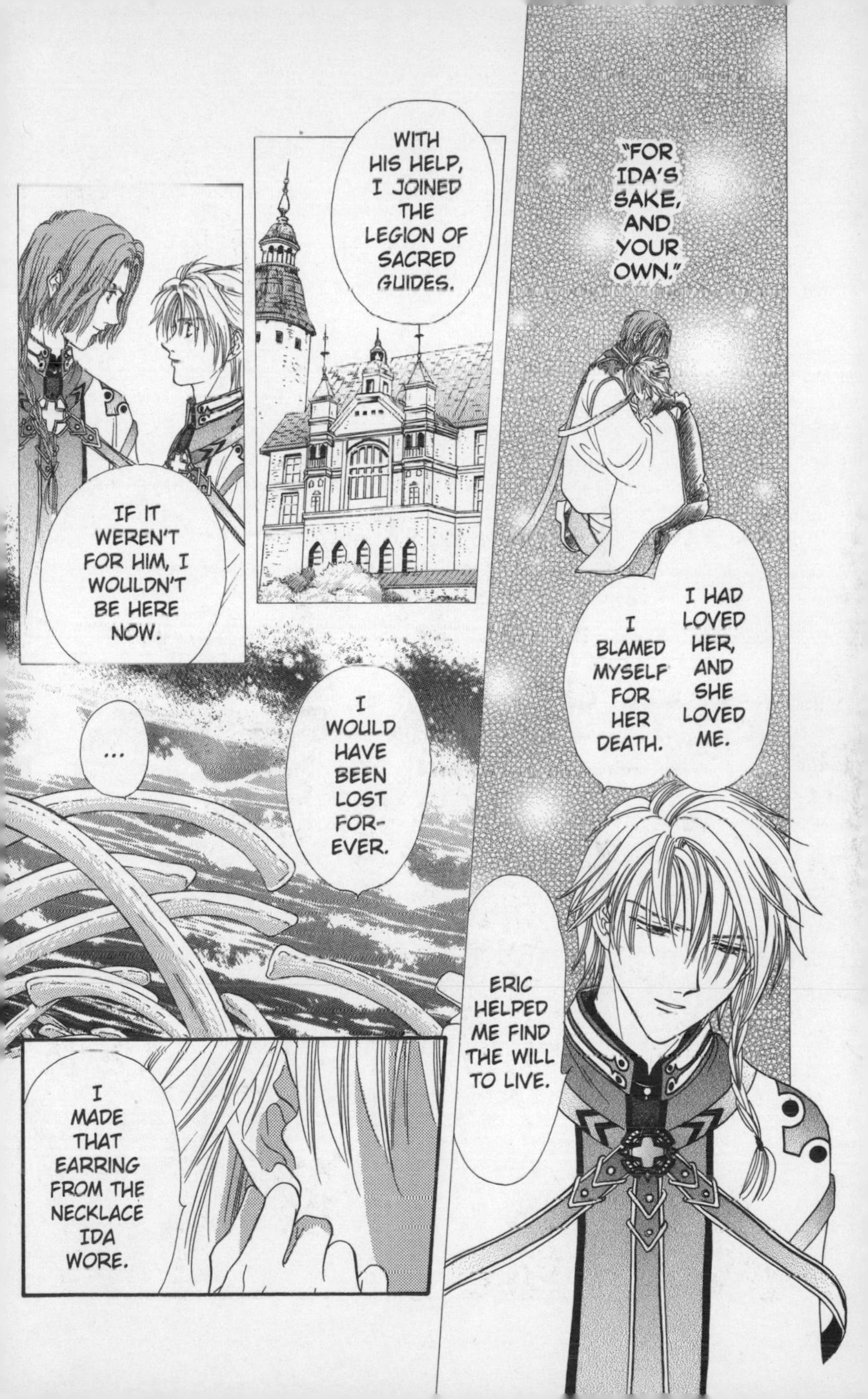
"FOR IDA'S SAKE, AND YOUR OWN."
I HAD LOVED HER, AND SHE LOVED ME.
I BLAMED MYSELF FOR HER DEATH.
ERIC HELPED ME FIND THE WILL TO LIVE.
WITH HIS HELP, I JOINED THE LEGION OF SACRED GUIDES.
IF IT WEREN'T FOR HIM, I WOULDN'T BE HERE NOW.
I WOULD HAVE BEEN LOST FOR-EVER.
...
I MADE THAT EARRING FROM THE NECKLACE IDA WORE.

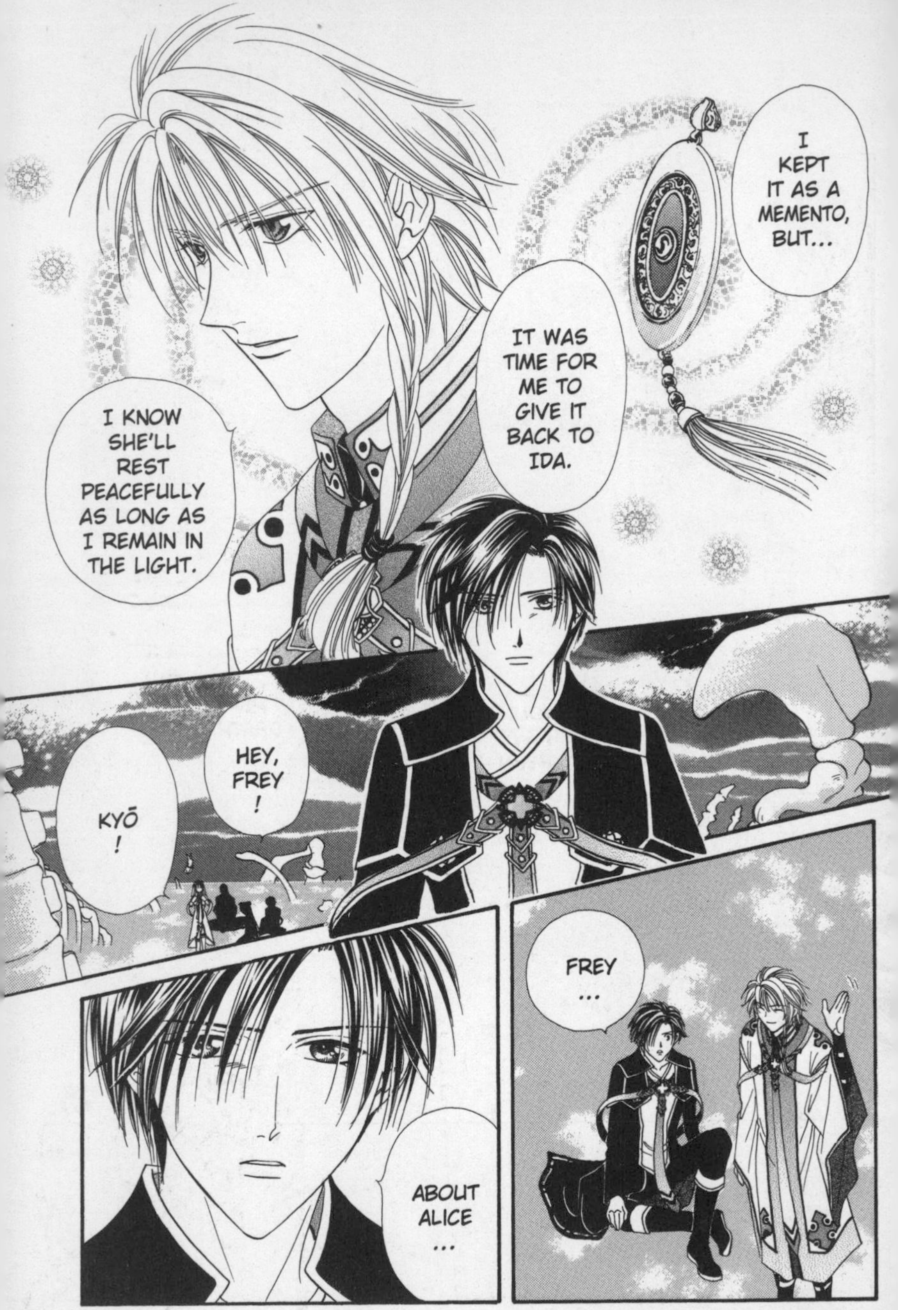
I KEPT IT AS A MEMENTO, BUT...
IT WAS TIME FOR ME TO GIVE IT BACK TO IDA.
I KNOW SHE'LL REST PEACEFULLY AS LONG AS I REMAIN IN THE LIGHT.
HEY, FREY!
KYŌ!
FREY ...
ABOUT ALICE ...

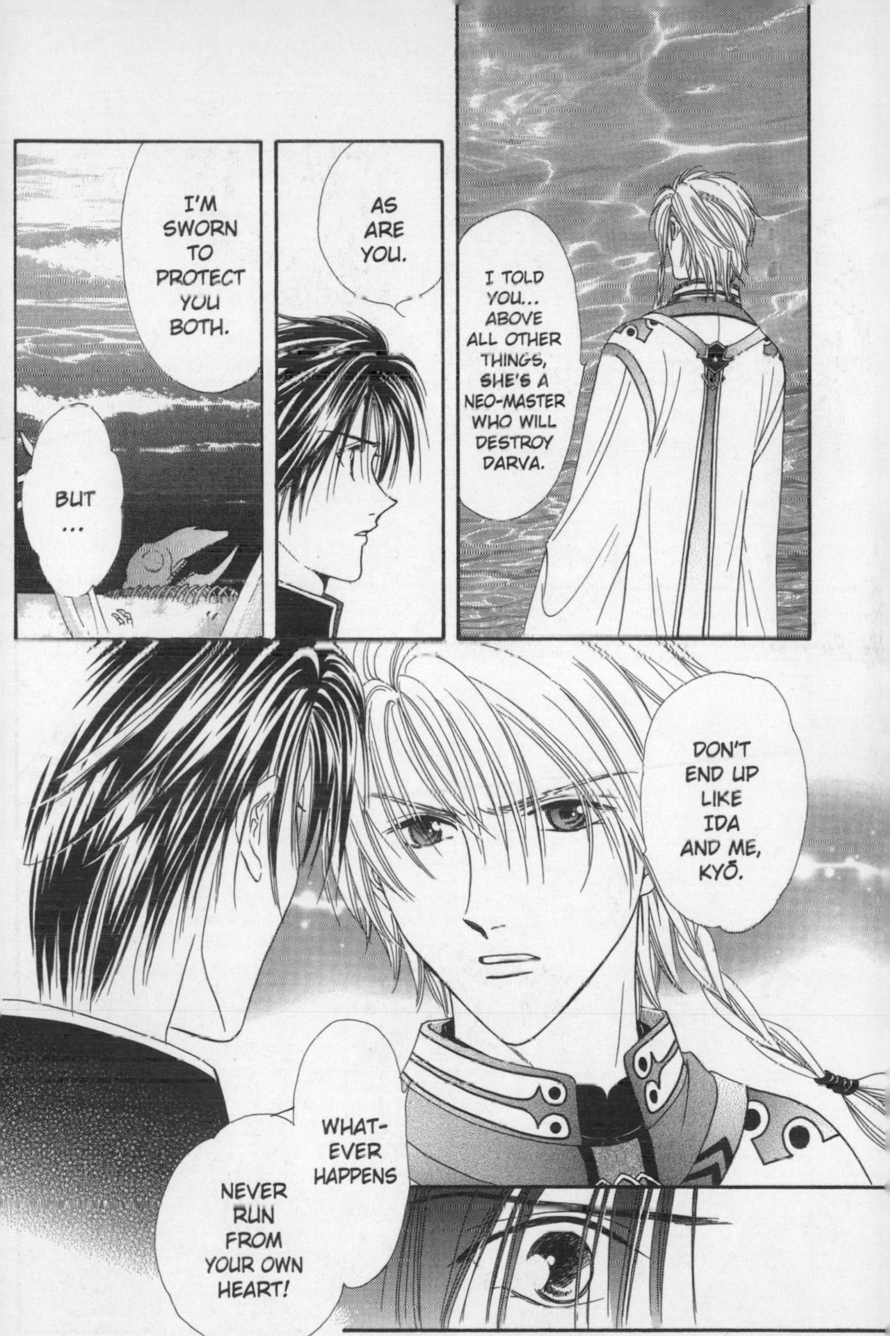
I TOLD YOU... ABOVE ALL OTHER THINGS, SHE'S A NEO-MASTER WHO WILL DESTROY DARVA.
AS ARE YOU.
I'M SWORN TO PROTECT YOU BOTH.
BUT ...
DON'T END UP LIKE IDA AND ME, KYŌ.
WHAT-EVER HAPPENS
NEVER RUN FROM YOUR OWN HEART!

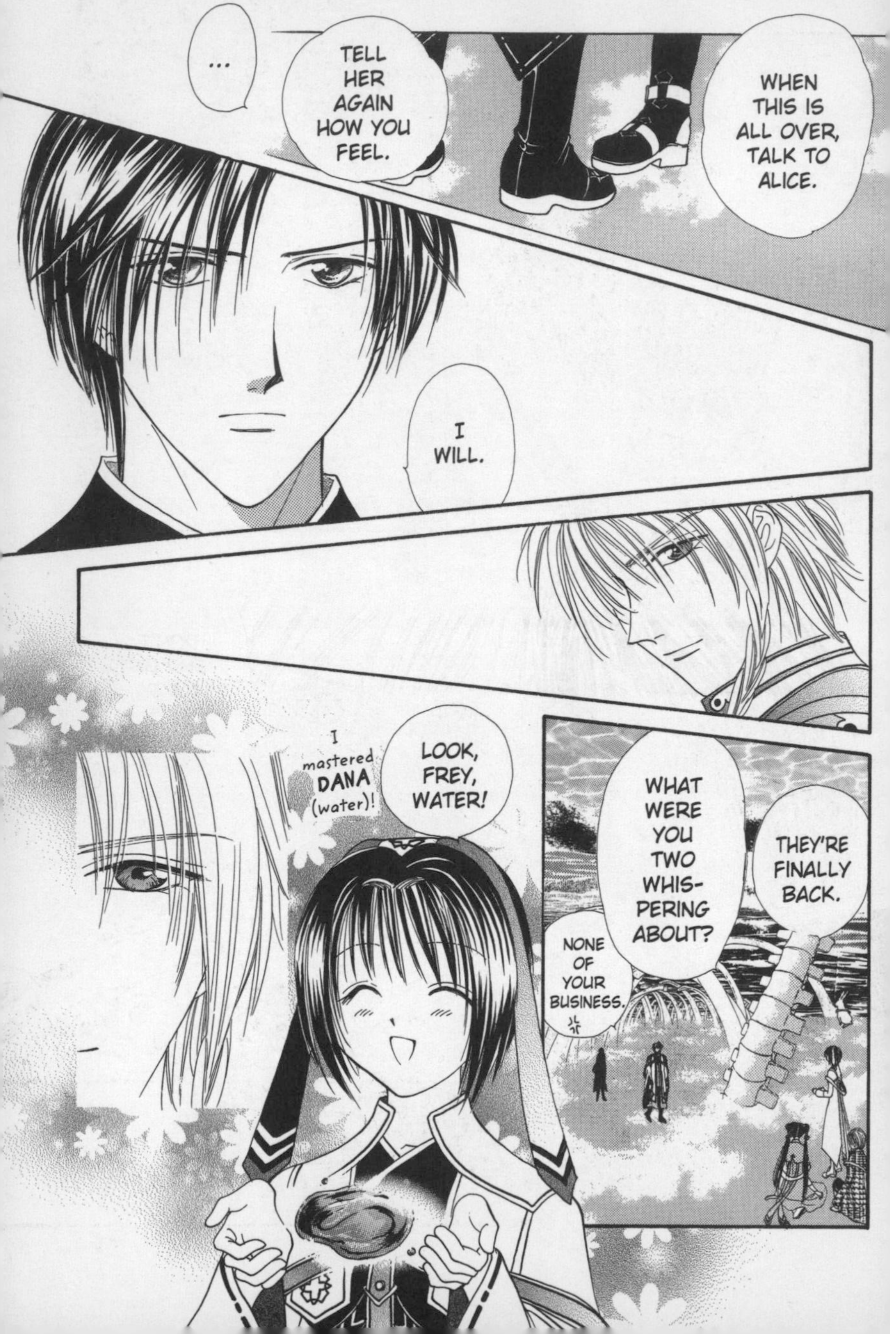
WHEN THIS IS ALL OVER, TALK TO ALICE.
TELL HER AGAIN HOW YOU FEEL.
...
I WILL.
THEY'RE FINALLY BACK.
WHAT WERE YOU TWO WHIS-PERING ABOUT?
NONE OF YOUR BUSINESS.
LOOK, FREY, WATER!
I mastered DANA (water)!

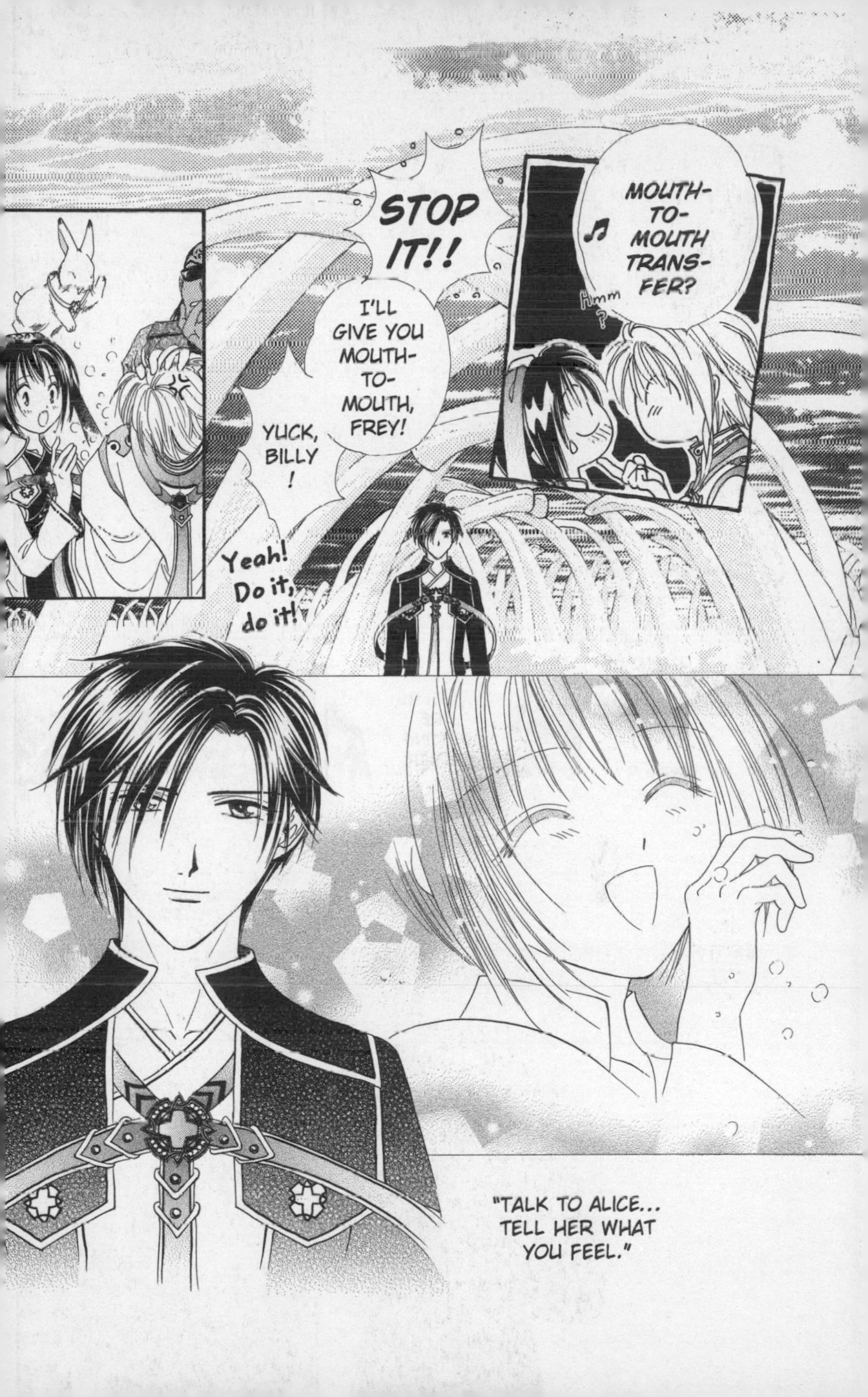

MOUTH-TO-MOUTH TRANSFER? ♪
Hmm?
STOP IT!!
I'LL GIVE YOU MOUTH-TO-MOUTH, FREY!
YUCK, BILLY!
Yeah! Do it, do it!
"TALK TO ALICE... TELL HER WHAT YOU FEEL."

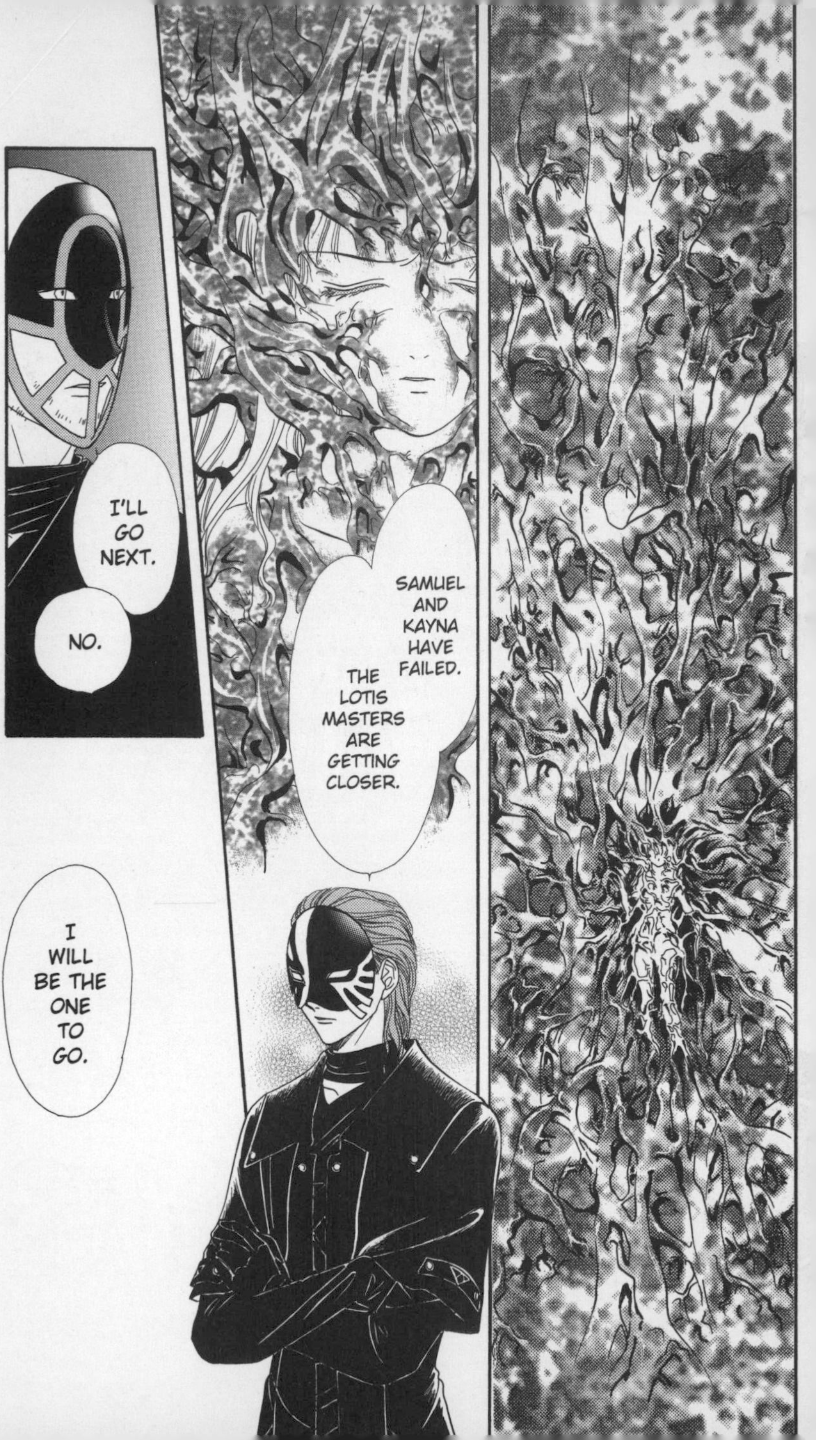
SAMUEL AND KAYNA HAVE FAILED.
THE LOTIS MASTERS ARE GETTING CLOSER.
I'LL GO NEXT.
NO.
I WILL BE THE ONE TO GO.

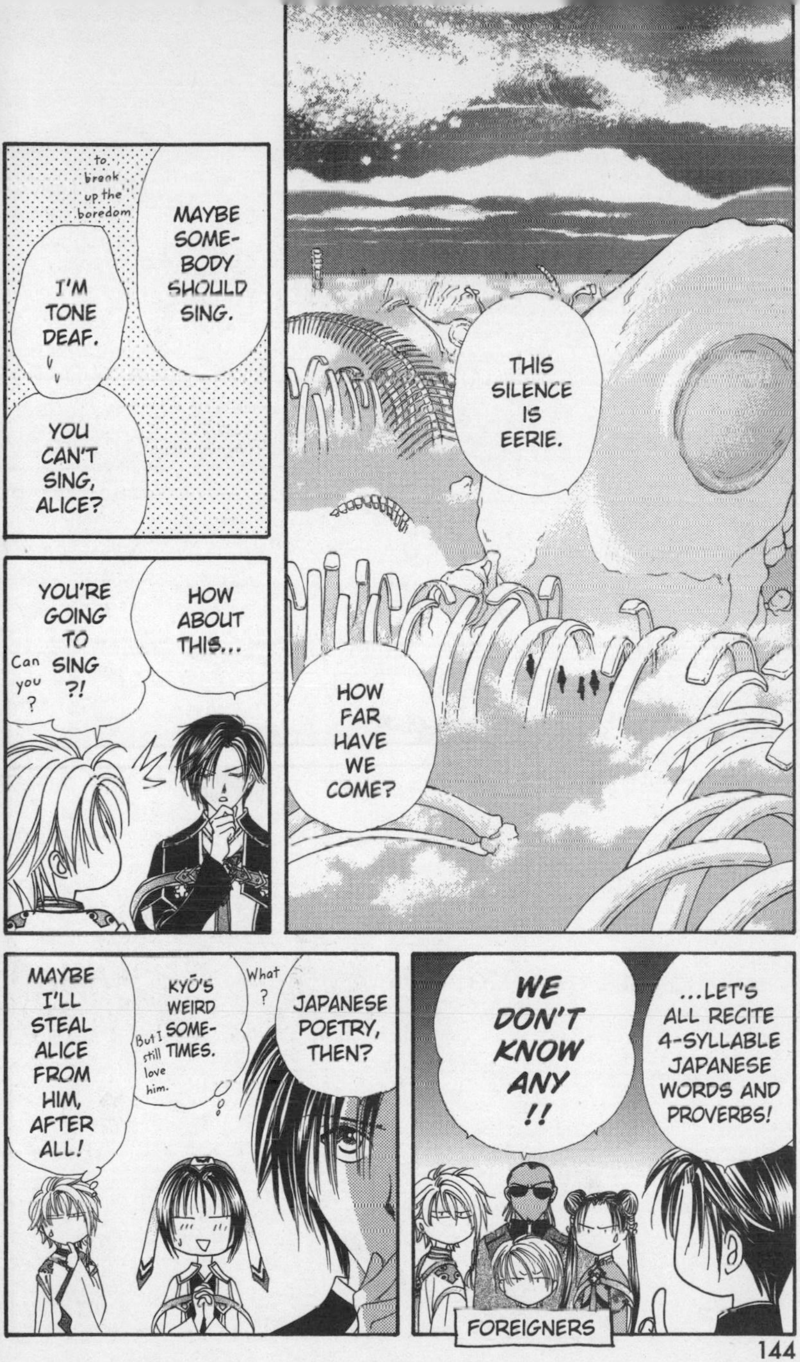
THIS SILENCE IS EERIE.
HOW FAR HAVE WE COME?
MAYBE SOME-BODY SHOULD SING.
to break up the boredom
I'M TONE DEAF.
YOU CAN'T SING, ALICE?
HOW ABOUT THIS...
YOU'RE GOING TO SING ?!
Can you ?
...LET'S ALL RECITE 4-SYLLABLE JAPANESE WORDS AND PROVERBS!
WE DON'T KNOW ANY !!
FOREIGNERS
JAPANESE POETRY, THEN?
What ?
KYŌ'S WEIRD SOME-TIMES.
But I still love him.
MAYBE I'LL STEAL ALICE FROM HIM, AFTER ALL!

HEY, MEI LIN, YOU'VE GOT A REALLY CUTE FIGURE.
You're pretty, too.
YOU SHOULD BE A MOVIE STAR.
WELL, I AM A STARLET.
HUH?! REALLY? COOL!
I HAVE AN AGENT IN SHANGHAI.
WHAT DO YOU DO, BILLY?
TRY TO GUESS.
BASKET-BALL PLAYER?
Kyō
D.J.!
Frey
I BET HE'S A BAR-TENDER...
Mei Lin
BOXER?
Chris
LAWYER!
Alice
BODY-GUARD!
Nyozeka
I'M A POSTAL WORKER.
HOW BORING!!

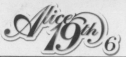

Now, when we went into the Metropolitan Building (my depiction), I planned to tell about the past, or Inner Heart, of all the characters, bad and good. But I changed my mind, because of space limitations, and because it might be good to leave something to the readers' imagination. So I'm not doing the stories of Billy and Mei Lin. I've focused on characters that are important to the development and meaning of the story. Billy is an African-American, so his story had a lot of possibilities, but if I'd made a mistake, people might have complained.
Mei Lin comes from a long line of Lotis Masters, so that was dangerous, too.
By the way, the heroine of *Bunny Heart*, the complete-in-one-issue story published in *Chu Chu*, is Po Lo Yuan. She's Mei Lin's ancestor. For those who haven't read it, it'll be included in the next volume of *Alice 19th*.
Right now, Mei Lin and her ancestor have the same hairstyle. I created it and played with it all on my own. None of my assistants noticed. Of course, they wouldn't.
Somehow, these 1/3-page spaces are gradually decreasing, and that's because there're more large frames! I wonder how the climax will turn out... There's one more volume to go. Please stay with us to the end. *Appare Jipangu!* is due to end, too. I hope I can finally put out the third volume after all

Later, then!

Ah, I'm dying to play video games...

02.12.

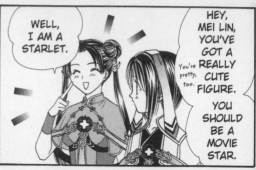

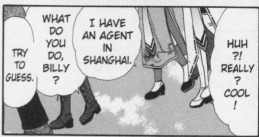

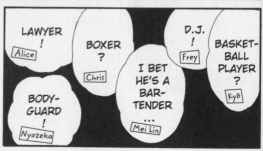

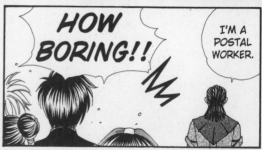

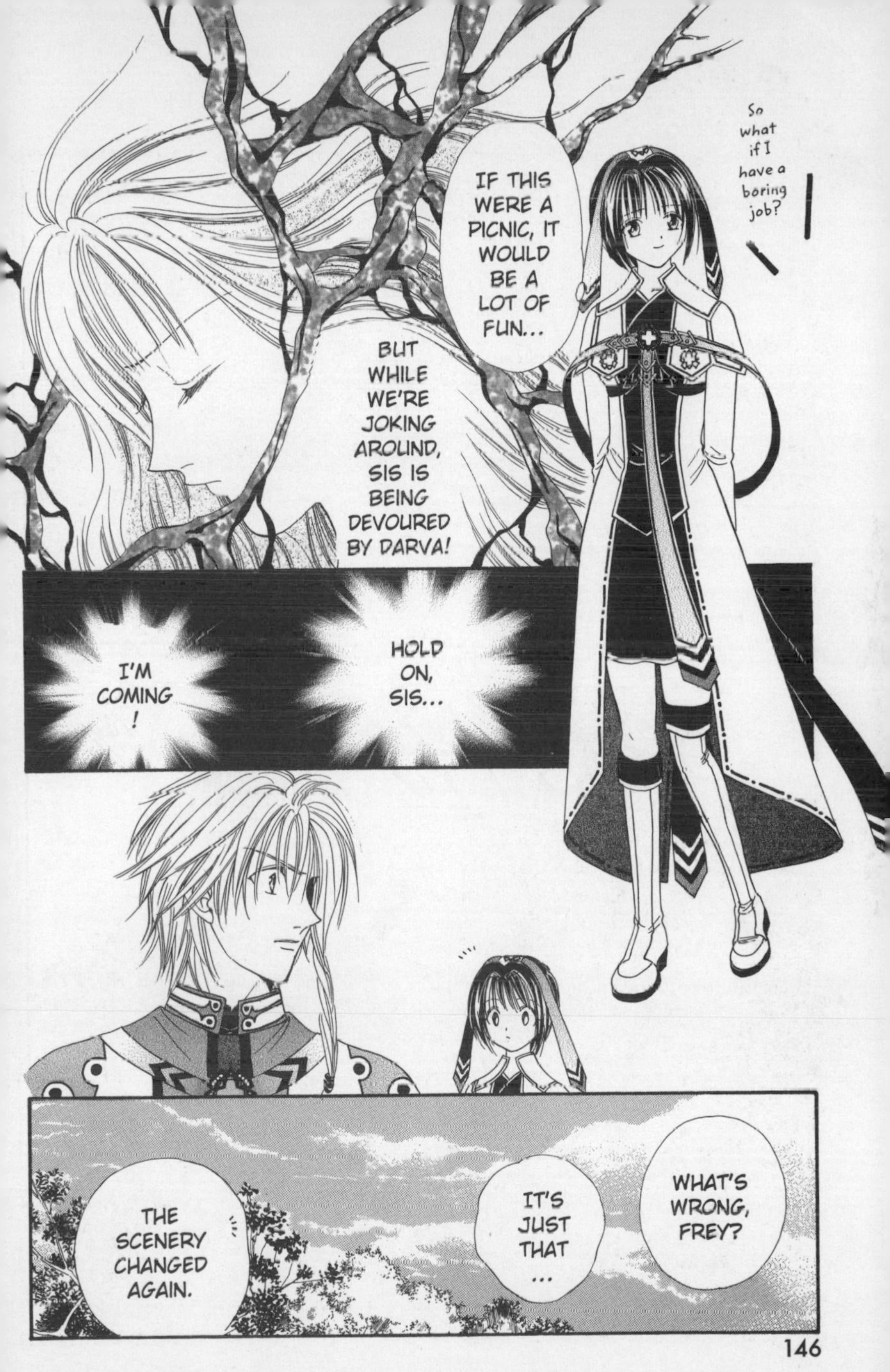
So what if I have a boring job?
IF THIS WERE A PICNIC, IT WOULD BE A LOT OF FUN...
BUT WHILE WE'RE JOKING AROUND, SIS IS BEING DEVOURED BY DARVA!
HOLD ON, SIS...
I'M COMING!
WHAT'S WRONG, FREY?
IT'S JUST THAT...
THE SCENERY CHANGED AGAIN.

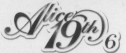

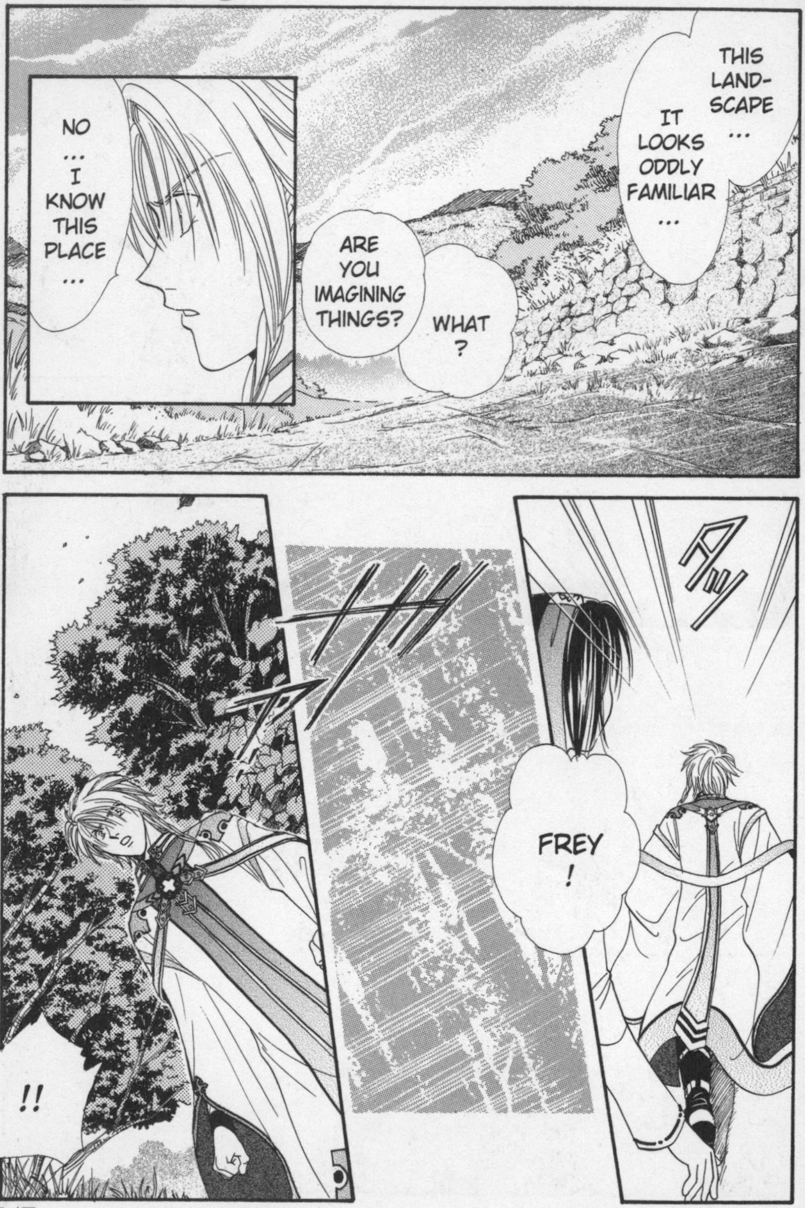
THIS LANDSCAPE ...
IT LOOKS ODDLY FAMILIAR ...
WHAT?
ARE YOU IMAGINING THINGS?
NO ... I KNOW THIS PLACE ...
FREY!
!!

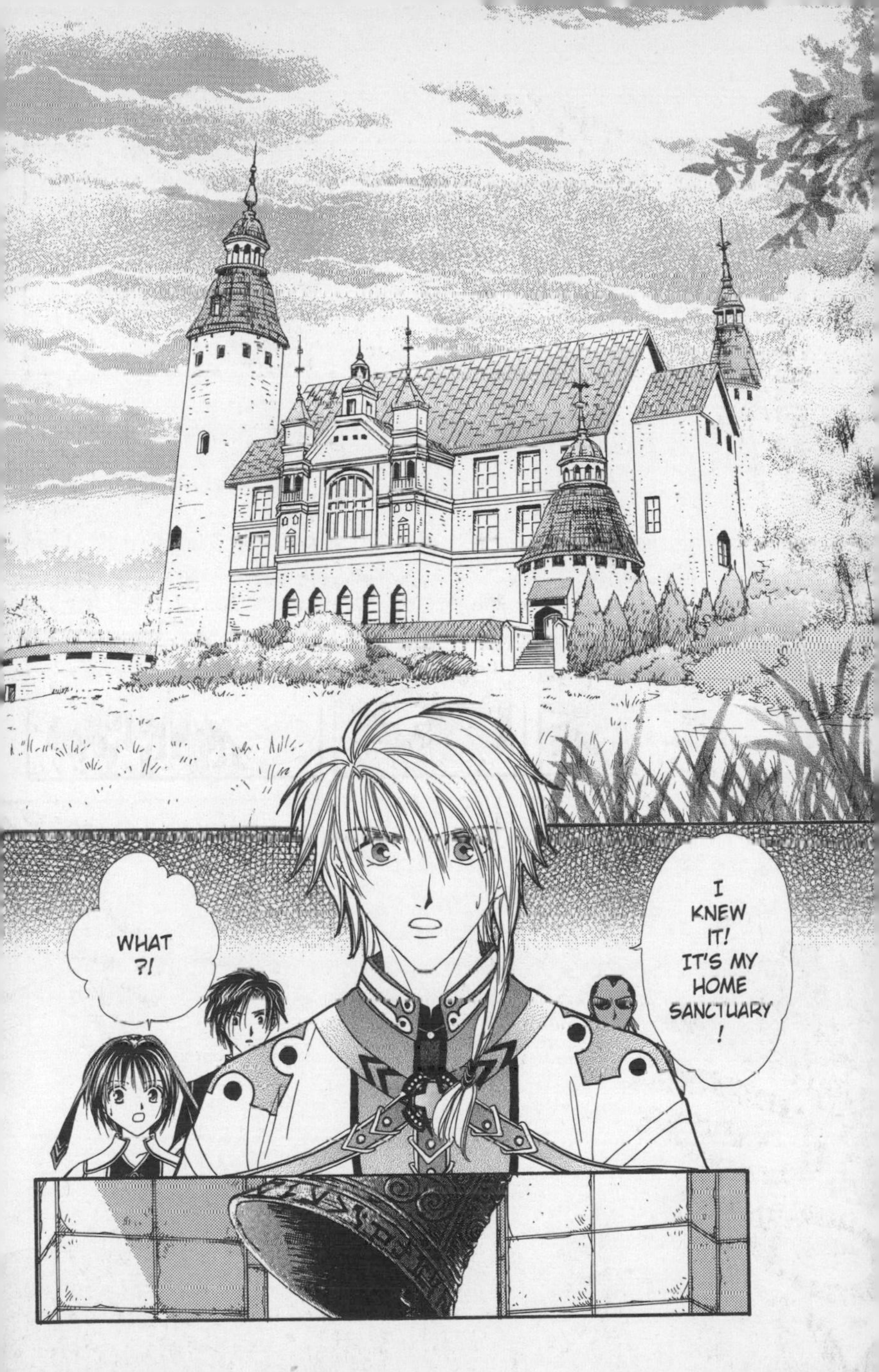
I KNEW IT! IT'S MY HOME SANCTUARY!
WHAT?!

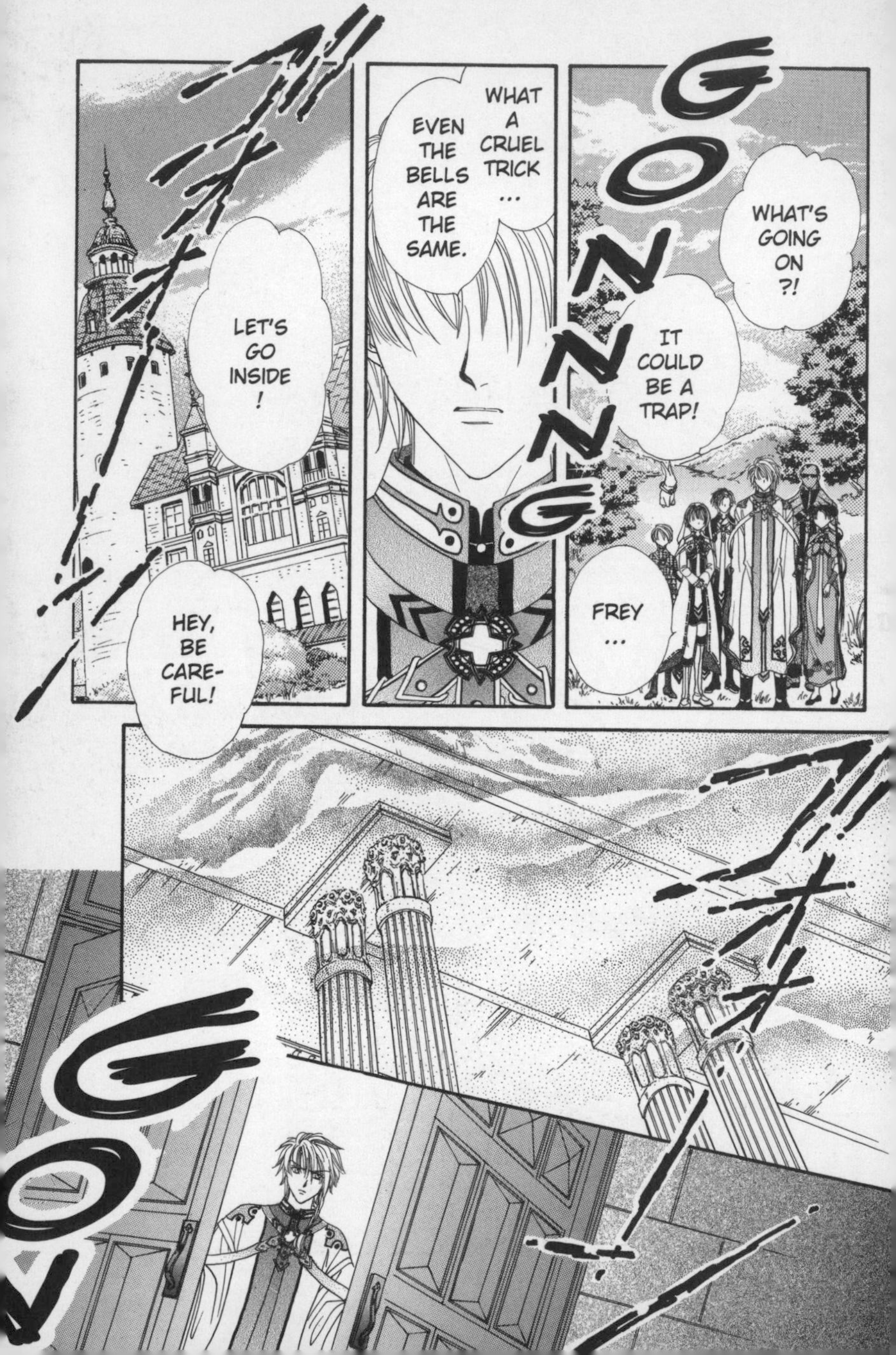
GONNNG
WHAT'S GOING ON ?!
IT COULD BE A TRAP!
FREY ...
WHAT A CRUEL TRICK ...
EVEN THE BELLS ARE THE SAME.
LET'S GO INSIDE !
HEY, BE CARE-FUL!
GO

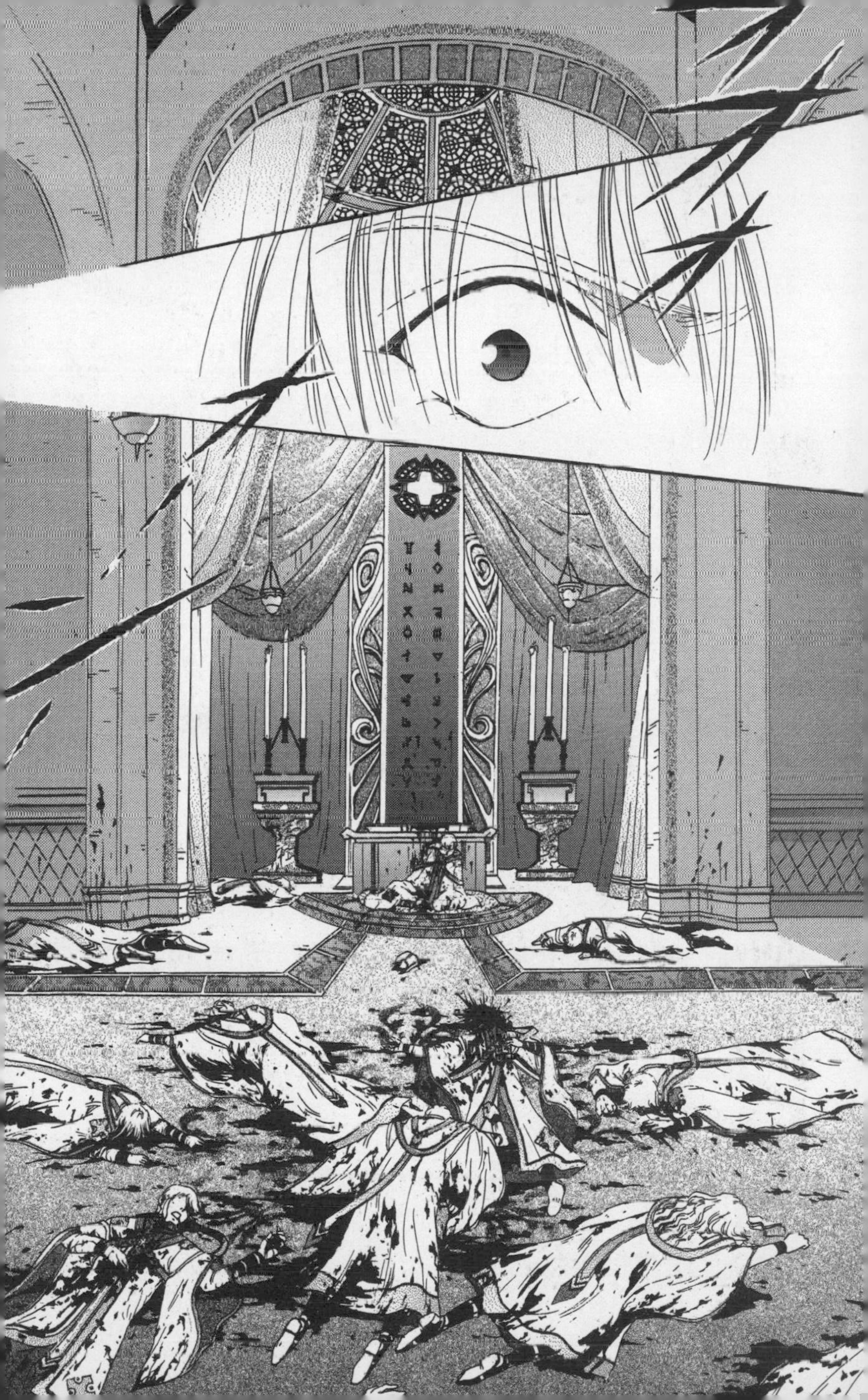

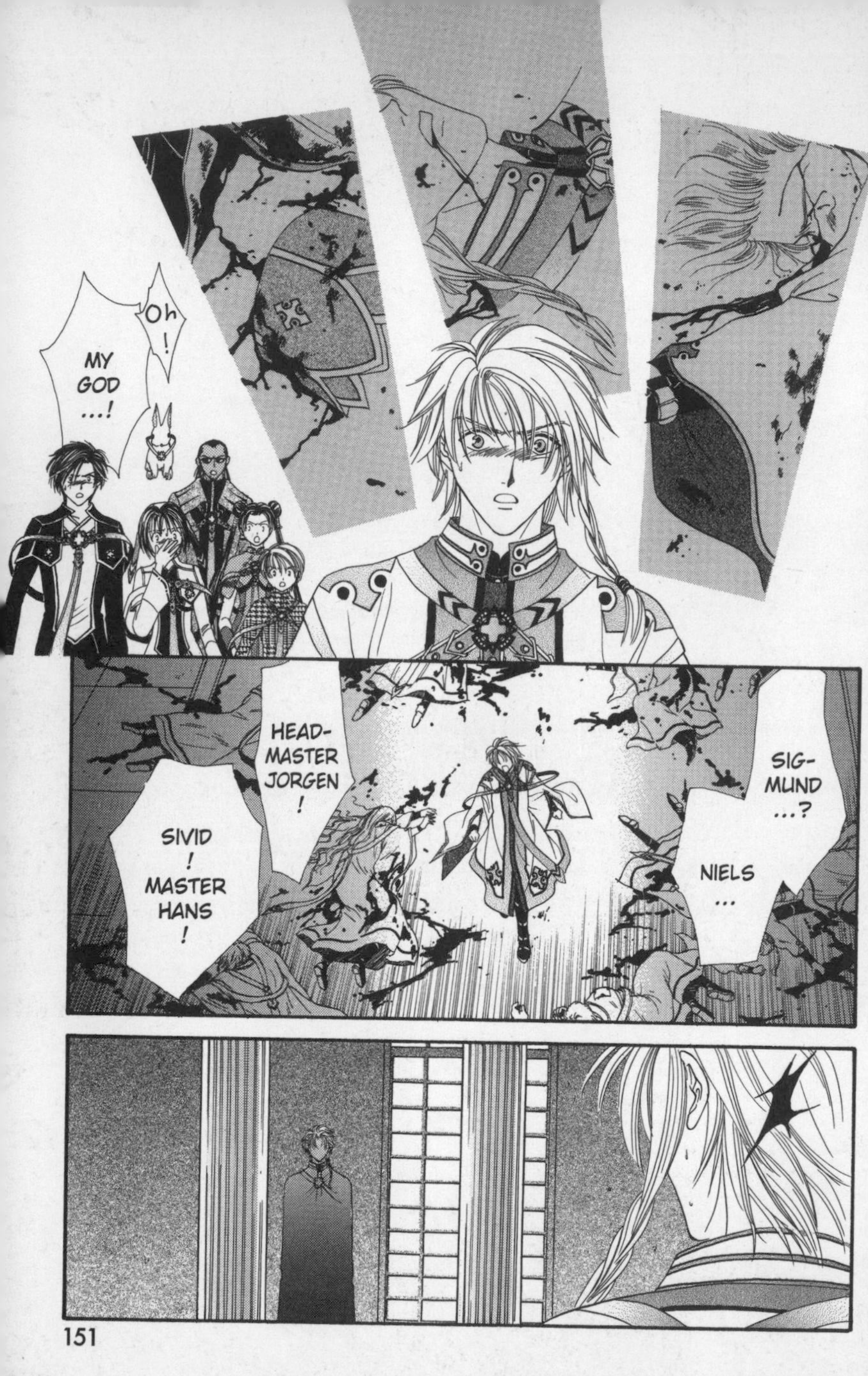
Oh!
MY GOD ...!
SIG-MUND ...?
NIELS ...
HEAD-MASTER JORGEN!
SIVID! MASTER HANS!

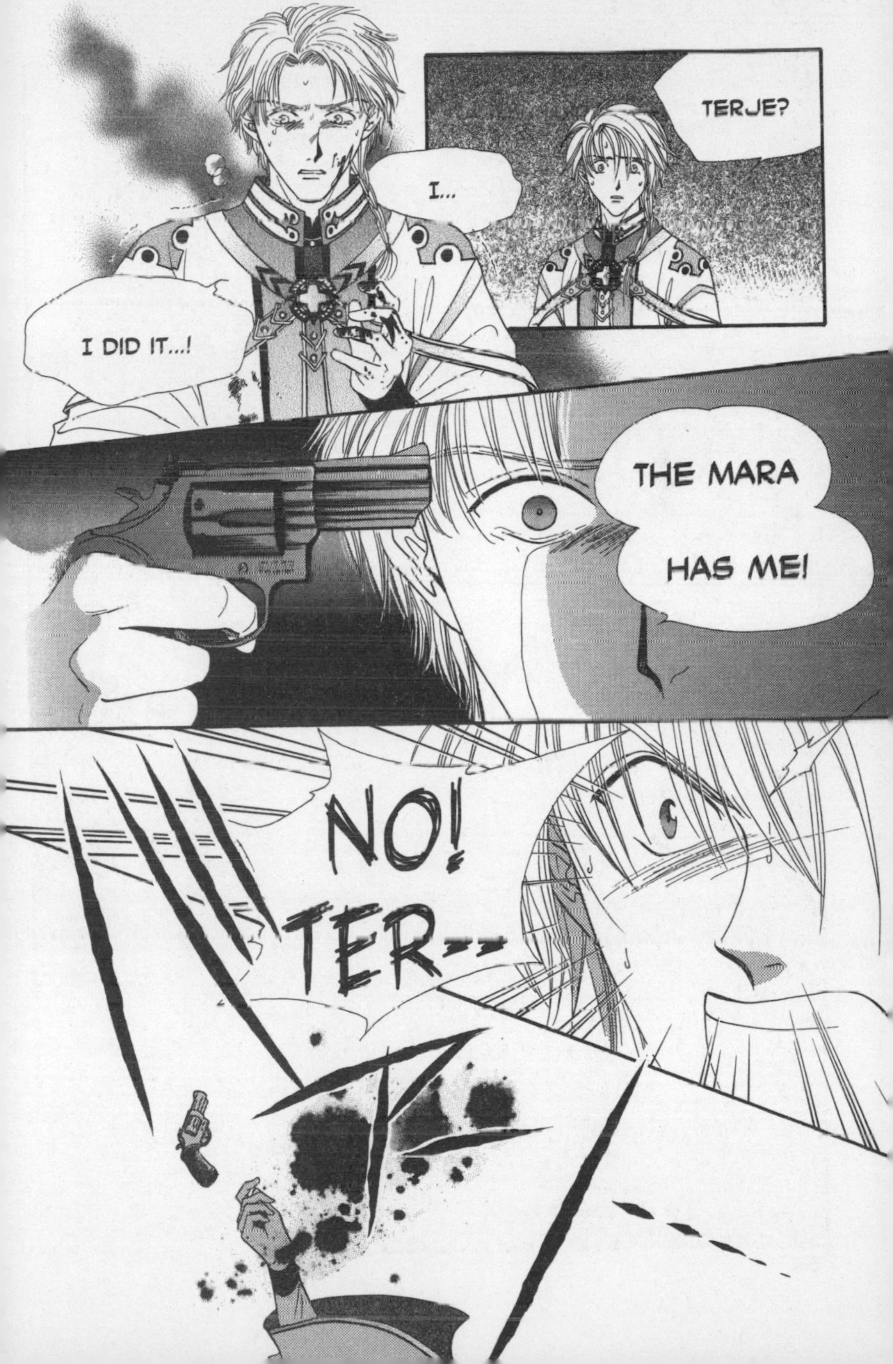
TERJE?
I...
I DID IT...!
THE MARA HAS ME!
NO! TER--

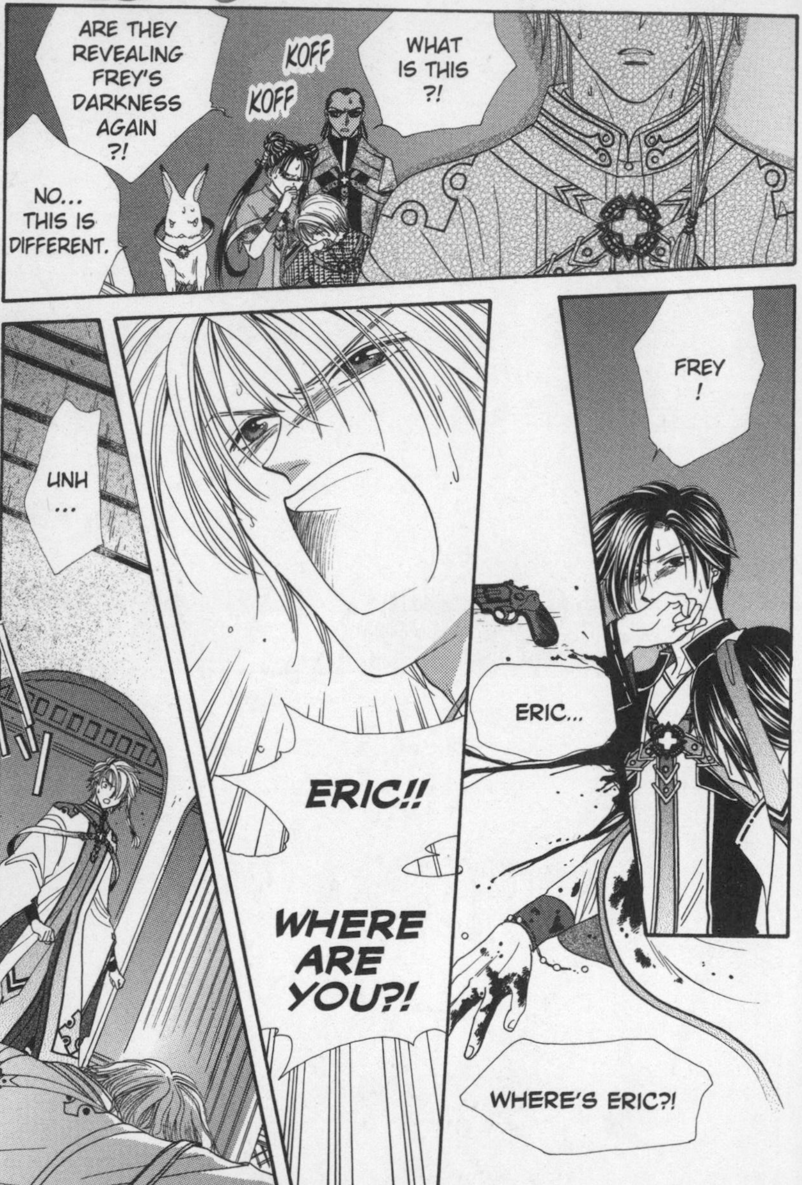
WHAT IS THIS ?!
KOFF
KOFF
ARE THEY REVEALING FREY'S DARKNESS AGAIN ?!
NO... THIS IS DIFFERENT.
FREY !
ERIC...
WHERE'S ERIC?!
ERIC!!
WHERE ARE YOU?!
UNH ...

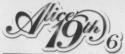

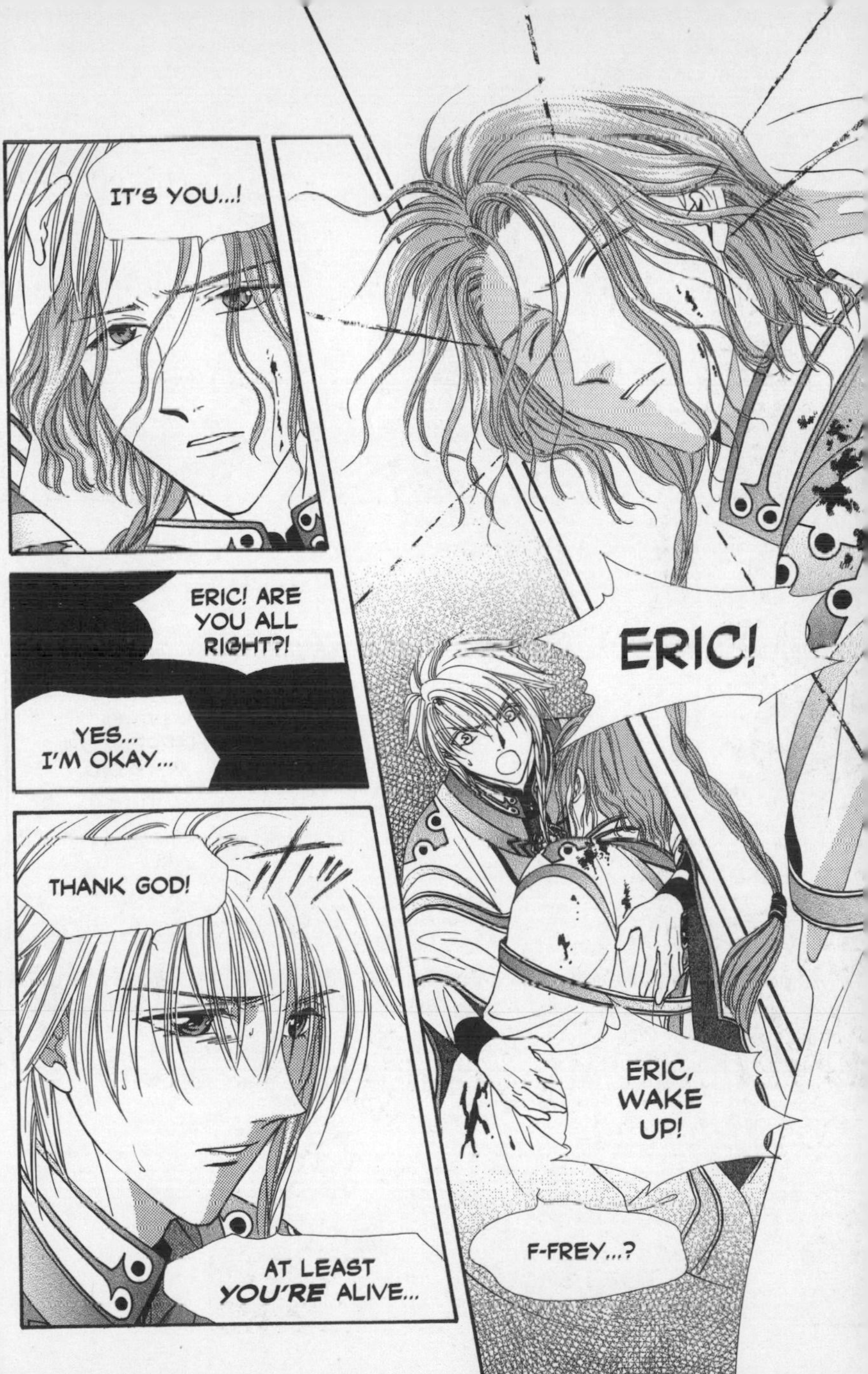
ERIC!
ERIC, WAKE UP!
F-FREY...?
IT'S YOU...!
ERIC! ARE YOU ALL RIGHT?!
YES... I'M OKAY...
THANK GOD!
AT LEAST *YOU'RE* ALIVE...

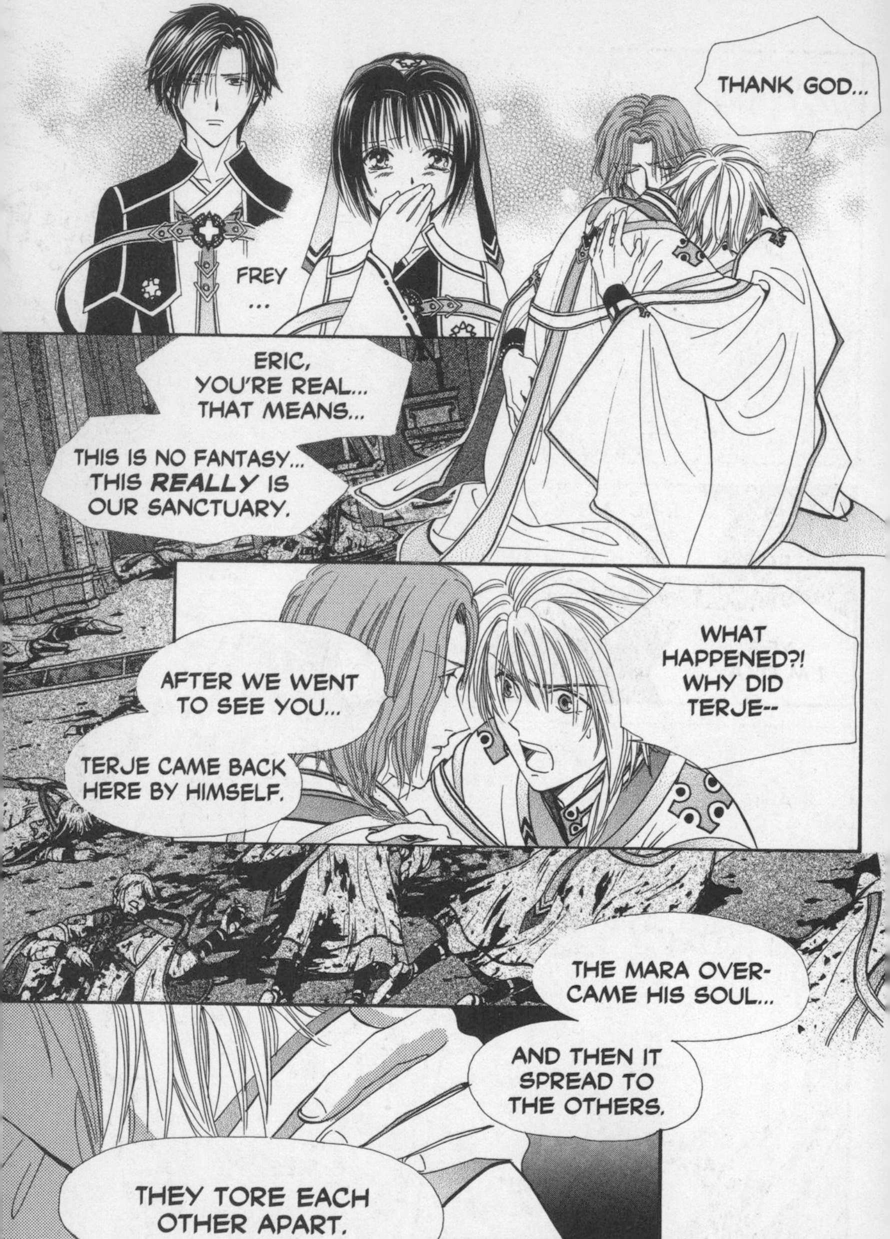
THANK GOD...
FREY ...
ERIC, YOU'RE REAL... THAT MEANS...
THIS IS NO FANTASY... THIS **REALLY** IS OUR SANCTUARY.
WHAT HAPPENED?! WHY DID TERJE--
AFTER WE WENT TO SEE YOU...
TERJE CAME BACK HERE BY HIMSELF.
THE MARA OVER-CAME HIS SOUL...
AND THEN IT SPREAD TO THE OTHERS.
THEY TORE EACH OTHER APART.

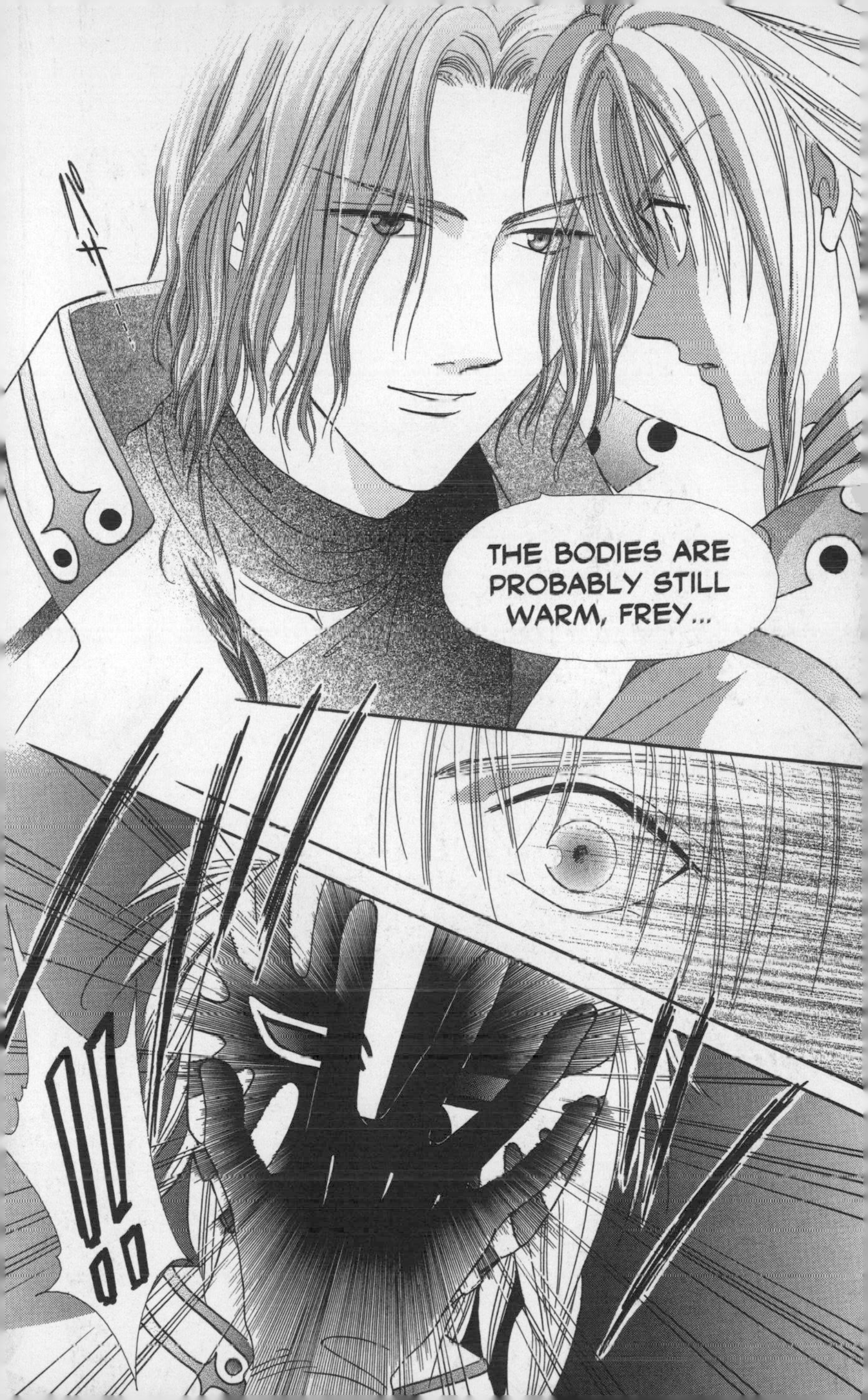
THE BODIES ARE PROBABLY STILL WARM, FREY...

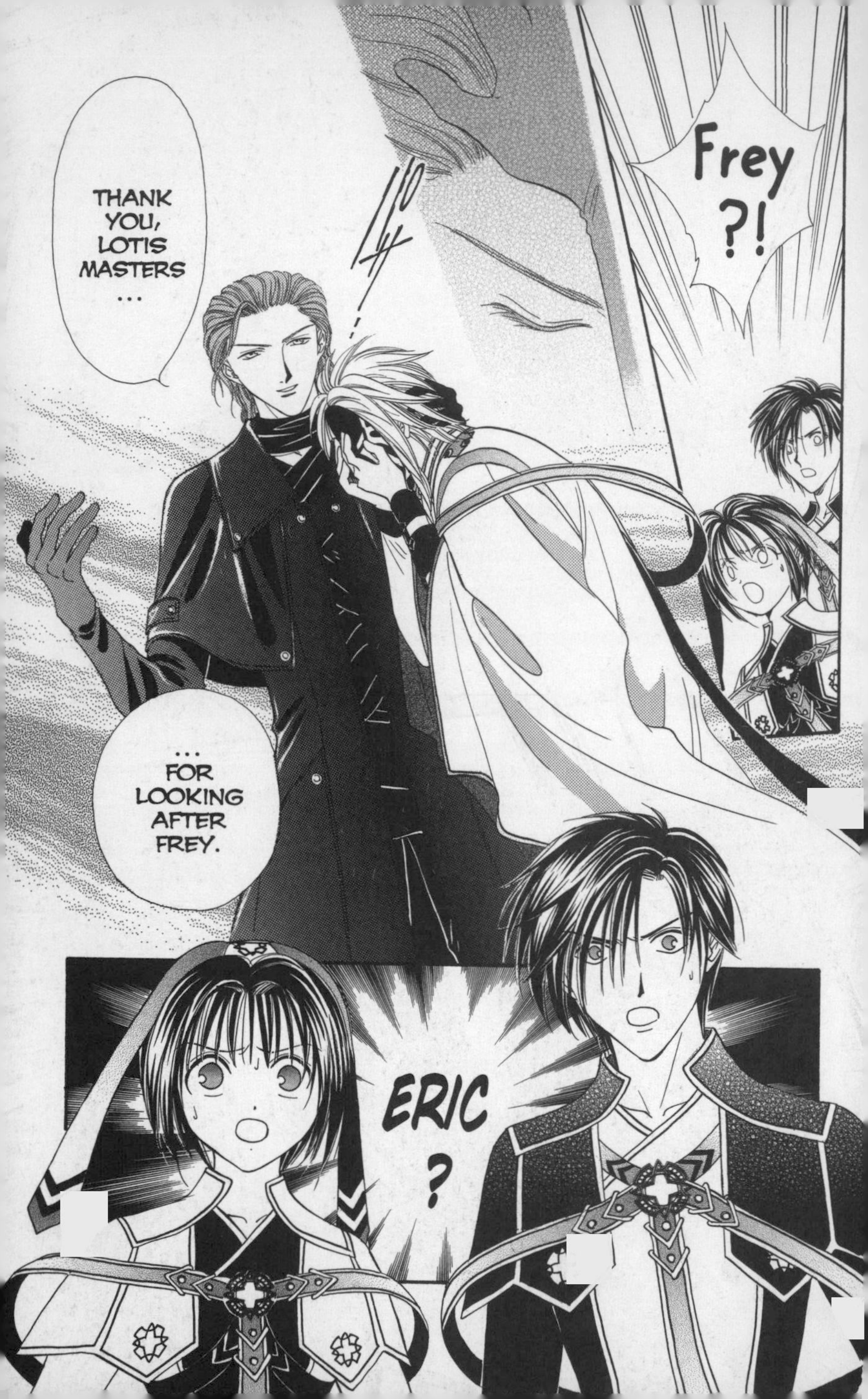
Frey ?!
THANK YOU, LOTIS MASTERS ...
... FOR LOOKING AFTER FREY.
ERIC ?

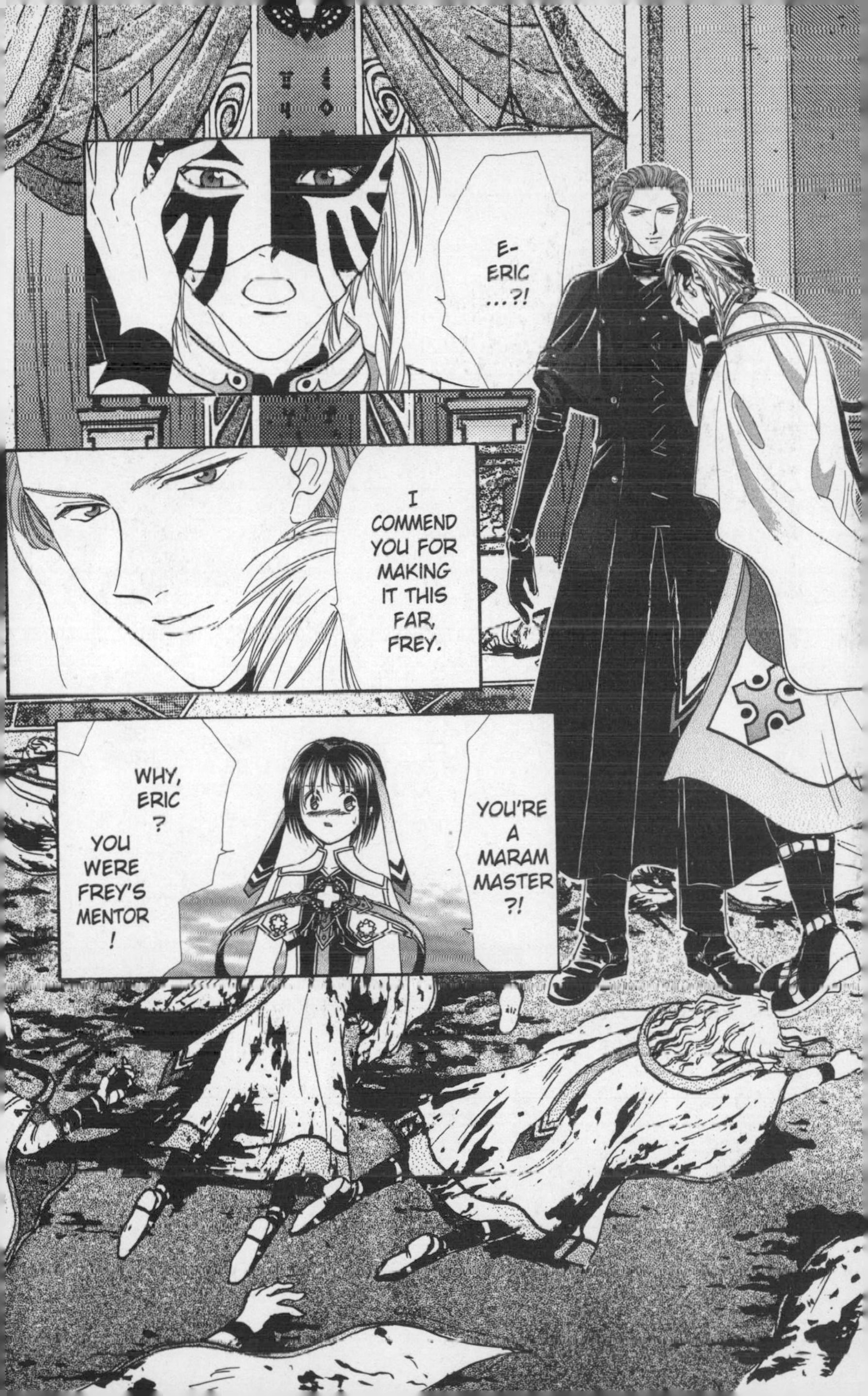
E-ERIC...?!
I COMMEND YOU FOR MAKING IT THIS FAR, FREY.
YOU'RE A MARAM MASTER?!
WHY, ERIC?
YOU WERE FREY'S MENTOR!

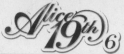

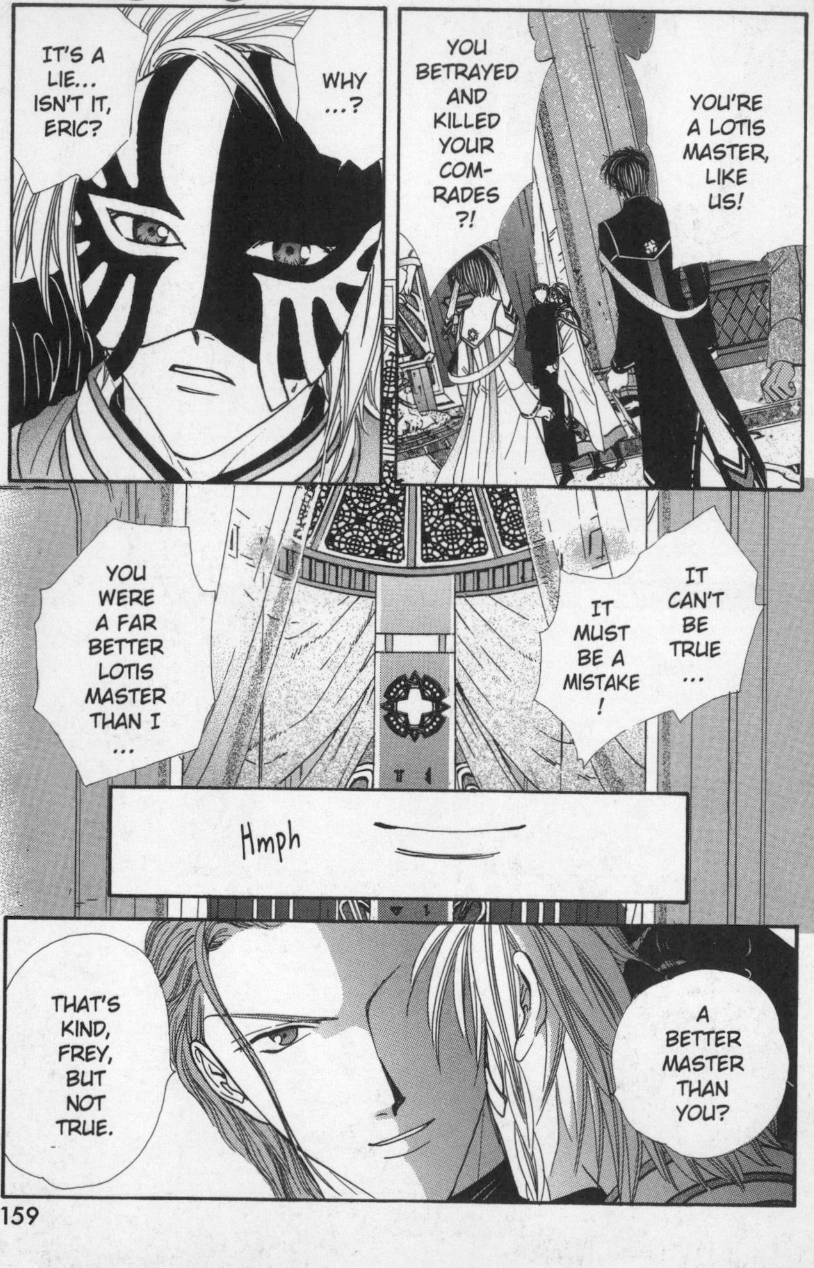
YOU'RE A LOTIS MASTER, LIKE US!
YOU BETRAYED AND KILLED YOUR COM-RADES?!
WHY...?
IT'S A LIE... ISN'T IT, ERIC?
IT CAN'T BE TRUE...
IT MUST BE A MISTAKE!
YOU WERE A FAR BETTER LOTIS MASTER THAN I...
Hmph
A BETTER MASTER THAN YOU?
THAT'S KIND, FREY, BUT NOT TRUE.

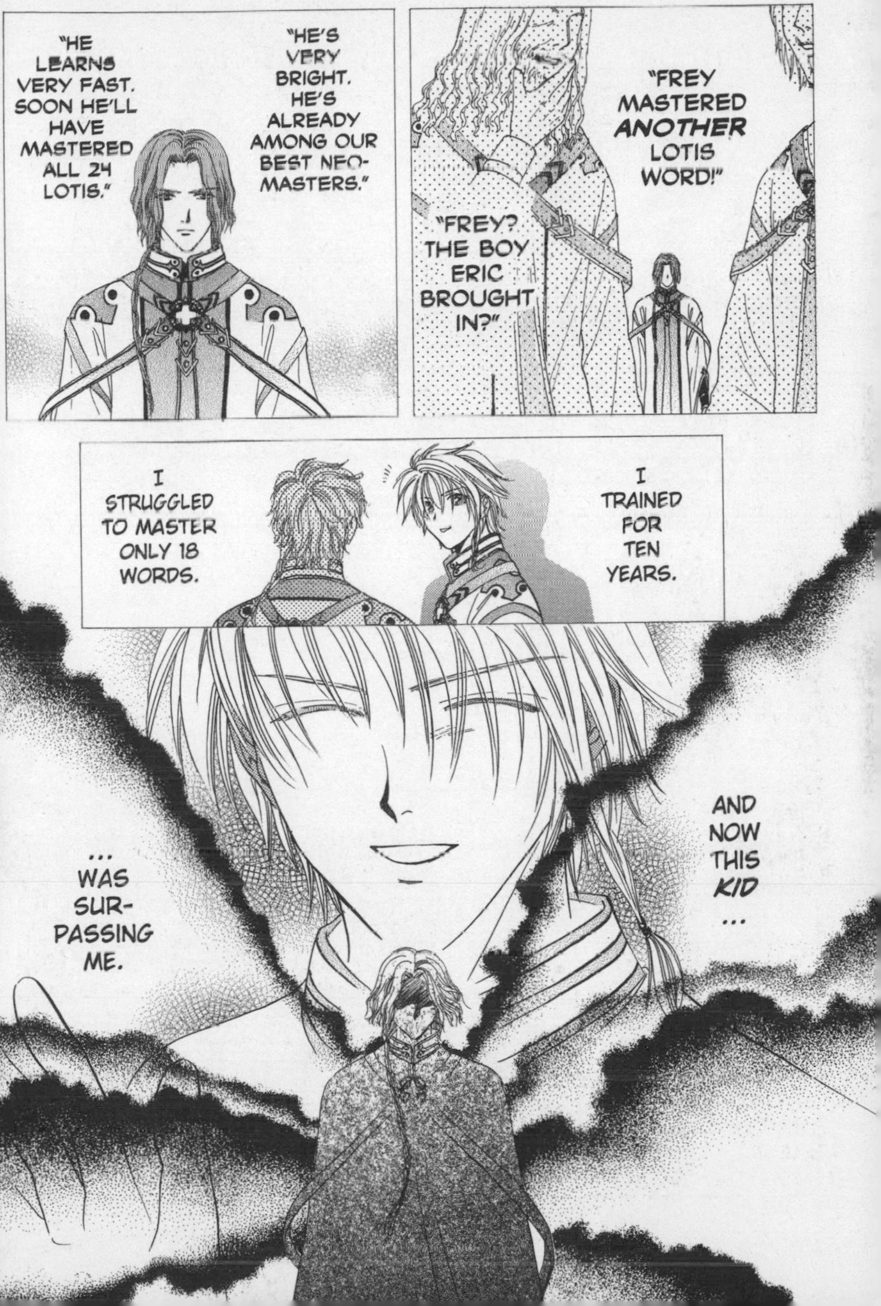
"FREY MASTERED *ANOTHER* LOTIS WORD!"
"FREY? THE BOY ERIC BROUGHT IN?"
"HE'S VERY BRIGHT. HE'S ALREADY AMONG OUR BEST NEO-MASTERS."
"HE LEARNS VERY FAST. SOON HE'LL HAVE MASTERED ALL 24 LOTIS."
I TRAINED FOR TEN YEARS.
I STRUGGLED TO MASTER ONLY 18 WORDS.
AND NOW THIS *KID* ...
... WAS SUR-PASSING ME.

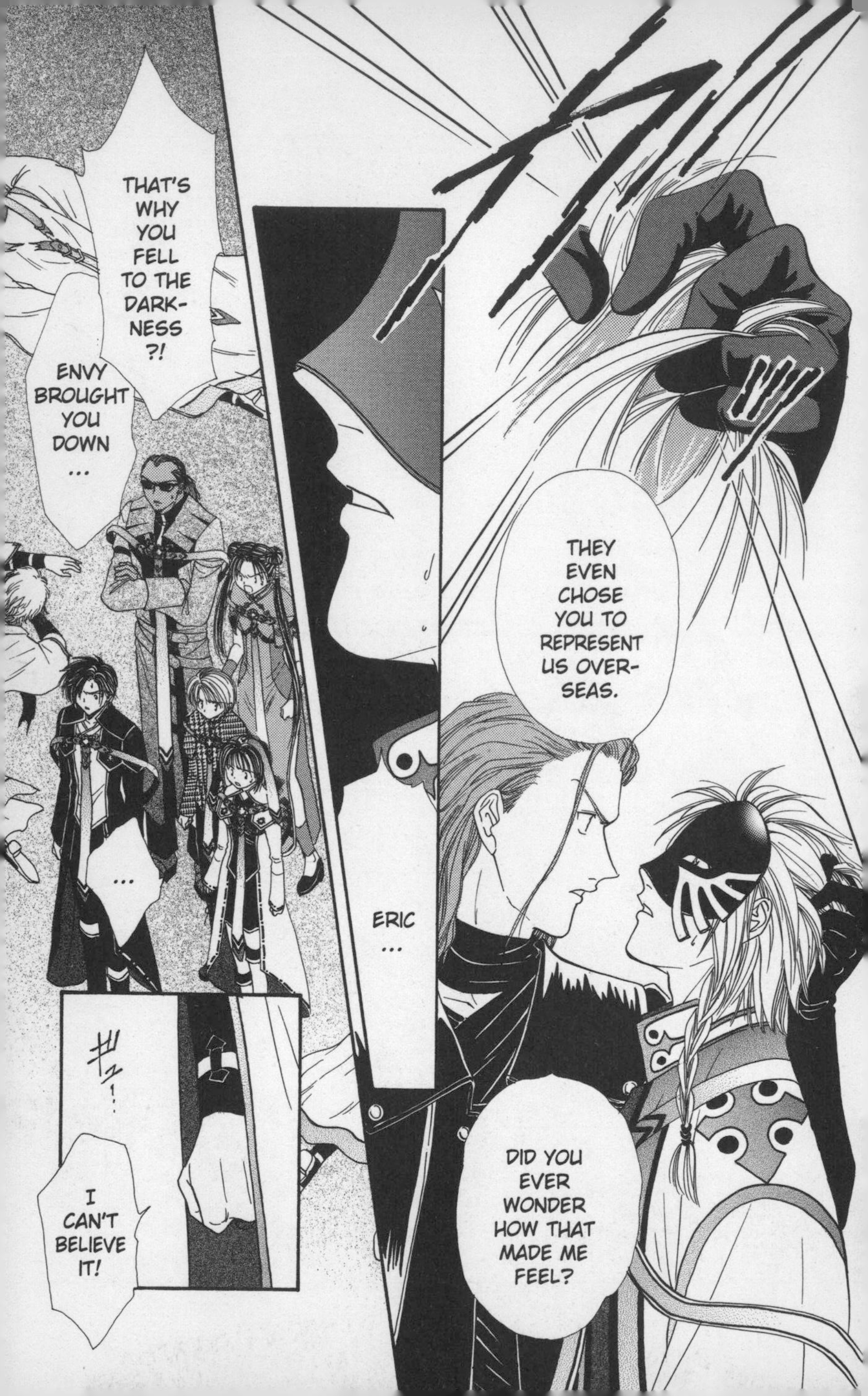
THEY EVEN CHOSE YOU TO REPRESENT US OVER-SEAS.
DID YOU EVER WONDER HOW THAT MADE ME FEEL?
ERIC ...
THAT'S WHY YOU FELL TO THE DARK-NESS ?!
ENVY BROUGHT YOU DOWN ...
...
ギュ
I CAN'T BELIEVE IT!

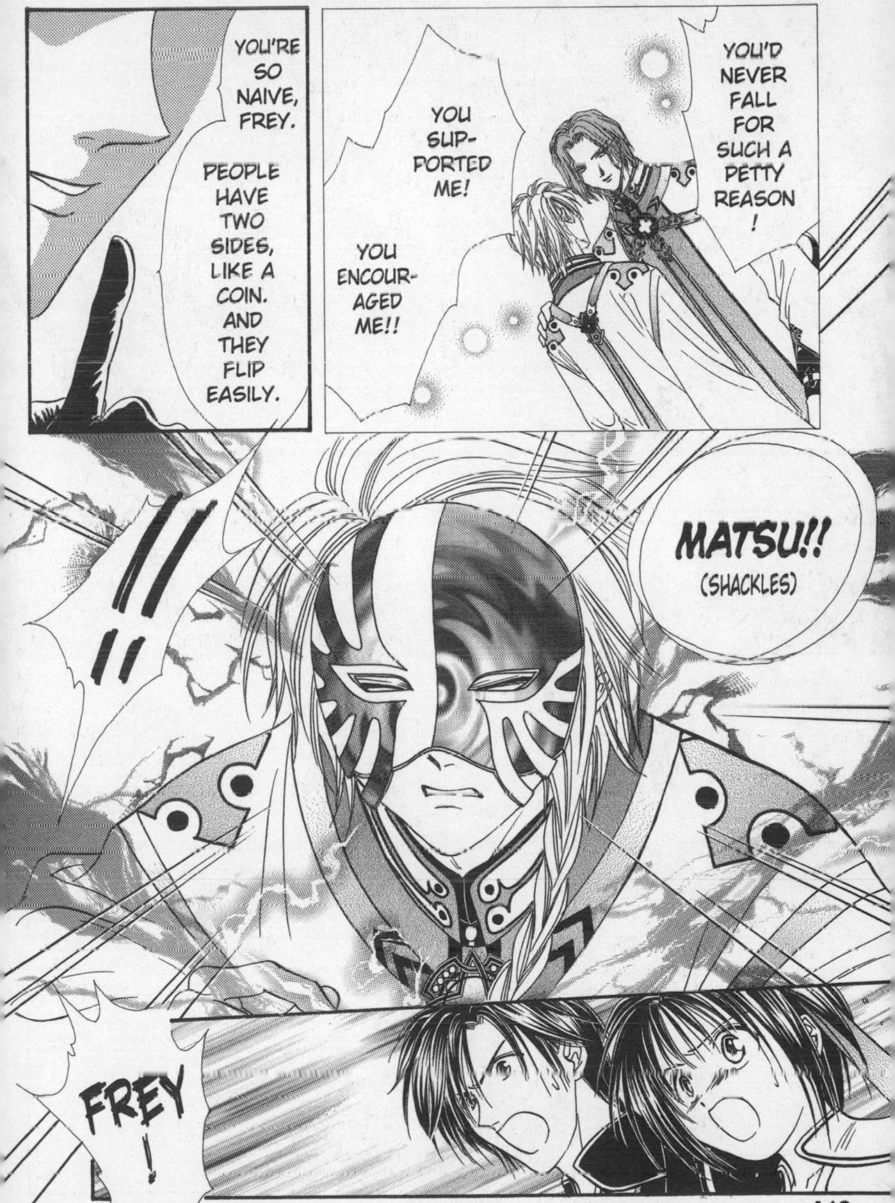
YOU'D NEVER FALL FOR SUCH A PETTY REASON!
YOU SUP-PORTED ME!
YOU ENCOUR-AGED ME!!
YOU'RE SO NAIVE, FREY.
PEOPLE HAVE TWO SIDES, LIKE A COIN. AND THEY FLIP EASILY.
MATSU!!
(SHACKLES)
!!
FREY!

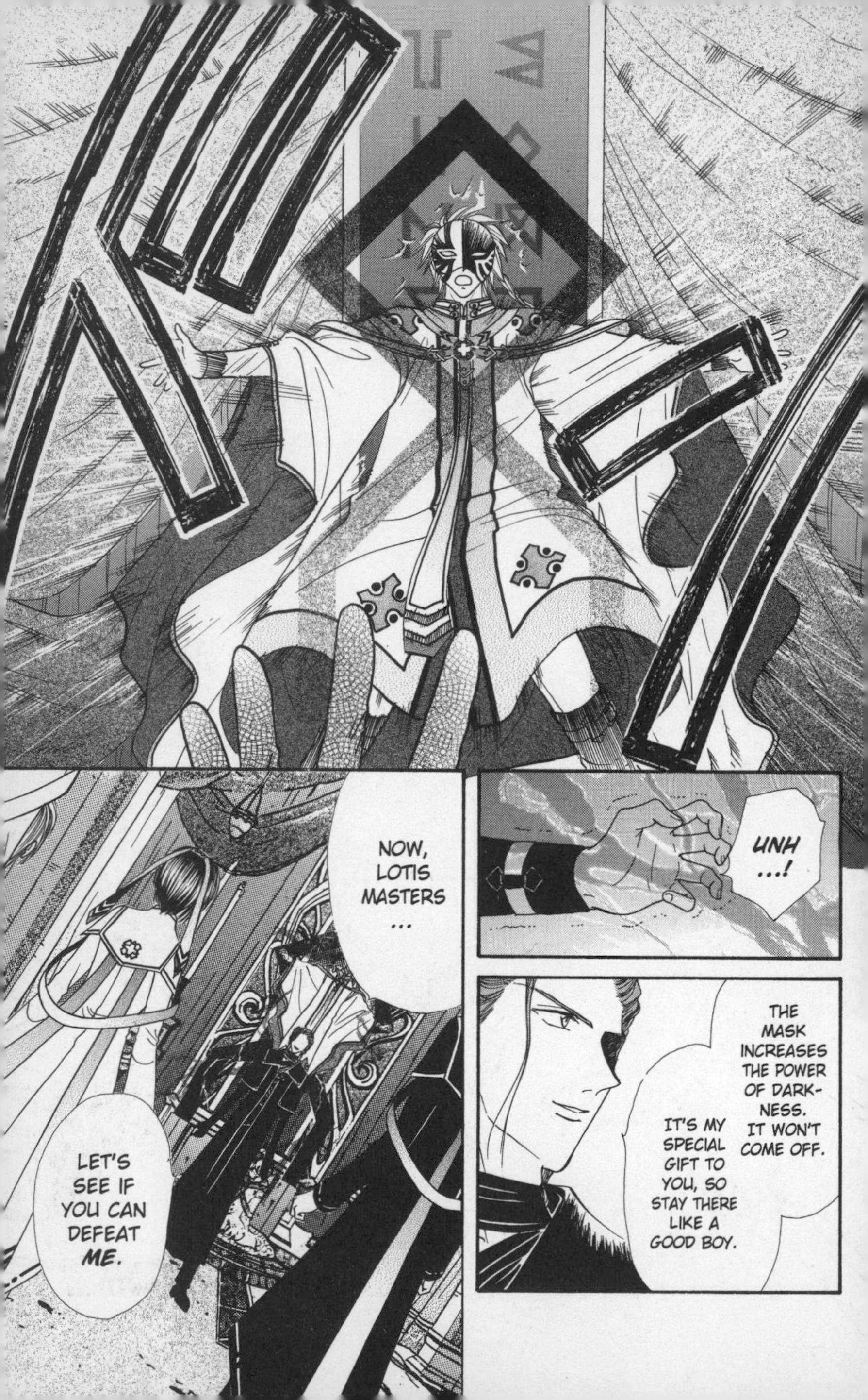
UNH ...!
THE MASK INCREASES THE POWER OF DARK- NESS. IT WON'T COME OFF.
IT'S MY SPECIAL GIFT TO YOU, SO STAY THERE LIKE A GOOD BOY.
NOW, LOTIS MASTERS ...
LET'S SEE IF YOU CAN DEFEAT ME.

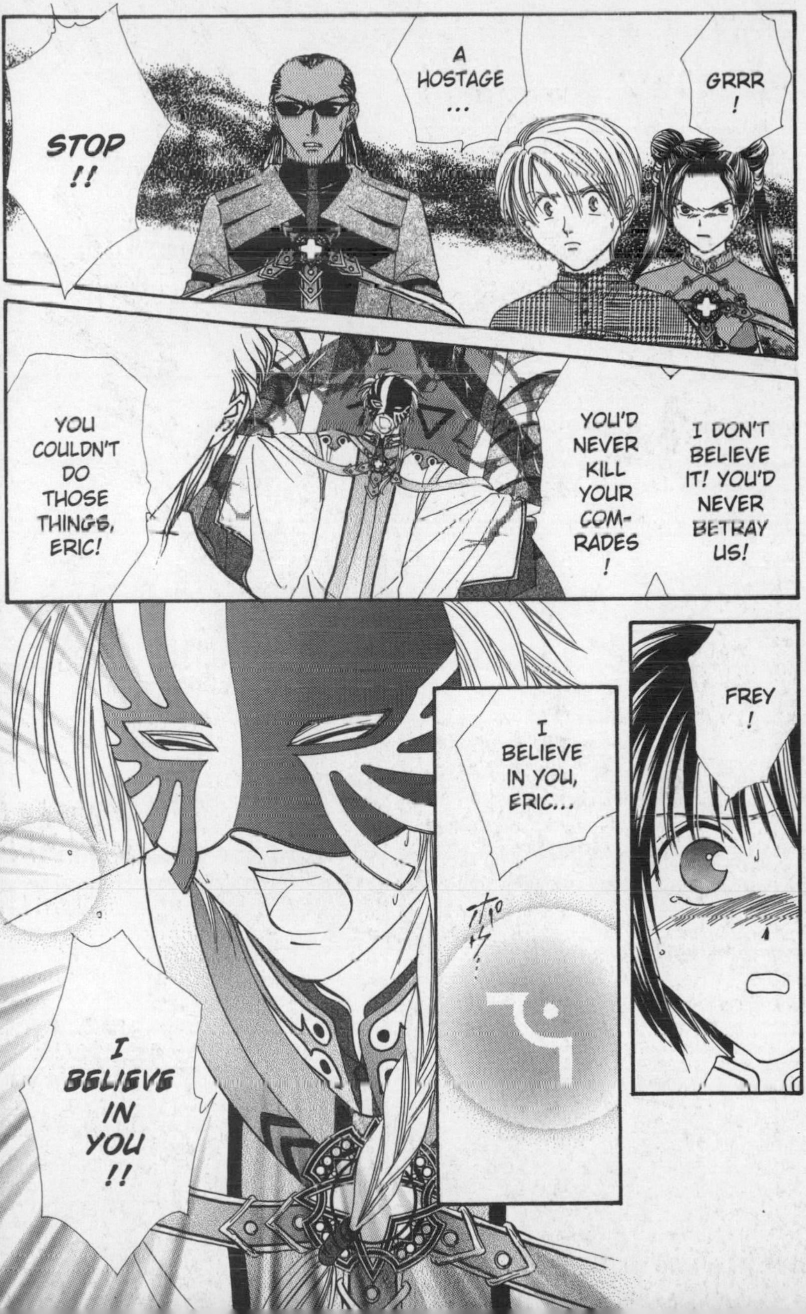
GRRR!
A HOSTAGE...
STOP!!
I DON'T BELIEVE IT! YOU'D NEVER BETRAY US!
YOU'D NEVER KILL YOUR COM-RADES!
YOU COULDN'T DO THOSE THINGS, ERIC!
FREY!
I BELIEVE IN YOU, ERIC...
I BELIEVE IN YOU!!

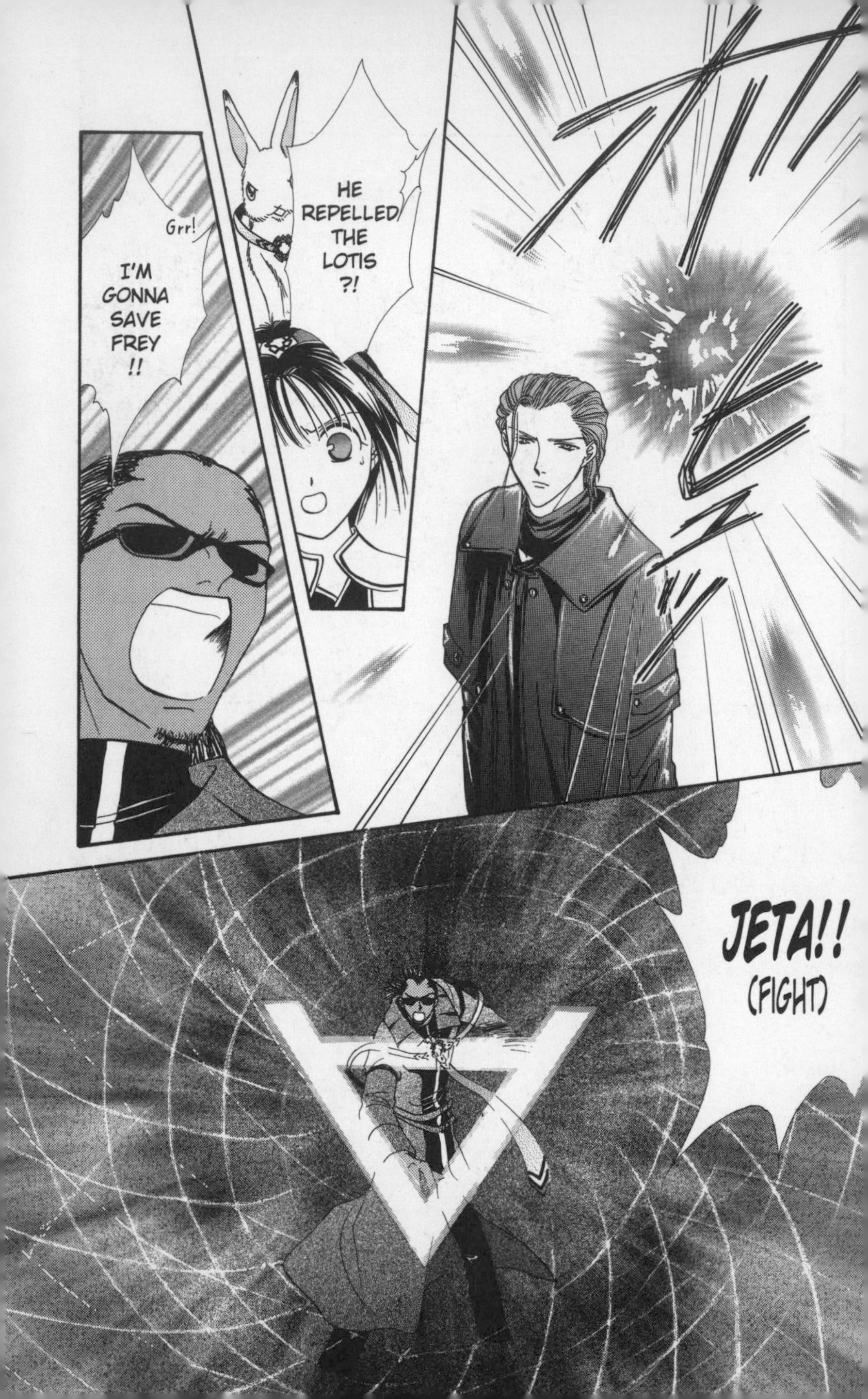
HE REPELLED THE LOTIS ?!
Grr!
I'M GONNA SAVE FREY !!
JETA!!
(FIGHT)

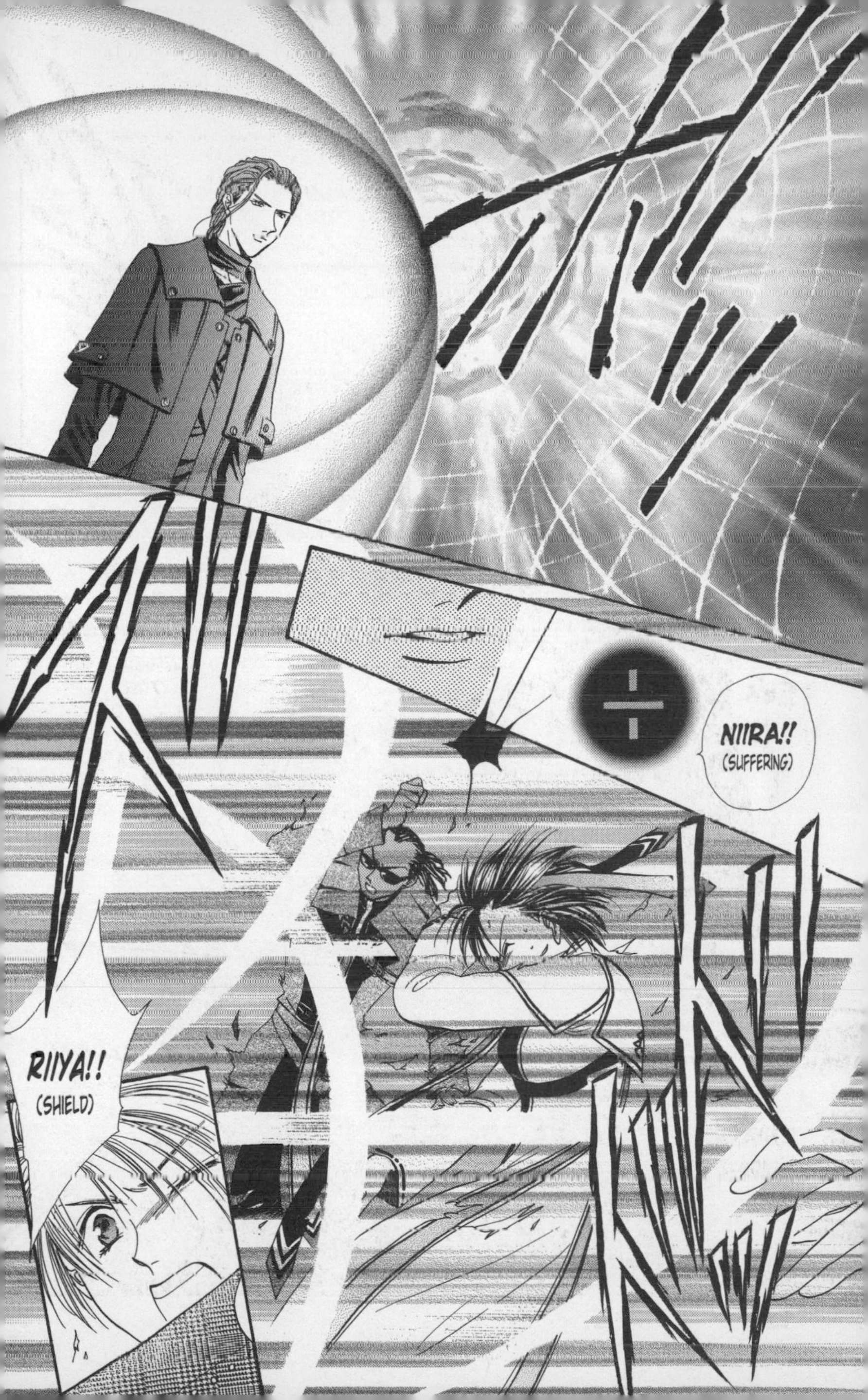
NIIRA!!
(SUFFERING)
RIIYA!!
(SHIELD)

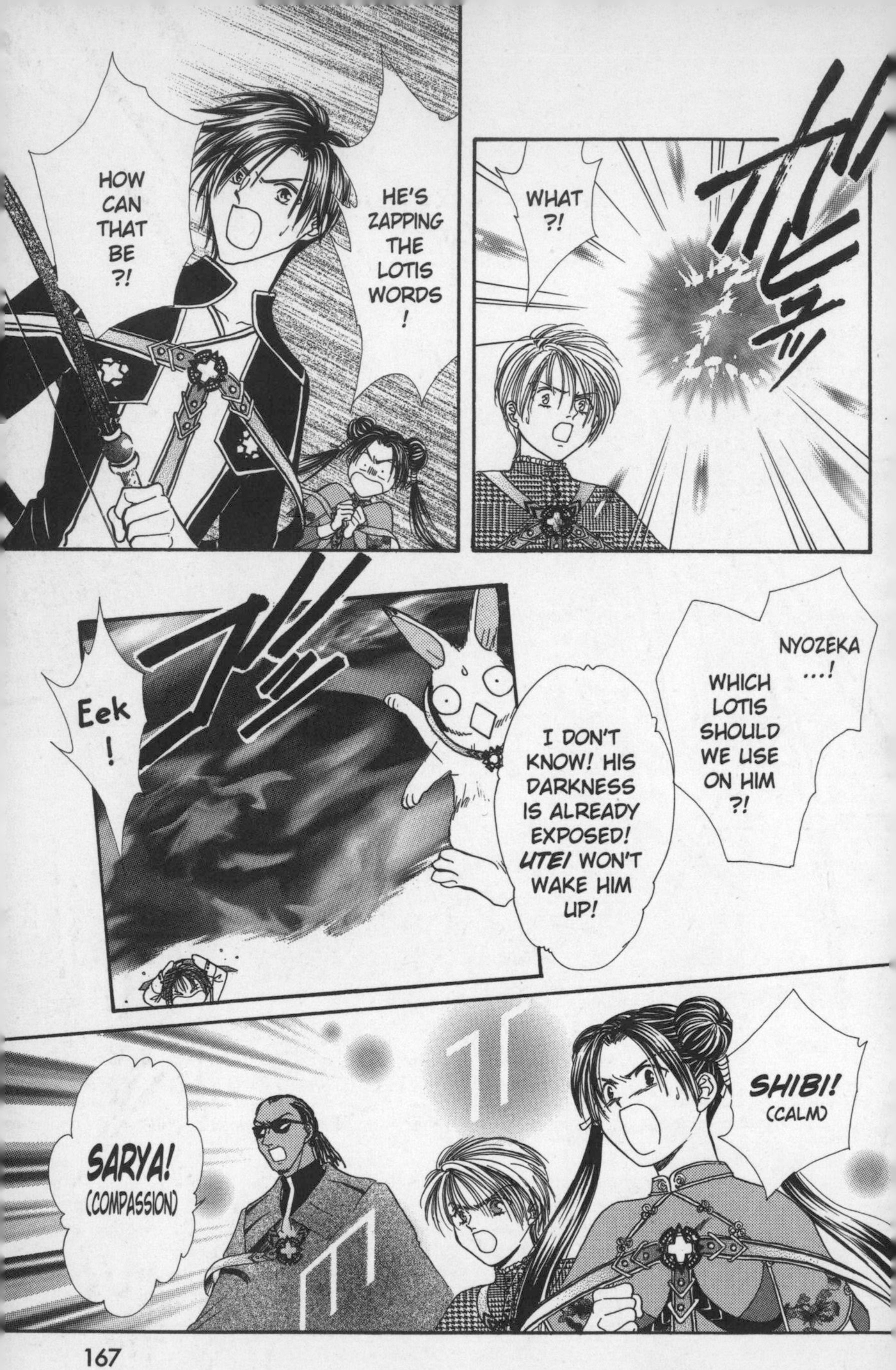
WHAT ?!
HE'S ZAPPING THE LOTIS WORDS !
HOW CAN THAT BE ?!
NYOZEKA ...!
WHICH LOTIS SHOULD WE USE ON HIM ?!
I DON'T KNOW! HIS DARKNESS IS ALREADY EXPOSED! *UTEI* WON'T WAKE HIM UP!
Eek !
SHIBI! (CALM)
SARYA! (COMPASSION)

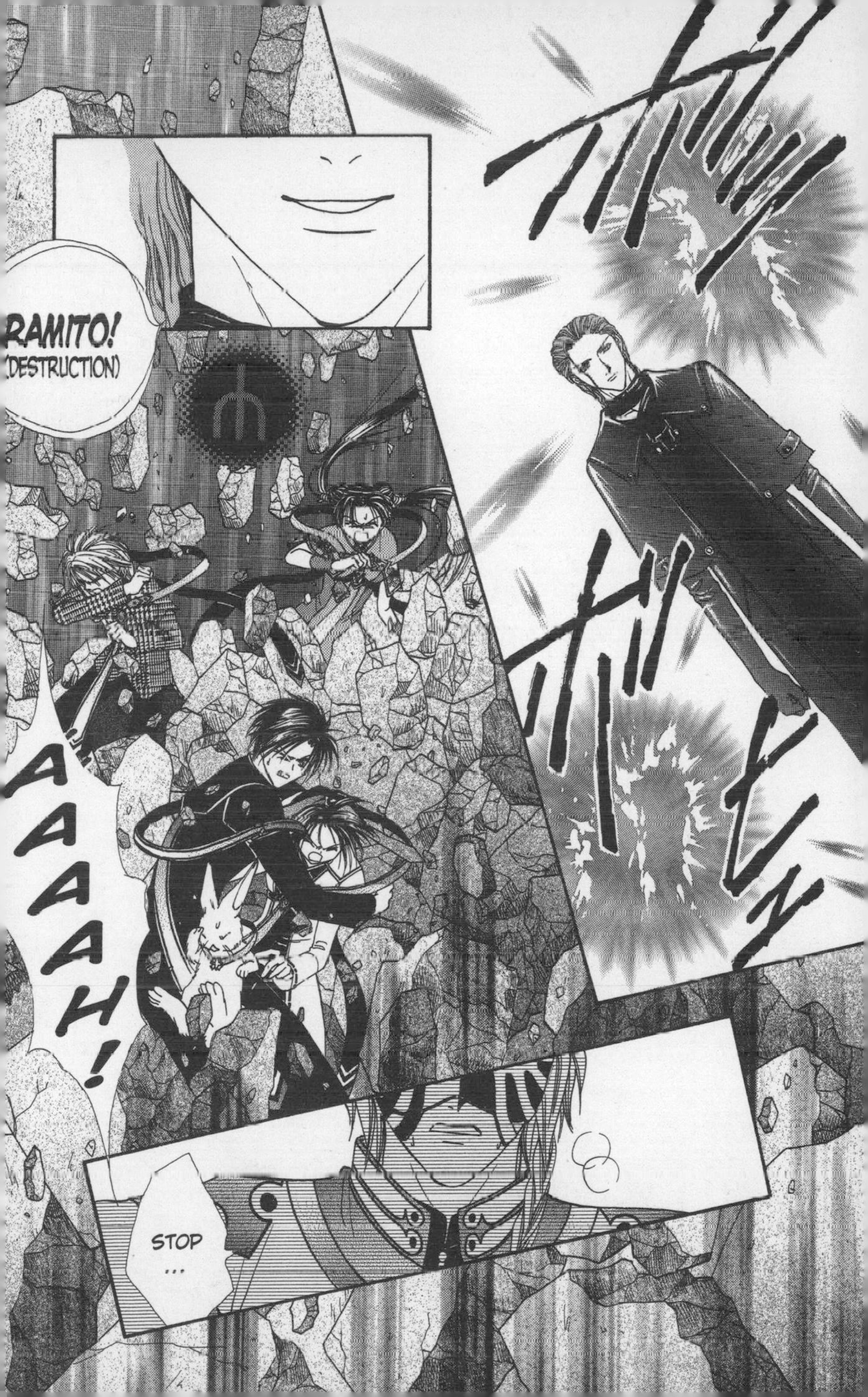
RAMITO!
(DESTRUCTION)
AAAAH!
STOP ...

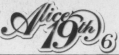

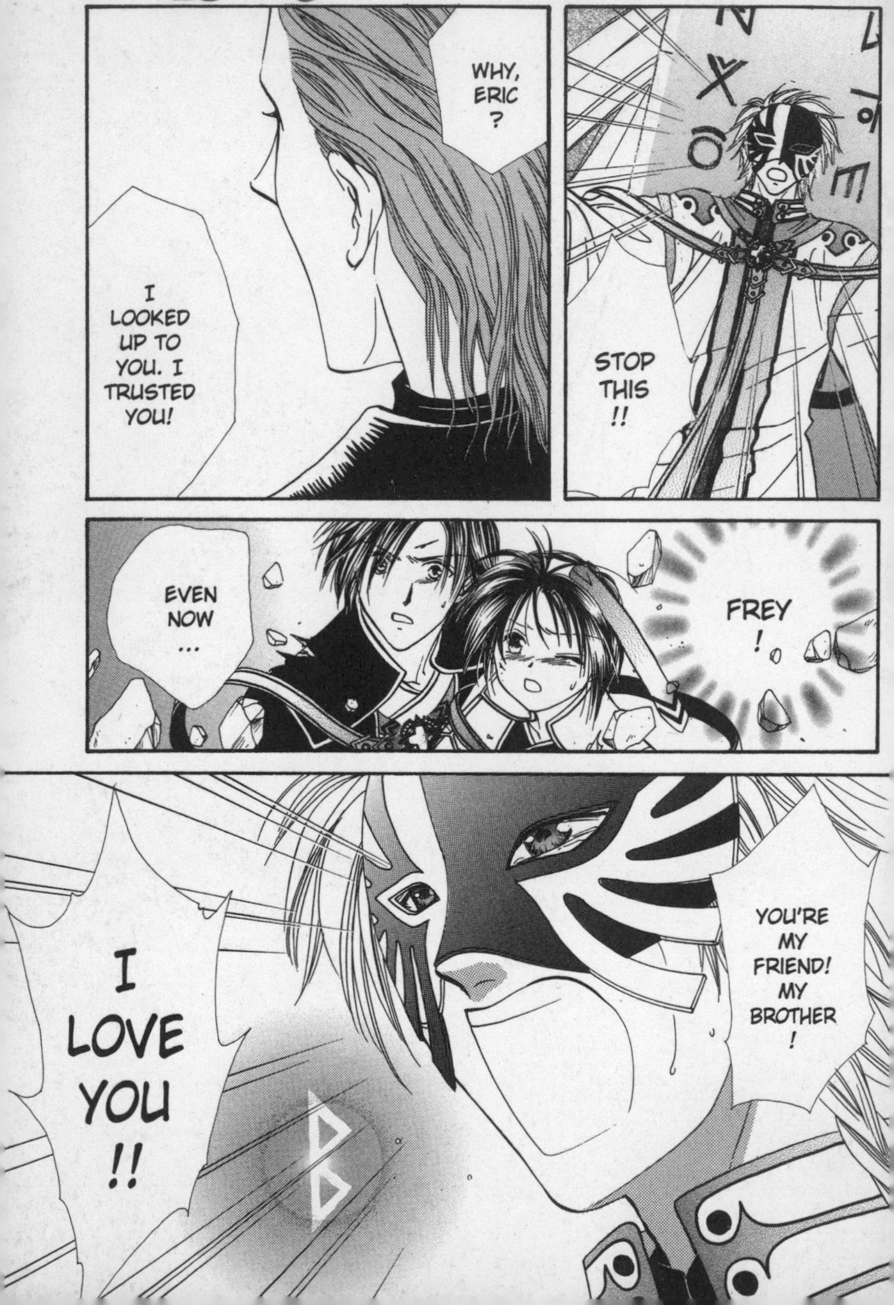
STOP THIS!!
WHY, ERIC?
I LOOKED UP TO YOU. I TRUSTED YOU!
FREY!
EVEN NOW...
YOU'RE MY FRIEND! MY BROTHER!
I LOVE YOU!!

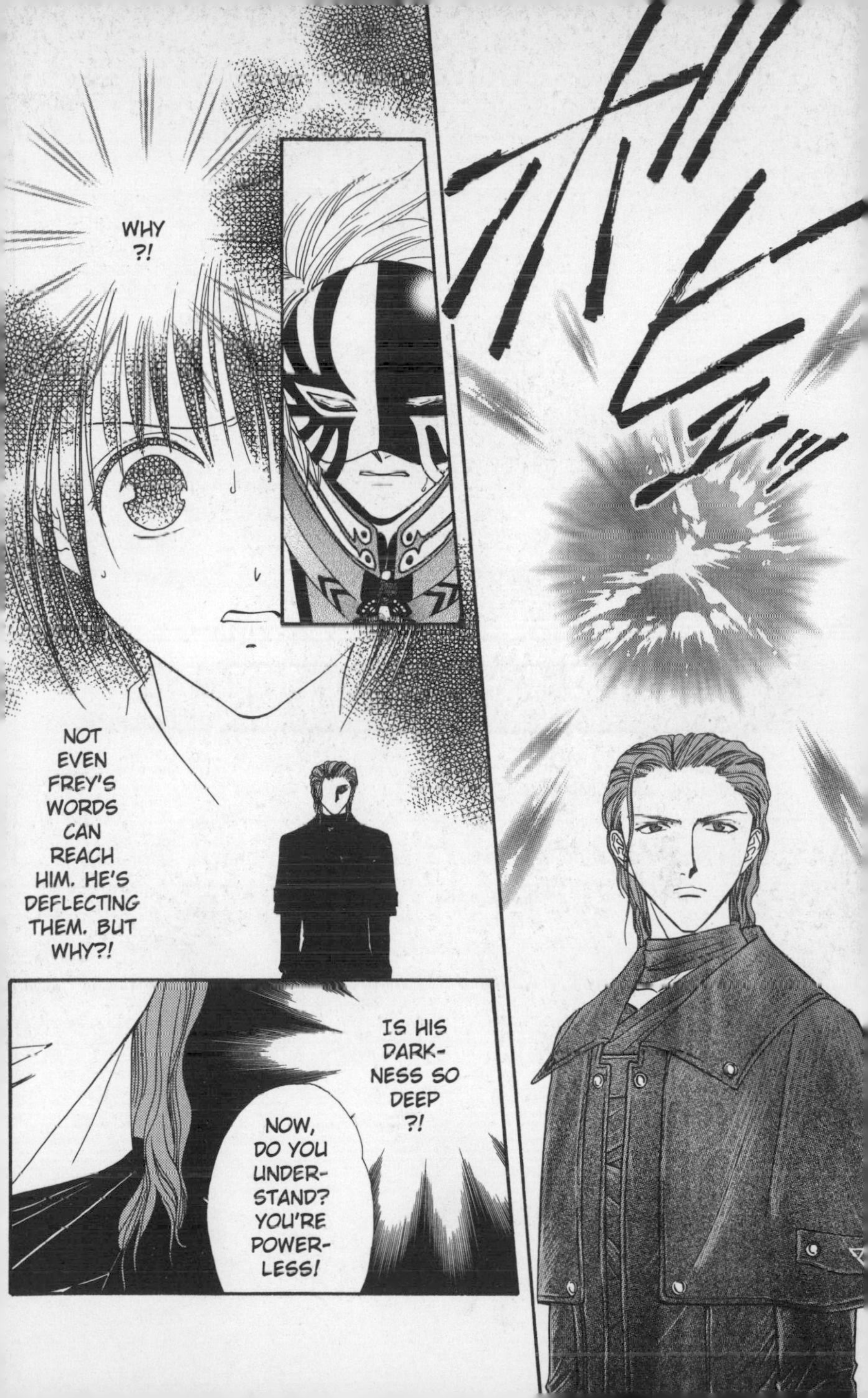
WHY ?!
NOT EVEN FREY'S WORDS CAN REACH HIM. HE'S DEFLECTING THEM. BUT WHY?!
IS HIS DARKNESS SO DEEP ?!
NOW, DO YOU UNDERSTAND? YOU'RE POWERLESS!

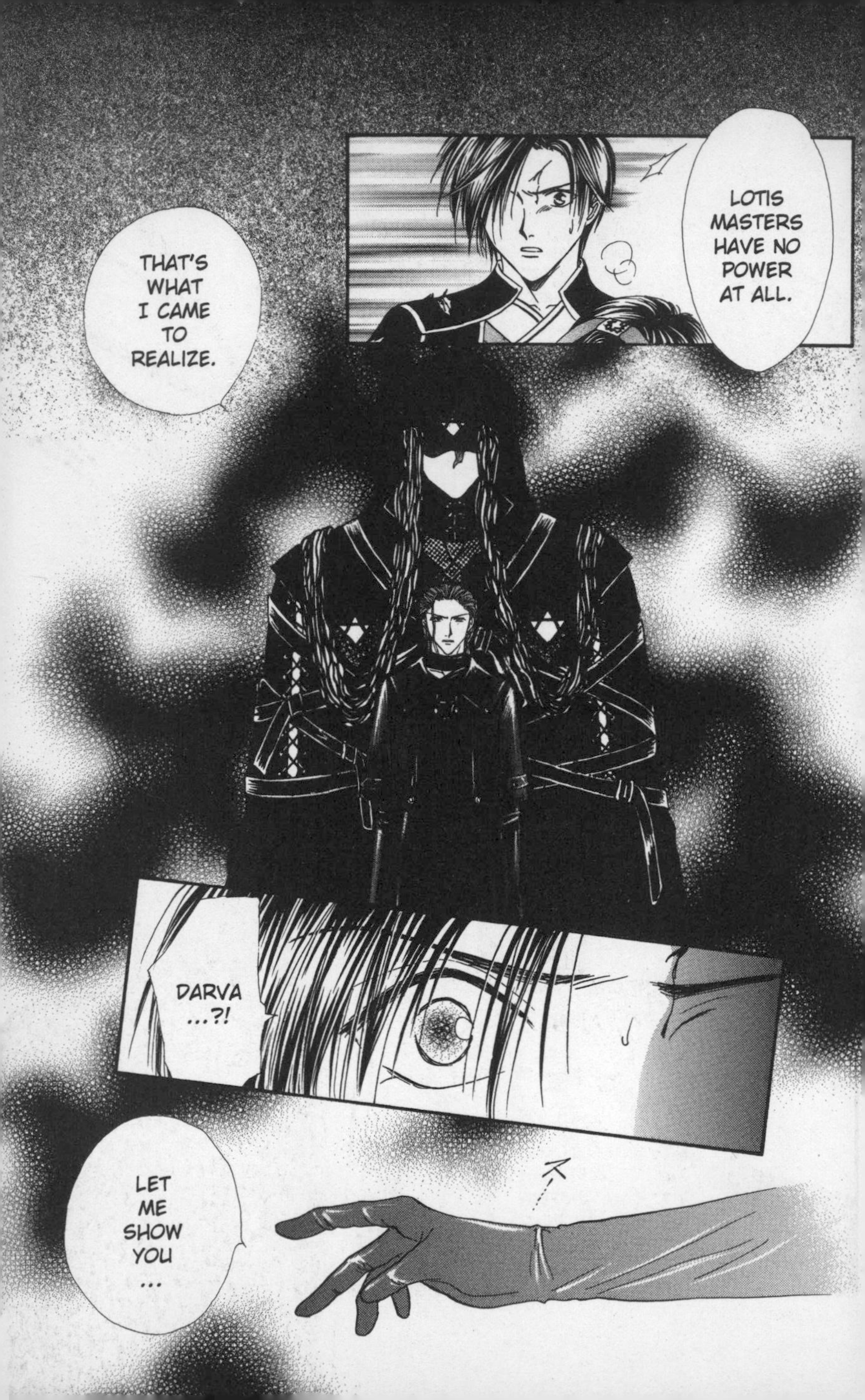
LOTIS MASTERS HAVE NO POWER AT ALL.
THAT'S WHAT I CAME TO REALIZE.
DARVA ...?!
LET ME SHOW YOU ...

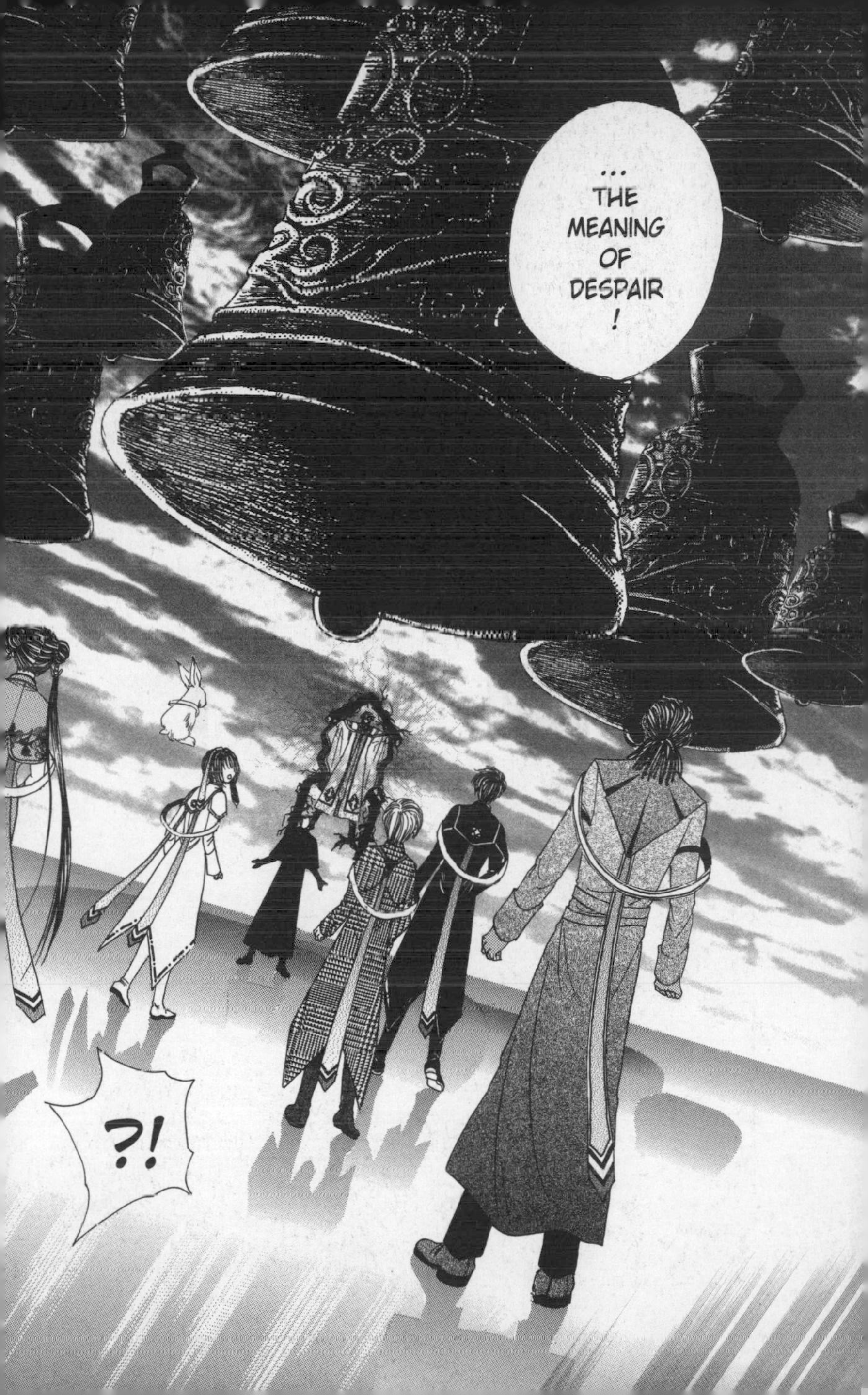
... THE MEANING OF DESPAIR !
?!

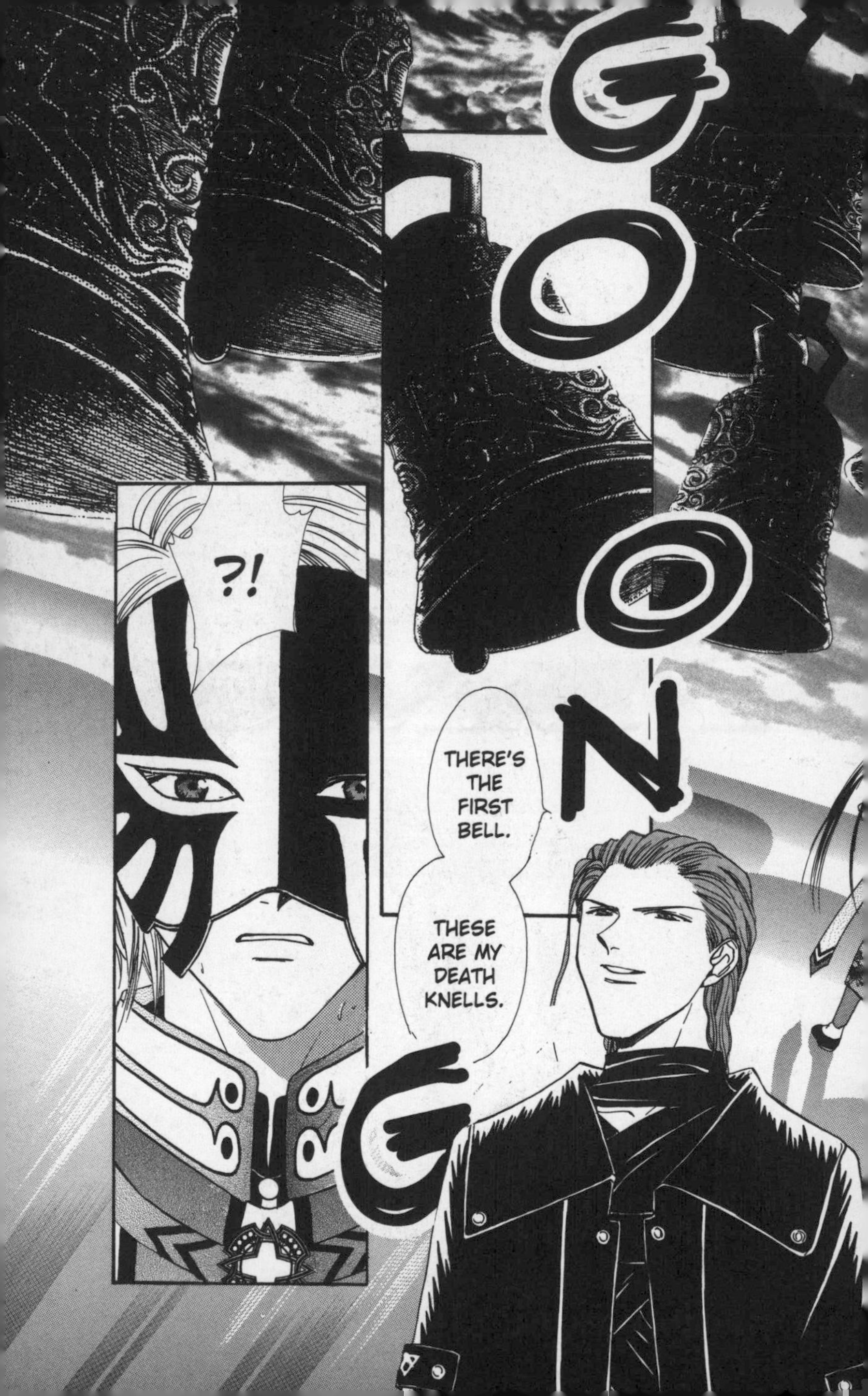
GOOONG
THERE'S THE FIRST BELL.
THESE ARE MY DEATH KNELLS.
?!

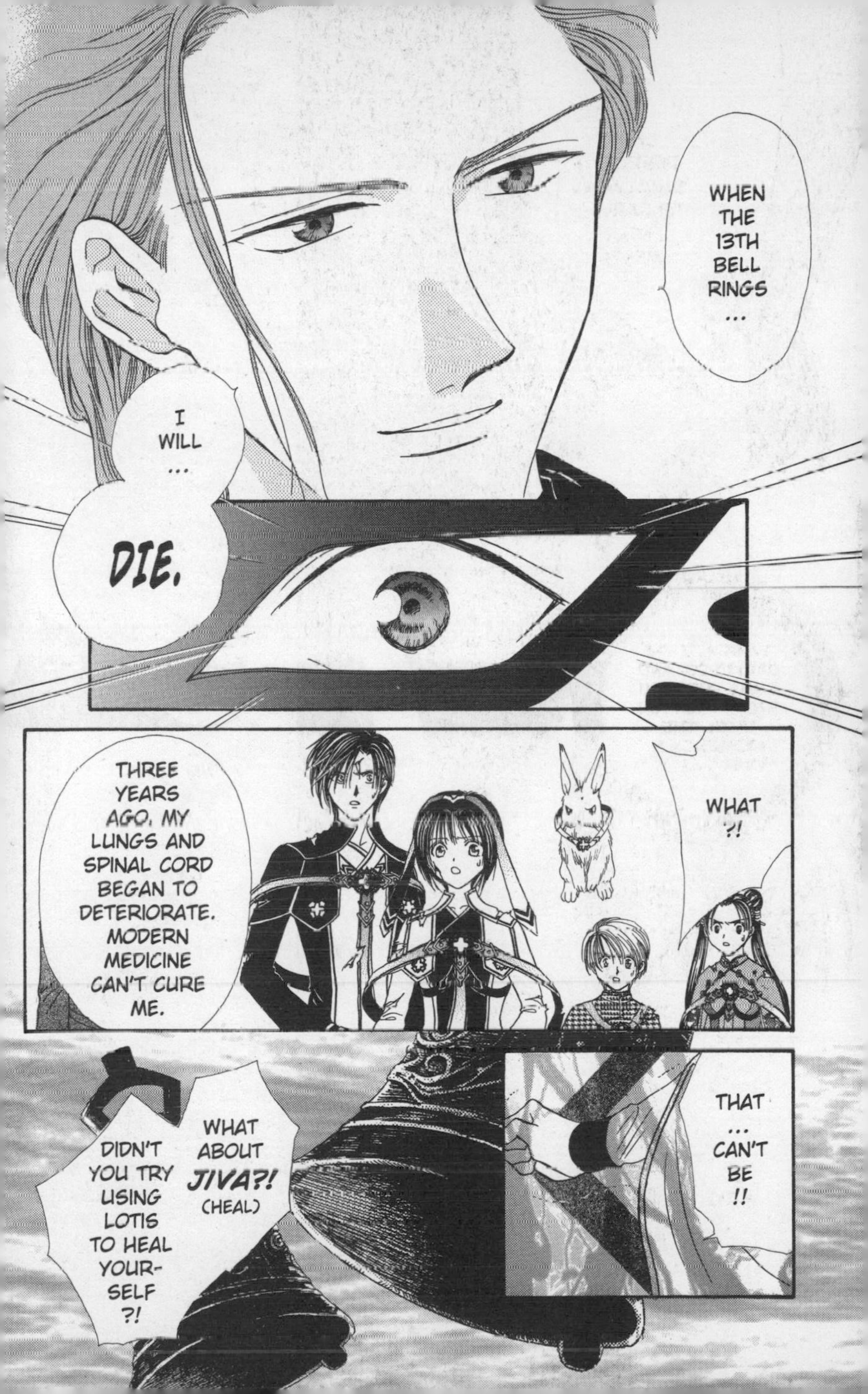
WHEN THE 13TH BELL RINGS...
I WILL... DIE.
WHAT?!
THREE YEARS AGO, MY LUNGS AND SPINAL CORD BEGAN TO DETERIORATE. MODERN MEDICINE CAN'T CURE ME.
THAT... CAN'T BE!!
WHAT ABOUT JIVA?! (HEAL)
DIDN'T YOU TRY USING LOTIS TO HEAL YOURSELF?!

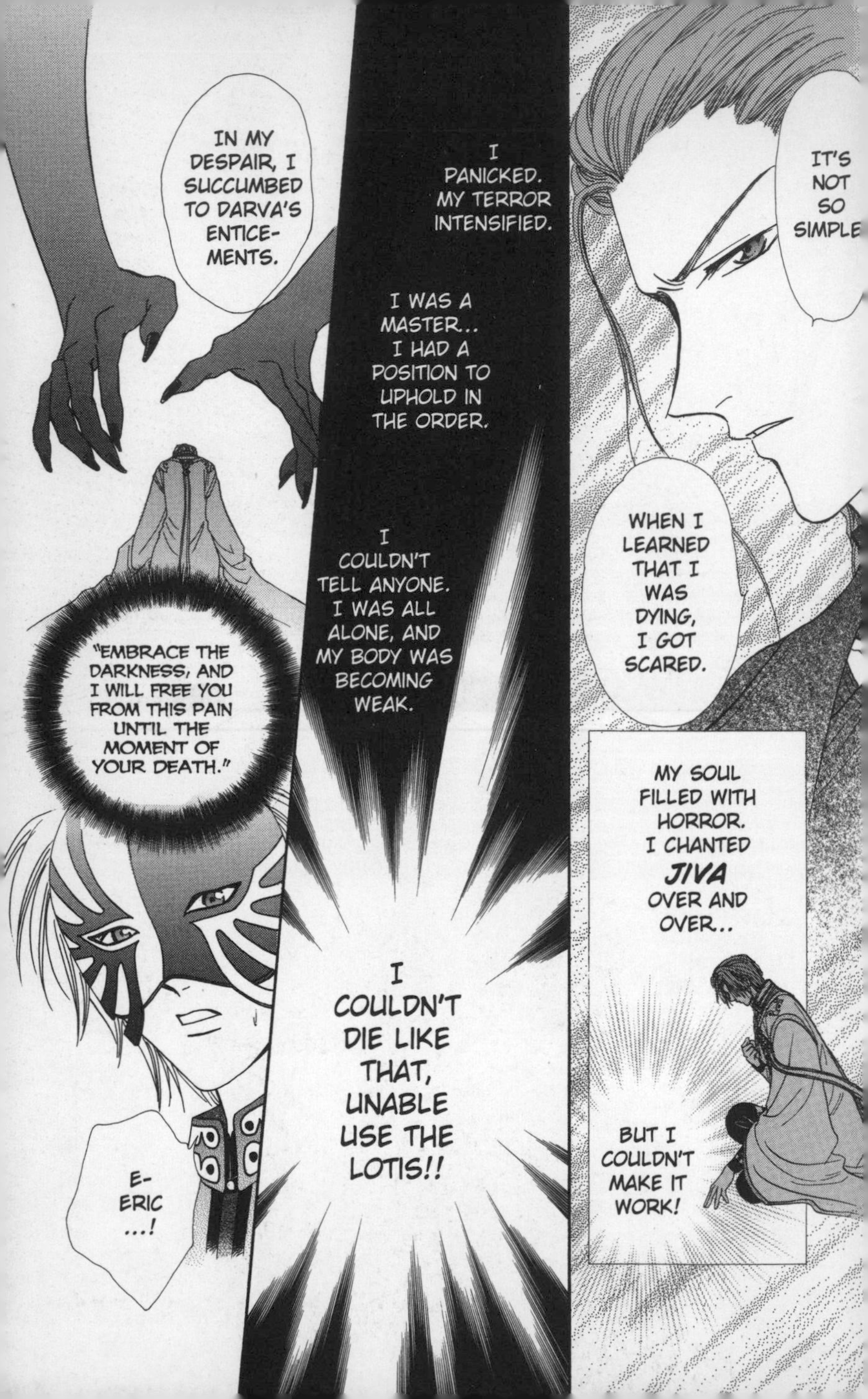

IT'S NOT SO SIMPLE
WHEN I LEARNED THAT I WAS DYING, I GOT SCARED.
MY SOUL FILLED WITH HORROR. I CHANTED *JIVA* OVER AND OVER...
BUT I COULDN'T MAKE IT WORK!
I PANICKED. MY TERROR INTENSIFIED.
I WAS A MASTER... I HAD A POSITION TO UPHOLD IN THE ORDER.
I COULDN'T TELL ANYONE. I WAS ALL ALONE, AND MY BODY WAS BECOMING WEAK.
I COULDN'T DIE LIKE THAT, UNABLE USE THE LOTIS!!
IN MY DESPAIR, I SUCCUMBED TO DARVA'S ENTICEMENTS.
"EMBRACE THE DARKNESS, AND I WILL FREE YOU FROM THIS PAIN UNTIL THE MOMENT OF YOUR DEATH."
E-ERIC...!

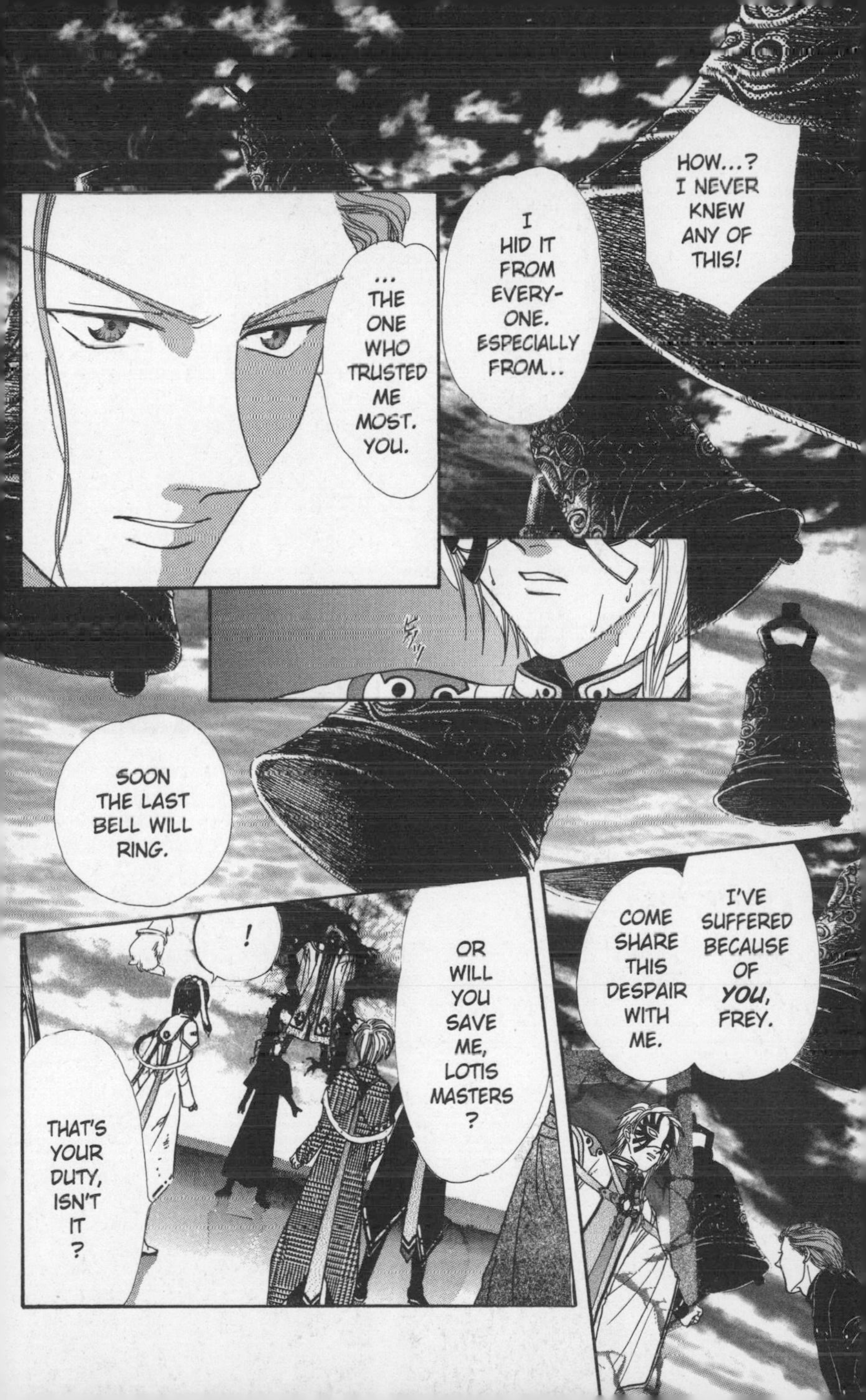
HOW...? I NEVER KNEW ANY OF THIS!
I HID IT FROM EVERY-ONE. ESPECIALLY FROM..
... THE ONE WHO TRUSTED ME MOST. YOU.
SOON THE LAST BELL WILL RING.
I'VE SUFFERED BECAUSE OF *YOU*, FREY.
COME SHARE THIS DESPAIR WITH ME.
OR WILL YOU SAVE ME, LOTIS MASTERS?
!
THAT'S YOUR DUTY, ISN'T IT?

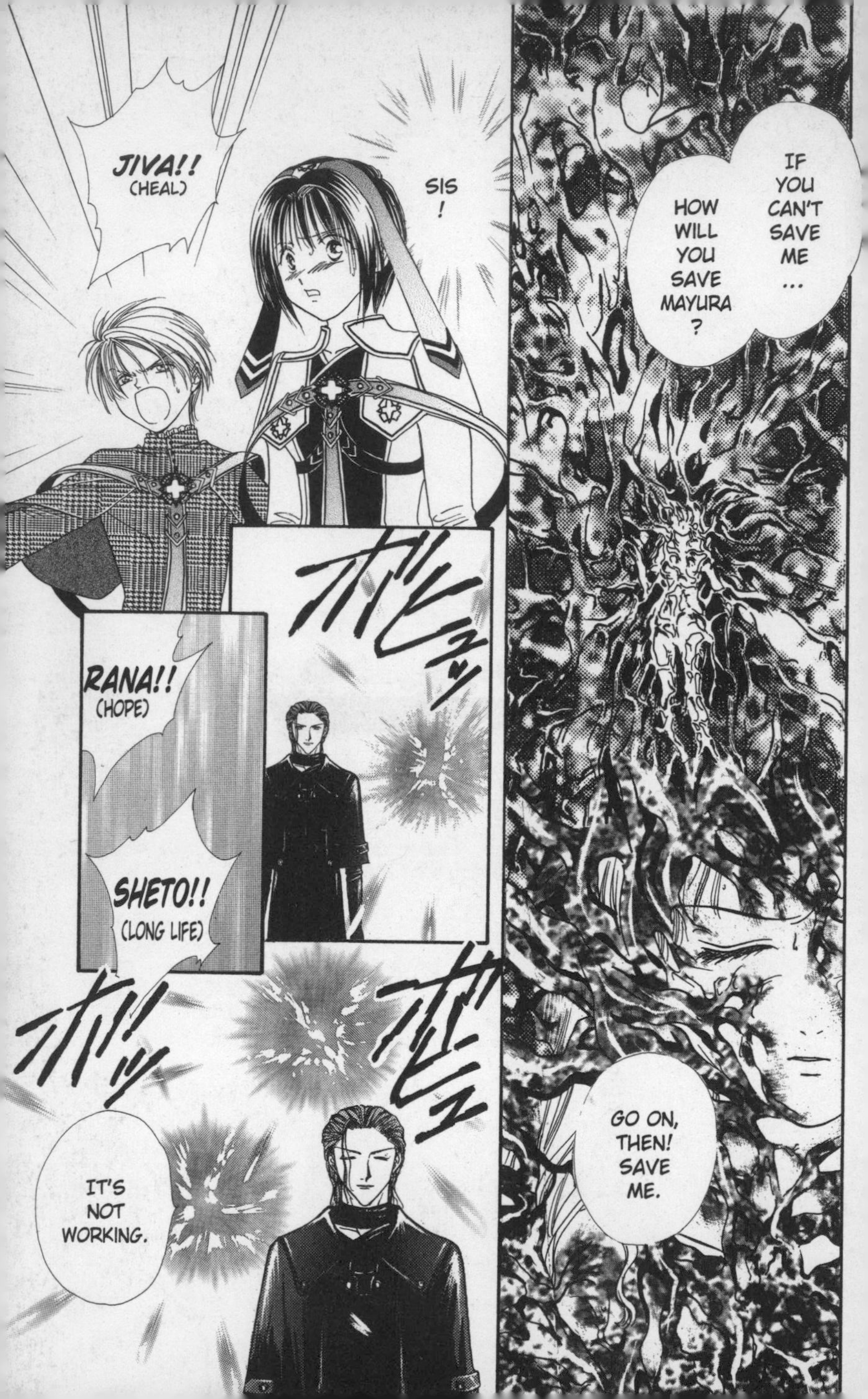
IF YOU CAN'T SAVE ME...
HOW WILL YOU SAVE MAYURA?
GO ON, THEN! SAVE ME.
JIVA!! (HEAL)
SIS!
RANA!! (HOPE)
SHETO!! (LONG LIFE)
IT'S NOT WORKING.

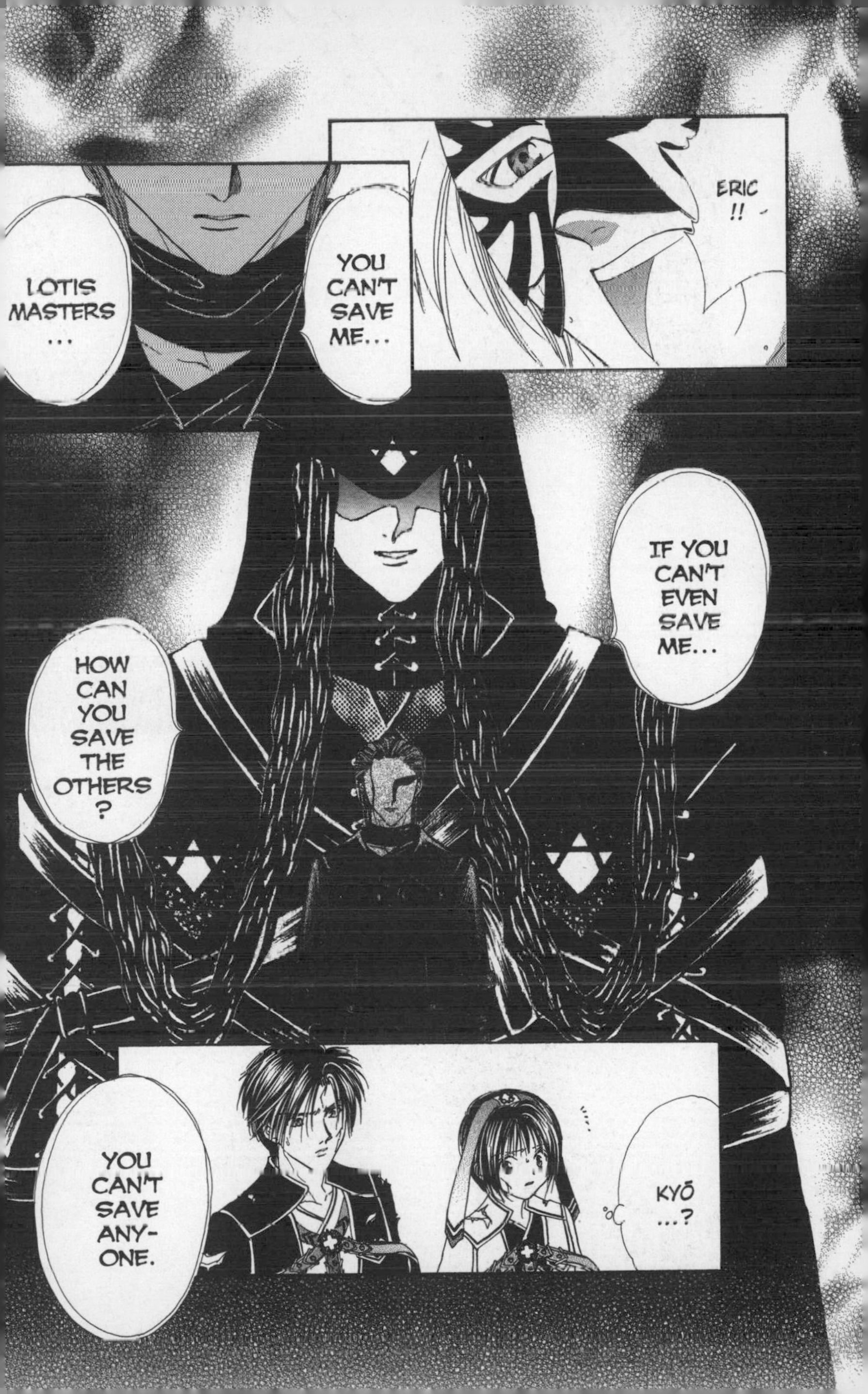
ERIC !!
YOU CAN'T SAVE ME...
LOTIS MASTERS ...
IF YOU CAN'T EVEN SAVE ME...
HOW CAN YOU SAVE THE OTHERS ?
...
KYŌ ...?
YOU CAN'T SAVE ANY-ONE.

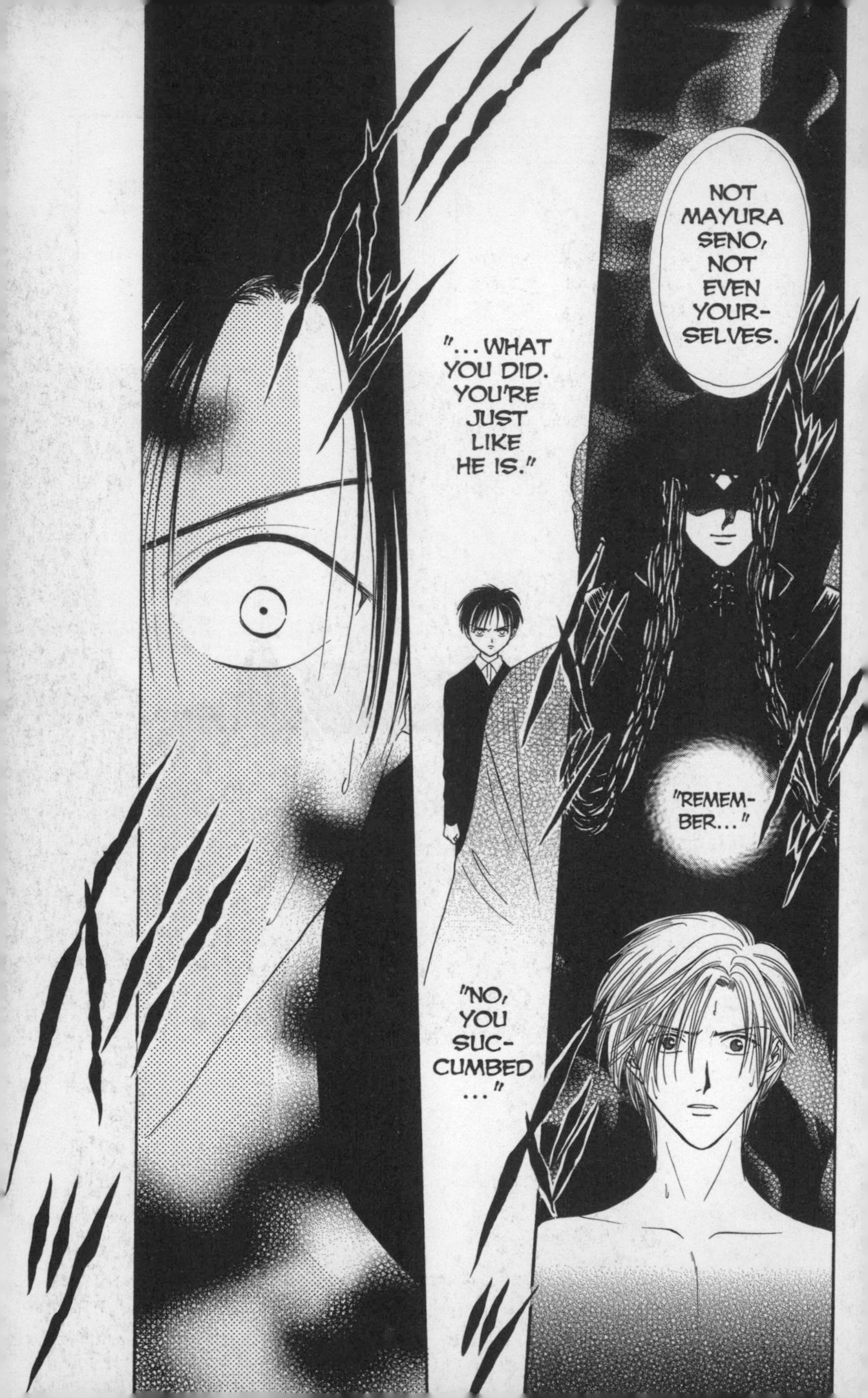
NOT MAYURA SENO, NOT EVEN YOURSELVES.
"REMEMBER..."
"...WHAT YOU DID. YOU'RE JUST LIKE HE IS."
"NO, YOU SUCCUMBED..."

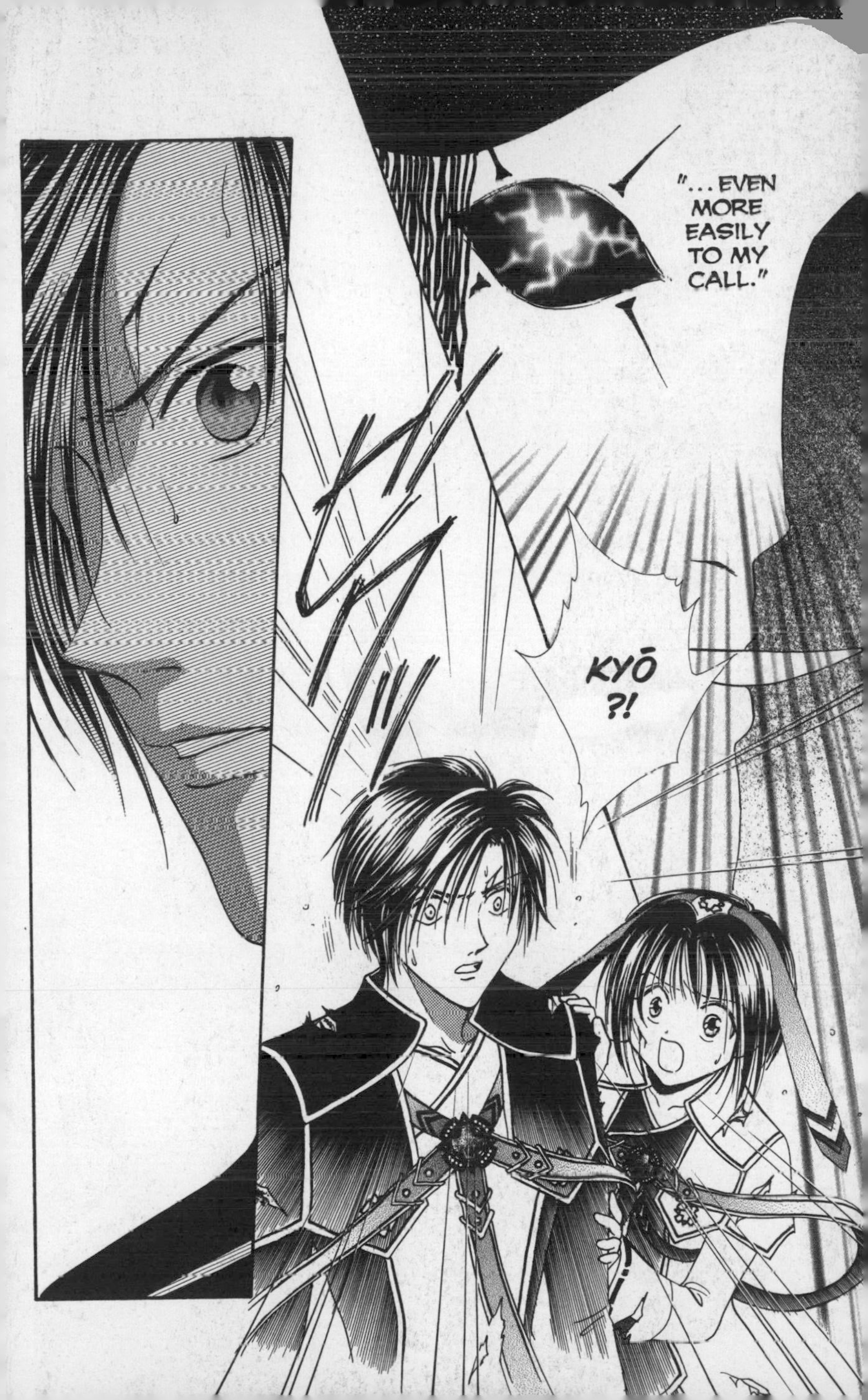
"...EVEN MORE EASILY TO MY CALL."
KYŌ ?!

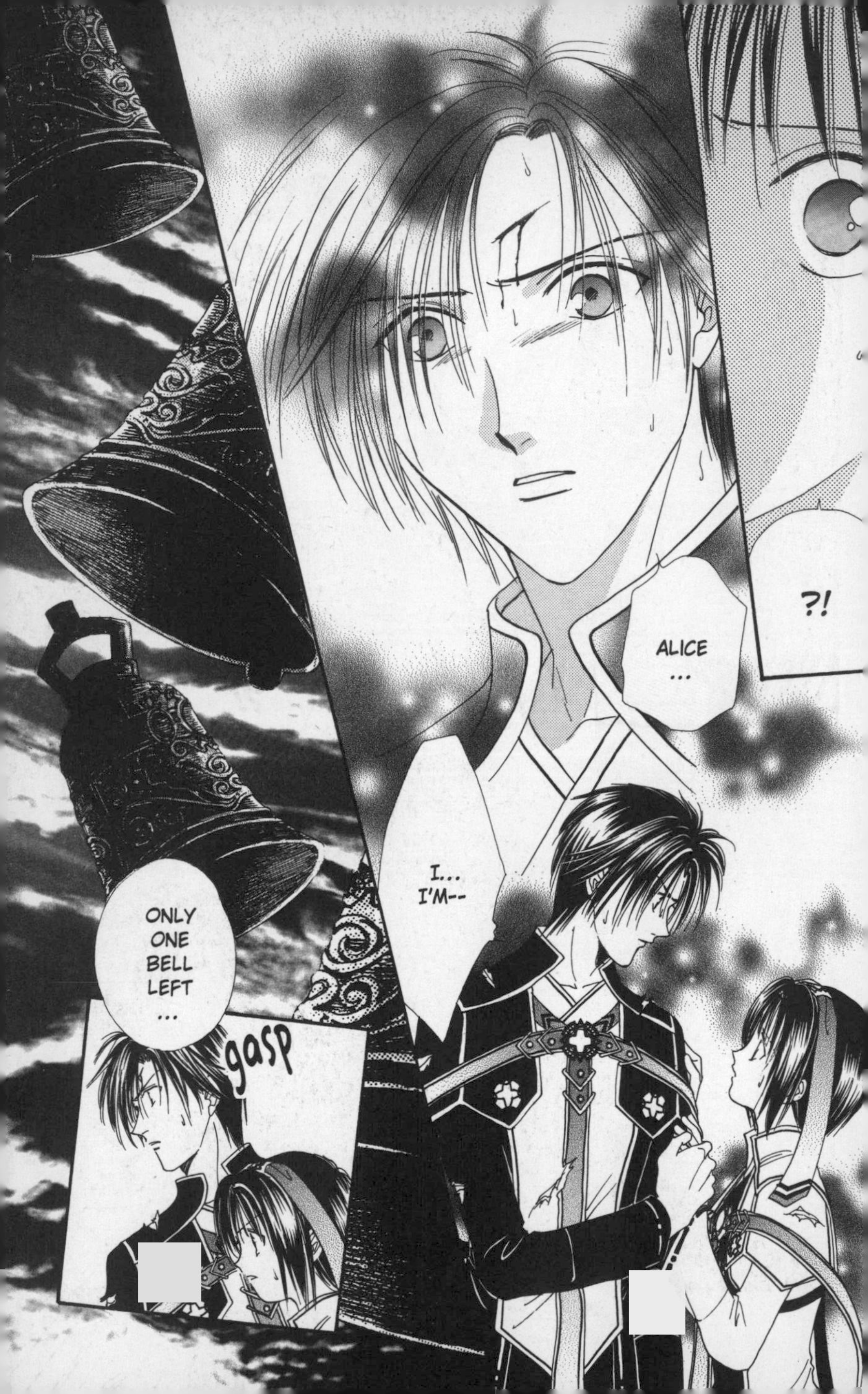
?!
ALICE ...
I... I'M--
ONLY ONE BELL LEFT ...
gasp

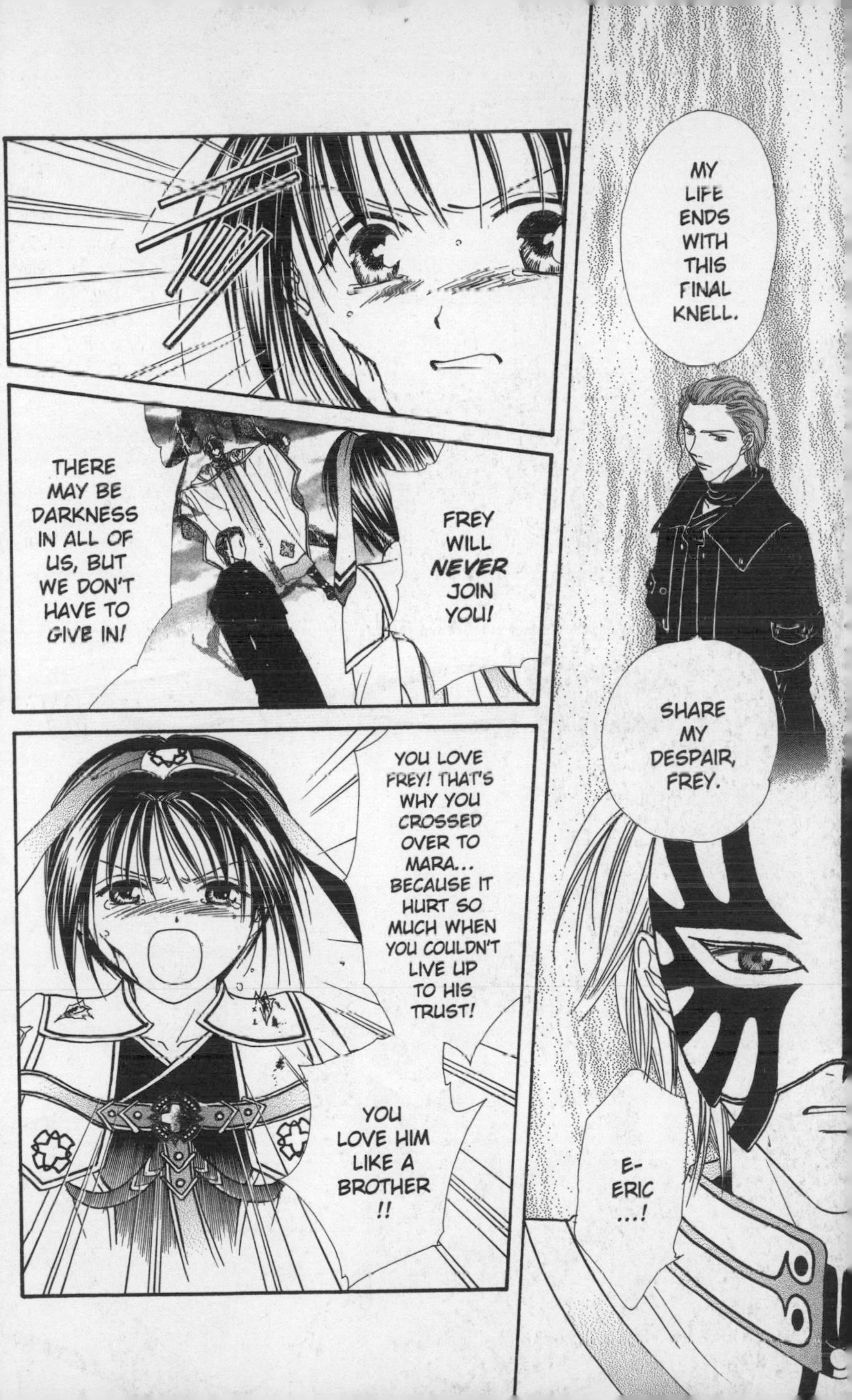
MY LIFE ENDS WITH THIS FINAL KNELL.
SHARE MY DESPAIR, FREY.
E-ERIC...!
FREY WILL ***NEVER*** JOIN YOU!
THERE MAY BE DARKNESS IN ALL OF US, BUT WE DON'T HAVE TO GIVE IN!
YOU LOVE FREY! THAT'S WHY YOU CROSSED OVER TO MARA... BECAUSE IT HURT SO MUCH WHEN YOU COULDN'T LIVE UP TO HIS TRUST!
YOU LOVE HIM LIKE A BROTHER!!

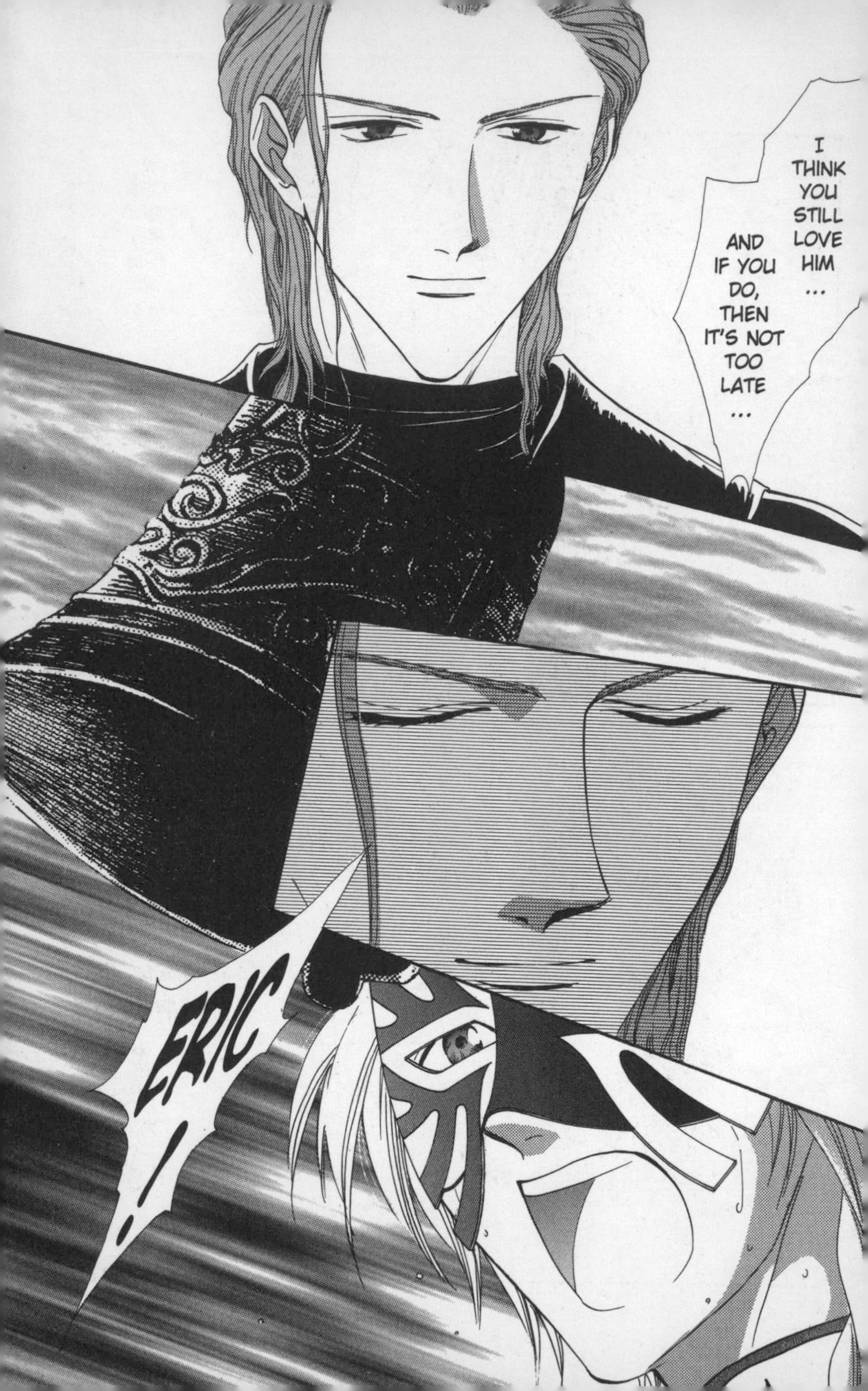
I THINK YOU STILL LOVE HIM ...
AND IF YOU DO, THEN IT'S NOT TOO LATE ...
ERIC ...!

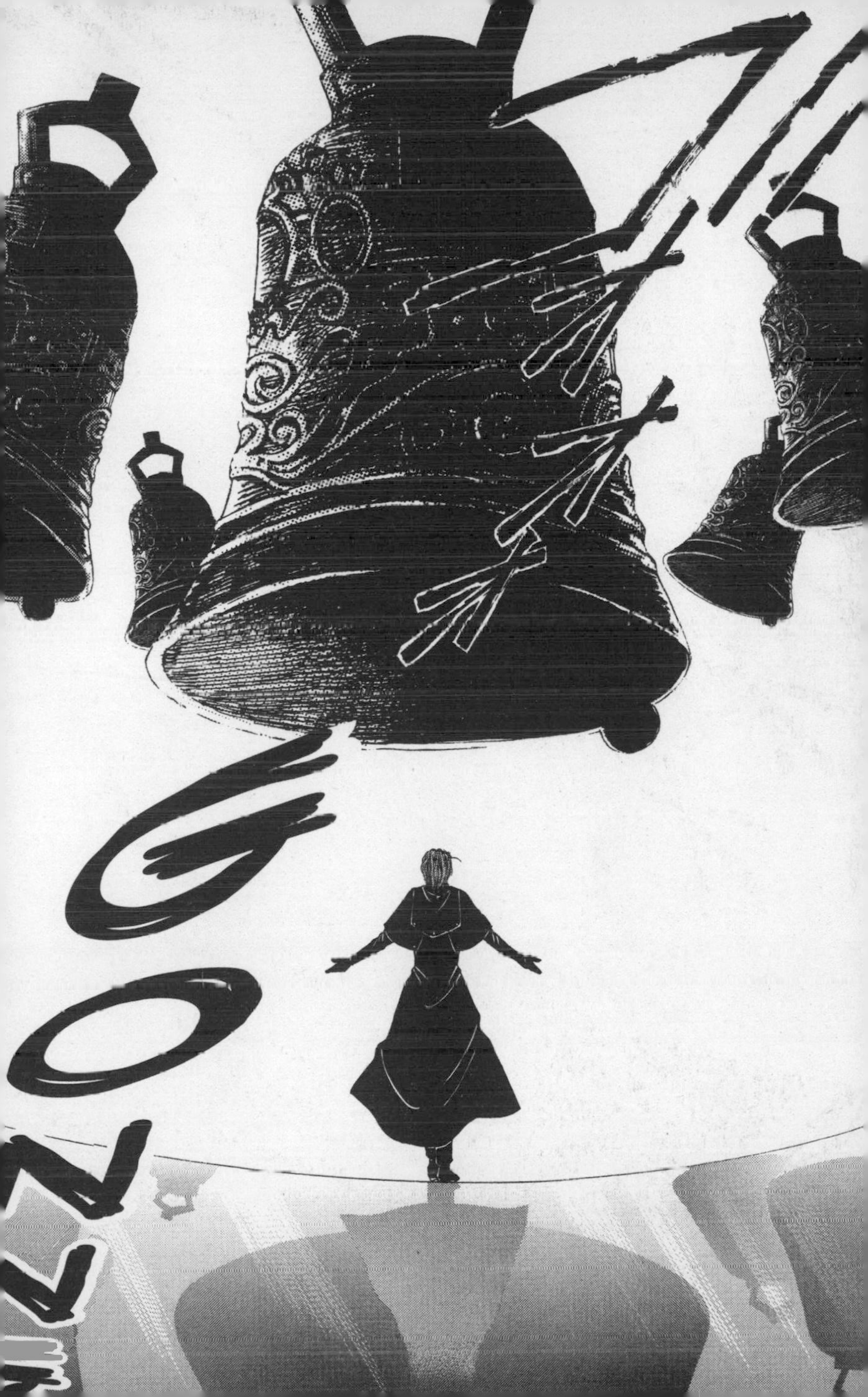

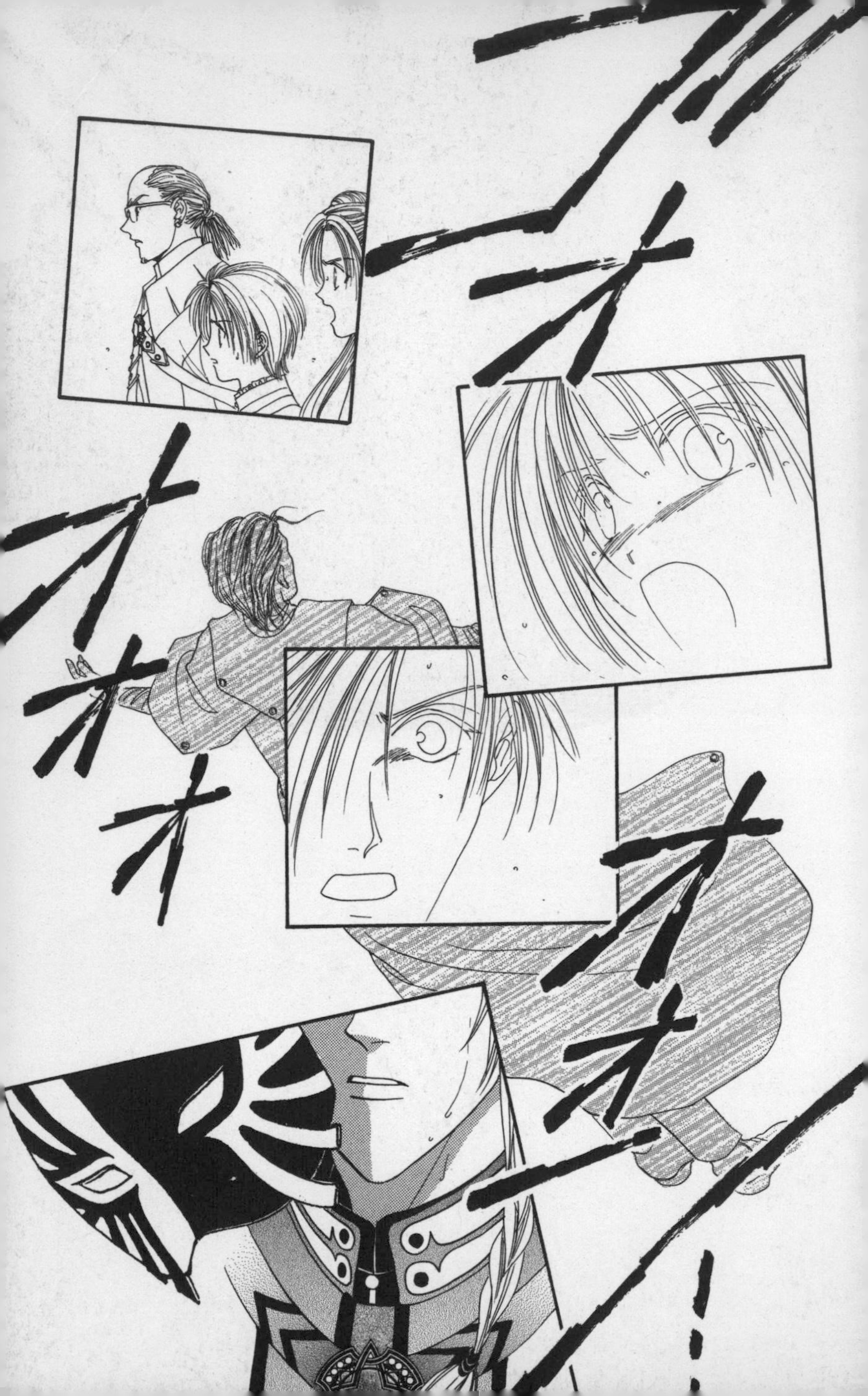
ブーオオオオオオー!

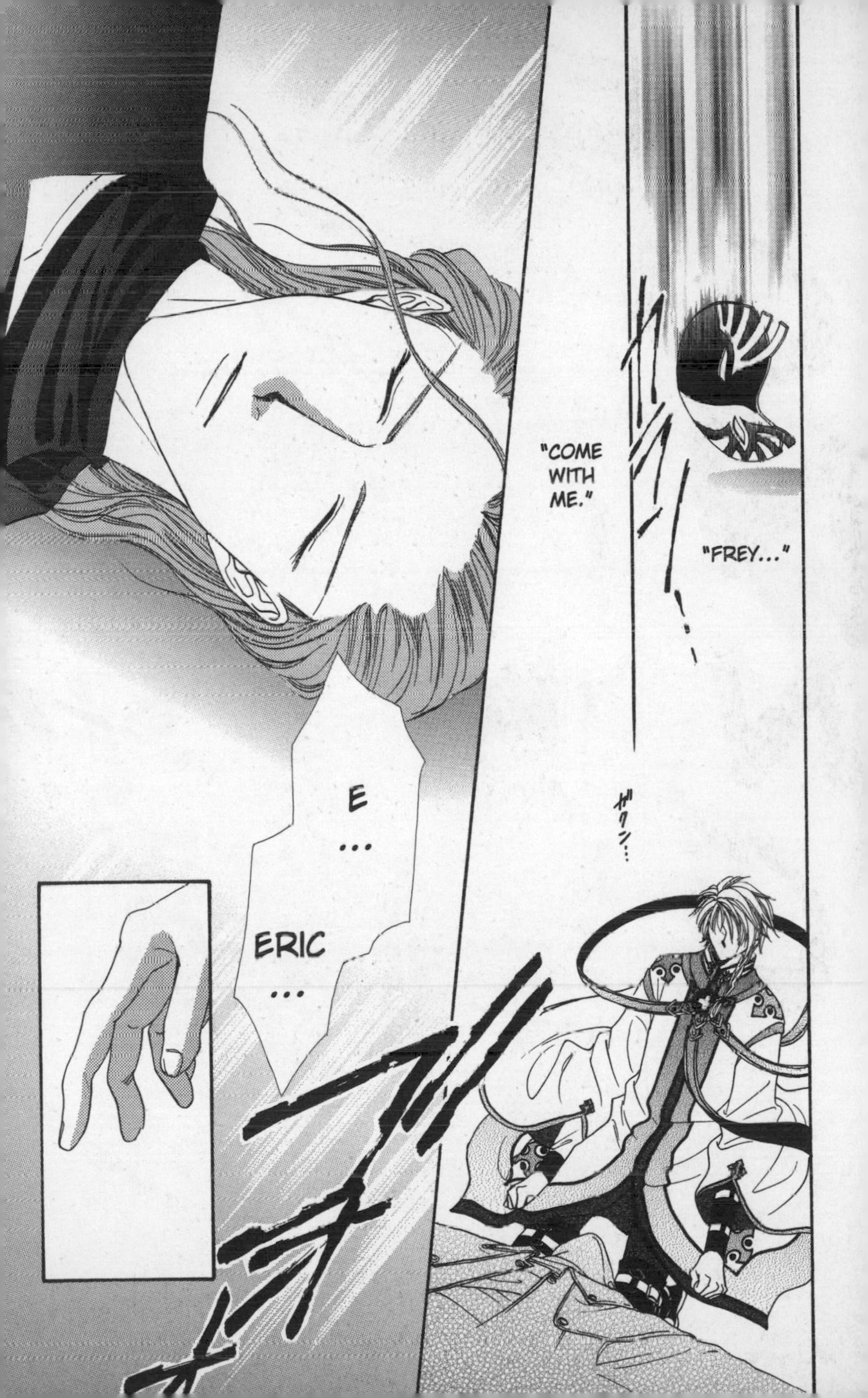
"FREY..."
"COME WITH ME."
ガクン…
E
...
ERIC
...

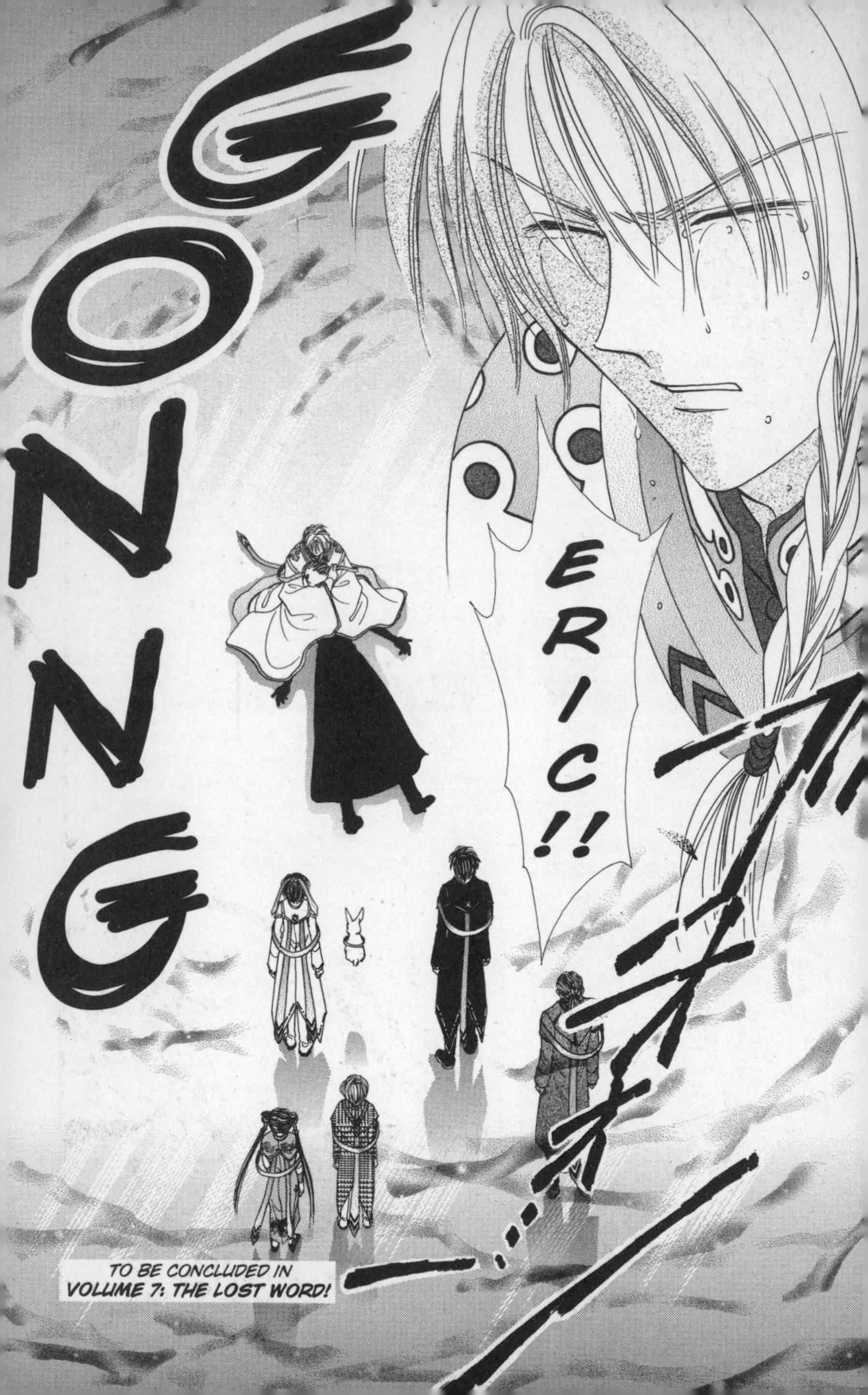
GONNG
ERIC!!
TO BE CONCLUDED IN
VOLUME 7: THE LOST WORD!

EDITOR'S NOTE

We're all susceptible to dark feelings — jealousy, rage, guilt, self pity — but the characters in *Alice 19th* show us that bottling up our painful memories allows those emotions to fester inside. It's important to expose the difficult experiences that haunt our pasts to the light of day, and to allow the people we love and trust to help us deal with them and defuse the power those memories exert over us. As the Lucksmiths say in their fabulous song, "Synchronized Sinking":

Come on, please get it off your chest, it's a commonplace, but I'd suggest a problem shared is a problem halved.

It's hard to believe that the next volume of *Alice 19th* — volume 7 — is the final one in the series! How will it end? What is the secret surrounding the death of Kyô's father? It's exciting, but it's also sad. Which manga will be your new favorite when Alice 19th is over?

—Frances E. Wall
Editor, *Alice 19th*

If you're enjoying this story and are in the mood for more, here are three manga titles that you should check out:

© 2000 Yuu WATASE/
Shogakukan Inc.

IMADOKI! (Nowadays) The newest series from Yuu Watase available in America, *Imadoki!* follows the trials and tribulations of Tanpopo Yamazaki, a budding young horticulturist, as she makes her way down the winding road to friendship. Snubbed by the rich kids at her new school, the elite Meio Academy, Tanpopo starts up a gardening club. But will this help her survive in an environment where superficiality and nepotism reign supreme?

VIDEO GIRL AI ©1989 by
Masakazu Katsura/
SHUEISHA Inc.

VIDEO GIRL AI When Moemi, the object of Yota's incurable crush, turns out to be in love with the dashing and popular Takashi, poor Yota is devastated. He rents a video to distract himself, but Ai, the hottie featured on the tape, magically bursts out of the TV and into Yota's world. Ai's mission is to fix Yota's hopeless love life, but when Ai develops romantic feelings towards Yota, things get complicated. A true manga classic, sweet and hilarious!

© 2002 Koho MIYASAKA/
Shogakukan Inc.

KARE FIRST LOVE Sixteen-year-old plain-Jane Karin finds herself torn between keeping the friendship of her classmate Yuka and entertaining the advances of a boy named Kiriya, who also happens to be the object of Yuka's affections. Living happily ever after in high school isn't on the curriculum, as Karin soon finds herself the center of Kiriya's attention, as well as the bull's-eye in embittered pal Yuka's dartboard of hate. Experience the spine-tingling roller coaster ride of Karin's first experiences in love!

Glossary of Sound Effects, Signs, and other Miscellaneous Notes

Each entry includes: the location, indicated by page number and panel number (so 3.1 means page 3, panel number 1); the phonetic romanization of the original Japanese; and our English "translation"—we offer as close an English equivalent as we can.

11.5—FX: Da! (dash!)

15.3—FX: Shiin (silence, nothing)

15.6—FX: Shiin... (silence)

17.2-3—FX: Dokun dokun dokun (thumping heartbeat)

18.4—FX: Ba ba ba! (blam, blam, blam)

18.5—FX: Boto boto (plop, plop)

19.1—FX: Ba! (breaking free)

19.4—FX: Ka! (blasting snakes)

20.2—FX: Pata pata (running footsteps)

20.3—FX: Pata pata (running footsteps)

22.2—FX: Ha! (gasp)

23.4—FX: Zaa (room changes)

27.3—FX: Ha! (gasp)

28.5—FX: Zuzu (wrenching leg)

30.5—FX: Patata (flap, flap, flap)

31.5—FX: Gu! (squeeze!)

34.1—FX: Dosa (falls)

37.1—FX: Ka! (glow!)

39.1—FX: Za! (the gang's all here!)

40.1—FX: Ha! (gasp!)

41.3—FX: Su! (walking)

44.3—FX: Buchyu (smooch)

46.2—FX: Goh! (loud rumble)

46.3—FX: Goh goh goh goh (crumble, crumble, crumble)

46.5—FX: Goh goh (crumble, crumble)

47.2—FX: Gura! (lurch!)

47.4—FX: Tan (leap)

48.1—FX: Ba! (flap!)

48.3—FX: Bashi! (bash!)

48.4—FX: Basa! (wings flap)

49.1—FX: Gohhh! (roar!)

50.3—FX: Bo! (pow!)

50.4—FX: Dosa (Alice & Kyô sink to the floor)

51.1—FX: Haa haa (huf huf - labored breathing)

51.2—FX: Po! (pop!)

51.3—FX: Katsun, katsun (footsteps on stone)

51.6—FX: Dota! (thud!)

52.1—FX: Gaba! (springs up)

53.3—FX: Doh! (thok!)

79.3 —FX: Van van... (doink - nothing happens)

79.5—FX: Za (appears)

80.3 —FX: Za! (sand hits head)

81.2 —FX: Gon (bonk)

81.4 —FX: Fuwa (floats up)

82.1 —FX: Gi gi gi gi (claws slowly crushing)

83.1—FX: Ba-a! (voom!)

83.2—FX: Gi gi! (twist, squeeze)

85.4 —FX: Zoku! (creepy feeling)

85.5 —FX: Su (raises hand)

86.1-2—FX: Shu-uu (fwoosh)

87.1 —FX: Suu... (Lotis fading)

87.3 —FX: Su (finger points)

88.2 —FX: Gan gan (banging on glass)

88.3 —FX: Gan gan (banging on glass)

88.4 —FX: Zaa (sand rushing)

89.2 —FX: Shuu (skin getting wrinkled)

89.4-5 —FX: Zaaaa (sand pouring in)

91.4—FX: Shara (tinkle - pendant falling)

92.1—FX: Shara (tinkle)

95.1 —FX: Pachi (eyes open)

54.1 —FX: Zuzaa! (slide!)

54.5—FX: Suu (wound fades)

56.5 —FX: Piku (Mayura begins to react)

58.5—FX: Ka (jolt)

59.2 —FX: Fu (fwoom - vanishing)

60.1—FX: Ba! (appears)

60.4 —FX: Poro poro (tears falling)

63.1 —FX: Gyu (clench fists)

65.4 —FX: Ha! (gasp)

69.3—FX: Zashu! (slash!)

70.2 —FX: Ba! (thock)

71.3 —FX: Su (hand goes up)

71.4 —FX: Su (appears)

72.4—FX: Guh! (roar!)

72.5 —FX: Ha! (gasp!)

72.6—FX: Ka! (screech!)

73.1—FX: Do-on (crash!)

74.1 —FX: Boshu! (goes up in flames)

75.1 —FX: Zaa! (whoosh!)

75.2 —FX: Ha! (gasp)

76.1-3—FX: Go-oh! (roar!)

76.4—FX: Ba! (shields Alice)

77.1 —FX: Za! (engulfs Kyô)

77.4—FX: Saa aa (whoosh of petals)

78.1—FX: Za aa (whoosh)

152.4-5 –FX: Ban (bang!)

153.5 —FX: Ha! (gasp)

154.5—FX: Ho! (phew!)

156.1 —FX: Pasa (braid comes off)

156.3 —FX: Ba! (bap!)

157.2 —FX: Pasa (Eric runs fingers through his hair)

161.1 —FX: Ga! (grab!)

163.1 —FX: Don (blam!)

164.4 —FX: Poh... (pop)

165.1 —FX: Bohyu! (repels power)

166.1 —FX: Bo! (repels Lotis)

166.3 —FX: Zudodo! (ba-blam!)

167.1 —FX: Bohyu! (repels)

167.4 —FX: Go! (roar of flames)

168.1 —FX: Bo! (pop!)

168.1 —FX: Bohyu! (pow!)

170.1 —FX: Bohyu! (pow!)

171.4 —FX: Su (hand stretches out)

176.3—FX: Hiku! (tenses up)

177.3—FX: Bohyu! (pow!)

177.5 —FX: Bo! (pop!)

177.5 —FX: Bohyu! (pow!)

179.1 —FX: Do! Do! Do! (heartbeats)

179.3—FX: Do! Do! (heartbeats)

95.2 —FX: Dokun dokun dokun (heart beating)

97.2 —FX: Paki paki paki paki (crack crack)

98.1 —FX: Paki paki paki paki (crack crack)

98.2—FX: Ba-am (blam!)

100.2 —FX: Kura (reeling)

101.2-3—FX: Pan (pow)

101.4—FX: Ban (blam)

103.1 —FX: Ka! (flash of light)

103.4-5—FX: Ba! (blam!)

104.2 —FX: Zuzu (creeping into sight)

104.3 —FX: Zuzu (creeping into sight)

107.6 —FX: Gasha—n (krash)

112.4-5—FX: Zuzu (creeping closer)

113.4—FX: Gu! (clench!)

119.4 —FX: Goshi! (wipe tears away)

132.2—FX: Saku! (crunch of snow under foot)

132.4 —FX: Fuwa (warmth enveloping)

147.3 —FX: Ta! (running off)

147.4 —FX: Zaa (fwoom)

149.3 —FX: Goohn (bell tolling)

149.4 —FX: Goohn (bell tolling)

150.1-2 –FX: Ooohn (tail end of bell tolling)

180.2 —FX: Biku! (jolted awake)

182.2—FX: Ki! (fierce look)

184-185–FX: Goohn Goohn (bell ringing)

186.1 —FX: Karan (mask falls)

186.2 —FX: Gakun (falls to knees)

186.3 —FX: Goohn (bell rings)

187—FX: Goohn (bell rings)

About the Author:

Yuu Watase was born on March 5 in a town
near Osaka, Japan, and she was raised there
before moving to Tokyo to follow her dream of
creating manga. In the decade since her debut
short story, "Pajama De Ojama" (An Intrusion in
Pajamas), she has produced more than 50 com-
piled volumes of short stories and continuing
series. Watase's beloved works *CERES:*
CELESTIAL LEGEND, IMADOKI! (Nowadays),
ALICE 19TH, ABSOLUTE BOYFRIEND, and
FUSHIGI YÛGI: GENBU KAIDEN are now available in North America in English editions published by VIZ Media.

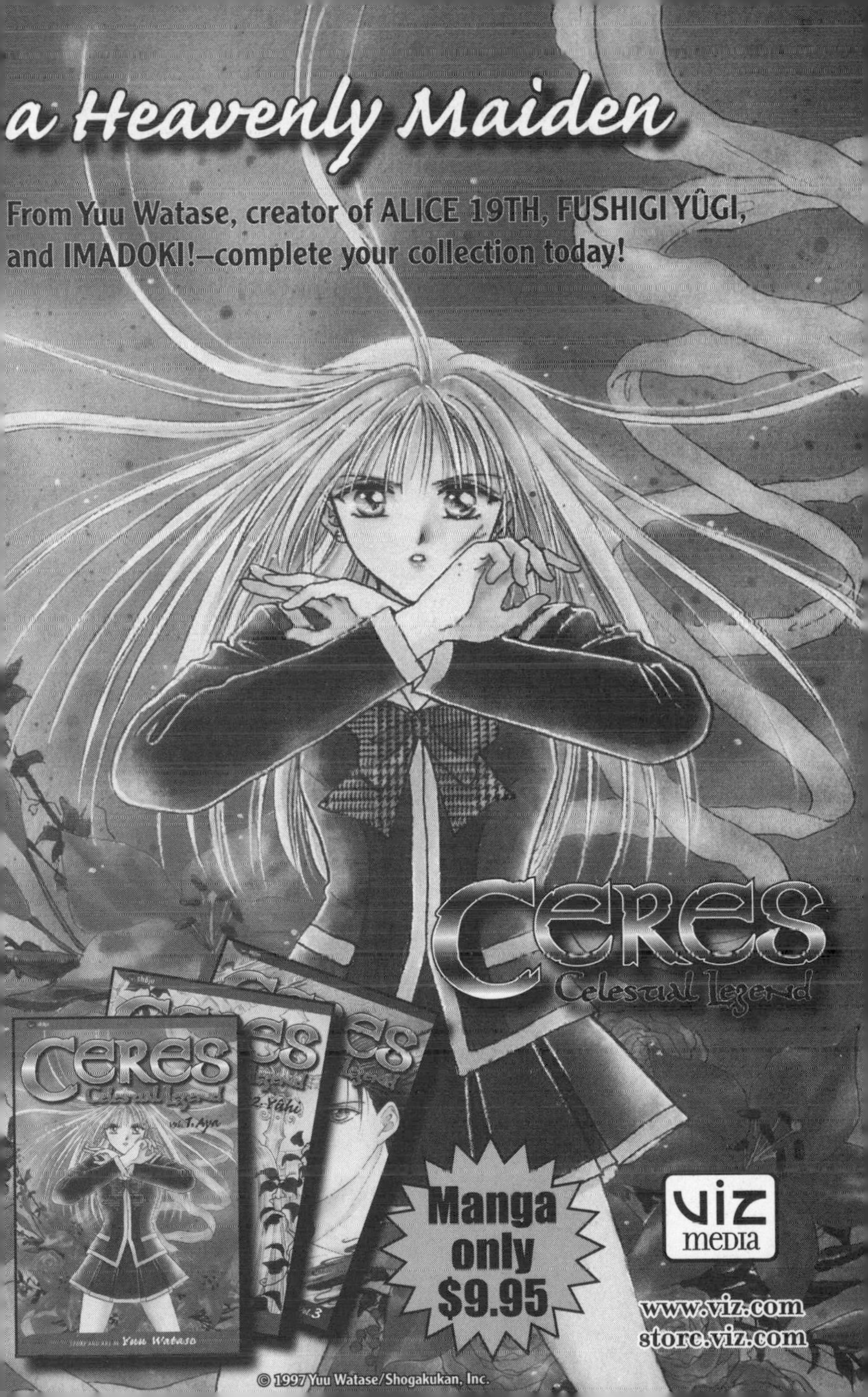
a Heavenly Maiden
From Yuu Watase, creator of ALICE 19TH, FUSHIGI YÛGI, and IMADOKI!—complete your collection today!
CERES
Celestial Legend
Manga only $9.95
viz media
www.viz.com
store.viz.com
© 1997 Yuu Watase/Shogakukan, Inc.

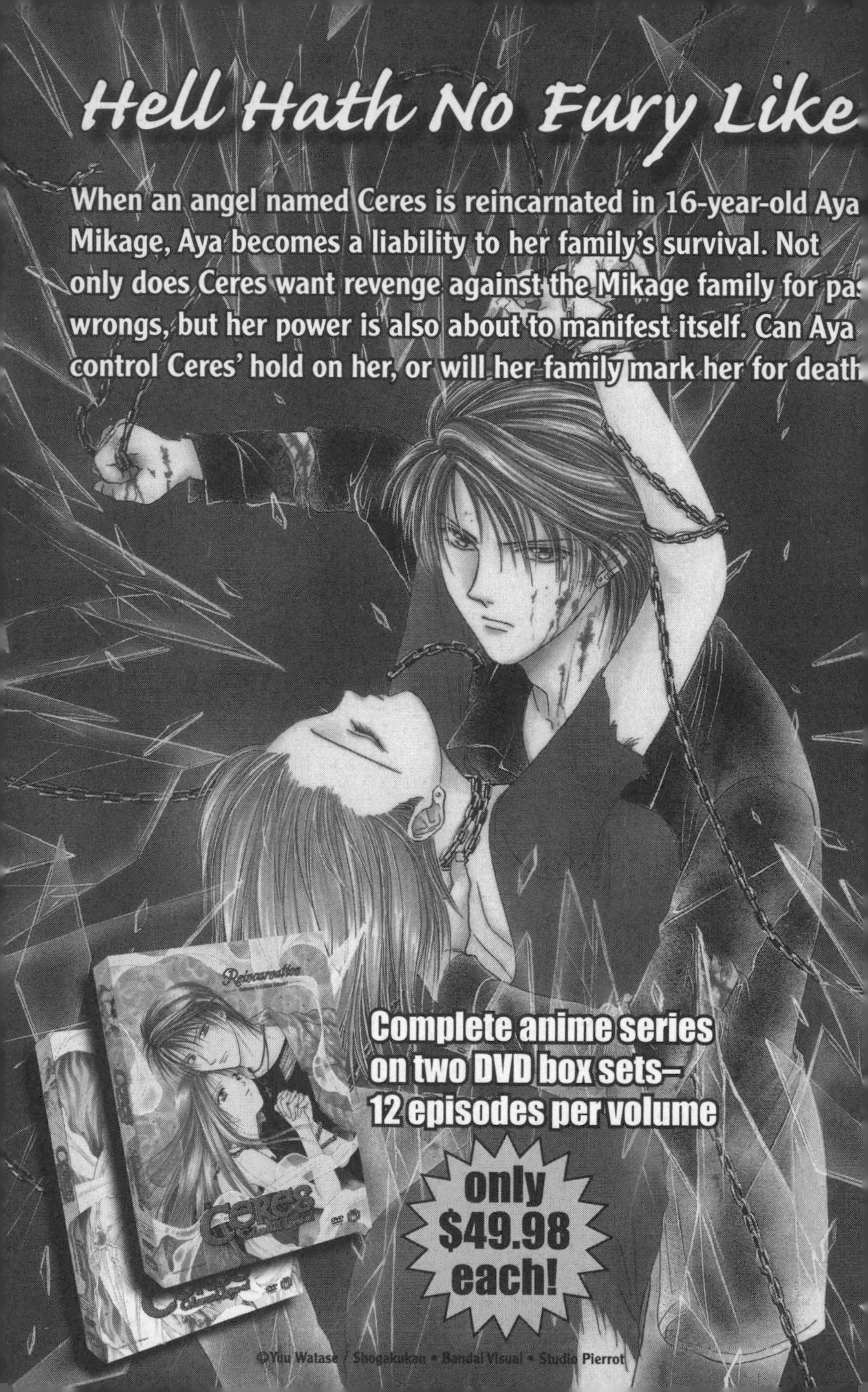
Hell Hath No Fury Like
When an angel named Ceres is reincarnated in 16-year-old Aya Mikage, Aya becomes a liability to her family's survival. Not only does Ceres want revenge against the Mikage family for pa wrongs, but her power is also about to manifest itself. Can Aya control Ceres' hold on her, or will her family mark her for death
Complete anime series on two DVD box sets– 12 episodes per volume
only $49.98 each!
©Yuu Watase / Shogakukan • Bandai Visual • Studio Pierrot

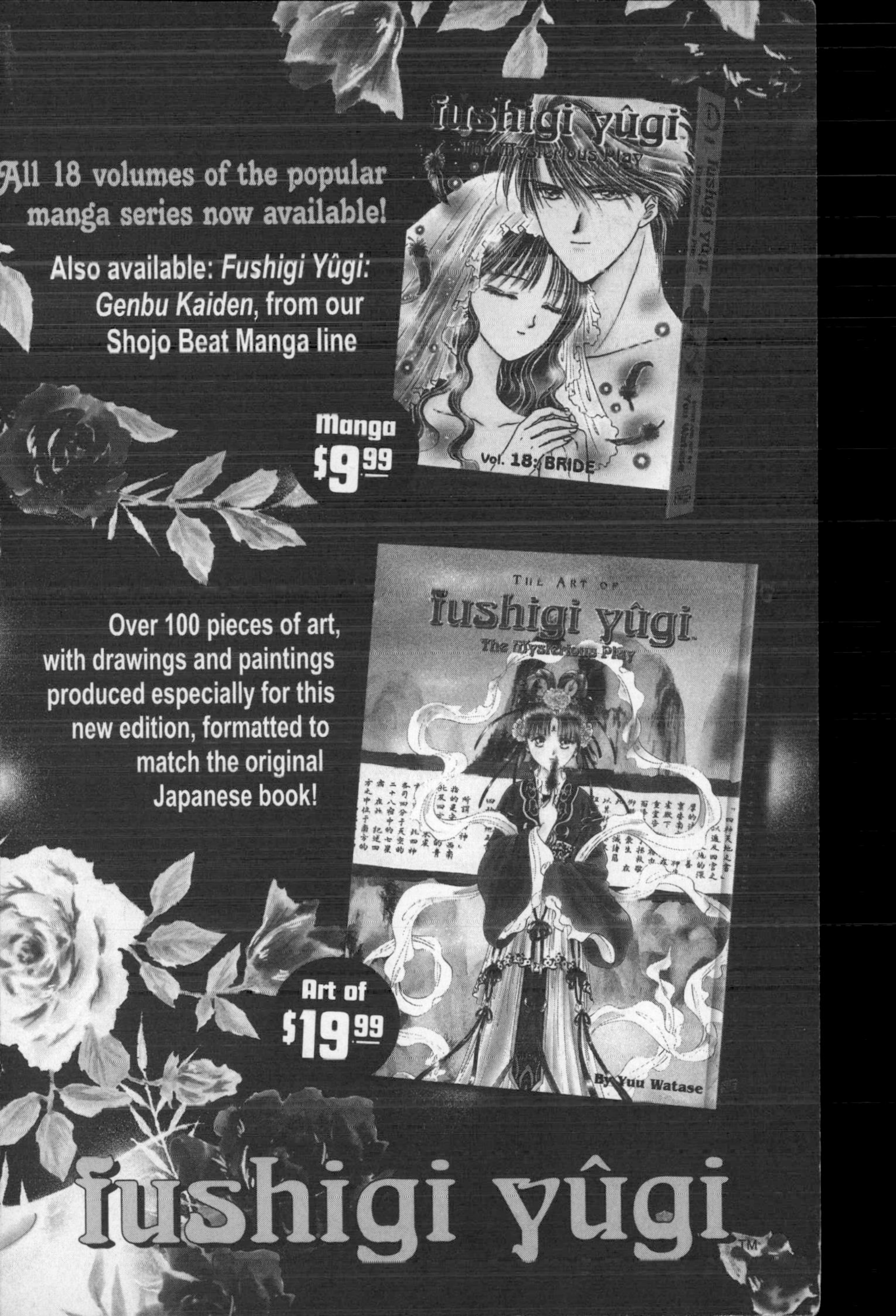

All 18 volumes of the popular manga series now available!
Also available: *Fushigi Yûgi: Genbu Kaiden*, from our Shojo Beat Manga line
fushigi yûgi
The Mysterious Play
Vol. 18: BRIDE
Manga
$9.99
Over 100 pieces of art, with drawings and paintings produced especially for this new edition, formatted to match the original Japanese book!
The Art of
fushigi yûgi
The Mysterious Play
By Yuu Watase
Art of
$19.99
fushigi yûgi™

GET THE COMPLETE
FUSHIGI YÛGI COLLECTION

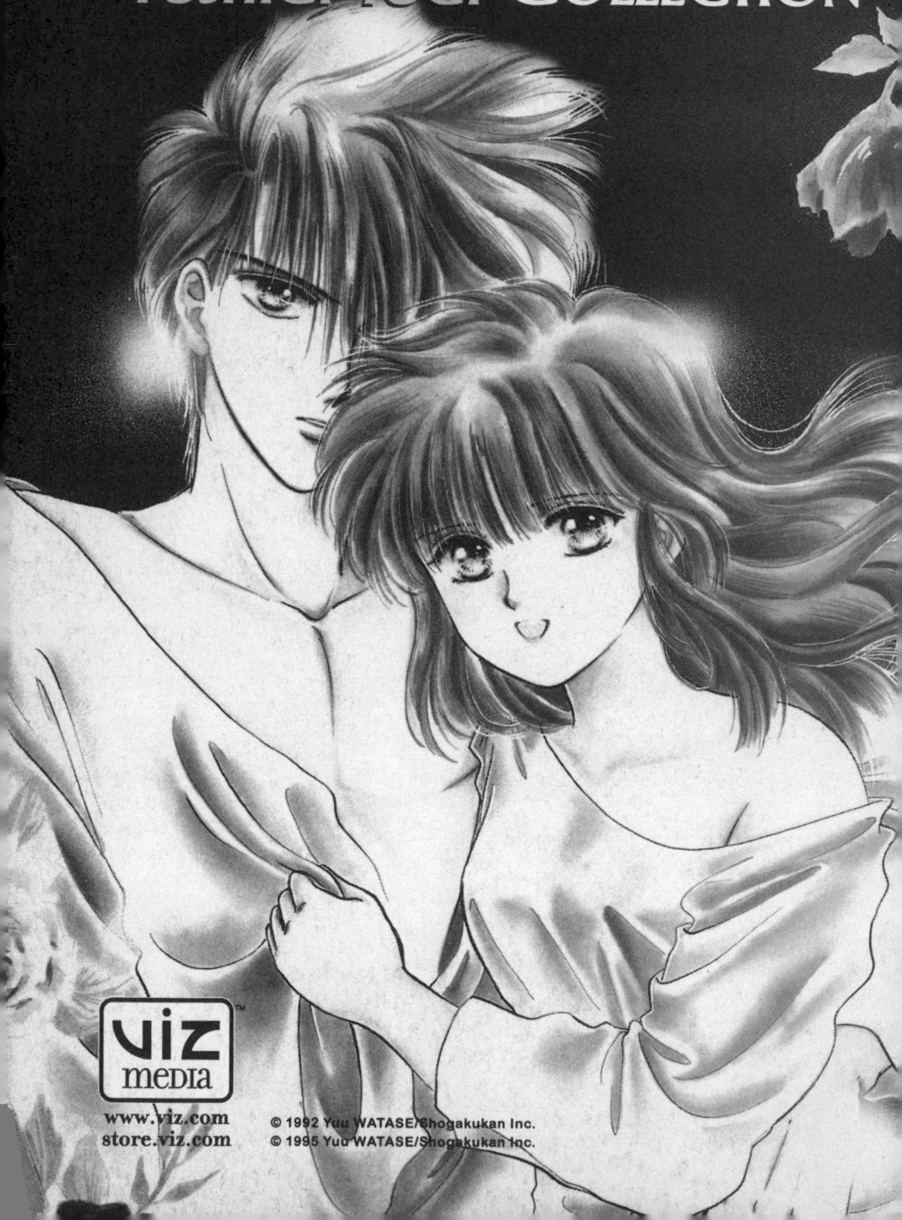

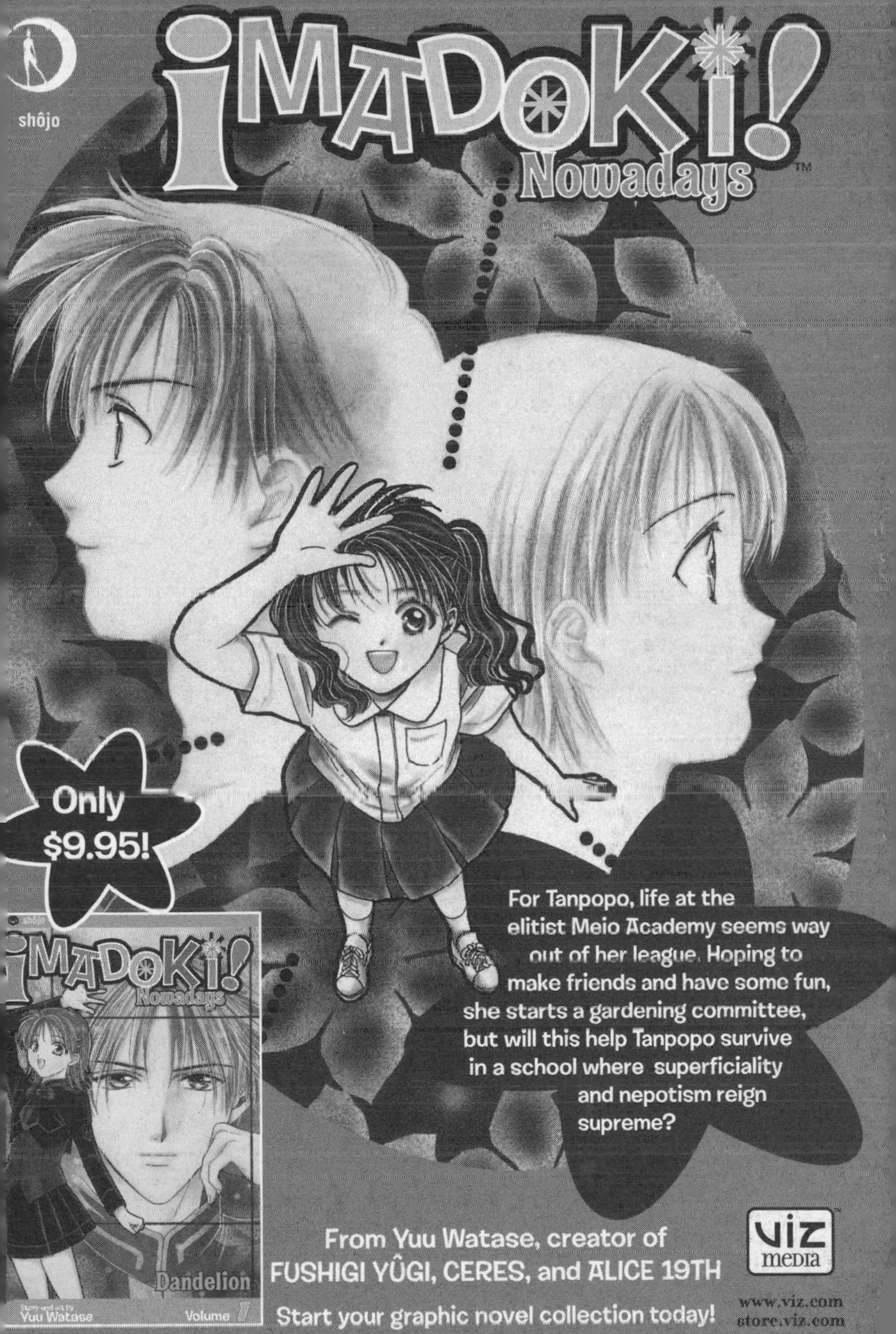
shôjo
IMADOKI! Nowadays™
Only $9.95!
For Tanpopo, life at the elitist Meio Academy seems way out of her league. Hoping to make friends and have some fun, she starts a gardening committee, but will this help Tanpopo survive in a school where superficiality and nepotism reign supreme?
IMADOKI! Nowadays
Dandelion
Story and art by Yuu Watase
Volume 1
From Yuu Watase, creator of FUSHIGI YÛGI, CERES, and ALICE 19TH
Start your graphic novel collection today!
VIZ media
www.viz.com
store.viz.com
000 Yuu Watase/Shogakukan, Inc.

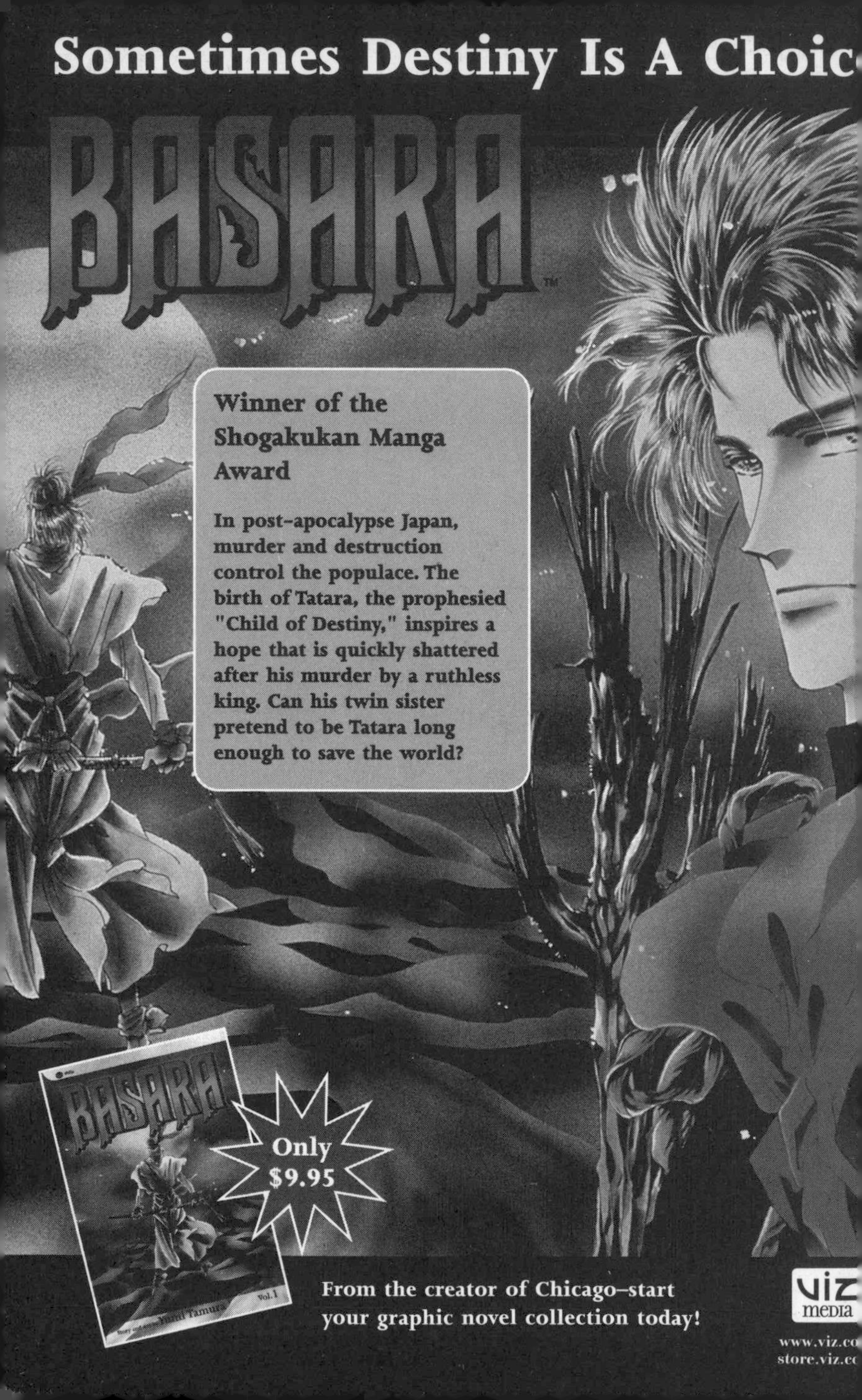
Sometimes Destiny Is A Choic
BASARA
Winner of the Shogakukan Manga Award
In post-apocalypse Japan, murder and destruction control the populace. The birth of Tatara, the prophesied "Child of Destiny," inspires a hope that is quickly shattered after his murder by a ruthless king. Can his twin sister pretend to be Tatara long enough to save the world?
BASARA
Only $9.95
From the creator of Chicago–start your graphic novel collection today!
VIZ media
www.viz.co
store.viz.co

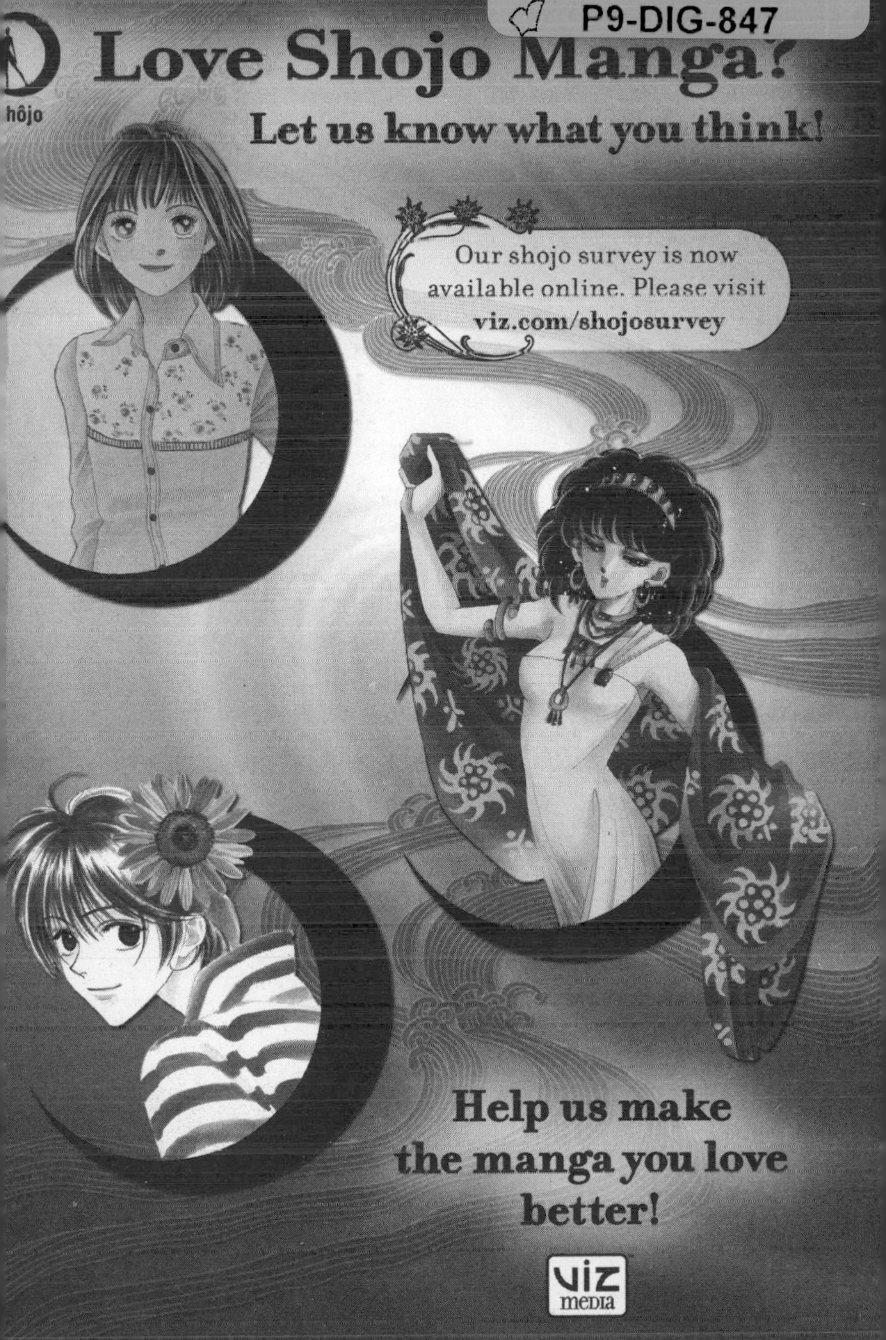
Shôjo
Love Shojo Manga?
Let us know what you think!
Our shojo survey is now available online. Please visit viz.com/shojosurvey
Help us make the manga you love better!
VIZ media

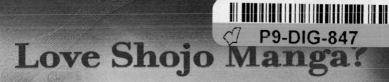